SPEAKING TO SENTENCE:

A PRACTICAL GUIDE

Justice Gilles Renaud

National Library of Canada Cataloguing in Publication Data

Renaud, Gilles, 1958-
    Speaking to sentence : a practical guide / Gilles Renaud.

Includes index.
ISBN 0-459-24122-2

1. Sentences (Criminal procedure)—Canada. I. Title.

KE9355.R47 2004   345.71'0772   C2004-900785-8
KF9685.R47 2004

Composition: Computer Composition of Canada Inc.

THOMSON
™
CARSWELL

One Corporate Plaza
2075 Kennedy Road
Toronto, Ontario
M1T 3V4

Customer Relations:
Toronto 416-609-3800
Elsewhere in Canada/U.S. 1-800-387-5164
Fax 1-416-298-5082

Dedication

This book is dedicated to the memory of Clarey B. Sproule, Q.C.: A teacher, scholar, friend, patriot, aviator, lover of puns, mentor, and so much more . . . he taught a generation of students the Law's majesty.

This book is also dedicated to my loving wife Sharon and our wonderful children, and to Doug and Carol Miller, in partial thanks for their love and affection.

Preface

In this practical guide, Justice Gilles Renaud provides an exhaustive and fair review of the relevant Canadian jurisprudence on sentencing. His selection of cases and commentaries is conveniently organized under a detailed list of the relevant factors and principles that inform the Court in the sentencing of convicted persons. The author also brings to this excellent piece of work years of experience as a trial judge in a busy jurisdiction and offers useful tips to counsel on how to present their client's case in the most favourable light. As the title suggests, this practical guide will undoubtedly provide counsel, Crown and defence alike, with a most useful tool in preparing for the difficult task of speaking to sentence.

Justice Louise Charron
Court of Appeal for Ontario

Introduction

Speaking to sentence is a skill, an art, and a science. When practiced by an advocate who has given the matter considerable thought and who has identified all of the relevant mitigating and aggravating principle, it is a joy to behold. And when one considers that 95% of all criminal accusations result in a guilty plea of some kind, "speaking to sentence" is an essential part of the working day of both defence counsel and Crown prosecutors.

The goal of this book is to enhance the ability of advocates to select the correct sentence from the vast animating case law *and* to assist them in persuading the Court as to the profound merits of the proposed sanction. Indeed, the chapters in *Speaking to Sentence: A Practical Guide* are organized to track the reasoning process commonly followed by sentencing judges. Accordingly, it is of signal importance to the advocate to structure sentencing submissions that parallel this thought process and that enjoy a substantial likelihood of being well received and favourably applied.

In Chapter 1, attention is drawn to a number of fundamental principles that undergird all sentencing decisions, notably Parliament's injunction restraining the selection of imprisonment and the principle according to which sentencing is an individualized process. In the second chapter, the offender's situation is the subject of the inquiry. The advocate is encouraged to discuss the presence of any presumptive leniency as in the case of youthful offenders. The focus of Chapter 3 turns to the potential for reformation as opposed to recidivism, as evaluated by the offender's maturity, character, behaviour, attitude and willingness to make amends. By far the longest of the book, the discussion is framed in such a way as to underscore the moral blame attached to the conduct and to the offender. The final chapter will consider a number of other relevant principles and circumstances such as totality, the guilty plea and the impact of secondary penalties.

It is my goal to assist counsel in identifying all of the principles, circumstances, and factors, whether mitigating or aggravating, that are at play in any given situation.

Table of Contents

Dedication iii

Preface v

Introduction vii

Table of Cases xxiii

Chapter 1 THE ANIMATING PRINCIPLES OF SENTENCING

1. Balancing of the factors 1
2. The need for an individualized sentence 1
3. The general principle of restraint in sentencing 2
4. Degree of wrongdoing: Seeking to place the offence at the favourable range of the scale 4
5. Proof of aggravating elements: Onus cast upon the prosecution 5
6. Proof of aggravating elements: Knowledge of harm 5

Chapter 2 DISTINCT OFFENDER GROUPS: PRESUMPTIVE MITIGATION

1. Youthful Offenders: 7
   a) Introduction 7
   b) Parliament's long-standing objective is to protect youths from the dangers of imprisonment 7
   c) The general principle that directs allowance for diminished moral blameworthiness 9
   d) Defining a youth 11
   e) The general exception to the principle of leniency in the case of youthful offenders: Little allowance for serious or violent offences 11
   f) The rationale for leniency in the case of young persons: They may be taught pro-social values .. 12
   g) The "teaching" of pro-social values to youthful offenders may require elements of coercion 13
   h) The "prodigal child" principle 16
   i) The degree of moral blameworthiness is the deciding factor, in the final analysis 17
   j) Youthful offenders and the advocate: Combining mitigating features 20

2.   Elderly offenders: 22
    a)   Introduction 22
    b)   The general rule: To spare elder offenders the
          rigours of punishment 23
    c)   The fundamental rule: No one should die in jail 24
    d)   No one should die in jail, but the punishment must
          fit the crime: The need for a proportionate
          penalty 26
    e)   A lengthy period of offending suggests the offender
          lacks good character 27
    f)   Advanced age and the passage of time since the
          commission of the offence 29
    g)   Advanced age and parole authorities 30
    h)   Elderly offenders and elderly dependants 31
    i)   Elderly offenders and the selection of a custodial
          facility 32
    j)   The latest word 32
    k)   Summary for advocates: Seek additional mitigating
          circumstances such as poor health 32
3.   Aboriginal offenders: 34
    a)   Introduction: S. 718.2(e) and the legacy of *R. v.*
          Fireman 34
    b)   The need to balance the desire for leniency with
          the need to protect the community in the
          immediate 35
    c)   Recent instruction: As a general rule, the moral
          blameworthiness for aboriginal offenders is
          attenuated 39
    d)   Summary for advocates: Parliament has recognized
          the special status enjoyed by aboriginal
          offenders 42
4.   Systemic racism and African Canadian offenders: 43
    a)   Breaking new ground: Mitigation based on
          attenuated moral blameworthiness 43
    b)   The need for compelling evidence of the offender's
          difficulties in life 44

Chapter 3   **THE MORAL BLAME ATTACHED TO AN
                OFFENDER'S CONDUCT AS IT SUPPORTS
                REFORMATION OR RECIDIVISM**

1.   An examination of the offender's maturity: The sad life
    principle and diminished moral blameworthiness: 47
    a)   Introduction 47

b)   The "sad life" principle and society's failure to equip the offenders with a "moral compass", thus ensuring immature actions: 49

     i)   Some preliminary questions for advocates 49

     ii)   The offender's sad life is relevant to sentencing 50

     iii)   The "sad life" and a perverted understanding of pro-social values 54

     iv)   The controversial question: Is it aggravating to repeat the cycle of sexual or other violence? 57

     v)   The allowance for leniency is not endless 59

     vi)   May sexual victimization in youth discount a sentence for a non-sexual offence? 60

     vii)   The impact of deprivations in childhood and the inability to develop a moral compass 60

     viii)   The significance of a fortunate background 62

     ix)   Sentencing must consider the offender and the offence 63

     x)   Pulling at the heart-strings of the Court 64

     xi)   Summary for advocates: The degree of moral blame is the ultimate question, the lack of a moral compass the immediate one in cases of a "sad life" 64

     xii)   A further word on advocacy 67

2.   An examination of the offender's character and moral blameworthiness: 69

   a)   Introduction 69

   b)   The offender is generally of good character 69

   c)   Character and overcoming great challenges in the past 74

   d)   Good character and entrapment 74

   e)   Good character and isolated offences: 75

     i)   Introduction 75

     ii)   Isolated offences and young persons 76

     iii)   The guidance from "distant" cases 78

     iv)   The contrary view: Non-isolated offending 78

3.   An examination of the offender's behaviour and moral blameworthiness: 80

   a)   Introduction 80

   b)   Successful therapy or counselling 81

   c)   Employment 81

   d)   Education 82

e) Behaviour and the passage of time since the
offence(s): 82
i) Has the offender demonstrated that further
correctional intervention is no longer
required? 82
ii) The passage of time and the reluctance to re-
incarcerate 87
iii) The thorny issue: Historical prosecutions in
which the offender made no overt threats or
acted to prevent prosecution 88
iv) The passage of time and learning the
necessary lesson 89
v) The situation of delayed arrest 90
vi) The offender cannot seek a therapeutic
remand 90
vii) The passage of time may not serve to
ameliorate the offender's situation 91
viii) Overcoming addiction 91
ix) Progress in the institution 92
x) Progress with treatment 92
xi) Summary for advocates: The passage of time
in general 93
f) Behaviour and the "gap" principle in sentencing: 94
i) Introduction 94
ii) The presence of a "gap" in the criminal record
may be mitigating 95
iii) The general principle of restraint in sentencing
.... 96
iv) A word on historical antecedents 98
v) Context is everything: The repetition of certain
offences may be quite troubling 98
vi) A "gap" may be in evidence, but severity is
still justified 99
vii) Focusing on the presence of a "gap" should
not trump the evaluation of the seriousness
of the prior record 100
viii) Has the offender shown that the "gap"
demonstrates the assimilation of pro-social
values? 101
ix) The extreme position: Any "gap" may be
seized upon as a sign of possible
reformation 103
x) A "gap" and achieving "first offender" status
once again 104

xi)   The "gap" principle and offences of violence ..   105
xii) May a "gap" be seen as aggravating?   106
xiii) The obvious question: How lengthy must the
        gap be to garner mitigating weight?   106
   A)   Older cases suggest that a quite lengthy
          period is required   106
   B)   A lesser relative period for youthful
          offenders   107
   C)   A lesser period may be found suitable if
          other mitigating elements are present
            108
   D)   A general review   108
xiv) The Court may credit more than one "gap":   110
   A)   In general   110
   B)   With reference to particular offences   111
xv)   Gaps created by prosecutorial policy   112
xvi) Gaps created by imprisonment?   113
xvii) Gaps followed by a serious period of
        offending   114
xviii) The influence of a pre-sentence report   114
xix) The impact of a "gap" between as yet
        unprosecuted offences: The "spree"
        principle   115
xx)   Expert evidence and "gaps" in the offender's
        record   115
xxi) Summary for advocates   115
g)   Behaviour and the trivial nature of the wrongdoing:
          116
   i)   The legislative background   116
   ii)   Behaviour and silly offences   117
h)   Behaviour and delay in sentencing   118
i)   Behaviour and the escalation of violence: An
        aggravating factor as it marks poor behaviour
        with a high degree of moral blame   119
j)   Behaviour while on parole   120
k)   Behaviour while on probation   121
l)   Behaviour and the impact of provocation   121
m)   Callous behaviour   124
n)   Behaviour behind the wheel   124
o)   Behaviour and planning   124
4. An examination of the offender's attitude and moral
      blameworthiness: 127
a)   Introduction   127
b)   Examples of a positive attitude: 128

	i)	A positive attitude as shown by an apology	128
	ii)	A positive attitude as shown by co-operation with the police	129
	iii)	The desire to reform shows a positive attitude	132
	iv)	The impact of a favourable pre-sentence report in demonstrating a positive attitude ..	133
c)		Attitude and remorse:	134
	i)	The impact of remorse in sentencing	134
	ii)	Lack of remorse as an indication of recidivism	137
	iii)	Lack of remorse as an indication of a lack of potential for reform	137
d)		Attitude as reflected by breach of court orders	138
e)		Attitude and test cases	139
f)		Attitude and religious scruples	139
g)		An examination of the offender's willingness to make amends and moral blameworthiness:	140
	i)	Introduction	140
	ii)	The presence of a support network as it influences the ability to make amends	141
	iii)	Support from the victim	144
	iv)	Support from the offender's family	145
	v)	Family support and a desire to reform	145
	vi)	Early attempts to repay for the damage or the loss	146
	vii)	The lack of a resolve to "make amends" is not aggravating, but it is not mitigating	146
	viii)	The offender has vowed to reform	147
	ix)	Making amends as opposed to being ordered to perform community service work or pay restitution	148

Chapter 4 MITIGATING AND AGGRAVATING PRINCIPLES AND CIRCUMSTANCES

1.		The guilty and not guilty pleas:	151
	a)	Introduction	151
	b)	The mitigation, if any, inherent in the guilty plea at various stages of the trial	152
	c)	The guilty plea: Is it always mitigating?	152
	i)	As a general rule, mitigation is awarded to an offender who pleads guilty, irrespective of remorse	152

ii) As a general rule, greater mitigating weight is
assigned to a guilty plea advanced at an
early stage of the proceedings 154
d) The early guilty plea: 155
i) An early guilty plea after an early admission of
responsibility 156
ii) The early guilty plea and apology 157
e) The not so early guilty plea: 157
i) Introduction 157
ii) The credit to be assigned to a guilty plea after
multiple court appearances but before a
trial date 159
iii) The credit to be assigned to a guilty plea after
the preliminary hearing 160
iv) The credit to be assigned to a guilty plea on
the day of trial 160
v) The credit to be assigned to a guilty plea after
the start of the trial 161
vi) The credit that arises in the case of a late
guilty plea after an adverse ruling 162
vii) The credit that arises in the case of a late
guilty plea to a lesser offence 162
viii) The credit that arises in the case of a late
guilty plea in situations in which the
prosecution withdraws one or more of the
accusations 164
ix) The credit to be assigned in cases of some
guilty and some not guilty pleas: 164
A) The guilty plea and calling the victim(s)
to testify at the sentence hearing 164
B) The lack of remorse and a guilty plea 165
C) The guilty plea and a discount based on
a fixed percentage 166
D) The guilty plea and a discount based on
a fixed formula 168
E) The guilty plea and the waiver of the
chance of being acquitted 168
F) The not guilty plea that is tantamount to
a guilty plea 169
G) The guilty plea and affirming the truth of
the victim's complaint 170
H) The guilty plea and societal interests 171

I) Credit for sparing victims and other witnesses from the ordeal of testifying 171

J) The issue of guilty pleas and the savings to the administration of justice in money terms 173

f) The mitigation, if any, arising from a guilty plea in a case of overwhelming evidence of guilt: 174

i) Introducing the rule in *R. v. Spiller*, [1969] 4 C.C.C. 211, 1969 CarswellBC 42, 6 C.R.N.S. 360, 68 W.W.R. 187 (C.A.) 174

ii) Discussing the application of the *Spiller* doctrine: 175

A) The course of justice is not advanced by a guilty plea where no successful defence is possible 175

B) What if the guilty plea does advance the course of justice by saving court time? 177

C) What if the guilty plea does advance the course of justice, by promoting a sense of responsibility? 178

D) What if the guilty plea does advance the course of justice, by evidencing remorse? 179

E) What if the guilty plea does advance the course of justice, by sparing victims the trauma of testifying? 180

F) What if the guilty plea does advance the course of justice, by promoting the search for the truth? 180

G) The emerging challenge to the *Spiller* doctrine 181

g) The mitigation, if any, arising as a result of a not guilty plea: 183

i) Introduction 183

ii) The ruling in *R. v. Kozy*: 183

A) The application of the rule in Ontario 187

B) The application of the rule in Québec 190

C) The application of the rule in Alberta 193

D) The minority view: *R. v. V. (J.T.)* (1998), [1998] B.C.J. No. 549, 105 B.C.A.C. 42, 1998 CarswellBC 751, 171 W.A.C. 42 (C.A.) 196

h) A summary for advocates 198
2. Mitigation inherent in secondary penalties: 198
a) Introduction 198
b) Sentencing requires a balancing of competing
factors 199
c) Punishment arising out of the mere fact of a public
prosecution 200
d) "Dead time": Mitigation as a result of secondary
penalties associated with pre-trial detention: 208
i) Introduction 208
ii) The recent instruction of the Supreme Court
of Canada 208
iii) The normal rule is for credit on a "two for one"
basis 209
iv) "Two for one" is the normal rule, not the
inflexible rule: 214
A) As an exercise of discretion 214
B) To promote other sentencing principles .. 216
v) May pre-trial detention be granted nil credit? .. 219
vi) Dead time and the maximum sentence 220
vii) Any period of imprisonment is to be excluded
from the credit to be assigned for "dead
time" 222
viii) Rationales for the rule of crediting "dead time":
.... 222
A) The absence of a statutory "credit"
scheme 222
B) The absence of programmes of
rehabilitation 222
C) The conditions at the jails are trying 223
D) Dead time is a form of punishment 225
E) To not credit dead time may lead to
disparity 225
F) The denial of credit might lead to
unfairness 226
ix) What of a mathematical formula? 226
x) The fixing of credit is to occur on a case-by-
case basis 227
xi) Pre-trial credit and minimum jail sentences: 228
A) Are sentencing courts empowered to
give credit even if it serves to reduce
a minimal period of incarceration? 229
xii) A word for advocates 231
e) Restrictive bail conditions as a secondary penalty .. 232

f)   Secondary penalties and ostracism 233
g)   Secondary penalties and poor health 235
h)   Secondary penalties and harm to the innocent
     members of the offender's family 236
i)   Secondary penalties and immigration
     consequences 239
j)   Secondary penalties and "automatic" fines 240
k)   Confiscation as a secondary penalty 241
l)   Compensation, not restitution, to the victim 242
m)   Civil driving penalties 242
n)   Professional disqualifications 243
o)   The adverse consequences of being convicted 243
p)   The impact of improper or flawed proceedings 244
q)   Injuries suffered by offender in course of offence 244
r)   Summary for advocates: Any element of
     punishment inherent in the proceedings must be
     considered to be mitigating 245
3.   Expert Evidence: Capacity for rehabilitation 246
4.   Moral blame: The degree of violence 246
5.   Violence: Placing the harm on a scale 248
6.   Individualized sentences and drinking and driving
     offences 251
7.   Range of sentences and exceptional cases 252
8.   Hardship: Avoiding undue hardship as a justification for
     leniency 253
9.   Aggravating feature: The length of time the offence
     occurred 254
10. Secondary harm: Obligation to move to be free of
     potential harm and to lessen fears 256
11. Victim's vulnerability 257
12. Neutral feature: The absence of a record in the case of
     drinking and driving: The typical offender is law-
     abiding 257
13. Road rage 261
14. The tragic consequences of the offender's actions 261
15. Breach of court orders designed to protect the public 263
16. The moral blame associated with drug offences: 264
     a)   The scale of offending and moral blame 264
     b)   The scale of the offence in terms of value 265
     c)   The potential for profit and moral blameworthiness
          265
     d)   Drug offences lead to destruction of individuals and
          communities 265
17. The worst-case analysis: The reformed rule 266

18. Cases of "Stark horror" 269
19. Harm to members of protected classes: 270
    a) Peace officers 271
    b) Internationally protected individuals 272
    c) Employees of businesses targeted for robbery 272
    d) Persons enjoying the protection of court orders as members of a protected class 273
20. Taking into account other wrongdoing 274
21. Harm to administration of justice 276
22. First offenders to incorrigible offenders: An examination: 276
    a) Introduction 276
    b) First offenders: The absence of a prior record demonstrates a capacity for pro-social conduct: 277
        i) In the case of no prior blameworthy conduct .. 277
        ii) In the case of prior blameworthy conduct not resulting in a record: If the offender can cease harmful conduct? 279
    c) Prior blameworthy conduct not resulting in a record: Domestic violence 280
    d) Prior blameworthy conduct not resulting in a record: Sexual and other violence advanced as similar fact 280
    e) Sprees: Prior misconduct not resulting in a record but that is aggravating at sentencing 281
    f) Unprosecuted prior offences and pre-sentence reports: An examination: 283
        i) Introduction 283
        ii) May the probation officer report that an offender has engaged in a pattern of misconduct? 284
            A) The traditional view: The Rule in *R. v. Bartkow* 284
            B) The emerging view: Prior misconduct is germane 285
            C) Whether pre-sentence reports may describe the abuse of alcohol by an offender not leading to offences "so found"? 288
    g) First offenders guilty of serious offences: The elevated moral blame may require severe sentences 288

h)   Repeat offenders: Assessing the blameworthiness
      of the misconduct: 291
      i)   Introduction 291
      ii)   The impact of a youth record 291
      iii) The impact of a minor record 292
      iv)   The impact of a recent but minor prior record
            292
      v)   The impact of a recent substantial record 292
      vi)   The impact of an unrelated record 293
      vii) The impact of a lengthy but unrelated record
            294
      viii) Repeat offenders and their motivation: The
            profit motive 295
      ix)   Repeat offenders who continue to offend by
            reason of addiction 296
      x)   Repeat offenders who continue to offend by
            reason of some animus 296
      xi)   Repeat offenders who continue to offend in
            cases of driving prohibitions 298
      xii) Repeat offenders who continue to offend in
            general 298
      xiii) Career criminals with extensive records: 299
            A)   The general rule 299
            B)   The exceptional disposition 300
            C)   The emerging rule 300
23. Vigilantism: 301
      a)   Introduction 301
      b)   Taking the law into one's hands: The fear of
            general lawlessness 301
      c)   Violence begets violence "Rambo-style" 307
      d)   Concerns over mob violence 308
      e)   Vigilante justice: A form of extortion 309
      f)   Vigilantism and deliberation 309
      g)   Vigilante justice: The multi-national perspective 310
      h)   Gang warfare 310
      i)   Vigilantism and the wrong person 310
      j)   Summary for advocates 311
24. The totality principle 311
25. Offender a good provider 312
26. Little profit was obtained from the offence(s) 313
27. Limited or minor role in the offence 313
28. Unblemished background 314
29. Economic hardship led to offence 314
30. Favourable employment history: 315

a)   In general 315
b)   Exceptional situations: Even a fair work record
      suffices 317
31.   Favourable family background: 318
a)   Provision of love from offender to family 318
b)   Provision of support and encouragement from
      family to offender 318
c)   Provision of financial support from offender to
      family 319
d)   Avoiding hardship on family 319
32.   Good citizenship 319
33.   Academic pursuits 320
34.   Favourable reputations 320
35.   The relative absence of serious injury 321
36.   The "jump" or "step" principle 321
37.   Spontaneous or "unplanned" wrongdoing 323
38.   Perceived unfairness in the prosecution to some degree
      324
39.   Avoiding the collateral harm resulting from incarceration
      324
40.   A technical breach of the law 327
41.   The presumption of good behaviour during a period of
      non-offending 327
42.   The prior record may show the "ability to go straight" 328
43.   The need for training to enhance employment skills: 328
a)   Introduction 328
b)   The general policy: Employment is an important
      mitigating factor in sentencing 329
c)   The issue of lack of employment 329
d)   Overcoming challenges in achieving employment ... 330
e)   The sliding scale of descriptions of a work history .. 331
f)   Employment and the issue of welfare benefits 332
g)   Unemployment and no apparent (lawful) means of
      support 333
h)   Employment and temporary absence 333
i)   Unemployment as a neutral factor if the offender is
      challenged 334
j)   Jail to enhance employment skills 334
44.   A casual, versus a professional, offence 334
45.   Proportionality 335
46.   Sentencing an offender guilty of committing a different
      offence than the one thought to be committed 337
47.   Experimentation 338
48.   No hope of success in offence: Any significance? 338

49.	Voluntary return to jurisdiction after fleeing	339
50.	The Crown's election	339
51.	The Crown's position on sentencing	339
52.	Dysfunctional background	340
53.	Disparity	340
54.	Offender acted impulsively	342
55.	Personality defects	343
56.	Change in residence	346
57.	The strict application of the law hinders rehabilitation	346
58.	Good character as a conduit to fraud offences	347
59.	Kicking	347
60.	Brazen offence: Any significance?	347
61.	Planning: What if the plan is to avoid injury?	348
62.	Racially motivated offences	348
63.	Consuming narcotics while in a motor vehicle	349
64.	Use of a ruse	349
65.	Unforeseen consequences	349
66.	An offender must not be sentenced twice: "So much for the offence and so much for the record!"	350
67.	Repetitive misconduct	351
68.	Offending shortly after release	352
69.	Record for quasi-criminal misconduct	352
70.	If the offender can't abide by the rules, may the Court change the rules?	353
71.	Proof of aggravating elements: Knowledge of harm	354
Index		355

Table of Cases

Bogdane v. R. 243
Brock-Berry v. Registered Nurses' Assn. (British Columbia) 189
C., Re 319
Canada (Attorney General) v. Boulet (1990) 60
College of Physicians & Surgeons (Ontario) v. Gillen 189
Goodwin v. Hoffman 242
Hardy v. Alain 241
MacMillan Bloedel Ltd. v. Brown, sub nom MacMillan Bloedel Ltd. v.
     Simpson 9, 167, 174, 178, 179
Merrit v. Headon 112
Ontario (Attorney General) v. Brenton 240
Paulk, Re 110
R. c. Abenaim 191, 192, 193
R. c. Cheung and Chow 205
R. c. Gaudreault 205
R. c. Gervais 57
R. c. Lévesque 192
R. c. Ménard 281
R. c. Monette 25
R. c. Parent 172, 173
R. c. Rondeau 193
R. c. Savard 191
R. c. Scraire 205
R. v. A. 329
R. v. A. (F.) 265
R. v. A. (J.R.) 133
R. v. Abbott 112, 245
R. v. Abell 63
R. v. Adam 86
R. v. Adelman 79, 320
R. v. Ahmed-Saidi 123
R. v. Alagendra 71
R. v. Ali 181
R. v. Allison-McLeish (2000) 211
R. v. Allison-McLeish (2001) 272, 291
R. v. Anderson 307, 308, 309
R. v. Andre 110
R. v. Andrew 332
R. v. Aquino 235
R. v. Ashoona 62
R. v. Askov 232
R. v. Atkinson 114

R. v. Audette 49, 331
R. v. B 38, 340
R. v. B. (J.) 331
R. v. B. (M.) 337
R. v. B. (N.W.) 93, 317, 319, 346
R. v. B. (R.) (2001) 71
R. v. B. (R.) (2003) 62, 65, 73, 86
R. v. B. (R.H.) 75
R. v. B. (R.I.) 110
R. v. B. (T.E.) 303, 307
R. v. B. (W.) 31
R. v. B. (W.R.) 23
R. v. Bajada 98, 104, 238
R. v. Bannerman 107
R. v. Bartkow 284, 287
R. v. Barton 224, 297
R. v. Barry 29, 99
R. v. Barton 140
R. v. Bassett 55
R. v. Bates (1977) 284
R. v. Bates (2000) 119, 120, 164, 211, 344
R. v. Batte, 145 C.C.C. (3d) 498 281
R. v. Batte, 145 C.C.C. (3d) 449 281
R. v. Baxter 124, 297
R. v. Bayani 73, 87, 133
R. v. Beaulieu 154
R. v. Bell 292
R. v. Benjamin 121
R. v. Bernshaw 260
R. v. Bertoia 241
R. v. Better 86
R. v. Bevacqua 79, 315, 320
R. v. Beyo 207
R. v. Biancofiore 260, 263, 273
R. v. Bigelow 71
R. v. Bigg 205
R. v. Bigham 72
R. v. Biscombe 131
R. v. Bjellebo 335
R. v. Blackbird 100
R. v. Blackmore 311
R. v. Blancard 54, 147
R. v. Blind 156
R. v. Bogart 52, 74
R. v. Borde 12, 18, 39, 43, 68, 322
R. v. Bourassa 51
R. v. Boyd 144
R. v. Bromley 29

R. v. Brookes 90, 91
R. v. Brooks 56
R. v. Browne 331
R. v. Bruce 166, 181
R. v. Bullock 311
R. v. Bunn 234
R. v. Burgess 338
R. v. Burke (2001) 21, 82, 131
R. v. Burke (2001), 153 C.C.C. (3d) 97 .... 124, 125, 136, 211
R. v. Burke (May 3, 1989) 165
R. v. Butler 353
R. v. C. (A.) 58, 62
R. v. C. (A.C.) 108
R. v. C. (D.W.) 83, 235, 249, 253, 257
R. v. C. (E.) 24, 25
R. v. C. (H.W.) 56
R. v. C. (M.W.) 18
R. v. C. (S.P.) 201
R. v. C. (V.K.) 203, 204, 205
R. v. C.A.M. 220
R. v. Cabrera 175
R. v. Cameron (1991) 278
R. v. Cameron (1999) 27
R. v. Camkiran 212
R. v. Cann 236
R. v. Canning 178, 179
R. v. Carrier 332
R. v. Cartwright 129
R. v. Casey 111, 273
R. v. Cater 86, 237
R. v. Cerasuolo 50, 53, 155
R. v. Charna 64
R. v. Chavali 146
R. v. Cheddesingh 147, 269
R. v. Cheung and Chow 204
R. v. Ching 176
R. v. Chung 180
R. v. Cindler 78
R. v. Clarke 122, 212, 219
R. v. Code 200
R. v. Coelho 212
R. v. Cohen 145, 233, 236
R. v. Colbourne 95, 108, 262
R. v. Comeau 106
R. v. Condo 138, 287
R. v. Cornett 184
R. v. Corpus 120, 288
R. v. Cossette-Trudel 310

R. v. Craig 5
R. v. Cranwell 185
R. v. Crawford 342
R. v. Critton 310
R. v. Crockford 332
R. v. Crowe 272
R. v. Cunningham 289
R. v. Curran 15
R. v. Cuzner 79, 90, 313, 320
R. v. D. (B.K.) 92, 93, 316
R. v. D. (C.) 243, 276
R. v. D. (F.) 31
R. v. D. (L.R.) 176
R. v. D. (M.) 204
R. v. D. (M.J.) 109
R. v. D. (T.) 331
R. v. D'Amour 137
R. v. Dash 202
R. v. DaSilva 212, 224, 266, 300
R. v. Davis 168, 179
R. v. Davy 211
R. v. de Haan 174
R. v. De La Cruz 282, 351
R. v. Deane 190
R. v. Dekoning 81
R. v. Demeter 78, 203, 206
R. v. Denault 17
R. v. Deschamps 202
R. v. Dewald 126
R. v. Dharamdeo 142, 259
R. v. Dhesi 98
R. v. Dhillon 301, 310
R. v. Diez 173
R. v. Dinn 26, 30
R. v. Dixon 196
R. v. Dobbs 297
R. v. Doerksen 154
R. v. Doren 186
R. v. Dragomir 189
R. v. Drisdelle 158, 247
R. v. Drozdz 283
R. v. Duck 87
R. v. Dumont 119
R. v. Dunbar 185, 194
R. v. Dycko 196
R. v. E. (P.) 289, 312
R. v. Eakin 134
R. v. Echegoyen 81, 118

R. v. Edwards (2001) 276
R. v. Edwards (2003) 291
R. v. Emes 352
R. v. Estabrooks 28
R. v. F. (G.W.) 9
R. v. F. (J.) 92
R. v. F. (J.S.) 211
R. v. F. (M.) 190
R. v. Faulds 152, 176
R. v. Fazekas 298, 352
R. v. Fedick 67
R. v. Fernandes 114
R. v. Fice 86, 213
R. v. Finley 98, 168, 170, 171
R. v. Fireman 34, 42, 66
R. v. Fitzgerald 175
R. v. Fitzpatrick 61
R. v. Flores 20, 73, 87, 278, 289
R. v. Foley 148, 234
R. v. Foran 347
R. v. Forrest 127, 271
R. v. Fox 334
R. v. Francis 82, 119, 136
R. v. Freedman 199
R. v. Friesen 61
R. v. Frost 190
R. v. Fudge 83, 128, 141, 290
R. v. Fuentes (1997) 189
R. v. Fuentes (2003) 235
R. v. G. (A.J.) 31
R. v. G. (G.L.) 8, 284
R. v. G. (K.) 50, 330
R. v. G. (O.J.) 57
R. v. Gagnon 182
R. v. Galbraith 102
R. v. Gallizzi 100
R. v. Garcia and Silva 274, 275
R. v. Gardiner 5
R. v. Garrow 81
R. v. Garrod 127
R. v. Gauthier 353
R. v. Gerhard 177
R. v. Gianfelice 31
R. v. Gibson 288, 331
R. v. Gillan 94, 155, 342, 352
R. v. Gillis 178, 179
R. v. Gladue 35, 36, 37, 39, 43
R. v. Glassford 18, 134, 287

R. v. Godfree 136, 142, 251
R. v. Gonidis 10, 12, 17
R. v. Gottli 140
R. v. Goodings 58
R. v. Goyette 351
R. v. Granston 162
R. v. Graveline 100
R. v. Gray 144
R. v. Greene 332
R. v. Greffe 180
R. v. Gregorczyk 329
R. v. Grunerud 112
R. v. Guest 309
R. v. Gummer 263
R. v. Gutoski 352
R. v. H. (C.N.) 21, 129, 296
R. v. H. (D.A.) 36, 51, 82, 140, 142, 157, 340
R. v. H. (J.) 279
R. v. H. (K.) 62
R. v. H. (P.J.) 56
R. v. H. (T.) 266
R. v. Habib 253, 290
R. v. Hackney 288
R. v. Hadida 119
R. v. Hagen 241
R. v. Haggarty 316
R. v. Hall (2001) 212, 322
R. v. Hall (2002) 301
R. v. Hanifan 247
R. v. Hannibal 352
R. v. Hansen 188
R. v. Harcourt 345
R. v. Harkness 139
R. v. Harper 185
R. v. Harris 15
R. v. Hayes (1999) 189
R. v. Hayes (2001) 119
R. v. Hayward 277
R. v. Heaslip 70, 136
R. v. Hebert (1990) 180
R. v. Hebert (2002) 298
R. v. Helpard 176
R. v. Henry Heyink Construction Ltd. 240
R. v. Hernandez 167
R. v. Hewlett 99
R. v. Hicks 98
R. v. Higginbottom 212
R. v. Hindes 164

R. v. Hirnschall 85
R. v. Hoang 182
R. v. Holder 182, 189
R. v. Howlett 121, 232, 273, 274, 298
R. v. Hudson 339
R. v. Hurst 64
R. v. Huynh 310
R. v. Huywan 107
R. v. Innes 293
R. v. Iwaniw 243
R. v. J. (L.A.) 57, 58, 66
R. v. J. (O.) 26
R. v. J. (R.K.) 173
R. v. Jamieson 188
R. v. Jeffrey 4
R. v. John 15, 313, 314, 315, 318, 319, 328
R. v. Johnson (1915) 241
R. v. Johnson (1989) 348
R. v. Johnson (1993) 55
R. v. Johnston (1970) 174
R. v. Johnston (1990) 331
R. v. Johnston (2000) 73, 234
R. v. Jolin 80, 315
R. v. Jones 10
R. v. Jover 204
R. v. K. (B.S.) 182
R. v. K. (D.) 73, 126, 153, 165
R. v. K. (H.M.) 103, 111, 113
R. v. K. (M.) 210
R. v. K. (S.) 341
R. v. Kaup 10, 69, 132, 142
R. v. Keefe 337
R. v. Keeler 91
R. v. Keevil 19, 214
R. v. Kehoe 99
R. v. Kelly 72, 332
R. v. Kerr 70, 133, 145
R. v. Khamphila 161
R. v. Khan 202
R. v. Kimbley 78
R. v. King 145
R. v. Kirkland 108
R. v. Kittle 168
R. v. Knight 255
R. v. Koe 51, 330
R. v. Koppang 155, 157
R. v. Kovacs 313, 314, 339
R. v. Kozy 183, 185, 186, 187, 189, 190, 191, 193, 196, 197

R. v. Krushel 135, 249, 254, 274
R. v. Kubbernus 95, 113
R. v. L. (B.R.) 123, 127, 136
R. v. L. (C.) 80, 93, 346
R. v. L. (G.S.) 58, 70
R. v. L. (J.), [2000] O.J. No. 2789 .... 20, 251
R. v. L. (J.), [2000] O.J. No. 3806 .... 249, 254, 277, 279
R. v. L. (M.C.) 96
R. v. L. (T.P.) 1, 63, 199
R. v. Labbe 58
R. v. Lacroix 239
R. v. Larcenaire 342
R. v. Larocque 216, 348
R. v. Lascelle 313
R. v. Lasik 29
R. v. Lauzon 121, 136
R. v. Layte 168
R. v. Leach 246
R. v. Leask 206
R. v. LeBeau 261
R. v. Leduc 50, 53, 64
R. v. Lee 333
R. v. Legere 221, 335
R. v. Lelieveld 296
R. v. Levesque 258, 260, 285, 286
R. v. Lewis (1903) 139
R. v. Lewis (2000) 128
R. v. Liikane 341
R. v. Littler 144
R. v. Liu 202
R. v. Llorenz 248
R. v. Lockyer 95, 105
R. v. Lount 321
R. v. Lowery 244
R. v. Lui 178, 179
R. v. Lumley 312
R. v. Luther 337
R. v. Luxton 1, 63, 199
R. v. Lyons 167, 336
R. v. M. 62
R. v. M. (B.F.) 59, 60, 62
R. v. M. (C.) (1997) 29
R. v. M. (C.) (1998) 31
R. v. M. (C.) (2000) 292
R. v. M. (C.A.) 1, 24
R. v. M. (C.B.) 153, 165, 166
R. v. M. (D.) 22, 25, 88
R. v. M. (F.D.) 32

R. v. M. (J.N.) 16, 317, 318
R. v. M. (J.S.) 84
R. v. M. (N.) 203
R. v. M. (R.) 92, 94, 346
R. v. M. (R.A.) 66
R. v. M. (T.) 20, 121, 127
R. v. M. (T.E.) 110
R. v. M.N.T. 227
R. v. MacDougall 129, 278, 295
R. v. Mack 180
R. v. Macki 175
R. v. MacKinlay 312
R. v. Mahamud 115
R. v. Major 78, 115, 328
R. v. Makinaw 109
R. v. Malik 82, 237
R. v. Mallea 156
R. v. Mankoo 121
R. v. Marcott 74
R. v. Marin 332
R. v. Maritan 32
R. v. Martel 196
R. v. Maruska 185, 190, 192
R. v. Mascarenhas 81, 124, 262
R. v. Matral 272
R. v. McCalla 261
R. v. McCormick 206
R. v. McCrystal 23
R. v. McCullough 226
R. v. McDonald (1997) 101
R. v. McDonald (1998) 210, 215, 220, 222, 223, 225, 228, 230
R. v. McDonald (2000) 182
R. v. McDow 163
R. v. McDowell 115
R. v. McGill 342
R. v. McGregor 241
R. v. McIlwain 112
R. v. McKenzie 108
R. v. McKimm 118, 316, 318
R. v. McVeigh 257, 258, 288
R. v. Medeiros 88
R. v. Melanson (1998) 160
R. v. Melanson (2001) 212
R. v. Memarzadeh 53
R. v. Meneses 201
R. v. Merryweather 50, 330
R. v. Michigan Central Railway 242
R. v. Mikic 340

R. v. Miles 254, 319
R. v. Millar 198, 238
R. v. Miller (1997) 170
R. v. Miller (2002) 215, 271
R. v. Mills 225
R. v. Mitzel 102, 109
R. v. Moir 42
R. v. Monchka 69
R. v. Moore 117, 321, 338
R. v. Morelli 8
R. v. Morey 294
R. v. Morgan 84
R. v. Morin 232
R. v. Morrisey 214
R. v. Morrison 279
R. v. Moses 52
R. v. Mossip 95
R. v. Mould 260
R. v. Mulvahill 55, 56
R. v. Munro 322
R. v. Murray 107, 108
R. v. N. (J.) 187
R. v. Nagy 244
R. v. Nelles 141, 256
R. v. Nelson 21, 190, 211
R. v. Nguyen 295
R. v. Nikitin 29, 143
R. v. Njeim 31
R. v. Noble 100
R. v. Nurse 228
R. v. O. (E.) 224, 251
R. v. O. (J.) 203
R. v. O. (J.N.) 23, 33
R. v. Oliver 71
R. v. Olsen (1965) 348
R. v. Olsen (1999) 266, 267
R. v. Ormerod 75
R. v. Osbourne (1984) 271
R. v. Osbourne (1994) 11, 78
R. v. Ouillett 14
R. v. Owens 238
R. v. Oziel 89
R. v. P. (C.) 203
R. v. P. (C.A.) 153, 155, 160
R. v. P. (C.C.) 89
R. v. P. (D.) 255
R. v. P. (D.J.) 155
R. v. P. (J.) 8

R. v. P. (J.A.) 52
R. v. P. (L.) 84, 85, 122
R. v. P. (R.B.) 156
R. v. Packwood 164
R. v. Paquette 53
R. v. Paradis 185, 190, 191
R. v. Parent 341
R. v. Pasdari 126
R. v. Pasha 70
R. v. Patenaude 120
R. v. Patterson (1947) 215
R. v. Patterson (2003) 289
R. v. Pavich 135
R. v. Pearce 200
R. v. Pecoskie 88
R. v. Pellerin 333
R. v. Penasse 36
R. v. Persaud 213
R. v. Pham 265, 295
R. v. Phillips 350
R. v. Phun 159
R. v. Pierce 207, 347
R. v. Pisani 323
R. v. Playford 96, 352
R. v. Porco 17
R. v. Power 64, 153, 233
R. v. Price 5, 132, 246, 354
R. v. Prieduls 202
R. v. Priest 10, 11, 76, 284, 328
R. v. Proulx 2, 9, 96
R. v. Pupovic 83, 121, 127, 274, 292
R. v. Q. (M.T.) 329
R. v. Quance 211
R. v. R. (A.) 23, 30
R. v. R. (D.) 161, 238
R. v. R. (J.D.) 28
R. v. R. (J.J.) 339
R. v. R. (M.) (1998) 286
R. v. R. (M.) (2003) 42, 87
R. v. R. (R.) 68
R. v. R. (W.G.) 56
R. v. R.R.O. 85, 123
R. v. Ralph 160, 172
R. v. Randhile 157
R. v. Raycraft 189
R. v. Reid 147, 196
R. v. Remillard 101
R. v. Rey, [2002] M.J. No. 321 176

R. v. Rey, [2002] M.J. No. 26 176
R. v. Rezaie 209, 210, 215, 217, 220, 222, 223, 227
R. v. Rivet 331
R. v. Rizek 341
R. v. Robertson 28
R. v. Robinson 205, 207
R. v. Rockey 21, 53, 155, 291
R. v. Rodway (1964) 99
R. v. Rodway (1991) 15
R. v. Rohr 72
R. v. Roud 42
R. v. S. (A.) 332
R. v. S. (C.J.) 166, 172
R. v. S. (C.W.) 330
R. v. S. (D.) 135, 274
R. v. S. (D.C.) 35, 51, 55, 128, 136, 211
R. v. S. (D.W.) 311
R. v. S. (H.F.) 23
R. v. S. (J.) 143
R. v. S. (L.J.) 22
R. v. S. (M.) 22, 131, 136
R. v. S. (M.L.) 207
R. v. S. (S.) 166, 180
R. v. Sabloff 191
R. v. Sabourin 212
R. v. Sackanay 37
R. v. Sajna 171
R. v. Salituro 77
R. v. Sampson 323
R. v. Sandercock 171, 173
R. v. Santos 181, 182
R. v. Sarao 182
R. v. Sargefield 330
R. v. Satish 93
R. v. Sawchyn 184, 185, 197
R. v. Schan 4
R. v. Scherer 177
R. v. Schurman 200
R. v. Schwan 179, 180
R. v. Schwarz 289
R. v. Seaway Gas & Fuel Ltd. 207
R. v. Shahnawaz 50, 289
R. v. Shakes 131
R. v. Shott 215
R. v. Singh 255
R. v. Skinner 332
R. v. Skolnick 281
R. v. Skone 185

R. v. Skoro 353
R. v. Sloan 215
R. v. Slusar 349
R. v. Smallboy 101, 109, 113
R. v. Smith (1997) 188
R. v. Smith (1999) 333
R. v. Spellacy 173
R. v. Spence 29
R. v. Spiller 174-177, 179-181
R. v. Spinder 114
R. v. Squires 220
R. v. Standring 331
R. v. Stang 159
R. v. Stein 11, 76
R. v. Stewart (1989) 91
R. v. Stewart (2002) 100, 103, 106, 114, 138, 218
R. v. Stewart (2003) 350
R. v. Stockfish 316, 319, 320, 339
R. v. Stone 122, 341
R. v. Strachan (1986) 304
R. v. Strachan (1991) 311
R. v. Stuckless 329
R. v. Sturge 124, 125, 137, 156, 282, 293, 294
R. v. Swaby 131
R. v. Swan, Piper & Co. 324
R. v. Swanson 177
R. v. Syblis 289, 292
R. v. Syed 84, 134, 289
R. v. Synnuck 60
R. v. T. (G.) 169
R. v. T. (M.N.) 227
R. v. T. (S.L.) 254
R. v. Tait 191, 190
R. v. Tallman 227
R. v. Tallman, Laboucan and Auger 227
R. v. Tame 282
R. v. Tardif 326, 327
R. v. Taylor 117
R. v. Tews 184
R. v. Thomas 62, 292, 297
R. v. Thompson 210, 218
R. v. Thongdara 20, 268
R. v. Tkachuk 172
R. v. Tom 8
R. v. Totten 202
R. v. Torchia 146
R. v. Turcotte 56, 249
R. v. Tustin 104

R. v. Ulayuk 52
R. v. United Keno Hill Mines Ltd. 176
R. v. V. (J.T.) 196
R. v. V. (R.C.) 218
R. v. Valentini 188
R. v. Valle-Quintero 81, 120, 137, 144, 146
R. v. Vandale 15
R. v. Vandervoort 61, 132, 255
R. v. Veaudry 4, 219
R. v. Veen (No. 2) 336
R. v. Venn 159
R. v. Verral 108
R. v. W. (A.G.) 22, 26, 88, 127, 255
R. v. W. (D.R.) 72
R. v. W. (J.) 15, 324
R. v. W. (L.W.) (sub nom. R. v. Wust) 208
R. v. W. (L.W.) (sub nom. R. v. Arthurs) 209, 215, 219, 222, 223, 224,
                                                    225, 226, 228, 230
R. v. W. (L.W.) (sub nom. R. v. Arrance) 208
R. v. Walker 189
R. v. Wang 22, 125, 246
R. v. Ward 120, 121, 273
R. v. Wardrop 347
R. v. Warren 209, 216, 219, 227
R. v. Watkins 15
R. v. Webb 117
R. v. Weenusk 302
R. v. Wells 35, 36, 37, 39
R. v. White (1970) 78, 115, 327, 328
R. v. White (1971) 327
R. v. White (2003) 212, 239, 282, 322, 343
R. v. Williams (1970) 75
R. v. Williams (1971) 340
R. v. Williams (1989) 349
R. v. Willmott (1966) 186, 338
R. v. Wilmott (1967) 336
R. v. Wilson (1971) 347
R. v. Wilson (2003) 32, 125, 154
R. v. Woodcock 349
R. v. Wright 99, 349
R. v. Wu 264, 265
R. v. Y. (T.) 268
R. v. Yip 322
R. v. Young (1901) 89, 116
R. v. Young (January 15, 1971) 253
R. v. Young (November 25, 1971) 90
R. v. Young (1989) 305, 307, 308, 309
R. v. Zerb 161

R. v. Zhang 211, 240, 269, 280, 289
R. v. Zimmer 162
Sanchez v. Metropolitan Toronto West Detention Centre 223
Smith, Re 242

1

The Animating Principles Of Sentencing

1. BALANCING OF THE FACTORS

It may be of assistance at the outset to underline for counsel the cardinal importance of reminding the sentencing court of the observations of Mr. Justice La Forest in *R. v. L. (T.P.)*, [1987] 2 S.C.R. 309, 37 C.C.C. (3d) 1, 1987 CarswellNS 41, 1987 CarswellNS 342, [1987] S.C.J. No. 62, 80 N.R. 161, 44 D.L.R. (4th) 193, 82 N.S.R. (2d) 271, 61 C.R. (3d) 1, 32 C.R.R. 41, 207 A.P.R. 271, at p. 22 [C.C.C.], "[i]n a rational system of sentencing, the respective importance of prevention, deterrence, retribution and rehabilitation will vary according to the nature of the crime and the circumstances of the offender. No one would suggest that any of these functional considerations should be excluded from the legitimate purview of legislative or judicial decisions regarding sentencing."

In other words, no single sentencing principle may trump one or all of the others save if the facts surrounding the offence and the offender permit the Court to conclude that it must be given priority. As made plain in *R. v. Luxton*, [1990] S.C.J. No. 87, [1990] 2 S.C.R. 711, 112 N.R. 193, [1990] 6 W.W.R. 137, 76 Alta. L.R. (2d) 43, 111 A.R. 161, 58 C.C.C. (3d) 449, 79 C.R. (3d) 193, 50 C.R.R. 175, 1990 CarswellAlta 144, 1990 CarswellAlta 658 it is of cardinal importance for the Court to structure a sentence to take into account the individual accused and the particular crime to be sanctioned. The concept of individualization of sentence is discussed at pp. 457-458 [C.C.C.].

2. THE NEED FOR AN INDIVIDUALIZED SENTENCE

The Supreme Court of Canada advanced the following guidance as penned by Lamer C.J.C. in *R. v. M. (C.A.)*, 105 C.C.C. (3d) 327, 1996 CarswellBC 1000, 1996 CarswellBC 1000F, [1996] S.C.J. No. 28, 46

C.R. (4th) 269, 194 N.R. 321, 73 B.C.A.C. 81, 120 W.A.C. 81, [1996] 1 S.C.R. 500, at para 92:

> Appellate courts, of course, serve an important function in reviewing and minimizing the disparity of sentences imposed by sentencing judges for similar offenders and similar offences committed throughout Canada: ... But in exercising this role, courts of appeal must still exercise a margin of deference before intervening in the specialized discretion that Parliament has explicitly vested in sentencing judges. It has been repeatedly stressed that there is no such thing as a uniform sentence for a particular crime: ... Sentencing is an inherently individualized process, and the search for a single appropriate sentence for a similar offender and a similar crime will frequently be a fruitless exercise of academic abstraction. . .

3. THE GENERAL PRINCIPLE OF RESTRAINT IN SENTENCING

It will be useful to pause in order to underscore that any mitigating principle should be advocated against the legislative backdrop of the major sentencing reforms of September 3, 1996, popularly described as Bill C-41, notably the introduction of s. 718.2(d) and the better known s. 718.2(e) of the *Code*. In this respect, recall the guidance of Chief Justice Lamer for the unanimous Supreme Court of Canada in *R. v. Proulx*, [2000] 1 S.C.R. 61, [2000] S.C.J. No. 6, 140 C.C.C. (3d) 449, 30 C.R. (5th) 1, 2000 CarswellMan 32, 2000 CarswellMan 33, [2000] 4 W.W.R. 21, 2000 SCC 5, 182 D.L.R. (4th) 1, 249 N.R. 201, 49 M.V.R. (3d) 163, 142 Man. R. (2d) 161, 212 W.A.C. 161, at para. 1: "By passing the Act to amend the Criminal Code (sentencing) and other Acts in consequence thereof, S.C. 1995, c. 22 ("Bill C-41"), Parliament has sent a clear message to all Canadian judges that too many people are being sent to prison. In an attempt to remedy the problem of overincarceration, Parliament has introduced a new form of sentence, the conditional sentence of imprisonment."

Thereafter note how both the title and the contents of para. 16 seek to emphasize the imperative need for restraint in sentencing:

(1) Reducing the Use of Prison as a Sanction

[16] Bill C-41 is in large part a response to the problem of overincarceration in Canada. It was noted in *Gladue*, at para. 52, that Canada's incarceration rate of approximately 130 inmates per 100,000 population places it second or third highest among industrialized democracies. In their reasons, Cory and Iacobucci JJ. reviewed numerous studies that uniformly concluded that incarceration is costly, frequently unduly harsh and "ineffective, not only in relation to its purported rehabilitative goals, but also in relation to its broader public goals" (para. 54). See also Report of the Canadian Committee on Corrections, Toward Unity: Criminal Justice and Corrections (1969); Canadian Sentencing Commission, Sentencing Reform: A Canadian Approach (1987), at pp. xxiii-xxiv; Standing Committee on Justice and Solicitor General, Taking Responsibility (1988), at p. 75. Prison has been characterized by some as a finishing school for criminals and as ill-preparing them for reintegration into society: see generally Canadian Committee on Corrections, supra, at p. 314; Correctional Service of Canada, A Summary of Analysis of Some Major Inquiries on Corrections—1938 to 1977 (1982), at p. iv. At para. 57, Cory and Iacobucci JJ. held:

> Thus, it may be seen that although imprisonment is intended to serve the traditional sentencing goals of separation, deterrence, denunciation, and rehabilitation, there is widespread consensus that imprisonment has not been successful in achieving some of these goals. Overincarceration is a longstanding problem that has been many times publicly acknowledged but never addressed in a systematic manner by Parliament. In recent years, compared to other countries, sentences of imprisonment in Canada have increased at an alarming rate. *The 1996 sentencing reforms embodied in Part XXIII, and s. 718.2(e) in particular, must be understood as a reaction to the overuse of prison as a sanction, and must accordingly be given appropriate force as remedial provisions.* [Emphasis added]

As a last observation, para. 17 instructs us that "Parliament has sought to give increased prominence to the principle of restraint in the use of prison as a sanction through the enactment of s. 718.2(d) and (e). Section 718.2(d) provides that 'an offender should not be deprived of liberty, if less restrictive sanctions may be appropriate in the circumstances', while s. 718.2(e) provides that 'all available sanctions other than imprisonment that are reasonable in the circumstances should be considered for all offenders, with particular attention to the circumstances of aboriginal offenders'."

4. DEGREE OF WRONGDOING: SEEKING TO PLACE THE OFFENCE AT THE FAVOURABLE RANGE OF THE SCALE

In speaking to sentence, counsel must seek to place those elements of the harmful conduct that are at the favourable or non-aggravating range of the scale of wrongdoing. For example, it is important to stress that the offence of cultivation of marijuana does not necessarily embrace the activity of trafficking in that substance. See *R. v. Veaudry* (2000), [2000] O.J. No. 1818, 132 O.A.C. 258, 2000 CarswellOnt 1776 (C.A.), at para. 1. The moral obloquy that flows from cultivation is, all other things being equal, inferior to that which flows from trafficking and this must be stressed.

Counsel should aim to assist the Court not merely by suggesting the obvious—that the degree of involvement of the offender might have been far greater, but also by pointing out the absence of aggravating features often found in similar offences, such as the presence of weapons, the sophisticated nature of the operation, the obvious professionalism, the length of time the offence has occurred, the presence of traps, etc. In the final analysis, the moral obloquy that flows from cultivation is, all other things being equal, inferior to that which flows from trafficking and the nature of the cultivation itself must be evaluated in order that no "extra" aggravating weight be assigned.

The dynamics of sentencing for possession of child pornography serve to illustrate the importance of moral blameworthiness in assessing the proper placement of the offence on the scale of wrongdoing. As seen in *R. v. Jeffrey* (2002), [2002] O.J. No. 3143, 2002 CarswellOnt 2821 (C.A.) and *R. v. Schan* (2002), [2002] O.J. No. 600, 155 O.A.C. 273, 2002 CarswellOnt 511 (C.A.), the absence of evidence of distribution may be critical in placing the case on the mitigating side of the scale of misconduct. The greater the harm to children, and to our community, the greater the need for the assignment of correctional resources. But, by parity of reasoning, the less grave the misconduct, the less is the need for severity, all other things being equal.

5. PROOF OF AGGRAVATING ELEMENTS: ONUS CAST UPON THE PROSECUTION

In the analysis of each factual situation, it must be recalled that the onus is cast upon the prosecution to establish all aggravating features beyond a reasonable doubt, pursuant to *R. v. Gardiner*, [1982] 2 S.C.R. 368, 68 C.C.C. (2d) 477, 30 C.R. (3d) 289, 1982 CarswellOnt 90, 1982 CarswellOnt 739, 30 C.R. (3d) 289, 140 D.L.R. (3d) 612, 43 N.R. 361 and to s. 724 of the Code. A recent appellate case on point is *R. v. Craig* (2003), [2003] O.J. No. 3263, 2003 CarswellOnt 3165, 175 O.A.C. 82, 177 C.C.C. (3d) 321 (C.A.), at para. 30.

6. PROOF OF AGGRAVATING ELEMENTS: KNOWLEDGE OF HARM

In cases involving two or more offenders, counsel must contest any attempt to have aggravating features assigned to an offender unless shown beyond a reasonable doubt, notably the offender's knowledge as to the degree of harm that might result from the offence. In this respect, *R. v. Price* (2000), [2000] O.J. No. 886, 144 C.C.C. (3d) 343, 33 C.R. (5th) 278, 2000 CarswellOnt 837, 72 C.R.R. (2d) 228, 140 O.A.C. 67 (C.A.) provides the following guidance:

> [para. 54] The appellant was not in the store during the robbery. He was the driver of the car that transported all three accused to and from the robbery. There was no evidence that the appellant fired any of the shots.

> [para. 55] It would appear that the trial judge was of the view that both the appellant and the co-accused Montgomery should be treated identically in so far as sentence was concerned. In my view, in so doing the trial judge erred in principle, given the disparity between the criminal records of the two and the different roles that the appellant and Montgomery performed with respect to the robbery. Although the appellant may have played a significant role in the planning of the robbery, he was not directly involved in the assaultive behaviour and threats of bodily harm which, according to the victim impact statements, so traumatized those present in the store at the time of the robbery. Nor is there any evidence that he either countenanced or envisaged the violence that occurred.

The instruction to be drawn from this passage is that the facts of the offence must be scrutinized with care in order that no aggravating weight be assessed that is not fairly attributable to the offender and that no available mitigating weight be overlooked.

were not guilty of youthful exuberance or rash judgment, which are the usual hallmarks of first offenders. With foolish, herd bravery, the appellants chose to join in what they knew was an unlawful disobedience of the law ... Notwithstanding their personal beliefs, they do not qualify for the usual leniency that judges generally offer to first offenders." In *R. v. Jones* (May 20, 1994), Doc. Masset 3098 (B.C. Prov. Ct.), Barnett, Prov. Ct. J., spoke of the fact that foolish behaviour has always been a characteristic of young persons.

By reason of this "favourable prejudice" towards leniency, the cases are legion in which youthful offenders guilty of less serious crimes avoid the imposition of the type of imprisonment that would otherwise be selected in the case of more mature offenders. For example, in *R. v. Gonidis* (1980), 57 C.C.C. (2d) 90, [1980] O.J. No. 1510, 1980 CarswellOnt 1281 (C.A.), page 94, para. 21, sets out the following remarks: "It has been frequently held by this Court that in general young offenders should not be given long sentences of incarceration where some other appropriate sentence can be imposed, but rather that a short, sharp sentence and a fairly lengthy period of probation should be imposed."

Stated simply, offenders who act out of immaturity, impulsiveness, or other ill-considered motivation are not to be dealt with as if they were proceeding with the same degree of insight into their wrongdoing as more mature, reflective, or considered individuals. The less elevated the degree of moral blameworthiness, the greater the reach of leniency. By way of limited example, the relative youth of an offender will be emphasized in those cases in which an individualized disposition is selected as in the case of *R. v. Kaup* (2000), [2000] O.J. No. 120, 128 O.A.C. 301, 2000 CarswellOnt 93 (C.A.). The Court's judgment begins by underscoring that the youthful offender was only 18.5 years old. See para. 1.

For present purposes, it will be instructive to refer as well to the instruction of the Court of Appeal in *R. v. Priest* (1996), [1996] O.J. No. 3369, 30 O.R. (3d) 538, 93 O.A.C. 163, 110 C.C.C. (3d) 289, 1 C.R. (5th) 275, 1996 CarswellOnt 3588 (C.A.). On behalf of Laskin and Moldaver JJ.A., Mr. Justice Rosenberg penned a comprehensive review of the sentencing principles and procedures that must be considered and applied in cases of youthful offenders, with particular emphasis in the case of those who are unrepresented.

At para. 17, we are reminded of the time honoured principle that a penitentiary term will be meted out even to a youthful offender for the offence of rape gives adequate recognition to the doctrine of deterrence. However, in determining the length of the penitentiary term, regard must be had to all the circumstances of the case, the observations made in the pre-sentence report and the ultimate advantage to society of imposing a sentence which not only acts as a deterrent but will have greater likelihood of affording rehabilitative prospects.

c) The general principle that directs allowance for diminished moral blameworthiness

As a general rule, in light of the historical attention given to youthful immaturity, and the emerging statutory injunctions against recourse to incarceration save where no other option is open, as seen at section 38(2)(e) in particular of the *Youth Criminal Justice Act*, sentencing courts are vigilant to extend a significant degree of leniency when called upon to sanction the actions of young people.

Judges are quite ready to acknowledge and to weigh the "youthful lack of judgment" demonstrated by an offender. For example, in *R. v. Proulx*, [2000] S.C.J. No. 6, [2000] 1 S.C.R. 61, 182 D.L.R. (4th) 1, 249 N.R. 201, [2000] 4 W.W.R. 21, 142 Man. R. (2d) 161, 140 C.C.C. (3d) 449, 30 C.R. (5th) 1, 49 M.V.R. (3d) 163, 2000 CarswellMan 32, 2000 CarswellMan 33, 2000 SCC 5, Lamer C.J.C. emphasized the offender's youth at p. 504, para. 130 [C.C.C.].

Note as well how *R. v. F. (G.W.)* (February 15, 1982), Brooke, Martin and Cory JJ.A., [1982] O.J. No. 32 (C.A.) illustrates the general concerns raised in cases involving youthful offenders. In that judgment, Mr. Justice Brooke set out at para. 1 that "At the time of the commission of the offences the appellant was just past his 16th birthday. Having regard to his age, the information as to his background contained in the pre-sentence report and other material before the Court, I would grant leave and consider his appeal".

It is equally instructive to advance the reverse proposition: Older, presumably more mature individuals are thought capable of greater deliberation prior to adopting a course of action and are penalized for failing to apply this deemed maturity. The language found in *MacMillan Bloedel Ltd. v. Simpson*, 44 B.C.A.C. 241, 71 W.A.C. 241, 1994 CarswellBC 218, [1994] B.C.J. No. 268, 88 C.C.C. (3d) 148, [1994] 7 W.W.R. 259, 92 B.C.L.R. (2d) 1 (C.A.), at para. 45, is apposite: "These appellants tary guidance in sentencing. As noted by Professor Neil Boyd, the original Canadian legislation respecting probation directed courts to consider "... if it appears ... that regard being had to the youth, character and antecedents of the offender, to the trivial nature of the offence..." that the matter might be dealt by other than incarceration or monetary penalty. Refer to "An Examination of Probation", 20 C.L.Q. 355-381, at p. 358.

The 1900 amendments to former s. 971(1) led to a provision that directed courts to have regard to the "age" of the offender as opposed to the former clause that required consideration of the offender's "youth". This amendment was introduced in order that greater numbers of offenders would enjoy probationary periods.

Not only do the courts favour probation, they seek to avoid penitentiary terms, if possible, in the case of youthful offenders. *R. v. P. (J.)* (1970), Aylesworth, Laskin and Jessup JJ.A., [1970] O.J. No. 47 (C.A.) makes plain the generally adhered to principle that penitentiary terms should be avoided, if possible in the case of youthful offenders. At trial, the three offenders, aged 17 to 19, received penitentiary-length terms. The Court of Appeal underlined that the Crown agreed that prison terms in the penitentiary should not have been imposed in light of their ages and the absence of prior records, notwithstanding the seriousness of the crimes. . . The Court noted that "the ends of justice will be met. . ." by imposing reformatory sentences. Laskin and Jessup, JJ.A., elected to impose two years less one day definite in a reformatory while the minority would have added "an indefinite term of as much as nine months to one year to the definite term". See para. 1.

For example, the observation made in *R. v. Morelli* (1977), 37 C.C.C. (2d) 392, 1977 CarswellOnt 1178 (Prov. Ct.) is quite common: "The accused's pre-sentence report was positive and because of her youthful age, excellent background with no previous criminal convictions I granted her a conditional discharge notwithstanding the [breach of trust]..." See p. 393 and *R. v. Tom* (1991), 3 B.C.A.C. 175, 7 W.A.C. 175, [1991] B.C.J. No. 2617, 1991 CarswellBC 746 (C.A.), at p. 176, para. 3.

Note as well *R. v. G. (G.L.)* (January 11, 1982), Jessup, Dubin and Blair JJ.A., [1982] O.J. No. 193 (C.A.), at para. 16:

> The danger of a lengthy term of imprisonment in the penitentiary for a youth is that he is likely when released to become more antisocial than he was when first imprisoned. The fact that

2

Distinct Offender Groups: Presumptive Mitigation

1. YOUTHFUL OFFENDERS:

a) Introduction

Young persons enjoy a particularly favourable status in the eyes of the Court. In essence, the sentencing proceedings begin with the Court favouring leniency unless and until the facts surrounding the commission of the offence and respecting the offender suggest otherwise. This is not just an application of the principle that restraint should be shown in the recourse to incarceration. This is the application of the principle that restraint should be shown in exposing youthful offenders to any form of punishment.

At bottom, it is suggested that the moral blameworthiness that has been demonstrated by the youthful offenders may be discounted, chiefly by reason of their immaturity. In addition, it is presumed that they will respond favourably to the sentencing process.

The duty that defence counsel must discharge is to marshal information to justify not only the presumed lenient penalty, but a lenient disposition as a matter of utilitarian allocation of correctional resources. In so doing, it must be recalled that the favourable status enjoyed by youthful offenders may be displaced in appropriate instances in light of the nature of the wrongdoing and the question of the offender's likely recidivism. As the discussion will reveal, much of the allocation of mitigating and aggravating weight is based on moral blame, and the likelihood of reform.

b) Parliament's long-standing objective is to protect youths from the dangers of imprisonment

The courts have repeatedly emphasized favourable treatment of youthful offenders and this philosophy is not surprising in light of Parliamen-

The primary objectives in sentencing a first offender are individual deterrence and rehabilitation. Except for very serious offences and offences involving violence, this Court has held that these objectives are not only paramount but best achieved by either a suspended sentence and probation or a very short term of imprisonment followed by a term of probation. In *R. v. Stein* (1974), 15 C.C.C. (2d) 376 (Ont. C.A.) at page 377, Martin J.A. made it clear that in the case of a first offender, the Court should explore all other dispositions before imposing a custodial sentence ....

d)   Defining a youth

It is not without interest or purpose to pause to note that at para. 21, the Court in *R. v. Priest* (1996), 93 O.A.C. 163, 1 C.R. (5th) 275, [1996] O.J. No. 3369, 30 O.R. (3d) 538, 110 C.C.C. (3d) 289, 1996 CarswellOnt 3588 (C.A.) observed that "With the increase, in 1985, in the age limit to which the *Young Offenders Act* applies, the range to which the term 'youthful offender' can properly be invoked in the ordinary courts is somewhat more narrow. However, the term 'youthful offender' refers not simply to chronological age and must include some consideration of the offender's maturity. This again highlights the need to obtain either a pre-sentence report or other clear statement of the offender's background to ensure that the appropriate sentencing principles are brought to bear". In that case, the fact of being 19 was sufficient, in the absence of any other evidence, to conclude that this appellant was a youthful offender. See also *R. v. Osbourne* (1994), 75 O.A.C. 315, 94 C.C.C. (3d) 435, 1994 CarswellOnt 165, 21 O.R. (3d) 97 (C.A.), leave to appeal refused (1995), [1995] S.C.C.A. No. 91, 96 C.C.C. (3d) v, 23 O.R. (3d) xvi, 191 N.R. 237 (note), 88 O.A.C. 79 (note) (S.C.C.).

e)   The general exception to the principle of leniency in the case of youthful offenders: Little allowance for serious or violent offences

Recall that in *R. v. Priest* (1996), [1996] O.J. No. 3369, 30 O.R. (3d) 538, 93 O.A.C. 163, 110 C.C.C. (3d) 289, 1 C.R. (5th) 275, 1996 CarswellOnt 3588 (C.A.), para. 17 included these remarks: "The primary objectives in sentencing a first offender are individual deterrence and rehabilitation. Except for very serious offences and offences involving violence, this Court has held that these objectives are not only paramount but best achieved by either a suspended sentence and probation or a very short term of imprisonment followed by a term of probation. . ."

In this respect, it must be noted that in *R. v. Gonidis* (1980), 57 C.C.C. (2d) 90, [1980] O.J. No. 1510, 1980 CarswellOnt 1281 (C.A.), the Court of Appeal added to the general principle directing leniency for youthful offenders that "The principle does not apply to serious crime or where violence is involved." Refer to page 94, para. 22. Little leniency was shown to the 17-year-old male offenders who enjoyed positive backgrounds as they were guilty of a well-executed and planned armed robbery which involved locking persons in a cold freezer.

It seems that the Court feared that to grant any significant measure of leniency would result in trumping the imperative of maintaining the safety of the community by concerns that the immaturity of the offenders may have led them to the wrongful acts. Stated otherwise, our society can expect immature actions from young people and must make some allowance for these situations, but the scope of the allowance becomes progressively narrower as the harm to the community increases.

A recent and striking application of this exception to the general principle endorsing leniency, on account of immaturity, in the case of youthful offenders is seen in the case of *R. v. Borde* (2003), (*sub nom.* R. v. B. (Q.)) [2003] O.J. No. 354, 168 O.A.C. 317, 172 C.C.C. (3d) 225, 8 C.R. (6th) 203, 2003 CarswellOnt 345, 63 O.R. (3d) 417 (C.A.). Mr. Justice Rosenberg makes plain at para. 35 that leniency was not available in the case of this young Black Canadian, who had known a blunted life experience marked by poverty and racism, by reason of the commission by him of very serious nature offences of violence. Refer to para. 35. In other words, the elevated moral blameworthiness disentitles the offender to any significant leniency.

f) The rationale for leniency in the case of young persons: They may be taught pro-social values

On the assumption that leniency is the foremost concern or, at the very least, that a measure of leniency is possible by reason of the nature of the offence(s), it will be helpful to identify and assess the rational underpinnings for leniency in the case of youthful offenders.

In this respect, it is suggested that the fundamental and overarching animating principle is the belief that an appropriate disposition may serve to rehabilitate the young person by the inculcation of pro-social values and thus obviate further anti-social activity. The tenacity of this principle is seen in the case of *R. v. Borde* (2003), (*sub nom.* R. v. B. (Q.)) [2003] O.J. No. 354, 168 O.A.C. 317, 172 C.C.C. (3d) 225, 8 C.R.

(6th) 203, 2003 CarswellOnt 345, 63 O.R. (3d) 417 (C.A.), at para. 36 wherein Rosenberg J.A. juxtaposes the gravity of the offender's violent crimes with his relative youth. As we read, "[a]side from the gravity of the appellant's crimes, the overwhelming factor is his youth."

Justice Rosenberg emphasized the hope that rehabilitation would be fostered, and not imperilled, by the imposition of a jail sentence and thus, that care should be taken to select a period that adequately reflected the need to protect the community in the short term but without failing to consider that the long term safety of the community depends, to a large measure, on the successful reintegration of an individual who is possessed of a positive view of his place in society. As we are instructed at para. 37:

> In my view, the trial judge erred in principle in focusing almost exclusively on the objectives of denunciation and general deterrence, given the appellant's age and that this was his first adult prison sentence and his first penitentiary sentence. The length of a first penitentiary sentence for a youthful offender should rarely be determined solely by the objectives of denunciation and general deterrence. Where, as here, the offender has not previously been to penitentiary or served a long adult sentence, the courts ought to proceed on the basis that the shortest possible sentence will achieve the relevant objectives. The trial judge's repeated references to the need to send a message and his statement that the sentence was meant to deter others who resort to guns make it clear that general deterrence and to a less extent denunciation determined the length of the sentence. In my view, this error led the trial judge to impose an excessive sentence for the aggravated assault.

g) The "teaching" of pro-social values to youthful offenders may require elements of coercion

Although the point is no doubt obvious from the foregoing, it must be underlined that the sentencing court must take into account to what degree the offender has been recalcitrant in applying the general "teaching" of pro-social values by the community at large, in the first place, and by the administration of justice in particular, in the second place. In this analysis, the younger the offender, the less likely it is that sufficient opportunity has been presented for sufficient assimilation of society's teachings.

As will be discussed at greater length with respect to offenders who have known a "sad life", it is suggested that offenders whose maturity had not flowered fully are not to be held to the same degree of moral account as those otherwise situated. Nevertheless, the teaching of these pro-social values by the Court may well require the application of correctional elements including detention in appropriate cases being mindful of the case-law and statutory injunctions against detention save as a last resort.

Having advanced these comments, it must be noted that a number of cases decided prior to the introduction of the conditional sentence regime served to emphasize that brief periods of detention might be required, together with lengthy periods of community supervision, in order to "teach" youthful offenders the lesson that anti-social conduct had to be deterred. The rationale was that only "short, sharp" periods of detention were required to make this point, and that longer terms of custody might jeopardize eventual rehabilitation by exposing youthful offenders to more hardened criminals. It is submitted that these cases must now be read in light of the many injunctions by various courts at all levels to the effect that a sentence of imprisonment served within the community retains the elements of denunciation and deterrence traditionally seen as inherent within the jail sentence.

By way of illustration, reference is made to *R. v. Ouillett* (February 5, 1980), Howland C.J.O., [1980] O.J. No. 563 (C.A.). In giving the judgment of the Court Chief Justice Howland held, at para. 5:

> Normally, in the case of a first custodial sentence for a youthful offender the principles to which particular attention are to be paid are those of individual deterrence and rehabilitation, and a short sharp sentence is imposed by the Court. Where there is a serious offence involving violence, general deterrence then becomes a prime consideration. The offence in question gave the appearance of having been planned. Masks had been worn and there was some violence, although no physical injuries were suffered. ... It was conceded by counsel that a custodial sentence was appropriate in the circumstances.

Counsel ought not so easily to make such concessions, although this submission may be quite appropriate in serious cases.

Indeed, surely we have arrived at a point in our understanding of the interplay between the principles of sentencing, both codified and as expressed in the case law, that it is no longer required that youthful offenders be jailed to bring home the message that clanging of the jail-house door was meant to convey. Recall the discussion respecting "extremely negative collateral effects" of incarceration discussed by Rosenberg J.A. in *R. v. W. (J.)* (1997), 5 C.R. (5th) 248, 115 C.C.C. (3d) 18, 33 O.R. (3d) 225, 99 O.A.C. 161, [1997] O.J. No. 1380, 1997 CarswellOnt 969 (C.A.) at para. 49. See also the general remarks found in *R. v. Harris* (October 20, 1989), Borins D.C.J., [1998] O.J. No. 2721 (Dist. Ct.), affirmed (1992), 1992 CarswellOnt 1739, 52 O.A.C. 178 (C.A.), per Judge Borins, as he then was, at para. 13. Indeed, both the Criminal Code and the *Youth Criminal Justice Act* enjoin sentencing courts not to select incarceration unless no other option is available.

R. v. John (1999), [1999] O.J. No. 175, 117 O.A.C. 100, 1999 CarswellOnt 132 (C.A.) and *R. v. W. (J.)*, *supra*, at para. 6 are instructive in reminding us that ". . . general deterrence is neither inconsistent with a conditional sentence order nor is it a basis for reserving the conditional sentence for rare or exceptional cases. To the contrary, the objective of general deterrence can be achieved through the conditional sentence of imprisonment."

By way of brief digression, it must be noted that the earlier case law also emphasized that the "taste of jail" might well be satisfied by a brief period of detention following arrest. See *R. v. Rodway* (October 21, 1991), Fraser Prov. Div. J., [1991] O.J. No. 2510 (Prov. Div.), at the penultimate paragraph. For a further example, note *R. v. Watkins* (February 28, 1996), Blacklock Prov. J., [1996] O.J. No. 4975 (Prov. Div.) at para. 38. Indeed, if a youthful or other first offender is to be given a "taste of jail", why should there be any further imprisonment in such cases?

Moreover, the emergence of the principle of proportionality as a codified measure elevates the teaching of the Court of Appeal in *R. v. Vandale* (1974), 21 C.C.C. (2d) 250 (Ont. C.A.) to require that general deterrence not be the yardstick against which is measured the need for detention. Recall that Martin J.A. adopted the reasoning of MacKenna J. in the case of *R. v. Curran* (1973), 57 Cr. App. R. 945 (Eng. C.A.) where the learned judge stated at pages 947 and 948:

> As a general rule it is undesirable that a first sentence of immediate imprisonment should be very long, disproportionate to the gravity of the offence and imposed as this sentence was, for reasons of general deterrence, that is as a warning to others. The length of a first sentence is more reasonably determined by considerations of individual deterrence; and what sentence is needed

to teach this particular offender a lesson which he has not learnt from the lighter sentences which he has previously received.

By way of recapitulation, we are to understand that what is foremost in the case of youthful offenders is to address their need for a better understanding of their duty to the community. They must be taught the lesson that has escaped them earlier, but no more than that, all other things being equal. They are not to be punished chiefly in order to deter others or to further the goal of denunciation. It is suggested that the conditional jail regime is the perfect vehicle to achieve this purpose of correcting an anti-social bent by means of instruction in pro-social responsibility, backed up with the treat of imprisonment if the onerous conditions are not respected.

h) The "prodigal child" principle

On occasion, the desire of the sentencing courts to offer a youthful offender some measure of leniency will be predicated on the bare hope that having gotten into trouble, the offender is sincere in wishing to return home and to turn over a new leaf. For example, in *R. v. M. (J.N.)* (May 20, 1970), Aylesworth, McGillivray and Jessup JJ.A., [1970] O.J. No. 370 (C.A.), a 17-year-old was successful in appealing the four, three-month definite and twelve-month indefinite concurrent terms, for three counts of auto theft and one of attempted auto theft. The Court held at para. 2 that had the trial judge been in possession of the further evidence he would have committed an error in principle had he not suspended sentence "on all of the facts of the case".

The fresh information disclosed that the offender, although a good student, had decided to quit school quite against the wishes of his parents, people of good repute, and they invited him to leave their house. While living on his own, he became involved in these offences. After being released on bail, he returned to his parents' home and to his former employer, where he had a good or, at least, a noteworthy work record and prospects of continued employment. Refer again to para. 2. He was sentenced to time served, and placed on probation for 15 months on conditions including no alcohol, residence with parents unless consent of probation officer obtained, no association with co-accused cousin "save as reasonably may be necessary in the employment of the two by the same employer".

i) The degree of moral blameworthiness is the deciding factor, in the final analysis

As will have become evident at this point, it is not a simple task to identify those cases where leniency is an available option for youthful offenders involved in serious misconduct. Possibly the best means of placing cases on either side of a clear line of demarcation when considering youthful offenders is to address the question of the degree of moral blameworthiness. For example, in *R. v. Gonidis* (1980), 57 C.C.C. (2d) 90, [1980] O.J. No. 1510, 1980 CarswellOnt 1281 (C.A.), we read at page 95, para. 24: "In the present case the trial judge, while stating the general principle applicable to youthful first offenders, overlooked the corollary to that principle, that different considerations apply in serious crimes of violence, particularly where careful planning is evident." I wish to emphasize the element of planning. This serves to emphasize that the offenders had many opportunities to desist or draw back from their intended crime. Stated in other terms, they never demonstrated a moral compass that was sufficient to guide them away from anti-social behaviour having a great degree of potential harm, and with greed as the prime motivation.

At times, the distinction is rather fine. By way of contrast, note *R. v. Denault* (1981), 20 C.R. (3d) 154, 1981 CarswellOnt 44 (C.A.) and *R. v. Porco* (May 5, 1987), Doc. 177/86, [1987] O.J. No. 1746 (C.A.). In the former case, Howland C.J.O. observed: "The offences in question are the first charges with which the appellant has been faced since he became an adult. In the case of a young first offender in adult court, the principles of sentencing which are usually applicable are individual deterrence and rehabilitation, and a short sharp sentence is imposed. However, in the case of a serious offence where violence is involved, then the principle of general deterrence becomes the prime consideration." The Court went on to conclude that "The offence of conspiracy to commit armed robbery where a loaded revolver is found would fall within the category of offences where general deterrence must be given the prime consideration".

Turning to the latter judgment, Lacourcière J.A. opined that a short sharp sentence followed by a period of probation was appropriate to sanction a "threat of violence" by an offender who attempted to rob a convenience store while brandishing a knife. See para. 1. In other words, the offence of conspiracy necessarily involves more forethought and opportunity to resile from a course of action than does a more spontaneous decision to rob a corner store armed with a common kitchen utensil.

Further instruction is found *R. v. C. (M.W.)* (February 18, 1982), Kurisko D.C.J., [1982] O.J. No. 340 (Dist. Ct.), at para. 21: "While a gun was used, the evidence satisfies me that it was not loaded, thereby, significantly mitigating the implications of the use of this offensive weapon." In other words, the offenders were not so callous as to risk an injury or fatality by reason of the accidental or voluntary discharge of their firearm.

R. v. Glassford (1988), 42 C.C.C. (3d) 259, 27 O.A.C. 194, 63 C.R. (3d) 209, [1988] O.J. No. 359, 1988 CarswellOnt 59 (C.A.) is also instructive. The Court of Appeal remarked at page 265 [C.C.C.] that an intermittent sentence was inadequate in the case of a serious sexual assault committed by a 19-year-old who left his victim unconscious and partly clothed. To the contrary, the Court held that the offence required a substantial term of imprisonment in the penitentiary but that the maximum reformatory term was fit in light of special circumstances. See page 266 [C.C.C.]. The commission of a sexual assault involves a high degree of moral blameworthiness, leaving aside the callous actions after the assault. Although there was no evidence of planning, his actions including his after-the-fact conduct bespeak a need for severity.

As a further point, I again refer to the recent instruction found in *R. v. Borde* (2003), (*sub nom.* R. v. B. (Q.)) [2003] O.J. No. 354, 168 O.A.C. 317, 172 C.C.C. (3d) 225, 8 C.R. (6th) 203, 2003 CarswellOnt 345, 63 O.R. (3d) 417 (C.A.). In particular, Rosenberg J.A. remarked at para. 36 that "[a]side from the gravity of the appellant's crimes, the overwhelming factor is his youth." Justice Rosenberg added:

> In my view, the trial judge erred in principle in focusing almost exclusively on the objectives of denunciation and general deterrence, given the appellant's age and that this was his first adult prison sentence and his first penitentiary sentence. The length of a first penitentiary sentence for a youthful offender should rarely be determined solely by the objectives of denunciation and general deterrence. Where, as here, the offender has not previously been to penitentiary or served a long adult sentence, the courts ought to proceed on the basis that the shortest possible sentence will achieve the relevant objectives. The trial judge's repeated references to the need to send a message and his statement that the sentence was meant to deter others who resort to guns make it clear that general deterrence and to a less extent denunciation determined the length of the sentence. In my view, this error led the trial judge to impose an excessive sentence for the aggravated assault.

Having so found, the Court of Appeal went on to hold at para. 37 that "...this case called for a penitentiary sentence notwithstanding the appellant's age. His very serious youth record, his failure to respond to other measures and his repeated violation of court orders indicated that specific deterrence would be an important objective. The string of offences, two involving use of a loaded handgun, required a lengthy sentence. These circumstances, however, had to be balanced against the appellant's age and his chaotic background as part of a dysfunctional family being raised in poverty by a mother who unfortunately had few parenting skills and suffered from a mental illness. There was also some reason for optimism about the appellant's chances for rehabilitation. The pre-sentence report indicates that while the appellant did not respond particularly well to community-based programmes, he did do well in a more structured environment."

In the same vein, reference is made to *R. v. Keevil* (2003), [2003] O.J. No. 112, 2003 CarswellOnt 113, 167 O.A.C. 329 (C.A.). The offender committed three groups of offences and note that he was only 23 when sentenced to seven years and nine months after 326 days of "dead time" credited on a two-for-one basis.

In the view of the Court of Appeal, the trial judge's comprehensive reasons did not disclose any violation of this principle and are not to be upset. In this respect, note the comments of the trial judge set out at para. 16:

> I have considered the submission with respect to defence counsel that the sentence should not be one that is crushing, and I have struggled, I can tell you, with that concept. I have looked at every factor that I could look at to try and determine if there was any way the needs of society could be met and impose a sentence of less than this amount, because it is a long sentence. In my view, the protection of society cannot be met with any other sentence.

Although the Court of Appeal acknowledged that the sentence was "a long sentence" for a 23-year-old man, it saw no basis for interfering with the trial judge's conclusion on the totality issue. As made plain at para. 17: "The seven-year sentence for aggravated assault endangering life was not excessive. The additional sentences, mostly for break and enters, were certainly not excessive in light of the appellant's long criminal record and the large number of break and enter convictions. Taken together, we cannot say that the global sentence violated the totality principle."

Offences of violence involving youthful offenders may result in severe sentences by reason of the elevated moral blame attached to such conduct, as illustrated by *R. v. M. (T.)* (2000), [2000] O.J. No. 2619, 133 O.A.C. 169, 2000 CarswellOnt 2188 (C.A.). No credit was assigned to the youth of a 17-year-old guilty of a callous shooting in the course of a robbery. Foremost in the mind of the Court was the slight hope of reformation. See para. 12: "...given the dim prospects for rehabilitation, the need to protect the public and the requirement for denunciation of these brutal acts, a long period of incarceration was required despite the appellant's youth and limited prior record."

R. v. Thongdara (2000), [2000] O.J. No. 1832, 132 O.A.C. 256, 2000 CarswellOnt 1872 (C.A.) includes this observation, at para. 4: "It is difficult to imagine a worse case than this [of robbery and extortion] and the offender, despite his youth, approaches the worst offender status." Thus, the Court refused to interfere with a total sentence of 18 years, notwithstanding two years of pre-trial detention.

Note as well *R. v. Flores* (2000), [2000] O.J. No. 1991, 2000 CarswellOnt 1886 (C.A.). At para. 1, the Court of Appeal recorded that "This was a very serious offence. Despite the respondent's youth (18), his first offender status, the positive pre-sentence report and his immediate and deep remorse, a significant custodial term was necessary." Para. 3 sets out, "Although the crime involved extreme violence, it was an isolated act borne of adolescent jealousy. There is nothing to suggest that the offender has a propensity for violence or that he will re-offend." Given certain exceptional circumstances, he received a lengthy conditional sentence.

In the same vein, certain offences are so offensive to the welfare of the community that little weight may be attached to youth and leniency, as made plain in *R. v. L. (J.)* (2000), [2000] O.J. No. 2789, 135 O.A.C. 193, 147 C.C.C. (3d) 299, 2000 CarswellOnt 2649, 5 M.V.R. (4th) 76 (C.A.), at para. 5. Notwithstanding his young age and genuine remorse for his actions, his contempt for the safety of others in driving recklessly for a great deal of time after consuming alcohol to excess, leading to the death of the victim, called for a denunciatory penalty of five years.

j) Youthful offenders and the advocate: Combining mitigating features

Counsel may achieve better success when representing a youthful offender who is guilty of a serious offence if able to point to the presence of mitigating features in addition to the "status" enjoyed by a youth. In other words, that the favourable view taken of youths may be augmented by the presence of other mitigating features is seen in *R. v. H. (C.N.)* (2002), [2002] O.J. No. 4918, 2002 CarswellOnt 4327, 170 C.C.C. (3d) 253, 62 O.R. (3d) 564, 167 O.A.C. 292, 9 C.R. (6th) 103 (C.A.). The judgment includes the observation that "[a]n important factor is the respondent's youth. He was only 19 years of age at the time of the offence. He was otherwise of prior good character. He had been performing volunteer work since 1995 with the Youth Outreach Program and was described as a 'tremendous, positive impact' on the youths with whom he worked. He was employed and financially assisting his mother, a single parent of three children. Finally, he pleaded guilty and was genuinely remorseful." Refer to para. 52.

On the other hand, as discussed herein, the well understood principle that an offender's youth is generally held to be a mitigating feature, and that imprisonment is typically judged to be counter-productive to rehabilitation, will be displaced in cases in which denunciation or deterrence must be expressed by means of a jail sentence. In other words, although restraint in imprisonment is required, if the facts at play do not permit this result, then the period of imprisonment should be as brief as possible, commensurate with the gravity of the offence.

Thus, in *R. v. Rockey* (2001), [2001] O.J. No. 1672, 2001 CarswellOnt 1447 (C.A.), the Court's oral endorsement noted that "[t]he trial judge gave no reasons for so significantly departing from [the Crown's submission of 12 months' imprisonment]". See para. 1. Recognizing that the offences were very serious, and that the offender had a lengthy youth record, it emphasized his early guilty plea, that he is still quite young, and that he suffered terrible abuse as a child. Hence, 18 months was held to be a fit sentence, given the pre-trial custody, not otherwise described.

A further example of leniency is seen in a "weapons case", *R. v. Burke* (2001), [2001] O.J. No. 3281, 2001 CarswellOnt 2789, 149 O.A.C. 272 (C.A.), leave to appeal allowed (August 9, 2001), Doc. C36396, [2001] O.J. No. 3299 (C.A.).

Of course, this does not result in precluding penitentiary-length sentences if the gravity of the offence requires such a penalty. The Court of Appeal noted in *R. v. Nelson* (2001), [2001] O.J. No. 2585, 147 O.A.C. 358, 2001 CarswellOnt 2297 (C.A.) at para. 14: "Although the appellant is a young man (21 years old) and has only a minor criminal record, a lengthy penitentiary term was fully warranted. [He] assaulted, terrorized and humiliated [the victim] over a prolonged period of time. His attack was premeditated and marked by repeated and egregious acts of gratuitous violence. [He] also confined and assaulted [the victim's friend]. To make a bad situation even worse, the attack occurred in [the victim's home]. No doubt, she will live with the terror of that afternoon for the rest of her life." At para. 19, the Court held that "[a] sentence closely approaching nine years was entirely appropriate in this case". See also *R. v. S. (M.)* (2001), [2001] O.J. No. 211, 140 O.A.C. 306, 2001 CarswellOnt 175 (C.A.), at para. 6-7 and *R. v. Wang* (2001), [2001] O.J. No. 1491, 153 C.C.C. (3d) 321, 144 O.A.C. 115, 2001 CarswellOnt 1321 (C.A.), additional reasons at (2001), 2001 CarswellOnt 1773 (C.A.).

2. ELDERLY OFFENDERS:

a) Introduction

Recall the general instruction touching upon young people. In broad terms, it applies to elderly offenders who enjoy a privileged "presumptive" status in the eyes of sentencing courts. That is not to say that proportionate sentencing does not occur. The traditional view of sentencing courts is that some leniency is granted to older offenders, but it is of little consequence unless the offender is also frail or in poor health. For example, in a case of historical sexual violence, *R. v. W. (A.G.)* (2000), [2000] O.J. No. 398, 130 O.A.C. 78, 2000 CarswellOnt 358 (C.A.) Rosenberg and MacPherson JJ.A. noted that "[t]his Court has consistently held that the range of sentencing for an incestuous relationship between a parent and a young child involving acts of sexual intercourse is between three to five years in the penitentiary. See for example *R. v. M. (D.)* (1999), [1999] O.J. No. 1829, 121 O.A.C. 322, 136 C.C.C. (3d) 412, 1999 CarswellOnt 1518 (C.A.)." Refer to para. 4.

On the other hand, their Lordships noted that the offender was very frail, being a "hapless, pathetic, feeble man" of 78 years of age. See para. 5. The fear was that the offender would die in jail, having seen his already frail health deteriorate while serving 52 days of pre-trial detention. In upholding a suspended sentence, the majority of the Court of Appeal commented that they were of the view that deference should be shown to the views of the trial judge in this "unique case". Refer again to paras. 5-6. The dissenting judgment observed that frail health did not prevent the Court of Appeal from concluding that custody was appropriate in cases of elderly offenders in *R. v. S. (L.J.)* (1997), [1997] O.J. No. 2286, 101 O.A.C. 34, 116 C.C.C. (3d) 477, 1997 CarswellOnt

1896 (C.A.), leave to appeal refused (1997), 106 O.A.C. 320 (note), 225 N.R. 237 (note) (S.C.C.) and *R. v. B. (W.R.)* (1994), [1994] O.J. No. 1108, 70 O.A.C. 346, 1994 CarswellOnt 2196 (C.A.).

An exceptional instance involving an elderly offender in extremely fragile health is found in the case of *R. v. McCrystal* (1992), 55 O.A.C. 167, 1992 CarswellOnt 1041 (C.A.). As noted at para. 11: "The appellant's health has deteriorated since the time of sentencing and the risk of incarceration is higher now than it was then. Our concern is that to require the appellant to serve a custodial term could well amount to the imposition of a death sentence." There was unchallenged medical evidence to the effect that the 71-year-old physician, guilty of fraud against a medical health plan, would not survive incarceration.

I acknowledge that s. 721(3)(a) does not refer to advanced age as a precise factor; however, it does refer to age. Nevertheless, it is recognized as a mitigating feature in sentencing, especially if it is considered together with evidence of an offender's poor health. Indeed, in "Sentencing", an unpublished paper of Mr. Justice Houlden dated January of 1981, His Lordship remarked at p. 29 that advanced age is a strong mitigating element.

b) The general rule: To spare elder offenders the rigours of punishment

Not unlike youthful offenders who receive lenient consideration as a result of their immaturity, elder offenders receive favourable treatment ostensibly by reason of their maturity, but fundamentally as a result of a deeply held belief that they ought to be spared punishment if possible, especially in situations of poor or declining health.

A judgment of note in this respect is that of *R. v. R. (A.)*, 92 Man. R. (2d) 183, 61 W.A.C. 183, [1994] 4 W.W.R. 620, 88 C.C.C. (3d) 184, 1994 CarswellMan 114 (C.A.), at para. 35: "Advanced age is usually a mitigating feature. There are two reasons for this. The older a person is the harder it is to serve a prison term and the less is that person's life expectancy after prison." Stated otherwise, "... it is common sense that a man of advanced age taken away from his own home and exposed to penitentiary life will in all likelihood be less flexible or able to adapt to the profound lifestyle change inherent in the loss of freedom". Refer to para. 25 of *R. v. S. (H.F.)* (1995), 136 Nfld. & P.E.I.R. 166, 423 A.P.R. 166, 1995 CarswellNfld 52 (T.D.), citing *R. v. O. (J.N.)* (1993), 103 Nfld. & P.E.I.R. 256, 326 A.P.R. 256, [1993] N.J. No. 9,

1993 CarswellNfld 60 (C.A.), at paras. 15 and 16. The offender in question was 73.

As a next step, it will be useful to define what is embraced by the term "elderly offender". It is noteworthy that at para. 19 of *R. v. M. (C.A.)*, counsel for the offender opined that a 55-year-old man was at an advanced age. The Supreme Court of Canada did not comment on that feature of the case. Further, in *R. v. C. (E.)* (1996), 113 Man. R. (2d) 33, 131 W.A.C. 33, 1996 CarswellMan 374 (C.A.), the "advanced age" principle was applied to a 61-year-old in quite frail health. See para. 42. Fragility and vulnerability were considered in the case of this individual.

c) The fundamental rule: No one should die in jail

In the landmark case of *R. v. M. (C.A.)*, [1996] 1 S.C.R. 500, 194 N.R. 321, 73 B.C.A.C. 81, 120 W.A.C. 81, 105 C.C.C. (3d) 327, 46 C.R. (4th) 269, 1996 CarswellBC 1000, 1996 CarswellBC 1000F, [1996] S.C.J. No. 28, the Supreme Court of Canada provided direct instruction on the issue of the sentencing of elder offenders, at para. 74. As will be seen, the Court was concerned that the fundamental values that undergird our régime of sentencing not be tainted by the possibility that an offender would be ordered imprisoned until death.

> However, in the process of determining a just and appropriate fixed-term sentence of imprisonment, the sentencing judge should be mindful of the age of the offender in applying the relevant principles of sentencing. After a certain point, the utilitarian and normative goals of sentencing will eventually begin to exhaust themselves once a contemplated sentence starts to surpass any reasonable estimation of the offender's remaining natural life span. Accordingly, in exercising his or her specialized discretion under the Code, a sentencing judge should generally refrain from imposing a fixed-term sentence which so greatly exceeds an offender's expected remaining life span that the traditional goals of sentencing, even general deterrence and denunciation, have all but depleted their functional value. But with that consideration in mind, the governing principle remains the same: Canadian courts enjoy a broad discretion in imposing numerical sentences for single or multiple offences, subject only to the broad statutory parameters of the Code and the fundamental principle of our criminal law that global sentences be "just and appropriate".

An illustration of the application of this principle is seen in *R. v. C. (E.)* (1996), 113 Man. R. (2d) 33, 131 W.A.C. 33, 1996 CarswellMan 374 (C.A.). At para. 53, Philp, J.A., opined:

> In *C.A.M.*, Lamer, C.J.C., had recognized that "[a]fter a certain point, the utilitarian and normative goals of sentencing will eventually begin to exhaust themselves once a contemplated sentence starts to surpass any reasonable estimation of the offender's remaining natural life span". That is what I think has happened in this case. A sentence of 25 years surpasses by large measure the "expected remaining life span" of the accused. In that sense, and only in that sense, can it be said that "traditional goals of sentencing have all but depleted their functional value", and that, therefore, the sentence in its totality was demonstrably unfit.

In the result, the total sentence of 25 years was reduced to one of 20 years.

A recent illustration of this rule being applied is the case of *R. c. Monette* (1999), [1999] O.J. No. 4750, 127 O.A.C. 276, 1999 CarswellOnt 4076 (C.A.). The first striking aspect of the case is that the offender is over 90 years of age: I know of no other criminal case involving a nonagenarian! Secondly, that he was sentenced in March of 1993 to five years' imprisonment for a number of sexual and other violent assaults. Labrosse, Weiler and Sharpe, JJ.A., reduced the total to a maximum reformatory term and ordered it to be served within the community without any special conditions, in the absence of any evidence suggesting that he represents a danger to the community. The Court noted his age, his frail state of health and the fear that "... en pratique, une sentence de cinq ans au pénitencier serait pour lui une sentence à perpétuité". Refer to para. 15. [Translation: "In practical terms, a five-year term in a penitentiary for this individual represents a life sentence."]

The Court of Appeal was divided on the question of sentencing in the case of historical sexual violence in *R. v. W. (A.G.)* (2000), [2000] O.J. No. 398, 130 O.A.C. 78, 2000 CarswellOnt 358 (C.A.).

On the one hand, Rosenberg and MacPherson JJ.A. noted that "This Court has consistently held that the range of sentencing for an incestuous relationship between a parent and a young child involving acts of sexual intercourse is between three to five years in the penitentiary. See for example *R. v. M. (D.)* (1999), [1999] O.J. No. 1829, 121 O.A.C. 322, 136 C.C.C. (3d) 412, 1999 CarswellOnt 1518 (C.A.)." Refer to p.

79, para. 4. On the other, their Lordships noted that the offender was very frail, being a "hapless, pathetic, feeble man" of 78 years of age. See pp. 78-79, para. 5. The fear was that the offender would die in jail, having seen his already frail health deteriorate while serving 52 days of pre-trial detention. In upholding a suspended sentence, the majority of the Court of Appeal commented that they were of the view that deference should be shown to the views of the trial judge in this "unique case". Refer again to paras. 5-6.

d) No one should die in jail, but the punishment must fit the crime: The need for a proportionate penalty

At this juncture, it will be instructive to refer to cases in which the extreme nature of the wrongdoing disentitled elderly, but otherwise reasonably healthy offenders, to any form of leniency. In this respect, the Newfoundland Court of Appeal has stated in *R. v. Dinn* (1993), 104 Nfld. & P.E.I.R. 263, 329 A.P.R. 263, 1993 CarswellNfld 62 (C.A.), at para. 15, that "...the point must also be made that there is no precept of law which states that because somebody is old, he or she cannot be sentenced to a prison term. Age may obviously be a factor for consideration in imposing sentence, and it is incumbent on a sentencing judge to consider both the offence and the offender. In this case we have a pattern of extremely serious offences amounting almost, as stated by Crown counsel before this Court, to torture. ... If she was so old and infirm that a prison term could seriously endanger her health, then that could well be a different matter". It is thus a matter of degree.

In my view, it appears undoubted that the general organizing principle of sentencing as applied to violent and other types of serious offences results in denying leniency to offenders guilty of such wrongdoing. Put simply, they do not command leniency.

In this respect, note the following comments, drawn from a report of an 80-year-old offender guilty of incest. The case is *R. v. J. (O.)* (1990), 94 Nfld. & P.E.I.R. 31, 298 A.P.R. 31, 1990 CarswellNfld 72 (Prov. Ct.), at para. 4.

> In passing sentence the Court has to consider the competing interest of denunciation, deterrence and rehabilitation. Because of the seriousness of the sexual assaults as well as the abuse of the position of trust by the father towards his daughter the emphasis in sentencing has to be on denunciation and deterrence. Under the circumstances a significant period of incarceration has

to be imposed. While the advanced age of the accused is a mitigating factor, I am unable to give it any degree of significance, as it would only condone elderly men sexually abusing their daughters. The message has to be quite clear, that is, sexual abuse by fathers against their daughters will attract a significant period of incarceration no matter what the father's age.

At all events, advanced age may incline the Court to a measure of mitigation, in light of an examination of all of the favourable circumstances. In this respect, note that the authors of the *Canadian Sentencing Handbook*, a 1982 publication of the Canadian Association of Provincial Court Judges, suggest the following, at p. 48: "While the effect of age may not be sufficient to warrant a non-custodial sentence in serious crimes such as robbery, it is a strong factor tending to reduce any period of imprisonment to a short term where there is no prior record and no physical harm...". Page 48 informs us that "In general ... old age ... will have a mitigating effect on sentence but not always ...".

e) A lengthy period of offending suggests the offender lacks good character

As a matter of common sense, if the offence is an isolated event, and is dwarfed by many years of blameless conduct, it might be entitled to less importance in the eyes of the sentencing court. The contrary view is also correct. On occasion, the advanced age of the offender is not considered significant in light of the lengthy period of wrongdoing. In other words, the commission of an offence or offences for a lengthy period of time does not tend to demonstrate attenuated moral blameworthiness.

For example, in *R. v. Cameron* (1999), 241 A.R. 87, 1999 CarswellAlta 181 (Q.B.), involving a 61-year-old woman who raised five children, Lee, J., rejected a joint submission for a conditional sentence and imposed a 30-day period of imprisonment to sanction a social assistance fraud spanning 60 months from 1989 to 1994. What is noteworthy is that she was in receipt of such benefits continuously since 1965. See paras. 32 and 39.

The best known example of the application of this sub-principle is the frequent denial of leniency to elderly sexual offenders who have been shown to have abused children over extended periods of time. The controversial nature of this concept is illustrated by means of the first example selected. In the case of *R. v. R. (J.D.)* (1998), 126 Man. R. (2d) 253, 167 W.A.C. 253, 1998 CarswellMan 245 (C.A.), the majority of the Court upheld the refusal of the trial judge to grant a conditional endorsement in the case of a 74-year-old man convicted of repeated offences of sexual violence involving young children 15 years earlier. Para. 11 sets out that the offender suffers from diabetes, has lost sight in one eye, and is not fluent in English.

In fact, a medical report outlined how his three-week stint in jail pending the filing of an appeal brought about great hardship and prophesied fatal consequences if he were to serve the balance of his 12-month term. Refer to para. 12. In the view of the majority, no grounds could be identified to justify interference with the conclusion of the trial judge that the safety of the community was jeopardized by the offender's refusal to accept responsibility and to obtain treatment. Although sharing the trial judge's reluctance to imprison a 74-year-old man, the majority could not be satisfied that any lesser disposition was fit to sanction such violent crimes.

On the other hand, Huband, J.A., was of the view that the offender no longer represented a threat to the safety of the community, chiefly by reason of the progress, albeit still minimal, in his perception of the harm he has brought about. Refer to para. 28. Para. 36 sets out that "He is beginning to suffer from the mental disabilities that often accompany old age". In the view of the dissenting member of the Manitoba Court of Appeal, "... this is the very kind of case where a sentence to be served in the community, subject to conditions, is completely appropriate. The accused is hobbled by the aging process and by illness. Effectively, he can go nowhere without being accompanied by his wife or, perhaps, a friend. If he was in the company of young girls, there would be genuine concern. But surely we have the ingenuity to so craft the terms of a conditional sentence to assure that that does not happen". Refer to para. 39. In the final analysis, as reflected in the observations recorded at para. 43, given the age and infirmities of the accused, conditions would be effective in ensuring the safety of the community.

Other examples include *R. v. Robertson* (1995), 157 N.B.R. (2d) 123, 404 A.P.R. 123, 1995 CarswellNB 350 (Q.B.), leave to appeal refused (1995), 167 N.B.R. (2d) 158, 427 A.P.R. 158, 1995 CarswellNB 266 (C.A.), in which a total of nine years in prison was meted out to a 71-year-old offender and *R. v. Estabrooks* (1999), 222 N.B.R. (2d) 55, 570 A.P.R. 55, 1999 CarswellNB 388 (Q.B.), in which a six-year term of imprisonment was imposed, also to a 71-year-old man. See also para.

2 of *R. v. M. (C.)* (1997), 158 Sask. R. 159, 153 W.A.C. 159, 1997 CarswellSask 500 (C.A.).

f) Advanced age and the passage of time since the commission of the offence

Having discussed rather extensively youthful first offenders, it will be of assistance to refer briefly to the situation of an older first offender. *R. v. Nikitin* (2003), [2003] O.J. No. 2505, 2003 CarswellOnt 2360, 176 C.C.C. (3d) 225, 38 M.V.R. (4th) 223, 173 O.A.C. 164 (C.A.) opens with these words: "This is a sad case. John Nikitin, a 64-year-old man with no criminal record, a good family life and a lifetime of steady employment, was convicted of manslaughter [for a motor vehicle offence]." The Court went on to uphold a lengthy conditional sentence, emphasizing among other factors the aberration of the conduct as judged against a lifetime of contribution to his family, employers and community at large. In terms of our analysis, the moral blameworthiness of his isolated misconduct at the wheel was not elevated, though the quite tragic consequences could not be ignored and justified the reach of a s. 742.1 endorsement, but not actual confinement.

A related question surrounds the passage of time since the commission of such offences, typically involving young children who did not disclose the abuse they suffered until reaching adulthood, discussed at greater length herein. As a general rule, courts tend not to assign any mitigating weight to the lengthy passage of time between the commission of the offence and the prosecution of the offender. See *R. v. Spence* (1993), (*sub nom.* R. v. F.) 131 A.R. 301, 25 W.A.C. 301, 78 C.C.C. (3d) 451, 1992 CarswellAlta 509 (C.A.). On the other hand, if the offender did not bring about the lack of complaint by means of threats, and the passage of time has been marked by no other anti-social act, it might be that greater leniency will be shown.

Consider the comments recorded by Dunn, J., at para. 36 of *R. v. Lasik* (1999), 180 Nfld. & P.E.I.R. 125, 548 A.P.R. 125, 1999 CarswellNfld 187 (Nfld. T.D.):

> Both the *Bromley* [(1998), 167 Nfld. & P.E.I.R. 212, 513 A.P.R. 212 (Nfld. T.D.)] and *Barry* [(1998), 167 Nfld. & P.E.I.R. 65, 513 A.P.R. 65 (Nfld. T.D.)] cases also consider the mitigating factor of age of the offender, along with the fact that he has no criminal record and appears to have lived productively and responsibly

since the occurrences of the offences. Neither judge appeared to place any great emphasis on these two areas in the sentencing process. Brother Barry was of a comparable age to Brother Lasik. He was charged with four offences involving gross indecency and indecent assault upon one complainant. The total sentence imposed was three years. Although the offender herein is of relatively advanced years, he is in good health. I am of the opinion that although age may be considered as a factor in sentencing, s. 718 mandates that similar sentences be imposed for similar offences upon similar offenders and the sentences be proportionate to the gravity of the offences. I am not persuaded that advancing age alone should cause any reduction in the normal range of sentence. I do not view this approach to be the "life sentence" argued by the defence. Rather, I recognize that the offender has had the benefit in his more youthful years of a free lifestyle without having been called upon to account for his criminal activities.

Nevertheless, "... where the delay in the reporting of the offence has not resulted from threats made by the offender, or from other attempts to suppress a complaint, the offender may be entitled to a somewhat reduced sentence if he has led an exemplary life during the intervening years and demonstrates genuine remorse. Such circumstances would obviate the need for individual deterrence and time for rehabilitation". Refer to para. 34 of *R. v. R. (A.)*, 92 Man. R. (2d) 183, 61 W.A.C. 183, [1994] 4 W.W.R. 620, 88 C.C.C. (3d) 184, 1994 CarswellMan 114 (C.A.).

g)   Advanced age and parole authorities

The dissenting opinion of Huband, J.A., in *R. v. R. (J.D.)* (1998), 126 Man. R. (2d) 253, 167 W.A.C. 253, 1998 CarswellMan 245 (C.A.), includes the common sense observation that "Realistically, parole authorities will release [a 74-year-old half blind diabetic first offender who is not fluent in English] from custody as soon as their regulations will permit. It makes little sense to re-arrest and imprison him, only to spend a further few months in jail. The accused has been ostracized by his family and shunned within his ethnic community. His health has been damaged. A community-served sentence, with these conditions, would constitute a continuing real and substantial punishment to a man of his age and health". See para. 45.

In *R. v. Dinn* (1993), 104 Nfld. & P.E.I.R. 263, 329 A.P.R. 263, 1993 CarswellNfld 62 (C.A.), at para. 15, one reads: "The same point may be made with regard to the appellant's state of health. While the appellant has for some time been subject to certain chronic disorders, it has not been shown that she is in any imminent danger from these disorders. It is thus not strictly relevant. If while she is in prison her state of health deteriorates, that may properly be looked at by the prison and correctional authorities and it will be their decision as to what should be done."

Note as well the dynamics of a worsening situation as made plain in the next example. In *R. v. B. (W.)* (1994), 122 Nfld. & P.E.I.R. 32, 379 A.P.R. 32, [1994] N.J. No. 259, 1994 CarswellNfld 197 (T.D.), Easton, J., observed of an 83-year-old man, "The pre-sentence report indicates that he is in good physical health, except for high blood pressure which is controlled by medication. Prior to his incarceration he was quite active and spent a lot of time out of doors. ... it also appears that a psychiatric nurse at Her Majesty's Penitentiary had reported that the accused, since his incarceration, had been disoriented and confused. She said that at times he was unaware of where he was or why he was there and does not understand why he cannot come home". Refer to paras. 5 and 6. He was sentenced to four years in all for a number of sexually violent offences. Doubtless he would be released in the very near future. See also para. 1 of *R. v. Njeim* (1986), 15 O.A.C. 198, 1986 CarswellOnt 1135 (C.A.) and *R. v. Gianfelice* (1992), 52 O.A.C. 243, 1992 CarswellOnt 1034, [1992] O.J. No. 2075 (C.A.), at p. 244, para. 3.

In closing, the comments in *R. v. D. (F.)* (1996), 149 N.S.R. (2d) 156, 432 A.P.R. 156, 1996 CarswellNS 95 (S.C.), are of interest. "At your age [66], I simply do not know whether there is any reasonable prospect for your rehabilitation. I leave that to the experts in the institution where you will be incarcerated." Refer to para. 21.

h) Elderly offenders and elderly dependants

On occasion, sentencing courts must grapple with the twin problems of an elderly offender and his or her elderly and vulnerable dependant(s). For example, in *R. v. G. (A.J.)* (1995), 168 N.B.R. (2d) 241, 430 A.P.R. 241, 1995 CarswellNB 186, [1995] N.B.J. No. 529 (Q.B.), Riordon, J., remarked at para. 18 of the 76-year-old offender: "Both he and his wife are senior citizens living alone in their own home and any order of detention would obviously have a severe impact upon Mrs. G. and I have difficulty in penalizing her for the improper and criminal action of her husband". See also para. 6 of *R. v. M. (C.)* (1998), 165 Nfld. & P.E.I.R. 124, 509 A.P.R. 124, 1998 CarswellNfld 175, [1998] N.J. No.

209, 127 C.C.C. (3d) 249 (C.A.), at paras. 6, 23, 29 and 30. This sort of situation might tip the scale in favour of an individualized disposition favouring the offender's liberty interest.

i) Elderly offenders and the selection of a custodial facility

In passing, note the curious case of *R. v. M. (F.D.)* (1995), 1995 CarswellAlta 1150 (C.A.). The Alberta Court of Appeal observed at para. 5 that "... age [76] has some general relevance to sentencing in the abstract. This is so with respect to the kind of institution in which he is to serve based upon humanitarian principles. He is not in the first flush of youthful vigour. That has some general relevance to sentencing in the abstract. It also has very great significance with respect to the kind of institution in which he is to serve." The Court went on to increase the unknown provincial reformatory period to one of four years' imprisonment and remarked, "We make a strong recommendation to the Federal and Provincial authorities that this man not, I repeat not, be moved out of a provincial institution...". Refer to para. 6.

For example, in the case of *R. v. Maritan* (2003), [2003] O.J. No. 1882, 2003 CarswellOnt 1821 (C.A.), the endorsement records the following at para. 2: "...we think the trial judge was entitled to give less weight to the character evidence filed on behalf of the appellant given that the appellant groomed the young complainant and was in a quasi-trust position towards her. Having regard to the gravity and seriousness of the crime, we are not persuaded that the trial judge erred in refusing to impose a conditional sentence." In few words, the good character evidence was discredited wholly.

j) The latest word

Refer to para. 5 of *R. v. Wilson* (2003), [2003] O.J. No. 1047, 2003 CarswellOnt 993, 174 C.C.C. (3d) 255, 170 O.A.C. 128 (C.A.): "Special circumstances that might justify a conditional sentence for OHIP fraud include . . . exceptional personal circumstances such as ill health or advanced age."

k) Summary for advocates: Seek additional mitigating circumstances such as poor health

By way of conclusion, although it appears undoubted that many judgments may be said to hold that advanced age is, without more, a factor tending to the exercise of leniency, it is suggested that the better view is that some other factor, often the poor health of the offender, must be present to justify an individualized disposition except in exceptional situations such as that involving a 90-year-old offender.

As made plain in *R. v. O. (J.N.)* (1993), 1993 CarswellNfld 60, [1993] N.J. No. 9, 103 Nfld. & P.E.I.R. 256, 326 A.P.R. 256 (Nfld. C.A.), a case involving a 74-year-old offender: "If the accused is considered elderly ... the sentencing judge is on notice to pay particular attention to the state of health and, to the extent it can be inferred, the life expectancy of the aging offender. As with the sentencing of a youthful accused, the seriousness of the offence and a criminal record are very important factors. Age is just another factor to be considered by the sentencing judge, its impact depending on all the circumstances of the case." Refer to p. 7.

As a matter of common sense, if the offence is an isolated event, and is dwarfed by many years of blameless conduct, it might be entitled to less importance in the eyes of the sentencing court. Again, an individual who has avoided all violent or dishonest behaviour for 75 years, by way of example, may be taken to have pro-social values and that one incident to the contrary must be taken to have been generated by extreme stress or pressure. In other words, such an individual need not be the subject of a deterrent penalty; his or her good character can be taken to guarantee future good comportment.

In practical terms, what useful purpose is served by incarcerating "to death" offenders? Indeed, such sentences may lead to discrediting the administration of criminal justice in the eyes of the general public. One can think of the situation involving an elderly and broken man, Rudolph Hess, in the Spandau Prison. On the other hand, who would argue that a feeble Adolph Hitler ought not to have been detained until his death, had the possibility arisen?

For ease of reference, the following factors are noteworthy in fixing a particular case on the scale of offenders, having in mind the cardinal principle that crimes of violence may disentitle offenders to leniency, even in the cases of elderly offenders, as in the case of young persons we have seen:

1)   An offence committed in one's elder years may be discounted as an isolated or aberrant act, often associated with health problems affecting judgment;

2)   A lengthy, almost blameless life, commands great mitigation;

3)   An offender's advanced age and frail health often combine to make that person sympathetic to the sentencing court;

4)   Elderly offenders may well be responsible for the care of dependants that are far more likely to suffer secondary harm if severity is exercised, whether by way of imprisonment or monetary penalty;

5)   There is little positive contribution to general deterrence in cases of sentencing involving elderly offenders; and

6)   There is a fear that too harsh a sentence (or the perception of this form of sanction) will diminish the prestige of the Court in the eyes of the public.

3.   ABORIGINAL OFFENDERS:

a)   Introduction: S. 718.2(e) and the legacy of *R. v. Fireman*

Comparatively little need be said as to the imperative need for individualized treatment when sentencing aboriginal offenders save to point to the little mentioned s. 718.2(d) directing that "an offender should not be deprived of liberty, if less restrictive sanctions may be appropriate in the circumstances", and to s. 718.2(e) directing that "all available sanctions other than imprisonment that are reasonable in the circumstances should be considered for all offenders, with particular attention to the circumstances of aboriginal offenders", and to refer to a few passages from *R. v. Fireman*, [1971] 3 O.R. 380, 4 C.C.C. (2d) 82, 7 C.N.L.C. 337 (C.A.).

It will be recalled that he was a First Nations member who was jailed thousands of miles away from his home and from anyone who could communicate with him. Indeed, page 84 [C.C.C.] records that ". . . he lived in a community where time is told only by seasons, that his sentence of ten years is something that he is not likely to fully understand for he is unfamiliar with the calendar measurement of time in terms of days, weeks, months or years." The Court of Appeal intervened to reduce his sentence substantially, but not without commenting that imprisonment not only failed to advance any of the recognized principles of sentencing that are meant to protect the community, it might well serve to destroy the offender while devaluing the administration of justice in the eyes of both the Native and non-Native communities.

That being said, there are a number of guiding principles that will serve to orient counsel in their advocacy. Once again, if there is any bright line of demarcation, it is that sentences tend to require the assignment of correctional resources in greater measure if the aggravating elements as measured by the moral blame assigned to the offender outweighs the mitigating elements. Further, in light of the signal guidance advanced of late by the Court of Appeal for Ontario, it is not necessary to review at length the seminal judgments of the Supreme Court of Canada interpreting s. 718.2(e), being *R. v. Gladue*, [1999] S.C.J. No. 19, [1999] 1 S.C.R. 688, 171 D.L.R. (4th) 385, 121 B.C.A.C. 161, 133 C.C.C. (3d) 385, [1999] 2 C.N.L.R. 252, 23 C.R. (5th) 197, 1999 CarswellBC 778, 1999 CarswellBC 779, 238 N.R. 1, 198 W.A.C. 161 and *R. v. Wells*, [2000] S.C.J. No. 11, [2000] 1 S.C.R. 207, 182 D.L.R. (4th) 257, [2000] 3 W.W.R. 613, 250 A.R. 273, 141 C.C.C. (3d) 368, [2000] 2 C.N.L.R. 274, 30 C.R. (5th) 254, 2000 CarswellAlta 95, 2000 CarswellAlta 96, 250 N.R. 364, 30 C.R. (5th) 254, 2000 SCC 10, 213 W.A.C. 273.

b) The need to balance the desire for leniency with the need to protect the community in the immediate

In *R. v. S. (D.C.)* (2000), [2000] O.J. No. 885, 47 O.R. (3d) 612, 131 O.A.C. 396, 2000 CarswellOnt 840 (C.A.), valuable guidance is provided on the interpretation of s. 718.2(e) in light of *Gladue* and *Wells*. In essence, the Court of Appeal directs trial judges to recognize the unique circumstances of aboriginal offenders and to sentence aboriginal offenders differently. See para. 10. The Court added, at para. 11, "Admittedly, both *Gladue* [and *Wells*] acknowledge that sentences should not be automatically reduced for aboriginal offenders, and that for more serious and violent offences sentences are likely to be similar whether the offender is aboriginal or not. Still, *Gladue* mandates a different approach to sentencing aboriginals because of the systemic or background factors that play a part in bringing them to Court."

The judgment went on to point out how the offender's background is a poignant example of just how much the upbringing of an aboriginal can differ from that of most Canadians. Paragraph 11 makes plain the debilitating effects of a home life characterized by horrific violence, alcoholism, and poverty. In sum, "Although the offender's crimes warrant a jail sentence, the hardships he has suffered should be taken into account in determining a fit sentence." In conclusion, the addiction to drugs and alcohol that led to the commission of two violent sexual offences was found to be linked to his sad home life as an aboriginal.

In preparing submissions for sentencing in the case of aboriginal offenders, some further guidance may be found in *R. v. Penasse* (2002), [2002] O.J. No. 4376, 2002 CarswellOnt 4024 (C.A.). The guidance provided is limited by reason of the paucity of facts. In brief, the Court refused to intervene, concluding that "[w]e have not been persuaded that [the trial judge] erred in balancing these important factors. The sentencing judge was in the best position to fashion an appropriate sentence." Refer to para. 2. Para 1 frames the litigation in these terms: "We consider that these offences are extremely serious as did the sentencing judge. The sentencing judge recognized that these were competing sentencing principles, namely the public's grave concern about domestic violence and predatory behaviour; and the need to consider all available sanctions other than imprisonment particularly in the case of aboriginal offenders."

Of note, the Court recommended that the offender immediately be considered for admission to Northern Treatment Centre in Sault Ste. Marie.

Note the valuable guidance in *R. v. H. (D.A.)* (2003), [2003] O.J. No. 143, 2003 CarswellOnt 148, 171 C.C.C. (3d) 309, 168 O.A.C. 176, 10 C.R. (6th) 109 (C.A.), on the selection of a fit and proper sentence in the case of aboriginal offenders, in light of s. 718.2(e) which provides as follows: (e) all available sanctions other than imprisonment that are reasonable in the circumstances should be considered for all offenders, with particular attention to the circumstances of aboriginal offenders. By way of brief background, the then 24-year-old offender pleaded guilty to incest involving his 14-year-old sister who was entrusted to his care as a foster parent. There were six acts of intercourse and other sexual acts over a period of time. Mr. H. was abusing alcohol quite heavily at the relevant time. The instruction of the Court in this respect begins at para. 36:

> [36] Notwithstanding the very serious nature of the offence, it is my view that this is a proper case to impose a reformatory sentence and that the sentence be served in the community as a conditional sentence. My primary reason for coming to that conclusion concerns the application of s. 718.2(e) of the Criminal Code as interpreted by the Supreme Court of Canada in *R. v. Gladue*, [1999] S.C.J. No. 19, 133 C.C.C. (3d) 385 and *R. v. Wells*, [2000] S.C.J. No. 11, 141 C.C.C. (3d) 368.

The Court then remarked, at para. 39:

> [39] As held in *R. v. Wells*, *supra*, at para. 30, "whenever a judge narrows the choice to a sentence involving a sentence of incarceration, the judge is obliged to consider the unique system or background circumstances which may have played a part in bringing the particular aboriginal offender before the courts." In short, *Gladue* and *Wells* require a different approach to the sentencing of aboriginal offenders because of systemic or background circumstances. In *R. v. Sackanay* (2000), 47 O.R. (3d) 612 at para. 9, this Court observed in relation to that offender that his background "is a poignant example of just how much the upbringing of an aboriginal can differ from that of most Canadians."

Noteworthy as well is the instruction found at para. 40:

> [40] In *Gladue*, *supra*, the Court described the impact of these kind of systemic and background factors, at para. 68.

> It is true that systemic and background factors explain in part the incidence of crime and recidivism for non-aboriginal offenders as well. However, it must be recognized that the circumstances of aboriginal offenders differ from those of the majority because many aboriginal people are victims of systemic and direct discrimination, many suffer the legacy of dislocation, and many are substantially affected by poor social and economic conditions. Moreover, as has been emphasized repeatedly in studies and commission reports, aboriginal offenders are, as a result of these unique systemic and background factors, more adversely affected by incarceration and less likely to be "rehabilitated" thereby, because the internment milieu is often culturally inappropriate and regrettably discrimination towards them is so often rampant in penal institutions.

Finally, note the guidance contained in the remarks consigned at para. 41:

> [41] *Gladue* also instructs the sentencing court as to how to use the evidence of these systemic and background factors, at para. 69: In cases where such factors have played a significant role, it is incumbent upon the sentencing judge to consider these factors in evaluating whether imprisonment would actually serve to deter, or to denounce crime in a sense that would be meaningful to the community of which the offender is a member. In many

instances, more restorative sentencing principles will gain primary relevance precisely because the prevention of crime as well as individual and social healing cannot occur through other means.

Having thus set out the law to be applied to the facts of the case, the Court of Appeal remarked on the particularly sad life history of the offender. Firstly, we read at para. 39 that "The respondent was subjected to alcohol as an infant. He began drinking with his mother when he was five. His father abused his mother and she in turn inflicted terrible physical abuse on him. His father was killed when he was seven. He suffered terrible sexual abuse from his own relatives." In addition, we are informed that "His mother was a prostitute and performed sexual acts in his presence. She would disappear for months at a time. As a child, the respondent was left to fend for himself for long periods and spent time in 20 different foster homes and in a group home. This has left the respondent psychologically damaged and with a serious alcohol addiction, a Grade 5 education, and few marketable employment skills."

The Court upheld the granting of a conditional sentence, but increased the length to the maximum, and doubled the period of probation to two years, while reinforcing the punitive elements of the conditional sentence order. The chief justification in addition to s. 718.2(e) is captured in the following quotation:

> [37] I will begin with a consideration of the factors that justify a reformatory sentence in this case, although I point out that many of these circumstances are also relevant to the decision to impose a conditional sentence. First, the circumstances leading to this conviction are quite unusual. As I have indicated, the offence came to light because of the respondent's voluntary disclosure to his psychologist when he was seeking treatment. Thereafter, the respondent was fully co-operative with the police, provided a videotaped statement to them and, of course, pleaded guilty. The respondent has only a minor unrelated criminal record. Second, the respondent's upbringing is simply one of the most horrendous that I have seen. He was subjected to terrible physical abuse at the hands of his own mother and extensive sexual abuse from other relatives. He was heavily addicted to alcohol, having begun to consume alcohol as an infant. Only recently has he been able to start to overcome some of the effects of this background by participating in counselling and various programmes and educational upgrading. In my view, these circumstances justify departure from the usual range [of three to five years] as set out in *R. v. B*, [1990] O.J. No. 36, 36 O.A.C. 307 (C.A.)] *supra*.

c) Recent instruction: As a general rule, the moral blameworthiness for aboriginal offenders is attenuated

Subsequently, Rosenberg J.A. provided signal instruction on the extent to which the unique situation involving aboriginal offenders in sentencing, and s. 718(2)(e), are to be considered in the case of quite violent offences in the judgment styled *R. v. Borde* (2003), (*sub nom.* R. v. B. (Q.)) [2003] O.J. No. 354, 168 O.A.C. 317, 172 C.C.C. (3d) 225, 8 C.R. (6th) 203, 2003 CarswellOnt 345, 63 O.R. (3d) 417 (C.A.).

Of interest, the offender was an African Canadian but in the course of addressing the sentence issues he raised, the Court of Appeal addressed in great detail aboriginal offenders.

As we read at para. 31, there is a positive duty of the trial judge to take judicial notice of the unique systemic and background factors that have contributed to the difficulties faced by aboriginal people in the criminal justice system. Note as well the earlier instruction, at para. 25: ". . . the courts have been directed by the Supreme Court of Canada in *R. v. Gladue* 133 C.C.C. (3d) 385 (S.C.C.) to take judicial notice of systemic racism against aboriginals."

Para. 28 reads as follows: "In *Gladue* and *R. v. Wells*, [2000] S.C.J. No. 11, 141 C.C.C. (3d) 368 (S.C.C.) the Court explained the approach courts must take to the sentencing of aboriginal offenders in light of s. 718.2(e). Section 718.2(e) of the *Criminal Code* provides that (e) all available sanctions other than imprisonment that are reasonable in the circumstances should be considered for all offenders, with particular attention to the circumstances of aboriginal offenders."

Of note, the instruction of para. 29 is relevant to many disadvantaged groups:

> The offenders in those two cases were aboriginals and the reasons of the Court naturally focused on the impact of s. 718.2(e) on such offenders given the special mention of aboriginal offenders in the provision. Some of the language used by the Court, however, could equally apply to the approach to sentencing other similarly disadvantaged groups. For example, in para. 65 of *Gladue* the Court summarizes the conditions that have led to the over-representation of aboriginal offenders in Canada's prisons:

The unbalanced ratio of imprisonment for aboriginal offenders flows from a number of sources, including poverty, substance abuse, lack of education, and the lack of employment opportunities for aboriginal people. It arises also from bias against aboriginal people and from an unfortunate institutional approach that is more inclined to refuse bail and to impose more and longer prison terms for aboriginal offenders. There are many aspects of this sad situation which cannot be addressed in these reasons. What can and must be addressed, though, is the limited role that sentencing judges will play in remedying injustice against aboriginal peoples in Canada. Sentencing judges are among those decision-makers who have the power to influence the treatment of aboriginal offenders in the justice system. They determine most directly whether an aboriginal offender will go to jail, or whether other sentencing options may be employed which will play perhaps a stronger role in restoring a sense of balance to the offender, victim, and community, and in preventing future crime.

Noteworthy as well is the guidance set out at para. 32:

Further, an important part of the *Gladue* analysis hinged on the fact that the traditional sentencing ideals of deterrence, separation, and denunciation are often far removed from the understanding of sentencing held by aboriginal offenders and their community. At para. 70 the *Gladue* Court noted, "most traditional aboriginal conceptions of sentencing place a primary emphasis upon the ideals of restorative justice. This tradition is extremely important to the analysis under s. 718.2(e)." . . . The importance that the Supreme Court attached to the sentencing conceptions of aboriginal communities results from the specific reference to aboriginal offenders in s. 718.2(e). In this regard, aboriginal communities are unique.

These comments led to the conclusion that is set out next, stressing the limits on this doctrine of leniency in cases of quite serious misconduct. As is recorded at para. 33-34:

...In *Gladue* and *Wells* the Supreme Court held that the more serious and violent the crime the less likely that the sentence for an aboriginal offender will differ from the sentence imposed on any other offender. This point is captured at paras. 79-80 of the *Gladue* reasons: Yet, even where an offence is considered serious, the length of the term of imprisonment must be considered.

In some circumstances the length of the sentence of an aboriginal offender may be less and in others the same as that of any other offender. Generally, the more violent and serious the offence the more likely it is as a practical reality that the terms of imprisonment for aboriginals and non-aboriginals will be close to each other or the same, even taking into account their different concepts of sentencing. As with all sentencing decisions, the sentencing of aboriginal offenders must proceed on an individual (or a case-by-case) basis: For this offence, committed by this offender, harming this victim, in this community, what is the appropriate sanction under the Criminal Code? What understanding of criminal sanctions is held by the community? What is the nature of the relationship between the offender and his or her community? What combination of systemic or background factors contributed to this particular offender coming before the courts for this particular offence? How has the offender who is being sentenced been affected by, for example, substance abuse in the community, or poverty, or overt racism, or family or community breakdown? Would imprisonment effectively serve to deter or denounce crime in a sense that would be significant to the offender and community, or are crime prevention and other goals better achieved through healing? What sentencing options present themselves in these circumstances?

The Court of Appeal restated this position from *Wells*, at para. 44:

Let me emphasize that s. 718.2(e) requires a different methodology for assessing a fit sentence for an aboriginal offender; it does not mandate, necessarily, a different result. Section 718.2(e) does not alter the fundamental duty of the sentencing judge to impose a sentence that is fit for the offence and the offender. Furthermore, in *Gladue*, as mentioned the Court stressed that the application of s. 718.2(e) does not mean that aboriginal offenders must always be sentenced in a manner which gives greatest weight to the principles of restorative justice and less weight to goals such as deterrence, denunciation, and separation (at para. 78). As a result, it will generally be the case, as a practical matter, that particularly violent and serious offences will result in imprisonment for aboriginal offenders as often as for non-aboriginal offenders (*Gladue*, at para. 33). Accordingly, I conclude that it was open to the trial judge to give primacy to the principles of denunciation and deterrence in this case on the basis that the crime involved was a serious one.

At para. 35, it was underscored that "[t]his appellant committed a crime of great violence and used a loaded handgun on two separate occasions. The *Gladue* approach would not lead to any different sentence for these violent and serious offences. This does not mean that the background factors as revealed in the pre-sentence report are irrelevant. To the contrary, they are very important, but they are important because, as was said by the Court in para. 80 of *Gladue*, the sentencing must proceed on an individual (or a case-by-case) basis: for this offence, committed by this offender, harming this victim, in this community."

The Court went on to comment, at para. 35: "To paraphrase a comment by Brooke J.A. in *R. v. Roud* (1981), [1981] O.J. No. 14, 58 C.C.C. (2d) 226, 1981 CarswellOnt 50, 21 C.R. (3d) 97 (C.A.), leave to appeal to S.C.C. refused 58 C.C.C. (2d) 226n, [1981] 1 S.C.R. xiii at 242 [S.C.R.], the trial judge has a duty to the public, and has a duty to the offender. The judge cannot discharge either without fairly complete information as to the offender, his background and his character. This necessarily includes whatever information is available about the background and other factors that have led to the offender being before the courts."

d)   Summary for advocates: Parliament has recognized the special status enjoyed by aboriginal offenders

Although many more cases could be reviewed under this heading, the foregoing should suffice to make understandable the special status enjoyed by aboriginal offenders. Starting with the wise words of Brooke J.A. in *R. v. Fireman*, [1971] 3 O.R. 380, 4 C.C.C. (2d) 82, 7 C.N.L.C. 337 (C.A.), and culminating in the present case law giving effect to Parliament's clear injunction to consider jail as an absolute last resort for aboriginal offenders, sentencing courts have come to understand that the need for restraint in sentencing First Nations members to detention is predicated upon a recognition of the diminished moral blameworthiness that is often at play.

As noted briefly in *R. v. R. (M.)* (2003), [2003] O.J. No. 2557, 2003 CarswellOnt 2461 (C.A.), the Court of Appeal at para. 3, the young person is of aboriginal heritage and this had not been taken into consideration at the time of disposition. To fail to note the aboriginal status of an offender may result in failing to acknowledge the possible difficulties encountered in childhood and subsequently. In this respect, note that in an earlier judgment, *R. v. Moir* (2000), [2000] O.J. No. 4523, 2000 CarswellOnt 4467 (C.A.), the Ontario Court of Appeal remarked that "...the appellant submits that the trial judge failed to consider his background as an aboriginal offender in determining an appropriate sentence." The Court held as follows: "We are not satisfied that the trial judge erred as contended. Express submissions were made to him about the appellant's background and on the need to address the principles in *R. v. Gladue*, [1999] 1 S.C.R. 688, [1999] S.C.J. No. 19, 171 D.L.R. (4th) 385, 121 B.C.A.C. 161, 133 C.C.C. (3d) 385, [1999] 2 C.N.L.R. 252, 23 C.R. (5th) 197, 1999 CarswellBC 778, 1999 CarswellBC 779, 238 N.R. 1, 198 W.A.C. 161. There is no reason to believe that this factor was not given due consideration by the trial judge. In all the circumstances, including the appellant's extensive criminal record for related offences, we are of the view that the sentence was fit." Refer to para. 5.

In other words, counsel must ensure that the sentencing court is made aware of all relevant aspects of the offender's background, including the signal relevance of s. 718(2)(e).

4. SYSTEMIC RACISM AND AFRICAN CANADIAN OFFENDERS:

a) Breaking new ground: Mitigation based on attenuated moral blameworthiness

The inclusion of this group within the class of offenders who should enjoy an initial claim or presumption to an individualized disposition together with young persons might appear to be controversial, at first blush. However, the case law cited below should support the view that the inclusion herein is proper. In the alternative, members of this group might qualify under the status of those who have suffered a sad life, if this is the case, of course.

As a starting point, refer to the discussion touching upon aboriginal offenders, for the broad principles are quite similar. Then, turn to the signal instruction advanced by the Court of Appeal for Ontario in *R. v. Borde* (2003), (*sub nom.* R. v. B. (Q.)) [2003] O.J. No. 354, 168 O.A.C. 317, 172 C.C.C. (3d) 225, 8 C.R. (6th) 203, 2003 CarswellOnt 345, 63 O.R. (3d) 417 (C.A.).

Without repeating all that was set out therein respecting the similarities as between aboriginal Canadians and African Canadians, it will be of assistance at the outset to repeat the following observation found in *R. v. Gladue*, [1999] S.C.J. No. 19, [1999] 1 S.C.R. 688, 133 C.C.C. (3d)

385, 23 C.R. (5th) 197, 171 D.L.R. (4th) 385, 121 B.C.A.C. 161, [1999] 2 C.N.L.R. 252, 1999 CarswellBC 778, 1999 CarswellBC 779, 238 N.R. 1, 198 W.A.C. 161 at para. 65 touching on the conditions that have led to the over-representation of aboriginal offenders in Canada's prisons:

> The unbalanced ratio of imprisonment for aboriginal offenders flows from a number of sources, including poverty, substance abuse, lack of education, and the lack of employment opportunities for aboriginal people. It arises also from bias against aboriginal people and from an unfortunate institutional approach that is more inclined to refuse bail and to impose more and longer prison terms for aboriginal offenders. There are many aspects of this sad situation which cannot be addressed in these reasons. What can and must be addressed, though, is the limited role that sentencing judges will play in remedying injustice against aboriginal peoples in Canada. Sentencing judges are among those decision-makers who have the power to influence the treatment of aboriginal offenders in the justice system. They determine most directly whether an aboriginal offender will go to jail, or whether other sentencing options may be employed which will play perhaps a stronger role in restoring a sense of balance to the offender, victim, and community, and in preventing future crime.

Para. 30 of *Borde* goes on to hold: "Some of the same things could be said of the over-representation of African Canadians in our jails and penitentiaries. I think that in an appropriate case a sentencing judge might find assistance from the approach described by the Court in *Gladue* and *Wells*, even though that approach is grounded in the special reference to aboriginal offenders in s. 718.2." Refer to para. 30.

b) The need for compelling evidence of the offender's difficulties in life

Additional comments that are relevant include the following. First, para. 17 makes plain that "[t]he appellant filed a number of reports prepared by various groups concerning systemic racism in Canada. These various reports chronicle a history of poverty; discrimination in education, the media, employment and housing; and overrepresentation in the criminal justice system and in prisons. Common among these reports is the assertion that aside from the experiences of aboriginal peoples, there is no other community in Canada that has faced and continues to face this combination of factors."

In addition, para. 18 and 19 record:

> [18] Among the reports filed by the appellant is the Report of the Commission on Systemic Racism in the Ontario Criminal Justice System (Toronto: Queen's Printer, 1995). This Commission was established in 1992 to inquire into and make recommendations about the extent to which criminal justice practise, procedures, and policies in Ontario reflect systemic racism toward racial minority, especially, black communities. One clear finding of the Commission is that there has been a dramatic increase in prison admissions for black offenders in Ontario in recent years. This increase is especially apparent with regard to drug offences.

> [19] Until this Report, research in the area of overrepresentation in the criminal justice system tended to focus on aboriginal Canadians. Research conducted by J.V. Roberts and A.N. Doob prepared for the Commission provided the first major empirical study on the treatment of black accused. See: "Race, Ethnicity, and Criminal Justice in Canada" in M. Tonry (ed.), *Ethnicity, Crime and Immigration* (Chicago: University of Chicago Press, 1997) 469. This study focused on the bail and sentencing stages of the criminal justice process in Ontario. The authors considered offence categories of robbery, sexual assault, drugs, serious assault and bail violations. The findings demonstrated racial disparities at both these stages of the process. More specifically, the greatest disparities were found for the drug offences. Chapter 4 of the Report explores the problem of the impact of the "war on drugs" on black offenders. Other relevant factors addressed in the Report that contribute to this problem of overrepresentation include social and economic inequalities, as well as differential enforcement.

We are then instructed at para. 20 that "[w]hile racial disparities were found, the authors highlight that the relationship between race, crime and imprisonment is difficult to demonstrate. Patterns of direct discrimination may be found with some offences, however they are unlikely to simply be a function of the differences in the seriousness of the offence. Rather, indirect discrimination arising from judges' reliance on neutral factors such as employment status and detention before trial contribute to the higher incarceration rates among black offenders [Chapter 8, p. 280; Roberts and Doob, p. 512]. In addition, the authors found unexplained race disparities that were not due to the gravity of the charge, record, plea, crown election, pre-trial detention, unemployment of other social factors. The Report attributes these results to direct racial discrimination."

In the final analysis, as noted already, the Court of Appeal emphasized the very serious nature of the violent offences, and that "[t]he *Gladue* approach would not lead to any different sentence for these violent and serious offences". See para. 35. Nevertheless, "[t]his does not mean that the background factors as revealed in the pre-sentence report are irrelevant. To the contrary, they are very important, but they are important because, as was said by the Court in para. 80 of *Gladue*, the sentencing must proceed on an individual (or a case-by-case) basis: for this offence, committed by this offender, harming this victim, in this community."

3

The Moral Blame Attached to an Offender's Conduct as it Supports Reformation or Recidivism

In Chapter 2, the presumption of leniency for certain offenders was the focus of the potential submissions that counsel might wish to advance in a given case. In the next chapter, attention will be drawn to the question of moral blameworthiness for the offender's conduct as it relates to the question of maturity, character, behaviour and willingness to make amends. The discussion seeks to alert counsel to those areas that justify leniency, such as the "immaturity" that may be the product of a "sad life" that has deprived the middle-aged offender of any moral compass typically provided and received in youth, and to those areas that justify severity, chiefly the violent attitudes and behaviours of those bent on ignoring the instruction of the courts. In the final analysis, it is the presence or absence of moral blameworthiness that drives the sentencing process and the following discussion will break down the preferred means of identifying the degree of blame attributable to the offender, and that may in fact be attributed to that person.

1. AN EXAMINATION OF THE OFFENDER'S MATURITY: THE SAD LIFE PRINCIPLE AND DIMINISHED MORAL BLAMEWORTHINESS:

a) Introduction

It is suggested that those who have known a sad life, one marked by alcoholism, violence and neglect in their youth, are often left without a functioning moral compass to guide their actions in life. Not unlike the youthful offender who is presumed to make rash judgments, as we have discussed, many offenders who have never been taught right from wrong, leaving aside having been taught to respond to any stressful situation by recourse to force, pills, liquids or lies, make choices that lead to anti-social actions. Throughout the discussion that follows in this initial part, counsel is reminded to evaluate the merits of a plea for mitigation on the grounds that the offender stands in the same footing as a youth, or has suffered deprivations, broadly speaking, in the same fashion as some aboriginal offenders or African Canadians.

In other words, particular emphasis will be placed on the potential impact of any hardships or difficulties in childhood that may account for a defective degree of maturity. In short, for a host of reasons explaining the presence of typically aggravating elements. For the reasons that follow, it is suggested that counsel should, in appropriate cases, urge that an offender who has experienced a "sad life" should not be assessed as to the presence of moral blameworthiness in the same manner as those who have been taught right and wrong from an early age.

In this light, the discussion in this part seeks to complement the review of the "special status" of the offenders discussed in the first part, as both groups receive some allowance or a diminished "moral compass" that serves to guide their actions. By reason of this impaired or lessened ability to select the correct moral choice, less aggravating weight may be assigned to the wrongdoing, all other things being equal, of course.

The justification for this position is that offenders who have enjoyed positive life experiences, and who have not had to suffer racism, poverty, violence, et cetera, may be seen as candidates for the selection of more punitive or coercive measures in sentencing on the footing that their maturity or character or attitude was such that they well knew that their actions were anti-social and yet they persisted in pursuing them nevertheless. In short, the moral obloquy is more elevated than in the case of those who have had a sad life or have been disadvantaged significantly.

This type of judgment may not be available, or only to a reduced extent, in the case of those who have endured a sad life. As has been discussed in the case of youthful offenders, leniency is often justified by reason of the reduced moral blame that can be attached to their immature indiscretions. On the one hand, we expect foolish behaviour and we demand soul-searching and a desire to avoid further offending coupled with a reduced exposure to coercive measures, on the other. The same general analytical framework operates in the case of more mature offenders: If it can be shown that the misconduct is a manifestation of an exceptional situation, and not the reflection of the normal mind-set, then it is not necessary to allocate the same proportion of coercive measures to bring about reformation, the ultimate means of protecting society.

In the present section, as set out, the discussion is aimed at answering the question whether the failure of the community to ensure an adequate moral instruction for certain offenders, with the result that they may be said to be immature as young persons, or entitled to sympathy as in the case of elderly offenders, or requiring individualized attention as in the case of addicts, or generally disadvantaged as in the case of certain aboriginal or black offenders, results in directing sentencing courts to select lenient sentences in all other similar cases unless imprisonment is necessary in the public interest.

b) The "sad life" principle and society's failure to equip the offenders with a "moral compass", thus ensuring immature actions:

i) Some preliminary questions for advocates

Is it relevant to the selection of a fit sentence that an offender has known but sadness in life? Does the lack of happiness one has experienced mitigate in any way the severity of the penalty to be imposed to sanction wrongdoing? What does happiness have to do with the standard of conduct expected of us all? If there is any significance to an offender's difficulties in life when it comes time to select an appropriate penalty for an offence, how is it to be measured? Does it matter that one co-accused got all the breaks while another got none?

In respect of these questions, note *R. v. Audette* (July 27, 1983), Doc. 354/83, [1983] O.J. No. 724 (C.A.), at para. 5:

> His most recent pre-sentence report, prepared in 1980, indicated that he has an alcohol and drug problem, which seems to be at the root of his troubles with the law. An earlier report describes him as dull and of impaired intelligence, quite possibly as a result of brain damage brought about by glue sniffing and other drug abuse. Generally the reports are not very encouraging.

The Court concluded at para. 6 that the 37-year-old unemployed multi-repeat offender who had shown a pattern of "going in and out of jail" is "... clearly at the point where only he can order a change in the present pattern of his life. With respect, one must question how he and so many other such offenders may stop the pattern of recidivism when their intellectual abilities are blunted to a degree such that they cannot find employment.

And, by way of contrast, it must be recalled that many individuals have overcome significant limitations of this nature and been successful in gaining employment. For example, in *R. v. G. (K.)* (1993), [1993] O.J. No. 1742, 63 O.A.C. 360, 1993 CarswellOnt 1502, 83 C.C.C. (3d) 140 (C.A.) the report of the case records these comments, at para. 3: "The appellant is now 61 years of age. ... He is virtually illiterate and of borderline intelligence, but during virtually all of his years in this country has been gainfully employed." In *R. v. Merryweather* (January 28, 1985), Doc. 552/83, 565/83, [1985] O.J. No. 21 (C.A.) Martin, J.A., noted: "The appellant Merryweather is below average intelligence. He comes from a deprived background, but notwithstanding his disadvantages he has, generally speaking, a favourable pre-sentence report."

In effect, the question to be answered by counsel is whether the injunction of the monster "Make me happy and I shall again be virtuous" is apt in sentencing? Refer to Mary Shelley's *Frankenstein*, at p. 100 [London, Oxford Universty Press, 1969].

ii)   The offender's sad life is relevant to sentencing

As noted in a thorough and poignant judgment, an offender's personal circumstances can properly be taken into account in reducing an otherwise appropriate sentence. See *R. v. Shahnawaz* (2000), [2000] O.J. No. 4151, 51 O.R. (3d) 29, 137 O.A.C. 363, 149 C.C.C. (3d) 97, 40 C.R. (5th) 195, 2000 CarswellOnt 4094 (C.A.), leave to appeal refused (2001), 2001 CarswellOnt 1378, 2001 CarswellOnt 1379, 270 N.R. 195 (note), 149 O.A.C. 395 (note) (S.C.C.), at p. 32 [O.R.], para. 6. Further, reference to this type of unfortunate background is now so common that it is advanced without any further information. For example, in *R. v. Cerasuolo* (2001), [2001] O.J. No. 359, 140 O.A.C. 114, 151 C.C.C. (3d) 445, 2001 CarswellOnt 323 (C.A.) Finlayson J.A. noted at para. 4 that the offender "was abused as a child." Indeed, it may be that the offender, as in *R. v. Leduc* (1995), [1995] O.J. No. 3372, 86 O.A.C. 64, 1995 CarswellOnt 1792 (C.A.), a prosecution for murder, did not receive appropriate love and affection. Indeed, the Court remarked that the offender's "...early childhood was marked by a 'dysfunctional and troubled environment.' His mother was described as an 'inadequate maternal role model'". See para. 2.

As the advocate may be in a position to argue, it may be that the impact of a chaotic, dysfunctional or brutal home has reverberated to the steps of the police station; that violence in childhood breeds violence in life. . ..

In an attempt to address this question, note the following cases. Firstly, *R. v. H. (D.A.)* (2003), [2003] O.J. No. 143, 2003 CarswellOnt 148, 171 C.C.C. (3d) 309, 168 O.A.C. 176, 10 C.R. (6th) 109 (C.A.) provides this guidance at para. 37: "...the respondent's upbringing is simply one of the most horrendous that I have seen. He was subjected to terrible physical abuse...".

Secondly, although discussed in the context of an aboriginal offender, it appears that the guidance found in *R. v. S. (D.C.)* (2000), [2000] O.J. No. 885, 47 O.R. (3d) 612, 131 O.A.C. 396, 2000 CarswellOnt 840 (C.A.) on the debilitating effects of a home life characterized by horrific violence, alcoholism, and poverty should be apposite to any discussion about an offender who has suffered similar hardships. Refer to para. 11 and 12.

Thirdly, consider how an offender's violent behaviour may have been conditioned by exposure to violence in childhood in the next case. As we read in *R. v. Bourassa* (1994), [1994] M.J. No. 203, 92 Man. R. (2d) 288, 61 W.A.C. 288, 1994 CarswellMan 401 (C.A.), at para. 1, the offender was a grandmother jailed for causing bodily harm to her five-year-old grandchild. "The circumstances leading up to the offence were such that the accused was at her wits' end, not knowing what to do to discipline the child for gross misbehaviour (involving setting fire to household items). She chose a highly inappropriate form of discipline, but as the probation officer pointed out, that was the product of her lack of sophistication, her frustration and own experiences of abuse." At para. 3, the Court observed: "Taking the accused's background and degree of sophistication (or more properly the lack of it) into account, we think the proper term is one of four months' imprisonment".

Note fourthly this last preliminary example, as a means of highlighting the terrible fact that the person to be sentenced for sexual violence was sexually abused in a place where he was to receive guidance and was to be in safety. In *R. v. Koe*, (1994), [1994] Y.J. No. 87, 47 B.C.A.C. 315, 76 W.A.C. 315, 1994 CarswellYukon 8 (C.A.), a pre-sentence report contained the following comments: "The children were also sexually abused by the father. Paul Koe attended residential school for 12 years suffering abuse there as well". Refer to para. 4.

We now return to our question, whether the impact of a chaotic, dysfunctional or brutal home has reverberated to the steps of the police station and whether that childhood violence breeds violence in life. If such is the case, based on this limited sampling and on the cases below, that violence in childhood breeds violence in life, may it not be argued that those who have been deprived of material advantages, if not abused outright, cannot be expected to behave as well as those who have never lacked for the essentials of life?

In the evaluation of this question, significant guidance has been found in the remarks of Mr. Justice de Weerdt: "Indeed, it is an all too common feature of the cases coming before this Court that violence breeds violence: children of violent parents or a violent environment growing up to repeat the cycle of violence on their own victims..." Consider *R. v. Ulayuk*, [1992] N.W.T.J. No. 453, [1992] N.W.T.R. 118, 1992 CarswellNWT 25 (S.C.), at p. 121, para. 13. The offender, guilty of manslaughter, was raised by a father who himself had killed. Indeed, the offender's father had killed an infant.

Further assistance is found in Chief Judge Lilies description of the offender's history in *R. v. Moses*, [1992] Y.J. No. 50, 11 C.R. (4th) 357, 71 C.C.C. (3d) 347, [1992] 3 C.N.L.R. 116, 1992 CarswellYukon 2 (Terr. Ct.), at p. 361, para. 13 [C.R.]: "The litany of desperate, destructive circumstances engulfing [his] early childhood are sadly typical of families caught in the turmoil of alcohol abuse and poverty. Abuse, and neglect within his home launched [him from age 10 to 16] in a series of foster homes, group homes, and ultimately into juvenile centres. Along this painful, destructive road of state-imposed care, [he] was physically and sexually abused."

In addition, His Honour has noted most aptly in speaking of certain Native communities: "Unfortunately, some of the children experienced neglect, abuse and even sexual abuse at the mission schools. They are now the adults who appear before this Territorial Court on a regular basis..." See *R. v. P. (J.A.)*, [1991] Y.J. No. 180, [1991] N.W.T.R. 301, 6 C.R. (4th) 126, 1991 CarswellYukon 2 (Terr. Ct.), at p. 304 [N.W.T.R.].

R. v. Bogart (2002), [2002] O.J. No. 3039, 2002 CarswellOnt 2537, 167 C.C.C. (3d) 390, 162 O.A.C. 347, 61 O.R. (3d) 75 (C.A.), leave to appeal refused (2003), [2002] S.C.C.A. No. 398, 2003 CarswellOnt 1027, 2003 CarswellOnt 1028 (S.C.C.) is of interest in demonstrating the elevated moral blameworthiness in the case of a massive OHIP fraud by a physician. In particular, it makes plain the need to deter this type of behaviour, which is often engaged in by well-educated individuals of prior good character, and who take advantage of a system based on self-reporting and an honour system.

A further example of a sad life is found at para. 22 of *R. v. Paquette* (2001), [2001] O.J. No. 5000, 2001 CarswellOnt 4528, 153 O.A.C. 149 (C.A.) where we read of the "...mitigating circumstances in this case, including the appellant's sad life and circumstances".

In *R. v. Rockey* (2001), [2001] O.J. No. 1672, 2001 CarswellOnt 1447 (C.A.), the Court's oral endorsement noted that "The trial judge gave no reasons for so significantly departing from [the Crown's submission of 12 months imprisonment]". See para. 1. Recognizing that the offences were very serious, and that the offender had a lengthy youth record, it underscored his early guilty plea, that he is still quite young, and that he suffered terrible abuse as a child. Hence, 18 months was a fit sentence, given the pre-trial custody, not otherwise described.

On occasion, one cannot discern what weight, if any, is placed on the offender's prior victimization. For example, at para. 4 of *R. v. Cerasuolo* (2001), [2001] O.J. No. 359, 151 C.C.C. (3d) 445, 140 O.A.C. 114, 2001 CarswellOnt 323 (C.A.), we read that "[h]e was abused as a child." Without any other comment, it appears that no weight was assigned to this factor.

Note also *R. v. Memarzadeh* (2001), [2001] O.J. No. 1022, 142 O.A.C. 281, 2001 CarswellOnt 826 (C.A.). As set out at para. 4, "[t]he appellant spent eight years in an Iranian jail as a political prisoner. As a result of interrogations, he was required to undergo three surgical operations on his brain to control bleeding. He was on medication in relation to ongoing mental problems. He was involved with the Centre for Victims of Torture."

Returning briefly to *R. v. Leduc* (1995), [1995] O.J. No. 3372, 86 O.A.C. 64, 1995 CarswellOnt 1792 (C.A.), a case of sexual assault leading to murder, there is found therein some support for the oft-expressed view that an individual whose childhood was marked by violence will go on to be a violent person in life. At para. 2, we read:

> ...[his] early childhood was marked by a "dysfunctional and troubled environment". His mother was described as an "inadequate maternal role model" and his father was an extremely violent alcoholic who had served time in custody for sexual assault. During his early years, the appellant together with his mother and sister suffered physical abuse at the hands of his father. He was also abused and mistreated while residing in foster homes and he exhibited suicidal tendencies.

iii) The "sad life" and a perverted understanding of pro-social values

Fundamental to the advocacy that counsel must advance in such cases is that the actions of the offender are contrary to what is expected of a mature individual, of one who should know right from wrong. What is being pressed is that the offender has a perverted sense of pro-social values and is thus not unlike a young person and entitled, all things being equal, to a substantial measure of leniency commensurate on the one hand with the deprivations that have been endured on grounds of fairness, and with the reduced assessment of moral blame by reason of the defective play of conscience, on the other.

To repeat, counsel should press the sentencing courts to extend a measure of leniency on the following grounds: An offender who has been physically abused in childhood may well be left with a perverted sense of right and wrong in reference to otherwise well-understood values such as the respect that must be shown for the physical integrity of others. Since the offender's physical (and, at times, sexual autonomy) was never respected, the theory goes, it is not surprising that s/he is incapable of respecting the bodily integrity of others.

In this respect, consider firstly the case of *R. v. Blancard* (1992), [1992] B.C.J. No. 762, 12 B.C.A.C. 90, 23 W.A.C. 90, 1992 CarswellBC 980 (C.A.), involving sexual offence by one physically abused in youth, but not by sexual violence. A former priest pleaded guilty to five indecent assaults and received a three-year sentence. On appeal, the total sentence was reduced to one year. He had abused a number of six- to seven-year-old girls who were members of his parish, in some cases after having been denounced and after having provided assurances that such behaviour would end. Blancard was diagnosed as a paedophile with a clear preference for female prepubescent children. Refer to p. 91, para. 5.

The professional evaluations and assessments that were drawn in his case included a report from his therapist, set out at p. 91, para. 10, that noted "...the dysfunctional nature of his early family life became clear and apparently the foundations were laid for a distorted sense of self and sexuality. There was much cruelty and physical and mental abuse in the home." There was not sexual abuse, it seems.

At the end of the day, to have reduced his sentence in this fashion notwithstanding his actions after being denounced and making promises of reformation, the Court must have accepted the opinion that

"There is reason to hope that his whole sexual orientation has matured."
See para. 7. See also *R. v. Johnson* (1993), [1993] B.C.J. No. 1547,
29 B.C.A.C. 69, 48 W.A.C. 69, 1993 CarswellBC 1038 (C.A.), at p. 69,
para. 4.

In advancing this submission, counsel must be alert to the opposite
views, as expressed most ably by Southin J.A. in these terms: "'The
sad life' principle appears to have no application to child abusers who
were themselves abused as children..." This was an obiter observation
in *R. v. Mulvahill* (1991), [1991] B.C.J. No. 3516, 5 B.C.A.C. 1, 11
W.A.C. 1, 69 C.C.C. (3d) 1, 1991 CarswellBC 953 (C.A.), at p. 11, para.
34(5). Further, it is observed that Her Ladyship did not refer to authority
for this proposition.

With respect, it is suggested that the great majority of the cases examined herein support the view that those offenders who were abused
in childhood are entitled to a measure of leniency. In *R. v. S. (D.C.)*
(2000), [2000] O.J. No. 885, 47 O.R. (3d) 612, 131 O.A.C. 396, 2000
CarswellOnt 840 (C.A.), the Court of Appeal took pains to underscore
the offender's tragic home circumstances. As recorded at paras. 11
and 12, the offender guilty of two offences of sexual violence and who
had a bad record had known but despair and hardship in youth. His
home life was characterized by horrific violence, alcoholism and poverty.

Briefly, it is noted that the cases are legion in which the sad home life
is taken into account in the sentencing process on the footing that
offenders are groomed to adopt anti-social values by their home milieu.
For example, in *R. v. Bassett* (1992), [1992] B.C.J. No. 1201, 13
B.C.A.C. 169, 24 W.A.C. 169, 1992 CarswellBC 989 (C.A.), sentence
appeals were heard involving two youths who had accumulated significant records before the Youth and adult courts. In a brief concurring
opinion, at p. 171, para. 10, McEachern C.J.B.C., underscored his belief
that "...there are very few bad people in this world but unfortunately
some unfortunate products of the environments to which individuals
have been exposed. The history of these two men make it easy to
identify them as probable repeat offenders unless something dramatic
is done to change their lifestyle."

As a general proposition, it appears appropriate to state that little mitigating weight will be assigned to the presence of a deprived childhood,
even one marked by violence, be it sexual or not, in cases of serious
wrongdoing. In this respect, the measure of leniency that may be extended is "capped", so to speak.

For example, in *R. v. H. (P.J.)*, [2000] N.S.J. No. 9, 181 N.S.R. (2d) 211, 560 A.P.R. 211, 2000 CarswellNS 12, 2000 NSCA 7 (C.A.), Glube C.J.N.S. remarked that the sentencing judge was correct to hold that the offender's sad life "...did not provide any justification or excuse for what he had done..." He had participated in a horrific home invasion robbery. Refer to paras. 67-68.

The same philosophy is in evidence in the case of *R. v. C. (H.W.)* (1999), [1999] N.S.J. No. 206, 176 N.S.R. (2d) 386, 538 A.P.R. 386, 1999 CarswellNS 184 (S.C.). MacDonald A.C.J.S.C. noted at para. 18, "[d]efence counsel quite candidly indicates that three years would otherwise be a reasonable disposition in the circumstances. However, he urges the Court to consider the 'sad life' principle and the unfortunate tragic past that Mr. Crann has had. I have heard from Mr. Crann directly regarding this." Nevertheless, the Court held that "...the need to emphasize general deterrence is just too important, too significant to detract from the Crown's recommendation of three years. I sincerely hope that there will be some glimmer of light so that Mr. Crann may turn his life around. However, the need for me to emphasize general deterrence is just too great and it commands a disposition of three years as submitted by the Crown." Refer to para. 19.

R. v. Turcotte (2000), [2000] O.J. No. 1316, 131 O.A.C. 311, 48 O.R. (3d) 97, 144 C.C.C. (3d) 139, 32 C.R. (5th) 296, 2000 CarswellOnt 1251 (C.A.), provides an interesting reference to the lack of significance of this principle in cases of truly repugnant behaviour. At para. 38 of his dissenting judgment, MacPherson J.A. remarked, "[i]n *R. v. Brooks,* [1993] O.J. No. 1396 (Gen. Div.), Moldaver J. (as he then was) imposed a six-year sentence in a manslaughter case where the accused had experienced a difficult and sad life." The terrible offence he committed had to be denounced. His Lordship went to underscore the extreme suffering of a victim of strangulation and the high degree of moral blameworthiness of an offender in such circumstances.

One other direct reference to this question is found in *R. v. R. (W.G.)* (1991), [1991] B.C.J. No. 3230, 8 B.C.A.C. 91, 17 W.A.C. 91, 1991 CarswellBC 1069 (C.A.), at p. 93, para. 8 and p. 94, para. 15. The Court of Appeal did not comment adversely on a trial judge's observations that the sexual and physical abuse suffered in childhood mitigated the sentence of an adult sexual offender. Although this is not a ringing endorsement of the principle, it does tend to negate the dicta in *R. v. Mulvahill, supra.*

The Quebec Court of Appeal has also advanced some guidance on this issue. In *R. c. Gervais* (1992), [1992] A.Q. No. 617, 1992 CarswellQue 204, 46 C.A.Q. 236 (C.A.), Mr. Justice Rothman observed at p. 3 that the "[a]ppellant was 25 years old ... his childhood had not been a happy one and he was frequently beaten by his parents. He had commenced both alcohol and drugs at an early age and had problems in both of these areas." Refer to para. 5.

iv) The controversial question: Is it aggravating to repeat the cycle of sexual or other violence?

One issue that defence counsel must consider at greater length is the question whether an offender who has suffered child abuse in the form of sexual or other violence at the hands of a relative is to be granted any measure of leniency if s/he goes on to act in the same fashion towards a younger relative, on the grounds of having been exposed to a deprived and depraved home milieu? May it not be said that the offender's poor socialization cannot be resorted to as a mitigating factor in a situation in which s/he ought to have known better.

Having been the victim of "sexual pollution", to track the language of Lacourcière J.A. in *R. v. J. (L.A.)* (July 4, 1983), Houlden J.A., Lacourcière J.A., Tarnopolsky J.A., [1983] O.J. No. 117 (C.A.), at para. 7: "Community standards will never tolerate sexual abuse and pollution of young children", may one not be in a far lesser position to claim the mercy of the Court?

Note the instruction of the Prince Edward Island Provincial Court on this issue. In R. v. G. (O.J.) (1988), 69 Nfld. & P.E.I.R. 176, 211 A.P.R. 176, 1988 CarswellPEI 108 (Prov. Ct.), Chief Judge Thompson convicted G. of having sexually assaulted his then seven-year-old daughter and a niece, who was 14 at the relevant time. The pre-sentence report contained references to G.'s unfortunate family circumstances including that his father was an alcoholic male batterer who abused his wife and that he was himself subjected to considerable sexual and physical abuse by an older sister and brother from ages five to thirteen.

The Court's approach with respect to this issue was described in these terms, at p. 184, para. 50:

> The accused proffers the foregoing abuse as an explanation for his conduct during the commission of the offences. The ab-

normal actions of the accused in committing the offences which are presently before the Court, in my view, are indicative that the accused, in the past, may well have been involved in sexual and physical abuse. In arriving at an appropriate disposition in these matters, the Court must, inter alia, consider the degree to which the accused should be held accountable for his actions, and to what extent, if at all, abuse to which the accused was himself subjected as a child should reduce his criminal accountability.

Refer to p. 184, para. 50. In the circumstances, the mitigating factor of this deplorable background was insufficient to warrant other than a two-year penitentiary term followed by probation for the maximum period.

At times, the fact that an offender was physically abused as a child is referred to but merely as a neutral circumstance, or as a matter of information. See *R. v. Goodings* (1991), [1991] B.C.J. No. 2126, 1 B.C.A.C. 44, 1 W.A.C. 44, 1991 CarswellBC 1086 (C.A.), at p. 45, para. 5. To the same effect is para. 15 of R. v. Labbe (2001), [2001] B.C.J. No. 184 (C.A.).

Hirshfield J. in *R. v. C. (A.)* (1997), [1997] Y.J. No. 137, 1997 CarswellYukon 52 (S.C.), added, at para. 7: "One would think that having had the sad life that you had, that you would go out of your way to protect and ensure that others do not suffer the same as you did; but on the contrary..." In the circumstances, no aggravating weight is to be placed on this aspect in the absence of any general support for the application of such a punitive element.

In the final analysis, may it be said of the offender in *R. v. L. (G.S.)* (2003), [2003] O.J. No. 1719, 2003 CarswellOnt 1686, 171 O.A.C. 117, 175 C.C.C. (3d) 564 (C.A.) that he is guilty of a crime of great moral obloquy by the very fact that he visited upon a child related to him the degree and nature of sexual violence visited upon him in childhood by a relative? As we read at para. 2, "The offender was raised in a dysfunctional home environment and was abused when he was young." Does he stand on an equal footing with the "mature professional" described by Lacourcière J.A. at para. 7 of *R. v. J. (L.A.)* (July 4, 1983), Houlden J.A., Lacourcière J.A., Tarnopolsky J.A., [1983] O.J. No. 117 (C.A.).

Sentencing courts may well conclude that prior sexual abuse suffered by a sexual offender may be considered, but the weight may not be significant.

v)   The allowance for leniency is not endless

Whatever may be the success enjoyed by counsel in addressing the above-noted question, it is suggested that as a general matter, the allowance for leniency may not be seen as being without limit, and counsel must be careful to delineate a reasonable demarcation point.

Of particular interest to this discussion having as its anchor an offender's degree of maturity, the Trial Division of the Newfoundland Supreme Court has also ruled that the fact that an offender was a victim of sexual abuse is a mitigating factor, but not without indicating that it may only serve to assist an immature offender. In *R. v. M. (B.F.)* (1993), [1993] N.J. No. 207, 109 Nfld. & P.E.I.R. 244, 343 A.P.R. 244, 1993 CarswellNfld 225 (T.D.), Mr. Justice L.D. Barry sentenced a 33-year-old male, who admitted to having committed gross indecency at the age of 21 with his nephew who was then aged 15. He was also found guilty of sexual assault with respect to his then ten-year-old nephew. At p. 246, para. 7, the Court observed that he was the ninth child of eleven, with an alcoholic father and a violent mother, who began to abuse alcohol at six and who was sexually assaulted for a period of five years commencing at approximately age five.

Of note, His Lordship remarked at p. 251, para. 39:

> The mitigating factors include ... the evidence that B.F.M. had been himself sexually abused and brought to a corrupt state of moral character by an unhealthy upbringing which saw him engage at an early age in the use of illegal drugs and alcohol and saw him exposed to violence in the home. Overcrowded sleeping quarters meant that he was accessible to the sexual attention of an uncle.

Refer to p. 251, para. 39. However, the sentencing judge went on to underscore that the unfortunate upbringing could not serve to displace wholly the principle of general deterrence, in that M. was guilty of sexual abuse with an adolescent at a time when he was a university student. In other words, "[h]e should by then have known that what he was doing was wrong, despite his unfortunate upbringing." Refer to p. 250, para. 27.

In *R. v. M. (B.F.)* (1993), [1993] N.J. No. 207, 109 Nfld. & P.E.I.R. 244, 343 A.P.R. 244, 1993 CarswellNfld 225 (T.D.), the Court rejected the Crown's submission that the offender's service in the Armed Forces would have permitted him to overcome his childhood abuse. As noted at p. 251, para. 39, "I do not accept the Crown's submission that B.F.M. had had the opportunity to break out of this cycle of drugs, alcohol and sexual abuse."

Of course, the Court or the prosecution may point out that not all those who are sexually abused commit sexual offences. In this respect, it is of interest to repeat the observations of Mr. Justice Barry at p. 251, para. 39 of *R. v. M. (B.F.)* (1993), [1993] N.J. No. 207, 109 Nfld. & P.E.I.R. 244, 343 A.P.R. 244, 1993 CarswellNfld 225 (T.D.): "There are many individuals who have it just as difficult during childhood as B.F.M. but who do not sexually abuse children...".

vi)   May sexual victimization in youth discount a sentence for a non-sexual offence?

If we assume that there is strong authority for the propositions that violence breeds violence, and thus that sexual violence breeds sexual violence, does it follow that sexual violence suffered in childhood is relevant to a sentence for a non-violent offence? It appears that it may well be in light of *Canada (Attorney General) v. Boulet* (1990), [1990] S.J. No. 330, 85 Sask. R. 93, 58 C.C.C. (3d) 178, 78 C.R. (3d) 309, 1990 CarswellSask 22 (C.A.).

In a dissenting opinion, Chief Justice Bayda considered the fact that the offender, a trafficker in narcotics, had been victimized by sexual abuse when in adolescence to be mitigating in nature. At p. 109, para. 59 and 60, [Sask. R.], p. 198, para. c [C.C.C.], His Lordship noted that: "He had what may be described as a tragic and tumultuous upbringing. The probation officer described him as coming from an extremely abusive, dysfunctional and deprived environment ... He was raised briefly by ... a perverted, alcoholic, foster dad ... He was physically abused as a child and raped at age ten."

vii)   The impact of deprivations in childhood and the inability to develop a moral compass

As discussed, this is the fundamental fulcrum for the present overview. In this respect, Taylor J.A. commented at p. 258, para. 5 of *R. v. Synnuck* (1991), [1991] B.C.J. No. 2834, 3 B.C.A.C. 257, 7 W.A.C. 257, 1991 CarswellBC 1110 (C.A.), that "...having in mind the intellectual abilities of the [offender] and the circumstances of his upbringing, which were apparently very deprived and appeared to have a lasting impact on his character, can I say that a denunciatory ingredient is called for...".

Thus, the presence of a "sad life" is not a credit towards future wrong-doing. In essence, at one point a sentencing court will conclude that an offender has had the opportunity to overcome whatever hardships have been encountered. In other words, it is not a credit in a "sentencing account," to be drawn from to discount sentences indefinitely. Once an offender has been given a fair opportunity to overcome the hardships of youth, no further leniency is to be shown.

For example, in *R. v. Vandervoort* (1991), [1991] B.C.J. No. 2413, 3 B.C.A.C. 317, 7 W.A.C. 317, 1991 CarswellBC 1111 (C.A.), there were two convictions for sexual assaults upon women. Mr. Vandervoort had an unfortunate history in that he was born to alcoholic parents and physically abused as an infant. Nevertheless, the Court of Appeal was of the view that it would not intervene to reduce the sentences, considered lenient in any event, and that were needed to assist him to mature and to recognize the error of his ways.

The British Columbia Court of Appeal returned to this issue, that a person cannot lay the blame for all criminal conduct at the feet of their dysfunctional parents, in *R. v. Friesen* (1992), [1992] B.C.J. No. 1787, 15 B.C.A.C. 76, 27 W.A.C. 76, 1992 CarswellBC 1034 (C.A.). On behalf of Justices of Appeal Taylor and Goldie, Proudfoot J.A. commented favourably, at p. 79, para. 9, on the trial judge's admonition to the offender that:

> Now, you have got to get it out of your mind that you can use your background as an excuse for your present behaviour because it is just not acceptable for 22-year-old adult male to be feeling that he can do these things because he was treated badly by his parents in the past. You have got to get that out of your mind because you are a responsible person and you will be treated as a responsible person. . .I mean, if we were dealing with an 11-year-old child, then there would be some credence to that. But we are not. We are dealing with a 22-year-old adult intelligence and I certainly hope you don't destroy that as you are very nearly doing now with the use of drugs.

Her Ladyship added the observation that one cannot forever draw on the difficulties experienced as a child to excuse criminal behaviour as an adult. In addition, refer to *R. v. Fitzpatrick* (1991), [1991] B.C.J. No. 3586, 5 B.C.A.C. 82, 11 W.A.C. 82, 1991 CarswellBC 951 (C.A.), at p. 86, para. 8: "One would be less than human if one was not sorry for the accused who apparently was made what he is by an unfeeling world but other people must be protected from him." To the same effect, see the holding of Hirshfield J. in R. v. C. (A.) (1997), [1997] Y.J. No. 137, 1997 CarswellYukon 52 (S.C.), at para. 7.

viii)   The significance of a fortunate background

By way of contrast, it will be of assistance to note that there is some support in the case law for the proposition that a person's inability to respond in a positive fashion to a proper and supportive upbringing may be taken into account. For example, in *R. v. Ashoona*, [1986] N.W.T.J. No. 130, [1986] N.W.T.R. 238, 1986 CarswellNWT 17 (S.C.), Marshall J. (now a member of the Ontario Superior Court) underscored how the offender "was brought up within a caring and concerned family. He was not exposed to alcohol abuse or physical or sexual abuse." Refer to p. 241, para. 16.

Note as well *R. v. M.* (1985), 64 N.B.R. (2d) 292, 165 A.P.R. 292, 1985 CarswellNB 407 (Q.B.), at p. 293, para. 4. Mr. Justice Miller remarked, "[i]t was the act of an intelligent young man obviously, granted 17 years of age, but with all the advantages that any young man could hope to have. Had an education, you obviously had a good home, had a good family life...".

Moreover, in *R. v. H. (K.)* (1994), [1994] N.B.J. No. 196, 146 N.B.R. (2d) 372, 374 A.P.R. 372, 1994 CarswellNB 211 (C.A.), the Court went to the trouble of pointing out that "[t]here was no suggestion of abuse within the family." Refer to para. 15. Consider as well R. v. Thomas (1994), [1994] M.J. No. 614, 97 Man. R. (2d) 205, 79 W.A.C. 205, 1994 CarswellMan 450 (C.A.), at para. 7. The Court observed: "[i]t is particularly important that [the assistance of probation] be offered to those who are young and otherwise without guidance from responsible elders."

The importance of a university education and of the training and insight into anti-social behaviour that a person should enjoy as a result of these studies, already noted above in *R. v. M. (B.F.)*, *supra*, at p. 250, para. 27, was highlighted in R. v. Ramsay (1992), [1992] B.C.J. No. 1184, 13 B.C.A.C. 176, 24 W.A.C. 176, 1992 CarswellBC 991 (C.A.), at p. 176, para. 4.

A further example is found in the case of *R. v. B. (R.)* (2003), [2003] O.J. No. 1959, 2003 CarswellOnt 1857, 172 O.A.C. 74 (C.A.), where it was emphasized at para. 6 that the young person was 17 years old at the time of the offence, and that neither he nor anyone in his family has had contact with the criminal justice system. Further, para. 6 sets out that "[h]e lives with his family and appears to have enjoyed a stable and happy upbringing in a good family. References submitted on his behalf confirmed that he was well-adjusted, polite and well-behaved. He does not appear to have a problem with alcohol, drugs or anger management. He is in the final stage of completing high school and plans to attend Mohawk College next September to learn a trade. He has held numerous part-time jobs."

Lastly, the courts do point out as well when offenders have had all of the advantages of growing up in well-to-do households. See R. v. Abell (1992), [1992] B.C.J. No. 419, 11 B.C.A.C. 26, 22 W.A.C. 26, 1992 CarswellBC 955 (C.A.), at p. 29, para. 7.

ix) Sentencing must consider the offender and the offence

It may be of assistance to digress in order to underline for counsel the cardinal importance of reminding the sentencing court of the observations of Mr. Justice La Forest in *R. v. L. (T.P.)*, [1987] 2 S.C.R. 309, 37 C.C.C. (3d) 1, 1987 CarswellNS 41, 1987 CarswellNS 342, [1987] S.C.J. No. 62, 80 N.R. 161, 44 D.L.R. (4th) 193, 82 N.S.R. (2d) 271, 61 C.R. (3d) 1, 32 C.R.R. 41, 207 A.P.R. 271, at p. 22 [C.C.C.], "[i]n a rational system of sentencing, the respective importance of prevention, deterrence, retribution and rehabilitation will vary according to the nature of the crime and the circumstances of the offender. No one would suggest that any of these functional considerations should be excluded from the legitimate purview of legislative or judicial decisions regarding sentencing."

Of course, note is taken of the instruction found in *R. v. Luxton*, [1990] 2 S.C.R. 711, 58 C.C.C. (3d) 449, 1990 CarswellAlta 144, 1990 CarswellAlta 658, [1990] 6 W.W.R. 137, 76 Alta. L.R. (2d) 43, 79 C.R. (3d) 193, 112 N.R. 193, 50 C.R.R. 175, 111 A.R. 161, that it is of cardinal importance for it to structure a sentence to take into account the individual accused and the particular crime must be applied. The concept of individualization of sentence is discussed at pp. 457-458 [C.C.C.].

In other words, the degree of maturity is a variable factor and whatever may be the Court's views as to the wisdom of discounting the otherwise fit sentence to reflect an offender's sad life, it must not be overlooked that injustice may result from a view of the offender as being a mature individual, if in fact s/he is not, for whatever reason.

Counsel must advance information suggesting immaturity where available. Of course, it will be easier for a court to accept that there was significant violence if there is some objective information to support the allegations. In this respect, note that in the case of *R. v. Leduc* (1995), [1995] O.J. No. 3372, 86 O.A.C. 64, 1995 CarswellOnt 1792 (C.A.), the claim of severe violence suffered as a child may have been more credible by reason of the fact that his father was jailed for sexual violence. See para. 2. Refer as well to R. v. Charna (October 26, 1990), Doc. CA011314, [1990] B.C.J. No. 2378 (C.A.), at p. 32.

x)   Pulling at the heart-strings of the Court

As has been revealed, on occasion, sentencing courts (and appellate tribunals) are swayed by the tragic circumstances of an offender even though the record may not reflect that any leniency was in fact accorded. For example, in *R. v. Hurst*, [1999] B.C.J. No. 2051, 130 B.C.A.C. 29, 211 W.A.C. 29, 1999 CarswellBC 1983, 1999 BCCA 510 (C.A.), Esson J.A. remarked that "[h]e is a man who suffers mental problems as a result of which his mental age is said by some to be that of about a child of ten years old—others would put it at more like five years old. He clearly is a man who has difficulty in learning from experience, and as a result, has lived an extremely sad life." Refer to para. 2.

Hence, the Court of Appeal upheld a six-month sentence for breach of probation, proceeded with by means of indictment, and dismissed the offender's sentence appeal. At first blush, this appears to be a severe sentence but the Crown had sought a two-year penitentiary term. Further, the Court appears to have de-emphasized specific deterrence by reason of Mr. Hurst's limited capacity to gain insight into his criminal activities.

xi)   Summary for advocates: The degree of moral blame is the ultimate question, the lack of a moral compass the immediate one in cases of a "sad life"

How often are sentencing courts faced with offenders such as the one described in *R. v. Power* (February 24, 1992), Locke J., [1992] O.J. No. 2005 (Gen. Div.), at para. 7 and 10: "The accused has lived a very sad life ... Mr. Power is a sad case. He has had no chance for any kind of a decent life from virtually the day he was conceived. He is obviously been abused in more than one way in his youth...". What is to be done with them is, as has been discussed herein, a difficult and complex issue. It is hoped that the discussion has served to provide some insight into this perplexing but critical issue in sentencing.

It is suggested that counsel should press the Court to extend a measure leniency in the case of diminished insight into wrongdoing. As a general observation, offenders who have not had much by way of socialization in their youth, who have not been shown right from wrong in few words, are often assigned some degree of leniency, all other things being equal. The theory behind this principle is often that the moral blameworthiness to be assigned to the misconduct is said to be lessened by reason of an inadequate (or absent) ability to understand fully the harm being done to the victim.

To understand fully the rationale being advanced, it may be of assistance to examine the opposite situation: that of an offender who has enjoyed a favourable home life and been exposed to pro-social values and attitudes, as made plain earlier. Recall the case of *R. v. B. (R.)* (2003), [2003] O.J. No. 1959, 2003 CarswellOnt 1857, 172 O.A.C. 74 (C.A.). It was emphasized at para. 6 that the young person was 17 years old at the time of the offence, and that neither he nor anyone in his family has had contact with the criminal justice system. Further, para. 6 sets out that "[h]e lives with his family and appears to have enjoyed a stable and happy upbringing in a good family. References submitted on his behalf confirmed that he was well-adjusted, polite and well-behaved. He does not appear to have a problem with alcohol, drugs or anger management. He is in the final stage of completing high school and plans to attend Mohawk College next September to learn a trade. He has held numerous part-time jobs."

Why would the Court underline these factors if not to make plain that having been made to understand right from wrong, his offence is more likely a momentary lapse in judgment than an indication of a negative disposition? In the result, he may be punished by means of a reduced allocation of correctional assets than would otherwise be the case if the offender had little insight into the wrongdoing and thus, was more likely to repeat the behaviour. Of note, para. 7 records that the Court characterized the misconduct as being an isolated incident that was totally out of character.

It is the duty of counsel to fashion an appropriate submission in cases of individuals who did not enjoy the upbringing described in *R. v. B. (R.)* (2003), [2003] O.J. No. 1959, 2003 CarswellOnt 1857, 172 O.A.C. 74 (C.A.) to underscore the lack of (or deficient) insight that might have resulted from this deficient home life. For example, although no one ignores that sexual violence is morally and legally wrong, some offenders have simply never been provided with any love, affection and tenderness in their lives. When they commit a sexual assault, by way of limited example, it may be fit to point out that although they knew the act was abhorrent, they stand on a lesser footing than those who enjoy a total understanding of such despicable behaviour.

This may be what motivated Lacourcière J.A. to remark at para. 7 of *R. v. J. (L.A.)* (July 4, 1983), Houlden J.A., Lacourcière J.A., Tarnopolsky J.A., [1983] O.J. No. 117 (C.A.): "Having regard to *the maturity and the professional standing* of the respondent and to the large number of offences over an extended period of time, the number and the age of the children involved and the abuse by the respondent of his position of trust with young children, we agree that a penitentiary term is necessary." The emphasized portion seeks to make plain that this individual well knew the harm he was inflicting. The question that defence counsel must address is whether the offender being represented in a sexual violence sentence hearing is similarly situated.

In fashioning a submission, it might be advantageous to argue from analogy from the principle surrounding guilty pleas. Not unlike the principle according to which no greater punishment is selected in the case of a not guilty plea, but a reduced sentence may be apt in the case of a guilty plea, an offender who did not labour under an impaired system of values may not qualify for any leniency in certain cases while the offender who did might be entitled to some diminished assignment of correctional resources.

In certain instances, there is a strong utilitarian component of the decision to exercise a measure of leniency. If the offender's development has been so blunted that s/he is unlikely to be able to draw much "instruction" from a jail term, than any period in excess of what serves denunciation and general deterrence is without purpose. Although the context is far from similar, this situation is not unlike the reaction of the offender in *R. v. Fireman*, [1971] 3 O.R. 380, 4 C.C.C. (2d) 82, 7 C.N.L.C. 337 (C.A.), a First Nations member who was jailed thousands of miles away from his home and from anyone who could communicate with him. Indeed, page 84 [C.C.C.] records that ". . . he lived in a community where time is told only by seasons, that his sentence of ten years is something that he is not likely to fully understand for he is unfamiliar with the calendar measurement of time in terms of days, weeks, months or years."

On the other hand, if the offender has drawn all that is available by way of instruction in a custodial setting, what purpose is achieved by further detention? In the case of *R. v. M. (R.A.)* (2003), [2003] O.J. No. 1489, 2003 CarswellOnt 1709 (C.A.), the Court endorsed the following remarks at para. 1: "While this was a very serious offence, it is not apparent from the trial judge's reasons what weight, if any, the trial judge gave to the appellant's prospects for rehabilitation. The appellant was a 15-year-old first offender when this offence was committed. He is now nearly 18 and has completed the secure custody portion of the disposition. He has done well during this period. In our view, no further purpose would be served by keeping the appellant in open custody." The probation period was upheld.

In the ultimate analysis, a "sad life" may demonstrate diminished moral blameworthiness as a vehicle for leniency: The offender who has received an inadequate degree of socialization should not be judged on the same footing respecting maturity as one who has, all other things being equal.

xii)   A further word on advocacy

Whatever may be the merits of this position, it is undoubted that the sentencing courts tend to discount the reach of the network of socialization that society entrusts to the family unit and to the schools in the case of those who have known a "sad life". They cannot be expected to have received, and to apply, this general instruction when confronted with the fact that the challenges of everyday life are exacerbated by crushing poverty, by way of limited example.

In any event, irrespective of one's view of the degree of moral blameworthiness associated with the reception or rejection of society's teachings as to respect for others and their property, the sentencing courts will evaluate the impact of prior socialization as a result of court sanctions.

Counsel must be prepared to address the animating rationale of sentencing in respect to immature offenders guilty of serious offences: Whatever may have been the deficits of the community in teaching right from wrong, offenders have a duty to heed the guidance of the courts, and the failure to do so may fairly be seen as an indication that a greater application of correctional resources, including custody, is necessary. How can it be objected that this is unfair in light of the moral blame associated with failing to respond to the lessons contained in earlier lenient sanctions? In the case of *R. v. Fedick* (May 20, 1980), MacKinnon A.C.J.O., Lacourciere and Goodman JJ.A., [1980] O.J. No. 919 (C.A.), MacKinnon, A.C.J.O. quoted the trial judge's comments to the effect that the offender had not taken advantage of the short, sharp sentences that had been previously imposed. See para. 6.

In this respect, it is instructive to return yet again to *R. v. Borde* (2003), (*sub nom.* R. v. B. (Q.)) [2003] O.J. No. 354, 168 O.A.C. 317, 172 C.C.C. (3d) 225, 8 C.R. (6th) 203, 63 O.R. (3d) 417, 2003 CarswellOnt 345 (C.A.). At para. 36, emphasis was placed on the offender's very serious youth record, his failure to respond to other measures and his repeated violation of court orders. These factors combined to demonstrate that specific deterrence would be an important objective and that a penitentiary sentence was fit notwithstanding the young man's age. Unfortunately for the young man, "The string of offences, two involving use of a loaded handgun, required a lengthy sentence." But these circumstances, however, had to be balanced against the appellant's age and his chaotic background as part of a dysfunctional family being raised in poverty by a mother who unfortunately had few parenting skills and suffered from a mental illness. There was also some reason for optimism about the appellant's chances for rehabilitation. The pre-sentence report indicates that while the appellant did not respond particularly well to community-based programmes, he did do well in a more structured environment.

Hence, in the final analysis, advocates must be mindful that mitigation may arise from the presence of individualistic circumstances, such as immaturity in general, and immaturity arising out of an inadequate exposure to socialization. A prime example is found in the majority opinion in *R. v. R. (R.)* (2001), [2001] O.J. No. 4254, 2001 CarswellOnt 3856, 151 O.A.C. 1, 159 C.C.C. (3d) 11 (C.A.), affirmed 2003 CarswellOnt 366, 2003 CarswellOnt 367, [2003] S.C.J. No. 3, 171 C.C.C. (3d) 575, 2003 SCC 4, 300 N.R. 230, 169 O.A.C. 180, 10 C.R. (6th) 1 wherein Abella J.A. noted that "[t]he eight month period of incarceration in these exploitative circumstances, far from representing an error in principle, represents a generous acknowledgement of the appellant's personal circumstances and background." Refer to para. 63. Having said that, the level of maturity may not be an obstacle to a severe sentence if the needs of the community require it, as seen in great detail.

Sentencing courts are of the view that at some point, to track the language of Félix Leclerc, offenders have passed the age of foolish, immature conduct. It is the duty of advocates to suggest that the sentence to be selected on this day is the last opportunity at individualization. In other words, leniency may once again be selected but for the final time as the offender now has the insight and the ability to overcome the inadequate or wholly negative lessons of the sad life s/he has encountered. ["Tu as passé l'âge des escapades". See page 20 of "Les péchés dans le hall", *Théâtre de village*, Fides: 1951, Montréal.]

2. AN EXAMINATION OF THE OFFENDER'S CHARACTER AND MORAL BLAMEWORTHINESS:

a) Introduction

Having examined at length the suggested submission according to which an offender's sad life may account for a diminished degree of moral blameworthiness on the grounds of immaturity, the focus of the discussion will now be turned on the offender's character and on the question whether the wrongdoing is in character or out of character. If it is in character, then little mitigation may be assigned even if there have been no prior convictions. For example, counsel for the binge drinker who gets drunk each weekend but who was never arrested until the fatal accident will be hard-pressed to assert as mitigating the first offender status of the accused; the same conclusion would flow for the individual who is guilty of domestic violence after an admission of regular corporal punishment. If it is not characteristic, however, leniency may be shown, as the Court will wish to assist offenders who are not wedded to anti-social behaviour.

Simply put, little emphasis need be placed on specific deterrence in the case of offences that are out of character. Refer to *R. v. Kaup* (2000), [2000] O.J. No. 120, 128 O.A.C. 301, 2000 CarswellOnt 93 (C.A.) at para. 1. The judgment begins by setting out that "The youthful appellant, who was only 18.5 years old at the time of the offence, has no criminal record. He has lived a non-violent, productive life and has lived at home with a stable and supportive family. He pleaded guilty to the offence and his post-apprehension conduct indicated significant remorse."

In *R. v. Monchka* (2000), [2000] O.J. No. 1069, 131 O.A.C. 9, 2000 CarswellOnt 1074 (C.A.), the Court of Appeal was influenced by the fact that the offender had an unblemished background. In particular, the record shows that the offence was completely out of character. Refer to para. 3. In addition, he had a positive pre-sentence report and he does not have a substance abuse problem and that he has strong family supervision.

b) The offender is generally of good character

One area of potential mitigation in which perhaps too little attention is placed by defence counsel in sentencing submissions surrounds the prior contributions to the community. Doubtless defence counsel quite often highlight awards and formal recognitions but all too often the very basic fact of being an otherwise law-abiding citizen is ignored or obscured. In the case of most drinking and driving offences, by way of limited example, the individual has never exhibited any anti-social tendencies and does not require the assignment of much, if any, correctional resources in order to guarantee future good behaviour.

In fact, it may be for this very reason that Parliament has elected, in the exercise of its undoubted wisdom, to direct the sentencing courts not to assign the normal mitigation that arises in cases of mature first offenders that are no threat to the community by reason of one aberrant mistake in judgment. As is well known, no discharge is possible by reason of the minimum fine, and there must be a driving prohibition no matter how sympathetic the offender.

In this vein, counsel might cite *R. v. L. (G.S.)* (2003), [2003] O.J. No. 1719, 2003 CarswellOnt 1686, 171 O.A.C. 117, 175 C.C.C. (3d) 564 (C.A.) as an example of an offender's prior good citizenship being taken into account. In that case, the offender committed a serious offence but it was still open to the Court of Appeal to observe that he has made contributions to his community. Refer to para. 2. Although little could be said of an offender who sexually abused his 13-year-old sister-in-law when he was 30 involving some 18 incidents over an 18-month period, it is counsel's duty to advance what can be said in his favour in mitigation.

What of an offender who not only has no record, but who also has been of exemplary character? Is this not mitigating? Some indirect support for this view may be found at para. 2 of *R. v. Kerr* (2001), [2001] O.J. No. 5085, 2001 CarswellOnt 4473, 153 O.A.C. 159 (C.A.). As noted by Abella J.A., "[t]he appellant was 27 years old at the time of sentencing and the youngest of three children in a close-knit family. He has a stable and close relationship with his parents and two sisters. He has no criminal record, and his family indicates that he has never been violent or verbally abusive."

On occasion, sentencing courts will seek to stress that offenders were of good character "prior to the commission of the offence". See page 322, para. 5 of *R. v. Pasha* (1981), 23 C.R. (3d) 320, 1981 CarswellOnt 74, 61 C.C.C. (2d) 340 (C.A.) with respect to trafficking in narcotics.

On the assumption that there is a nuance separating good character from the absence of any prior, unprosecuted offences, note that in *R.*

v. Heaslip (2001), [2001] O.J. No. 1043, 10 M.V.R. (4th) 220, 144 O.A.C. 107, 2001 CarswellOnt 850 (C.A.), the offender pleaded guilty to two counts of impaired driving causing death and one count of impaired operation of a motor vehicle causing bodily harm. At para. 10, the Court emphasized the fact that "the respondent is of generally good character." Of note, it had set out immediately above that he had no record. Hence, being of good character is somehow different, perhaps as it relates to his good work and family history.

For the sake of balance in reviewing these themes, note that in *R. v. Alagendra* (2001), [2001] O.J. No. 527, 141 O.A.C. 193, 2001 CarswellOnt 429 (C.A.), the accused was convicted of aggravated assault and sentenced to imprisonment for two years less one day. He appealed arguing that, given his young age, 21 at the time, background and prospects for rehabilitation, including his attendance at university, the sentence was manifestly unfit. He was not successful, as the Court of Appeal emphasized the very serious nature of the crime, including that it was racially motivated, unprovoked and gang-related. Note as well the findings at para. 15 that but for the defensive measures taken by the victim, the injuries might have been fatal. In sum, having caused serious and lasting injuries to the victim against this aggravating background, he could not expect any significant degree of leniency.

An endorsement of the Ontario Court of Appeal is also apposite. It includes the observation that: "The sentences were substantial and deservedly so. This was a vicious gang rape of a young girl by four men. The appellants are young, come from good families and have enjoyed academic success. Despite these mitigating factors, nothing short of a significant penitentiary term could adequately reflect the seriousness of the assault on the complainant." See para. 20 of *R. v. B. (R.)* (2001), [2001] O.J. No. 4643, 2001 CarswellOnt 4160, (*sub nom.* R. v. A. (G.)) 152 O.A.C. 116 (C.A.).

In most instances, our Court of Appeal has held that an offender's prior good character is a mitigating feature in that it makes it more likely than not that he or she will respond favourably to the sentence of the Court, it being the culmination of a public trial. For example, in *R. v. Oliver* (1997), (*sub nom.* R. v. G.O.) [1997] O.J. No. 1911, 99 O.A.C. 234, 1997 CarswellOnt 1562 (C.A.), note the comment that "It is no doubt because of the appellant's otherwise good character, that a reformatory sentence was imposed" in the case of repeated sexual abuse in a situation of trust. See para. 17. Consider as well *R. v. Bigelow* (1991), [1991] O.J. No. 1739, 1991 CarswellOnt 1780 (C.A.): "Having regard to all of the circumstances of this offence and the background and previous good character of the appellant, we think that the interests of justice would have been better served had this first offender been sentenced to a maximum reformatory term instead of one in the penitentiary." See p. 5.

As can be easily understood, the question whether an act is or not out of character for an offender is often crucial in the determination whether an individualized disposition is appropriate. In *R. v. Rohr* (1978), 44 C.C.C. (2d) 353, 1978 CarswellOnt 1224 (C.A.), Martin, J.A., observed that the offence of break and enter committed by the then 16-year-old offender "was entirely out of keeping with the character of the [offender]". See page 354, para. 3. The Court described the offenders in *R. v. Kelly* (1979), 48 C.C.C. (2d) 560, 1979 CarswellOnt 1410 (C.A.) at page 571, para. 3, as "... casual or accidental offenders as opposed to persons who had committed themselves to criminality". In considering the issue of character as it predicts potential recidivism, it will be of assistance to recall the useful admonition found in *R. v. W. (D.R.)* (1992), 100 Sask. R. 106, 18 W.A.C. 106, 1992 CarswellSask 99, [1992] S.J. No. 230 (C.A.) "As near as one can tell, though one can never be altogether sure of these things, he seems unlikely to reoffend." Refer to p. 107, para. 3. Professor Nigel Walker has opined that "nothing predicts future behaviour quite like past wrongdoing". See *Why Punish?*, Oxford, Oxford University Press, 1991, at p. 53.

In concluding this section, I wish to underline a further troublesome issue confronting the courts: May an offender claim a prior good character notwithstanding prior difficulties with the administration of justice? For example, in *R. v. Bigham* (1982), [1982] O.J. No. 614, 1982 CarswellOnt 13, 15 M.V.R. 206, 69 C.C.C. (2d) 221 (C.A.) the Court noted at para. 2 that the offender had a bad driving record to then remark that he "is a successful person of good character ... He is respected in his community". Refer to para. 3 and to the Court's opinion that this must have influenced the trial judge in fixing a four month jail term for the offence of dangerous driving causing two deaths by an impaired individual. Indeed, at para. 4, the Court observed: "... the case can be briefly summarized by saying it is a case of a man of good reputation, who has a bad driving record, who drank to the point where his ability to drive was impaired, and who drove in a manner that amounted to dangerous driving with the result that two people were killed."

This begs the question: Would he have such a good reputation within the community if his friends and neighbours knew of his constant disrespect for the driving laws?

An isolated incident, although serious, may be the subject of a lenient sentence. The Court of Appeal for Ontario has underscored that an individualized disposition is possible even in cases of extreme violence if it can be shown that it was an isolated instance of wrongdoing, as in the case of *R. v. Flores* (2000), [2000] O.J. No. 1991, 2000 CarswellOnt 1886 (C.A.). That was an "isolated act borne of adolescent jealousy." Refer to para. 2. See also the case of *R. v. B. (R.)* (2003), [2003] O.J. No. 1959, 2003 CarswellOnt 1857, 172 O.A.C. 74 (C.A.).

Of course, if a propensity for violence was shown, or some evidence to suggest the likelihood of further violence, different considerations might carry the day. Stated otherwise, it is not an isolated event, aggravating weight may be assigned, as was the case in *R. v. Johnston* (2000), [2000] O.J. No. 3539, 136 O.A.C. 190, 2000 CarswellOnt 3354 (C.A.), at para. 38. Further, *R. v. Bayani* (2003), [2003] O.J. No. 2437, 2003 CarswellOnt 2316, 173 O.A.C. 36 (C.A.) involved an offender who has a lengthy criminal record involving offences of violence, and was on probation for harassing the victim at the relevant time he attacked her with weapons and he was subject to a lifetime prohibition from possessing firearms at the time of the most recent wrongdoing.

R. v. K. (D.) (2003), [2003] O.J. No. 562, 2003 CarswellOnt 542, 169 O.A.C. 97 (C.A.) emphasizes that it is a serious aggravating element to commit "a horrific series of sexual assaults with various weapons over a protracted period." See para. 3. The victim was the then wife of the offender and she was assaulted five times over 12 years, twice with a gun, once with a hatchet and three times with knives. There were death threats and once she was forced, with a knife pointed at her, to fellate the offender. Para. 3 concludes that "...the offences reveal cruel, dehumanizing treatment ... and conduct designed ... to demean, terrorize, humiliate and subjugate [the victim]." As noted at para. 7, "[t]he admitted offences are horrendous in nature. They arose from a domestic relationship. They were carried out in a brutal and horrifying manner over a lengthy time. Thus, they were not isolated occurrences."

Counsel's duty, therefore, is to show that the offence is an isolated instance of wrongdoing and that such behaviour is not the norm. In so doing, it will be easier to secure a lenient sentence. As discussed, the main rationale for leniency is that the wrongdoing is an out-of-character offence.

c) Character and overcoming great challenges in the past

When counsel submits, as was the case in *R. v. Bogart* (2002), [2002] O.J. No. 3039, 2002 CarswellOnt 2537, 167 C.C.C. (3d) 390, 162 O.A.C. 347, 61 O.R. (3d) 75 (C.A.), leave to appeal refused (2003), 2003 CarswellOnt 1027, 2003 CarswellOnt 1028, [2002] S.C.C.A. No. 398 (S.C.C.), that the offender should be given credit for being a cancer survivor, how is the sentencing court to respond? By agreeing that all indications of character may be consistent with pro-social qualities that may be nurtured to assist in achieving reformation. After all, an offender who can display strength of character may be advantaged in attempting to demonstrate that there will be no further anti-social behaviour.

Hence, the Court in *Bogart* acknowledged a "powerful catalogue of mitigating circumstances", notably that the defendant was a cancer survivor who overcame tremendous obstacles to become an excellent doctor who provided much-needed psychotherapy to an under-serviced group, namely persons who are HIV positive or who have AIDS, and who pleaded guilty and expressed great remorse and who had made restitution of about 20% of the amount involved and who had served half of his sentence. See para. 20.

Nevertheless, the aggravating elements were such as to demand imprisonment, notably the elevated moral blame associated with a near unprecedented OHIP fraud, as measured in money terms and transactions. See para. 21. Dr. Bogart defrauded OHIP of $923,780.53 by means of fraudulent claims respecting 19,892 insured services over a period of seven years.

d) Good character and entrapment

Although we cannot tell whether it mattered to the selection of the penalty, it is noted that Osler J.A. advanced strong language in describing the actions of the authorities in *R. v. Marcott* (1901), [1901] O.J. No. 173, 2 O.L.R. 105, 4 C.C.C. 437 (C.A.), at para. 28, page 112: ". . . she undertook to tell [fortunes to witnesses] who were suborned by the policeman Irwin to entrap the accused into committing a breach of the law." This type of judicial disdain should result in a modest penalty, assuming a conviction is proper in the circumstances, for fear that a severe penalty will encourage improper investigative techniques.

It will be worthwhile to consider the lesser situation of police solicitation facilitating the commission of an offence but not giving rise to a defence. For example, in *R. v. Williams* (May 6, 1970), Aylesworth, McGillivray and Jessup JJ.A., [1970] O.J. No. 332 (C.A.), the Court ruled that the trial judge erred in imposing a suspended sentence and probation for trafficking in narcotics, in the absence of any special circumstances. "This Court has made it plain repeatedly that in cases of trafficking in narcotics suspended sentence ought not to be given unless there are special circumstances in the case. It will be rare, as has often been pointed out, that there are special circumstances warranting the suspension of sentence." See para. 1. It added that *R. v. Ormerod* is not to be taken as the equivalent of a special circumstance simply because there has been some solicitation by police officers leading to conviction. See para. 2. It added, again at para. 2: "Each case with respect to the conduct which may be complained of with respect to police officers must be determined on its own facts." Three months in jail were ordered.

If we take the instruction of the Court to be that the fact that police officers have solicited the sale is not, in and of itself, sufficient to raise special circumstances, it ought still to constitute an objective ground for leniency on the footing that the degree of moral blameworthy conduct is not as elevated.

e) Good character and isolated offences:

i) Introduction

In the course of the endorsement rendered in *R. v. B. (R.H.)* (2002), [2002] O.J. No. 2345, 159 O.AC. 217, 2002 CarswellOnt 1929 (C.A.) Catzman, Weiler and Feldman JJ.A. advanced these observations, at para. 14: "The appellant submits that we should impose a conditional sentence of 18 months as opposed to the sentence of 18 months in jail that was imposed. The appellant was in his 30s when the [sexual] offences were committed. They commenced when the complainant was a very young child; they were not isolated events and took place over a number of years. . .". In the result, the sentence of incarceration was upheld.

Stated otherwise, had the wrongdoing consisted of isolated events, it might have been mitigating; at the very least, it would not have been as aggravating as in the case of on-going abuse. One of the rationales is that in the case of an isolated offence, the offender's degree of moral blame is often not as elevated as in the case of a pattern of misconduct for in such a case, the refusal to take stock of what is happening is a crucial concern.

ii)   Isolated offences and young persons

It must be noted that the courts do not appear to invoke the "isolated" nature of the wrongdoing in any case involving youthful first offenders. In such instances, the traditional rule expressed in cases such as *R. v. Priest* (1996), [1996] O.J. No. 3369, 30 O.R. (3d) 538, 93 O.A.C. 163, 110 C.C.C. (3d) 289, 1 C.R. (5th) 275, 1996 CarswellOnt 3588 (C.A.).

By reason of the importance of the instruction provided by Mr. Justice Rosenberg, it may be opportune to pause in order to set out at length the passages found at paras. 17-22, pages 294-296 [C.C.C.], as it provides signal guidance on the limited reach of incarceration in contemporary sentencing:

> [17] The primary objectives in sentencing a first offender are individual deterrence and rehabilitation. Except for very serious offences and offences involving violence, this Court has held that these objectives are not only paramount but best achieved by either a suspended sentence and probation or a very short term of imprisonment followed by a term of probation. In *R. v. Stein* (1974), 15 C.C.C. (2d) 376 (Ont. C.A.) at page 377, Martin J.A. made it clear that in the case of a first offender, the court should explore all other dispositions before imposing a custodial sentence:

> It is the view of the Court that the sentence imposed upon the appellant does reflect an error in principle. In our view, before imposing a custodial sentence upon a first offender the sentencing Court should explore the other dispositions which are open to him and only impose a custodial sentence where the circumstances are such, or the offence is of such gravity that no other sentence is appropriate. In our view, this offence does not fall within the category of offences where a custodial sentence is the only appropriate sentence to be imposed upon a first offender, nor are there other circumstances which require the imposition of a custodial sentence. [Emphasis deleted]

> [18] As the *Stein* case shows, it has been an important principle of sentencing in this province that the sentence should con-

stitute the minimum necessary intervention that is adequate in the particular circumstances. This principle implies that trial judges consider community-based dispositions first and impose more serious forms of punishment only when necessary. These principles have now been codified in the recently proclaimed sections 718 and 718.2 of the Criminal Code. Section 718(c) instructs that separation of offenders from society is an appropriate objective of sentencing "where necessary". Section 718.2(d) directs that an offender should not be deprived of liberty "if less restrictive sanctions may be appropriate in the circumstances".

[19] The principle embodied in now s. 718.2(e) was of particular significance in this case. It provides that "all available sanctions other than imprisonment that are reasonable in the circumstances should be considered for all offenders, with particular attention to the circumstances of aboriginal offenders". Although these sections had not been proclaimed when the appellant appeared before [the trial judge], the provisions to a large extent codify existing practice and principles in this province, especially in relation to first offenders. See *R. v. Salituro* (1990), 56 C.C.C. (3d) 350 (Ont. C.A.) at page 373 per Galligan J.A.

[20] The duty to explore other dispositions for a first offender before imposing a custodial sentence is not an empty formalism which can be avoided merely by invoking the objective of general deterrence. It should be clear from the record of the proceedings, preferably in the trial judge's reasons, why the circumstances of this particular case require that this first offender must receive a sentence of imprisonment. The trial judge had no material before him from which he could possibly have made this determination. His reasons are barren of any lawful justification for such a radical departure from this well-established principle especially in the case of a youthful first offender.

[21] With the increase, in 1985, in the age limit to which the *Young Offenders Act*, R.S.C. 1985, c. Y-1, applies, the range to which the term "youthful offender" can properly be invoked in the ordinary courts is somewhat more narrow. However, the term "youthful offender" refers not simply to chronological age and must include some consideration of the offender's maturity. This again highlights the need to obtain either a pre-sentence report or other clear statement of the offender's background to ensure that the appropriate sentencing principles are brought to bear. The trial judge had no information concerning the offender's maturity, char-

acter, behaviour or any other information to assist in properly characterizing his level of maturity, save for his chronological age. Nevertheless, the fact that the appellant was only 19 years of age was sufficient, in the absence of any other evidence, to conclude that this appellant was a youthful offender. See *R. v. Osbourne* (1994), 94 C.C.C. (3d) 435 (Ont. C.A.).

[22] The rule laid down by this Court is that ordinarily for youthful offenders, as for first offenders, the objectives of individual deterrence and rehabilitation are paramount. See *R. v. Demeter and Whitmore* (1976), 32 C.C.C. (2d) 379 (Ont. C.A.). These objectives can be realized in the case of a youthful offender committing a non-violent offence only if the trial judge gives proper consideration to alternatives to incarceration.

iii)   The guidance from "distant" cases

What little direction is available on the issue of "isolated" cases may be found in the cases of *R. v. Kimbley*, 84 C.C.C. 310, [1945] 4 D.L.R. 413, [1945] 3 W.W.R. 232, 1945 CarswellSask 52 (C.A.) and *R. v. Cindler*, 98 C.C.C. 303, [1950] 2 W.W.R. 1088, 11 C.R. 34, 1950 CarswellMan 56 (K.B.).

In the former case, it is made plain that leniency may be appropriate in a case in which the offence, in this case a sale of an article at a price exceeding the wartime ceiling, is isolated and not as part of an ongoing pattern of misconduct. In particular, page 317 [C.C.C.] sets out that "[a]s it is conceded that he is a farmer and has not been making it a practice to commit breaches of the above Order in Council, I would also order that he pay only a moderate fine, which I place at $200. . .".

In the latter case, we read at page 308 [C.C.C.] that courts are concerned with the pattern of criminality over an offender's life and that an isolated pattern may be discounted.

iv)   The contrary view: Non-isolated offending

By way of contrast, note *R. v. White* (March 17, 1970), Aylesworth, MacKay and Kelly JJ.A., [1970] O.J. No. 212 (C.A.). The offender, 40 years of age, "shamefully defrauded an elderly lady" out of $83.00. The Court took pains to point out the particularly serious nature of the wrongdoing, having to do with preying upon the old, the infirm and the like, making reference to *R. v. Major* (1966), 48 C.R. 296, 1966 CarswellOnt

17 (C.A.). Refer to para. 2. It added that unlike the *Major* case, this was an isolated instance. Nevertheless, it highlighted in para. 1 that he had not committed an offence for seven years "and one must assume was a proper citizen". It then made plain at para. 2 that he "has demonstrated his ability to go straight, as it were, for a great length of time considering his previous record and his previous inclinations as indicated by that record."

It is instructive that in *R. v. Cuzner*, [1970] 3 O.R. 222, [1970] 5 C.C.C. 187 (C.A.), the Court observed at page 188 [C.C.C.]:

> It was strongly urged that because of his good character before the commission of the offences and his fine performance since and because he is in school, this respondent should receive some special treatment. In this respect, we adopt what was said by Tysoe, J.A., for the British Columbia Court of Appeal in the case of *R. v. Adelman*, [1968] 3 C.C.C. 311, at p. 322, 63 W.W.R. 294.

> The instances where a suspended sentence can properly be given for trafficking in drugs must be very rare indeed and arise only where there are exceptional circumstances. This is not such an instance. . .

In addition, it should be noted that the Court remarked at page 187 [C.C.C.]: "The respondent is 19 years of age and has no criminal record. Indeed, evidence adduced at his trial indicated that he was a person of very good character prior to the occurrence and the material which we granted leave to be filed and which relates to the time period following his sentence indicates that the respondent has apparently reformed and has a new outlook on life with respect to the use of and trafficking in marijuana and hashish."

In the case of *R. v. Bevacqua*, [1970] 5 C.C.C. 139, [1970] 2 O.R. 786, 11 C.R.N.S. 76, 1970 CarswellOnt 15 (C.A.), the Court was unanimous that the 18- and 19-year-old first offenders should serve only three months in jail, not the nine and six-month definite, and six-month indeterminate, terms imposed at trial for possession of offensive weapons. Para. 4 recorded that "Both have highly commendable reputations . . . in the community and with their employers. Both have records of steady, gainful employment." Note the further comment: "Obviously . . . there really is no room in a consideration of sentence with respect to these two for imposition of any sentence to answer to the element of their rehabilitation because they need none. The remaining elements for consideration are deterrence to them and deterrence to others." In the result, the Court emphasized their clear records, their youth, favourable employment histories, and highly commendable community reputations.

Consider *R. v. Jolin* (May 7, 1970), Doc. Toronto 471/69, [1970] O.J. No. 338 (C.A.) as an example of a case in which prior good character was noted, but without great weight being assigned to that factor, in light of the elevated moral blame associated with the grave domestic violence. In sum, the manslaughter victim was his estranged wife who had left him to live with another man, together with the couple's two children. "He discovered their whereabouts and sought with a sawed-off shotgun to persuade his wife to return home. Argument followed in the course of which he shot and killed his wife and injured her paramour." See para. 3. He was of good character and had an excellent work record. Refer to para. 4. Notwithstanding the claimed drunkenness and the provocation, the Court found the ten-year sentence unimpeachable.

Note as well *R. v. L. (C.)* (1989), [1989] O.J. No. 2397, 1989 CarswellOnt 2079 (C.A.). As was reported at para. 1, "Although a disposition of three months open custody for this offence was not too severe, we are all of the opinion that in the circumstances of this young offender, noting in particular, the reports of her previous good character and her present attempts to rehabilitate, including attending a special school program in Hamilton, and the impossibility of her being able to complete the current school term in Hamilton while she is in open custody in Brampton, all lead us to conclude that the disposition should be changed as to custody." The custodial disposition was reduced to time served, and she was to comply with a probation order providing for community service.

3. AN EXAMINATION OF THE OFFENDER'S BEHAVIOUR AND MORAL BLAMEWORTHINESS:

a) Introduction

The discussion in this section will be devoted to the behaviour of the offender, prior to and at the time of the offence. A number of individual themes will be examined with a view at revealing whether the moral blame attaching to the conduct suggests potential reform or recidivism. Many aspects of behaviour may feed into this part of the analysis.

For example, the passage of time was a feature in *R. v. Echegoyen* (2001), [2001] O.J. No. 1021, 143 O.A.C. 147, 2001 CarswellOnt 827 (C.A.). The Court granted a measure of leniency, chiefly on the grounds that "Four years have passed since the commission of this offence and, except for a breach of recognizance, the appellant has conducted himself as a responsible citizen and a good parent. He has served seven and one-half weeks of the sentence." Hence, "[i]n the circumstances, it is in the public interest to reduce the sentence to time served." Refer to para. 10.

In other words, good behaviour under any rubric is worthy of credit while bad behaviour is not.

b) Successful therapy or counselling

In the case of *R. v. Dekoning* (2002), [2002] O.J. No. 4363, 2002 CarswellOnt 3924 (C.A.), the Court agreed with the trial judge's conclusion that a custodial sentence was appropriate. Indeed, that decision had been motivated in large part by the finding that the offender was a risk to re-offend, thus posing a danger to the safety of children, notwithstanding his counselling. Subsequently, however, fresh evidence in the nature of two psychiatric reports made plain that "the risk of re-offending is much less significant than thought by the trial judge." Refer to para. 3. Of note, the treatment and counselling were instrumental in this respect. Accordingly, he was released from custody and ordered to comply with a conditional sentence of ten months.

In *R. v. Garrow* (2002), [2002] O.J. No. 3787, 2002 CarswellOnt 3333 (C.A.), the Court remarked that the potential for rehabilitation justified a measure of leniency. See para. 2. *R. v. Mascarenhas* (2002), [2002] O.J. No. 2989, 2002 CarswellOnt 2517, 60 O.R. (3d) 465, 162 O.A.C. 331, 29 M.V.R. (4th) 1 (C.A.) is also apposite.

The conclusion to be drawn from this modest review is that an offender whose behaviour, at any point, suggests a better hope of reformation than fear of recidivism is entitled to a degree of leniency.

c) Employment

Note that in *R. v. Valle-Quintero* (2002), [2002] O.J. No. 4107, 2002 CarswellOnt 3583, 169 C.C.C. (3d) 140, 165 O.A.C. 275 (C.A.) the Court of Appeal remarked at para. 74 that the trial judge reduced the sentence, which he otherwise would have imposed, in light of the offender's pre-trial custody and steady employment and positive work ethic.

Further, para. 1 of *R. v. Malik* (2002), [2002] O.J. No. 387, 2002 CarswellOnt 3346 (C.A.) records these observations: "When determining the appropriateness of a discharge, the sentencing judge had to have regard to the best interests of the accused as well as the public interest. The sentencing judge appears to have had insufficient regard to the interests of the accused." The Court went on to note at para. 2: "The accused essentially lost his ability to earn his livelihood as a consequence of the conviction. In his position as a chartered accountant, he was required to travel to the United States and Europe. The conviction has impeded his ability to travel. He had no prior criminal record. He was unemployed at the time of conviction and sentencing and has been unable to obtain employment since that time. It appears that the conviction has hindered his ability to find suitable employment."

d) Education

The impact of upgrading of educational skills is also of interest, as is any educational pursuit. In this respect, see *R. v. Francis* (2000), [2000] O.J. No. 5043, 2000 CarswellOnt 4881, 139 O.A.C. 385 (C.A.) and *R. v. Burke* (August 9, 2001), Doc. Toronto C36396, [2001] O.J. No. 3299 (C.A.) and *R. v. Burke* (2001), [2001] O.J. No. 3281, 2001 CarswellOnt 2789, 149 O.A.C. 272 (C.A.) involving a youthful offender resolved to return to school.

Para. 42 of *R. v. H. (D.A.)* (2003), (*sub nom.* R. v. D.A.H.) [2003] O.J. No. 143, 2003 CarswellOnt 148, 171 C.C.C. (3d) 309, 168 O.A.C. 176, 10 C.R. (6th) 109 (C.A.) emphasizes the efforts of the offender at improving the level of his education. Notably, the Court commented: "He had a Grade 5 education. He is now taking courses to upgrade his education at Confederation College. He has completed one course and is now taking a literacy and basic skills course."

e) Behaviour and the passage of time since the offence(s):

i) Has the offender demonstrated that further correctional intervention is no longer required?

In reviewing these cases, counsel is encouraged to pick out those elements suggesting that the behaviour post-offence is a true indication of a positive moral resolve that may not have been in operation at the time of the wrongdoing, but that is in evidence now, at the critical time of sentencing.

In an outstanding example of weight being assigned to the co-operation and compliance shown by an offender post sentence, the Court of Appeal refrained from setting aside a conditional term in a case of prolonged and grave sexual violence in the context of abuse of trust. In *R. v. C. (D.W.)* (2000), [2000] O.J. No. 3759, 2000 CarswellOnt 3519 (C.A.), it noted that the offender's behaviour during the first year of the conditional period was exceptional, and that his health had deteriorated somewhat due to the stress of the proceedings. It was not in the interests of justice to order him to be incarcerated at this time. Refer to para. 15.

In *R. v. Fudge* (2000), [2000] O.J. No. 2780, 2000 CarswellOnt 2628 (C.A.), the Court of Appeal emphasized in the first paragraph that the offender committed a crime of violence, having accumulated a record for crimes of violence, making her a significant danger to the community and to herself, not just by her prior conduct but also by reason of her addictions and her mental state. In sum, she was a real risk to the safety of the community.

Nevertheless, great leniency was shown to her by reason of the fact in the two years between the commission of the offence and the imposition of sentence, she turned her life around. "She is in a positive relationship with her husband, has developed a strong support network in the community and has remained drug and alcohol free. She has continued her progress since this sentence was imposed some six months ago." Refer to para. 2.

The Court of Appeal accepted that the trial judge had selected appropriate terms of a conditional sentence to guard against a return to her prior lifestyle. "She crafted a conditional sentence which was directed very much to the specific situation and concerns raised by this particular offender. The terms imposed by the trial judge also contain a significant punitive component." Refer to para. 4. It did not interfere with the sentence.

At para. 13 of *R. v. Pupovic* (2000), [2000] O.J. No. 4427, 138 O.A.C. 193, 2000 CarswellOnt 4112 (C.A.), leave to appeal refused (2001), 2001 CarswellOnt 872, 2001 CarswellOnt 873, 271 N.R. 192 (note), 149 O.A.C. 199 (note) (S.C.C.), the Court of Appeal noted that despite a related record for violence and a breach of a condition of probation to protect the same victim, leniency could be shown by reason of the seven years of good behaviour post-offence and awaiting appeal. A further great period of time was in evidence in *R. v. Syed* (2000), [2000] O.J. No. 3535, 22 C.C.L.I. (3d) 163, 2000 CarswellOnt 3291 (C.A.); "In considering what sentence we should now impose, we take into consideration that the [offender] and his family have had these charges hanging over their heads for some seven years. [He] has been through two trials and has been subject to significant bail terms throughout..." See para. 15.

In this vein, refer to the case of *R. v. P. (L.)* (2003), [2003] O.J. No. 251, 2003 CarswellOnt 193, 168 O.A.C. 170, 172 C.C.C. (3d) 195 (C.A.). In particular, refer to para. 26: "[he] has been under a form of house arrest since July 1999, that he has been on bail pending appeal on very strict terms including house arrest since March 2001..." In addition, we read: "The fresh evidence also indicates that the offence and its aftermath have had extraordinary adverse ramifications for R.B. and the rest of his family. R.B. is now 20 years old. It is fair to say that he is far removed from the young man who committed this heinous offence." See also *R. v. M. (J.S.)* (2003), [2003] O.J. No. 72, 2003 CarswellOnt 83, 32 M.V.R. (4th) 22, 168 O.A.C. 75, 171 C.C.C. (3d) 534 (C.A.).

In general, the passage of time without incident demonstrates an ability to act responsibly and thus, accentuates the possibility that the sentencing court may view the offender's wrongful behaviour as aberrant conduct. I repeat, counsel must strive to underscore that what took place at the time of the offence is an aberration and that the prior good record *and* subsequent good behaviour are the true indicators of the offender's underlying character. Thus, in *R. v. Morgan* (2003), [2003] O.J. No. 1776, 2003 CarswellOnt 1697, 171 O.A.C. 160 (C.A.), para. 2 includes the comment that in light of the fresh evidence indicating good conduct over the course of a year, the taking of treatment for impulse control and the resolve to support his common law wife and child, it was not necessary to incarcerate the offender even though the serious elements of the offence called for detention. Stated otherwise, it was not necessary to turn to the correctional authorities to ensure that the offender adopt a pro-social attitude and act in an appropriate manner.

This judgment may be of particular assistance to defence counsel as the offender was not inclined at first to respect court orders and was as unlikely a promising candidate for leniency as might be imagined. In fact, it appears that Mr. Morgan was convicted of sexual assault, involving intercourse with a 12-year-old, three breaches of recognizance including approaching the victim on the street, two counts of attempting to obstruct justice by attempting to convince the victim not to testify, and escape custody during which he attempted to run out of the court-room when his bail was revoked. Nevertheless, the Court of Appeal extended a large measure of leniency by reason of his subsequent reformation while on bail and after receiving a conditional sentence.

At the end of the day, counsel for an offender must exploit the observation of the Court of Appeal in *R. v. Hirnschall* (2003), [2003] O.J. No. 2296, 2003 CarswellOnt 2204, 176 C.C.C. (3d) 311, 173 O.A.C. 5 (C.A.): "As in other cases, the passage of time works against the Crown's position." Mr. Hirnschall having served his original inadequate conditional sentence without incident, the interests of justice were not served in directing his re-incarceration.

In the case of *R. v. P. (L.)* (2003), [2003] O.J. No. 251, 2003 CarswellOnt 193, 168 O.A.C. 170, 172 C.C.C. (3d) 195 (C.A.) para. 23 includes these observations: "The serious consequences of this offence for J. cannot be overstated. The trial judge properly gave these consequences significant weight in determining the appropriate disposition." See para. 24. Having so found, it went on to conclude that "We are satisfied, however, that the trial judge erred in finding that the injuries actually suffered by J. were reasonably foreseeable at the time of the assault. The evidence of the experts suggests that the tragic consequences were far from foreseeable." In addition, the trial judge erred in principle in failing to give sufficient weight to the circumstances surrounding the assault.

As we read at para. 25:

> On his findings, the confrontation between the appellants and J. was precipitated by the appellants' reasonable and genuine belief that J. was responsible for the disgusting racial graffiti which was appearing in the neighbourhood. Also on his findings, the appellants did not seek out J. intending to assault him. The violence which occurred at the time of the confrontation was spontaneous and very brief. The facts of this case, while no doubt serious, are clearly less serious than those outlined in *R. v. R.R.O.*, [1997] O.J. No. 341 (C.A.), where this Court upheld the disposition of one year secure custody for aggravated assault.

Turning to the question of the appropriate disposition, the Court held that "despite R.B.'s positive antecedence and his favourable prospects, we are satisfied that a significant period of secure custody is required to adequately reflect the seriousness of this offence." Mitigating weight was placed on the fact that he has been under a form of house arrest since July 1999, that he has been on bail pending appeal on very strict terms including house arrest since March 2001, and that the appeal should have been heard long ago through no fault of his. "The fresh evidence also indicates that the offence and its aftermath have had extraordinary adverse ramifications for R.B. and the rest of his family. R.B. is now 20 years old. It is fair to say that he is far removed from the young man who committed this heinous offence." See para. 26. In the result, a six-month closed custody term was selected, followed by probation for one year.

Note that in *R. v. Fice* (2003), [2003] O.J. No. 2717, 2003 CarswellOnt 2494, 13 C.R. (6th) 174, 65 O.R. (3d) 751, 177 C.C.C. (3d) 566 (C.A.), para. 23 records the Crown's concession that the Court might not wish to interfere with the sentence having regard to the lengthy passage of time since its imposition. This is followed by these comments, at para. 24: "... as was anticipated by Crown counsel, I find that the passage of time, when considered in the context of all the circumstances of this case, militates against appellate intervention." See also *R. v. Cater* (2003), [2003] O.J. No. 1781, 2003 CarswellOnt 1696, 171 O.A.C. 178 (C.A.) at para. 2 and *R. v. B. (R.)* (2003), [2003] O.J. No. 1959, 2003 CarswellOnt 1857, 172 O.A.C. 74 (C.A.), at para. 8.

In addition, note briefly the case of *R. v. Better* (2003), [2003] O.J. No. 806, 2003 CarswellOnt 702 (C.A.) on the importance of the passage of time in sentencing. Although the Court of Appeal had some concern as to the selection of a conditional sentence in a case of a serious offence (not otherwise described) and for the protection of the public, it was not prepared "at this point" to substitute incarceration for the conditional sentence. See para. 1. The Court remarked at para. 2: "We have come to this conclusion particularly having regard to the fact that the respondent's personal circumstances have changed significantly and have been maintained since the date of the offence approximately three years ago, the fact that he has served seven months of his conditional sentence in compliance with the strict conditions imposed, the fact that he has fully discharged the community service provision of those conditions, and the fact that he now understands the need for, and has entered into, the recommended treatment program."

Further guidance is found in *R. v. Adam* (1994), [1994] M.J. No. 6, 92 Man. R. (2d) 115, 61 W.A.C. 115, 1994 CarswellMan 218 (C.A.). The trial judge selected a 12-month period of imprisonment, followed by probation for 12 months, to sanction a first offender's involvement in the theft of a truck and a break and enter of a store. In so doing, "He made reference to the pre-sentence report which was extremely favourable, but placed little weight on the youthfulness of this offender, his previous positive history and the circumstances which led to the accused's involvement in the present offences", in the opinion of the Manitoba Court of Appeal. See para. 3. Indeed, the Court went on to underscore how "... a one-year term for this offender, whose involvement in criminal behaviour appears to be an aberration on an otherwise unblemished record, was unduly harsh." Refer to para. 4. See as well, *R. v. Duck* (June 16, 1989), Doc. 218/89, [1989] M.J. No. 325 (C.A.) at page 3 (Q.L.), a case involving a serious case of threatening conduct with a knife.

In closing, it will be of interest to comment on the situation of incarcerated offenders who have made good progress towards rehabilitation. It is obvious that good progress by an offender in assimilating the teachings advanced in a custodial setting may only be invoked successfully by appellate counsel, but the fact remains that such advances demonstrate a signal desire for reformation. In light of the utilitarian nature of allocating our scarce custodial resources, it may be fit for an appeal court to intervene as was done in *R. v R. (M.)* (2003), [2003] O.J. No. 2557, 2003 CarswellOnt 2461 (C.A.) to end the custodial part of the sentence to reward the progress shown by an offender. See para. 3.

In other words, once jail has taught the offender the necessary lesson, it is appropriate to consider what further gains society will make if detention is prolonged. By way of contrast, in the case of offenders who simply don't wish to reform, sentencing courts will generally find this elevated moral blameworthiness sufficient justification for a severe sentence. Hence, in *R. v. Bayani* (2003), [2003] O.J. No. 2437, 2003 CarswellOnt 2316, 173 O.A.C. 36 (C.A.), para. 4 refers to the following: ". . . the pre-sentence report was very negative, the respondent being described as being at risk for offending with violence and as not being amenable to counselling or community service. In addition, he expressed no remorse for his misconduct."

ii) The passage of time and the reluctance to re-incarcerate

Note the interesting result in *R. v. Flores* (2000), [2000] O.J. No. 1991, 2000 CarswellOnt 1886 (C.A.). Even though he was guilty of a serious offence of violence calling for a significant custodial term, the Court of

Appeal extended a great measure of leniency having regard to the "present circumstances" of the offender. In particular, it noted at para. 2, "This Court must impose a sentence which is fit under the present circumstances. Those circumstances include: 1) The respondent completed his incarceration [of six months] and was released about two months ago. 2) All of the other persons involved in the assault, although clearly less culpable than the respondent, received non-custodial terms. 3) The appellant's psychological state is fragile. He has attempted suicide twice, partially as a result of his fear of incarceration." A conditional period of detention was selected.

R. v. Pecoskie (2002), [2002] O.J. No. 4056, 2002 CarswellOnt 5289, 170 O.A.C. 396 (C.A.) demonstrates that delays attributable to the prosecution in perfecting an appeal may be decisive, on the footing that unfairness to an offender who is attempting to achieve rehabilitation may result from the undue passage of time. See para. 15. *R. v. Medeiros* (2002), [2002] O.J. No. 3396, 2002 CarswellOnt 2884, 163 O.A.C. 46 (C.A.) sets out a six-month jail term for a case of child abandonment resulting in an accidental death of a six-month-old. In addition, there was a concurrent period of six months for the abandonment offence. Further, a three-month consecutive term was selected for welfare fraud. As set out at paras. 10-11, the passage of time and other factors justified a total term of nine months within the community.

iii)   The thorny issue: Historical prosecutions in which the offender made no overt threats or acted to prevent prosecution

The Court of Appeal was divided on the question of sentencing in the case of historical sexual violence in *R. v. W. (A.G.)* (2000), [2000] O.J. No. 398, 130 O.A.C. 78, 2000 CarswellOnt 358 (C.A.). On the one hand, Rosenberg and MacPherson JJ.A. noted that "This Court has consistently held that the range of sentencing for an incestuous relationship between a parent and a young child involving acts of sexual intercourse is between three to five years in the penitentiary. See for example *R. v. M. (D.)* (1999), [1999] O.J. No. 1829, 121 O.A.C. 322, 136 C.C.C. (3d) 412, 1999 CarswellOnt 1518 (C.A.)." Refer to p. 79, para. 4. On the other, their Lordships noted that the offender was very frail, being a "hapless, pathetic, feeble man" of 78 years of age. See pp. 78-79, para. 5. The fear was that the offender would die in jail, having seen his already frail health deteriorate while serving 52 days of pre-trial detention. In upholding a suspended sentence, the majority of the Court of Appeal commented that they were of the view that deference should be shown to the views of the trial judge in this "unique case". Refer again to paras. 5-6.

Whatever may be thought of this position, offenders who have acted so as to cower the victims receive little leniency.

iv)   The passage of time and learning the necessary lesson

In the same vein, the passage of time may have resulted in teaching the lessons that the offender had failed to heed at the time of the offence(s). To illustrate this suggestion, note *R. v. Oziel* (1997), [1997] O.J. No. 1185, 1997 CarswellOnt 1118 (C.A.) wherein the Court of Appeal noted that the passage of time since the commission of the offences of sexual violence and the precarious nature of the offender's health in combination permitted a conclusion that he no longer represented a danger to society. See para. 12. Nevertheless, a total deprivation of liberty was required to reflect the nature and number of the offences; the only concession the offender received in light of his precarious health was a reduction of his five-year term to a period of 24 months. Refer to para. 14.

In *R. v. P. (C.C.)* (September 6, 1995), Doc. AY 95-30-02222, [1995] M.J. No. 596 (C.A.), one reads at para. 4 how the offender took advantage of the pre-trial period to transform himself and, as a result, the pre-sentence report could be qualified as "exceptional" whereas it might have been dreadful but for the resolve to act responsibly and a sufficient period of time within which to prove himself.

An outlandish example of the unfairness that may result from the passage of time between the entry of a conviction and the ultimate assignment of a penalty is seen in *R. v. Young* (1901), [1901] O.J. No. 198, 2 O.L.R. 228, 4 C.C.C. 580 (C.A.). The prosecutor moved for sentence to be imposed 14 years after the subject matter arose "because it is alleged [the offender] has broken a condition of his recognizance by not being of good behaviour [by defaming the prosecutor]". See para 13, page 230. He was convicted of libel on April 28, 1887, and the motion was decided on July 7, 1901. The Court left the matter to the civil courts, but without commenting on the maximum period for return of the offender to receive judgment.

v)   The situation of delayed arrest

It is instructive that concurrent sentences were selected for a series of similar offences wherein the police delay arrest in the case of *R. v. Cuzner*, [1970] 3 O.R. 222, [1970] 5 C.C.C. 187 (C.A.). The Court observed at page 188 C.C.C. that each of the jail sentences for trafficking in hashish be served in a concurrent fashion. Each instance of trafficking was similar in that it involved the same undercover officer, and relatively small amounts of narcotics and profits. In addition, the police did not arrest the offender upon his first offence.

vi)   The offender cannot seek a therapeutic remand

As a first point, the cases continue to hold that "therapeutic remands", that is to say adjournments granted to permit offenders to "prove themselves prior to sentence" by overcoming drug addiction, by returning to school or to employment, etc., are not consonant with the proper principles of sentencing, and may contravene s. 721 of the Code.

In this respect, *R. v. Brookes*, [1970] 4 C.C.C. 377, [1970] 3 O.R. 159, 10 C.R.N.S. 126, 1970 CarswellOnt 2 (C.A.) makes plain that "In postponing the imposition of sentence [for five months] the learned trial judge apparently acted upon the request of counsel for the respondent for such postponement in order to see how [he] would conduct himself in the meantime. Also, . . . the judge delayed the sentencing for the purpose of awaiting certain amendments to the Criminal Code that he felt would undoubtedly be introduced." It concluded that it was appropriate to postpone sentencing to obtain a pre-sentence report or additional information concerning the offence or the offender. It is not appropriate to postpone sentencing for a lengthy period simply for the purpose of determining whether an accused will behave himself during the period of postponement. The Court noted that Mr. Brookes had behaved well, but that was to be expected since he faced sentencing. Refer to para. 4, pages 378-379 [C.C.C.].

Thus, the Court emphasized that "respiting" of sentences is not proper, save for the briefer adjournments required to obtain a pre-sentence report, or to obtain further information about the offence or the offender. Further, little weight is to be assigned to good behaviour while awaiting sentence, as one is expected to be of good conduct during this phase of the proceedings.

Note also *R. v. Young* (November 25, 1971), Doc. Toronto 247/70, [1971] O.J. No. 889 (C.A.). The offender complained that the plea arrangement he had negotiated fell through. As set out at para. 2, after he had pleaded guilty, the prosecutor was to ask that he be sent to a treatment facility to combat his alcoholism, and that the sentence hearing occur after a 90-day respite period. Nothing prevented him, however, from attempting to obtain treatment prior to the plea, it seems.

vii)   The passage of time may not serve to ameliorate the offender's situation

R. v. Brookes, [1970] 4 C.C.C. 377, [1970] 3 O.R. 159, 10 C.R.N.S. 126, 1970 CarswellOnt 2 (C.A.) contains this passage, at para. 4, pages 378-379 [C.C.C.]: "Counsel for the respondent pointed out that his client has apparently behaved himself since his conviction, but one might expect that he would, having regard to the fact that he faced sentencing and, since sentence, an appeal has been confronting him. Accordingly, that single circumstance does not override the gravity of the offences which he committed, the fact that he has six previous convictions, and the fact that one offence was committed while he was on bail."

R. v. Stewart (1989), [1989] O.J. No. 2784, 1989 CarswellOnt 2083 (C.A.) also provides an example of an offender not receiving any reduced sentence notwithstanding post-sentence progress. As we read at para. 1, "His progress in its institution towards his own rehabilitation is commendable but his early release is really a matter of prison authority."

viii)   Overcoming addiction

R. v. Keeler (1989), [1989] O.J. No. 2452, 1989 CarswellOnt 1500 (C.A.) points to the fact that credit may be appropriate for overcoming an addiction, as one example of post-offence progress. As we read at para. 2, "We take note of the fact that the appellant has overcome his cocaine addiction, is now a resident of a halfway house and is permanently employed." The Court did not interfere, however, opining that in these circumstances, it is preferable to let the date of his release be determined by the corrections and parole authorities who are in a position to assess the appellant's success in his rehabilitation.

It will be useful to note the issue of the absence of progress in overcoming addiction, as it touches upon the potential for rehabilitation. In this respect, the line between a neutral factor and an aggravating one can be quite fine. For example, in respect to overcoming an addiction, reference is made to *R. v. F. (J.)* (1989), [1989] O.J. No. 2532, 1989 CarswellOnt 1575 (C.A.), at para. 1:

> In our opinion, the totality of the sentences imposed in the first instance was not unfit having regard to the nature of the offences, a prior record on the part of the offender and the contents of the pre-disposition report. In the absence of any evidence indicating that any progress has been made with respect to the offender's ability to cope with his drug addiction and mental problems and having regard to the fact that information supplied to us by Counsel is that the offender is not taking advantage of rehabilitation programs available to him in his custodial institution; although leave to appeal is granted, the appeal is dismissed.

ix)   Progress in the institution

Note *R. v. M. (R.)* (1989), [1989] O.J. No. 2346, 1989 CarswellOnt 2006 (C.A.). Para. 1 reads in part: "This disposition, which the trial judge imposed, was, at the time of its imposition, entirely appropriate. However, the information which we have received respecting the appellant's progress in open custody shows that at this point he has obtained all the benefit that could be accomplished by the disposition and that there is no useful purpose to be served by its continuation after the commencement of the next school year." As a result, the disposition was varied to substitute four and a half months open custody for the eight months open custody imposed with respect to the first count with the result that the total disposition was to be eight and a half months open custody.

x)   Progress with treatment

The brief endorsement in *R. v. D. (B.K.)* (1989), [1989] O.J. No. 2344, 1989 CarswellOnt 2010 (C.A.) makes plain at para. 1 that the offender was guilty of ". . . a serious offence involving sexual abuse of a child by a person in a position of trust. There were no exceptional circumstances and a custodial sentence was required." Para. 2 highlights that but for the ". . . passage of time since the commission of the offence, the extreme remorse of the respondent, the good progress he has made under psychological treatment, the absence of any criminal record, and his exemplary work record, the sentence we imposed would be longer." Unfortunately, the sentence was not recorded.

xi) Summary for advocates: The passage of time in general

An example of excellent post-sentence conduct being considered as a substantial mitigating factor is seen in *R. v. B. (N.W.)* (1989), [1989] O.J. No. 2538, 1989 CarswellOnt 1915 (C.A.). Although the disposition imposed on the young person was fit when it was made, it no longer was fit at the time of the hearing. As we read at para. 1, ". . . the excellent post-disposition report filed at the hearing, which reported on the appellant's performance in high school, the prospects of him attending university, arrangements for employment and residence with his brothers upon release have persuaded us that the public interest would best be served by his immediate release." He was to be the subject of a probation order for one year with a reporting condition ". . . at such times thereafter as the probation officer may direct and paragraph (e) shall be changed to provide that his residence may be altered at the discretion of his probation officer."

Note as well *R. v. L. (C.)* (1989), [1989] O.J. No. 2397, 1989 CarswellOnt 2079 (C.A.). As was reported at para. 1, "Although a disposition of three months open custody for this offence was not too severe, we are all of the opinion that in the circumstances of this young offender, noting in particular, the reports of her previous good character and her present attempts to rehabilitate, including attending a special school program in Hamilton, and the impossibility of her being able to complete the current school term in Hamilton while she is in open custody in Brampton, all lead us to conclude that the disposition should be changed as to custody." The custodial disposition was reduced to time served, and she was to comply with a probation order providing for community service.

R. v. Satish (1989), [1989] O.J. No. 2347, 1989 CarswellOnt 2106 (C.A.) appears to support the view that the passage of time may justify a reduced sentence. As we read at para. 1, "We think that the custodial term imposed was appropriate and that there is no reasonable basis on which we can interfere with it. It appears to us that at this time it would be appropriate for the probation period to be reduced by one year [from three years to two years]".

The brief endorsement in *R. v. D. (B.K.)* (1989), [1989] O.J. No. 2344, 1989 CarswellOnt 2010 (C.A.) makes plain at para. 1 that the offender was guilty of ". . . a serious offence involving sexual abuse of a child by a person in a position of trust. There were no exceptional circumstances and a custodial sentence was required." Para. 2 highlights that but for the ". . . passage of time since the commission of the offence, the extreme remorse of the respondent, the good progress he has made under psychological treatment, the absence of any criminal record, and his exemplary work record, the sentence we imposed would be longer." Unfortunately, the sentence was not recorded.

Note as well *R. v. M. (R.)* (1989), [1989] O.J. No. 2346, 1989 CarswellOnt 2006 (C.A.). Para. 1 reads in part: "This disposition, which the trial judge imposed, was, at the time of its imposition, entirely appropriate. However, the information which we have received respecting the appellant's progress in open custody shows that at this point he has obtained all the benefit that could be accomplished by the disposition and that there is no useful purpose to be served by its continuation after the commencement of the next school year." As a result, the disposition was varied to substitute four and a half months open custody for the eight months open custody imposed with respect to the first count with the result that the total disposition was to be eight and a half months open custody.

f)   Behaviour and the "gap" principle In sentencing:

i)   Introduction

One of the common mitigating elements raised in sentencing hearings concerns any gap in the record of offending. As a general statement, it is aggravating that an offender continues to offend as it makes plain that the sentences of the Court are not successful in bringing home individual deterrence; by contrast, it is mitigating that the offender has demonstrated some pro-social elements by avoiding criminal misconduct for an important period of time.

The disparity between the positions of two offenders, one who re-offends early on and one who does not, is illustrated in the case of *R. v. Gillan* (2003), [2003] O.J. No. 2315, 2003 CarswellOnt 2364 (C.A.). In the opinion of the Court of Appeal, the seemingly disparate sentences were justified by reason of the fact the offender pleaded guilty to more charges than the related offender, that his record for break and enter was much worse than the co-accused's and in particular, by reason of the fact the co-accused had an eight-year gap in his record while the offender was released three weeks before he committed these offences. See para. 2. In the pages that follow, attention is drawn to the various elements of the "gap" principle by means of a thematic overview of the case law in order to illustrate the importance of this mitigating element in appropriate sentence proceedings.

ii)   The presence of a "gap" in the criminal record *may* be mitigating

At the outset, it must be underscored that the offender's ability to avoid "trouble" for a period of time may be mitigating, depending on the circumstances. This demonstrates the ability to act in a pro-social manner and the means to gain a livelihood without crime. The rationale being advanced is that the original sentence did succeed in teaching the offender "right from wrong" and that the commission of a subsequent infraction is the manifestation of a temporary incapacity to recall and apply the Court's instruction, not of a criminal mindset.

This principle finds its practical application in cases such as *R. v. Colbourne*, [2002] A.J. No. 1525, 2002 CarswellAlta 1602, 2002 ABPC 141 (Prov. Ct.). As we see at para. 15, in reviewing the aggravating circumstances, the trial judge opined "The accused does not come before the Court as a first offender. Albeit there is a substantial gap of some eight years in his record prior to his most recent conviction in 2002." Stated otherwise, having first identified a prior record, the Court discounts, to a lesser or greater extent, the impact of this aggravating feature in light of the passage of time, and all other relevant principles.

In *R. v. Lockyer*, [2000] N.J. No. 306, 195 Nfld. & P.E.I.R. 1, 586 A.P.R. 1, 2000 CarswellNfld 311, 2000 NFCA 59 (C.A.), leave to appeal refused (2001), 2001 CarswellNfld 114, 2001 CarswellNfld 115, 270 N.R. 192 (note), 204 Nfld. & P.E.I.R. 180 (note), 614 A.P.R. 180 (note) (S.C.C.), the dissenting opinion of Marshall, J.A. contains these remarks at para. 142: "The so-called gap principle plays a role in some sentences where there has been an intervening period between a prior criminal conviction in which the offender has maintained a notable period of good behaviour. It operates to mitigate the effect that the record of a prior conviction would otherwise have on the sentencing at hand." A further example of a gap in the criminal record as evidence of partial rehabilitation is provided in *R. v. Mossip* (1992), 17 B.C.A.C. 81, 29 W.A.C. 81, 1992 CarswellBC 1059 (C.A.), at p. 82, para. 10.

In this respect, note as well the guidance found at para. 36 of *R. v. Kubbernus* (2000), [2000] A.J. No. 1054, 272 A.R. 99, 2000 CarswellAlta 978 (Q.B.): "This concept also relates to restraint in that it acknowledges that a person who has rectified past behaviour should also be considered as having better prospects for individual deterrence and rehabilitation." Of interest, the Court added, "There is no basis for making any such finding here . . . This offender re-offended twice while on parole, choosing, it is apparent to resume a life of crime and persist therefore in it. Rather than a embarking upon a lifestyle of crime avoidance, his propensity was toward a continuation of a life of crime. As a result he can no longer argue that he had a period of reformation." See paras. 36-37.

A further "contrary" case that is useful as a contrast to better evaluate the reach of the mitigation along these lines is *R. v. Playford* (2003), [2003] O.J. No. 954, 2003 CarswellOnt 874, 169 O.A.C. 300 (C.A.). Para. 2 records that "the previous conviction for extortion and the short period following the serving of the sentence on that conviction before this offence was committed were aggravating factors and we take them into account." In other words, the opposite of a gap situation.

It is also useful to underscore at the outset that sentencing courts will refer to the absence of a gap in the offender's history, as we see at para. 83 of *R. v. L. (M.C.)* (1997), [1997] A.J. No. 64, 193 A.R. 304, 135 W.A.C. 304, 1997 CarswellAlta 28 (C.A.), leave to appeal refused (1997), 212 A.R. 36 (note), 168 W.A.C. 36 (note) (S.C.C.): "So there is little gap between sentences and re-offences, and constant breach of probation."

iii)   The general principle of restraint in sentencing

It will be useful to pause in order to underscore that any mitigating principle should be advocated against the legislative backdrop of the major sentencing reforms of September 3, 1996, popularly described as Bill C-41, notably the introduction of s. 718.2(d) and the better known s. 718.2(e) of the *Code*. In this respect, recall the guidance of Chief Justice Lamer for the unanimous Supreme Court of Canada in *R. v. Proulx*, [2000] 1 S.C.R. 61, [2000] S.C.J. No. 6, 140 C.C.C. (3d) 449, 30 C.R. (5th) 1, 2000 CarswellMan 32, 2000 CarswellMan 33, [2000] 4 W.W.R. 21, 2000 SCC 5, 182 D.L.R. (4th) 1, 249 N.R. 201, 49 M.V.R. (3d) 163, 142 Man. R. (2d) 161, 212 W.A.C. 161, at par. 1: "By passing the Act to amend the Criminal Code (sentencing) and other Acts in consequence thereof, S.C. 1995, c. 22 ("Bill C-41"), Parliament has sent a clear message to all Canadian judges that too many people are being sent to prison. In an attempt to remedy the problem of overincarceration, Parliament has introduced a new form of sentence, the conditional sentence of imprisonment."

Thereafter note how both the title and the contents of para. 16 seek to emphasize the imperative need for restraint in sentencing:

(1) Reducing the Use of Prison as a Sanction

[16] Bill C-41 is in large part a response to the problem of overincarceration in Canada. It was noted in *Gladue*, at para. 52, that Canada's incarceration rate of approximately 130 inmates per 100,000 population places it second or third highest among industrialized democracies. In their reasons, Cory and Iacobucci JJ. reviewed numerous studies that uniformly concluded that incarceration is costly, frequently unduly harsh and "ineffective, not only in relation to its purported rehabilitative goals, but also in relation to its broader public goals" (para. 54). See also Report of the Canadian Committee on Corrections, Toward Unity: Criminal Justice and Corrections (1969); Canadian Sentencing Commission, Sentencing Reform: A Canadian Approach (1987), at pp. xxiii-xxiv; Standing Committee on Justice and Solicitor General, Taking Responsibility (1988), at p. 75. Prison has been characterized by some as a finishing school for criminals and as ill-preparing them for reintegration into society: see generally Canadian Committee on Corrections, supra, at p. 314; Correctional Service of Canada, A Summary of Analysis of Some Major Inquiries on Corrections—1938 to 1977 (1982), at p. iv. At para. 57, Cory and Iacobucci JJ. held:

Thus, it may be seen that although imprisonment is intended to serve the traditional sentencing goals of separation, deterrence, denunciation, and rehabilitation, there is widespread consensus that imprisonment has not been successful in achieving some of these goals. Overincarceration is a long-standing problem that has been many times publicly acknowledged but never addressed in a systematic manner by Parliament. In recent years, compared to other countries, sentences of imprisonment in Canada have increased at an alarming rate. *The 1996 sentencing reforms embodied in Part XXIII, and s. 718.2(e) in particular, must be understood as a reaction to the overuse of prison as a sanction, and must accordingly be given appropriate force as remedial provisions.* [Emphasis added]

As a last observation, para. 17 instructs us that "Parliament has sought to give increased prominence to the principle of restraint in the use of prison as a sanction through the enactment of s. 718.2(d) and (e). Section 718.2(d) provides that "an offender should not be deprived of liberty, if less restrictive sanctions may be appropriate in the circumstances", while s. 718.2(e) provides that "all available sanctions other than imprisonment that are reasonable in the circumstances should be considered for all offenders, with particular attention to the circumstances of aboriginal offenders".

iv)   A word on historical antecedents

Although it is neither possible nor necessary to determine the origins of this sentencing policy, it will be of assistance to note that in *R. v. Hicks*, [1925] 2 D.L.R. 1000, 44 C.C.C. 13, 1925 CarswellSask 52, 19 Sask. L.R. 359, [1925] 1 W.W.R. 1155 (C.A.) and *R. v. Finlay*, [1924] 4 D.L.R. 829, 43 C.C.C. 62, 1924 CarswellSask 135, [1924] 3 W.W.R. 427, 19 Sask. L.R. 43 (C.A.) reference is made to *Russell on Crimes*, 8th ed., vol. II., p. 1850, and to the quote that consideration must be given to evidence "that the accused had for a considerable time lived honestly." Refer to pages 14-15 [C.C.C.] of *Hicks, supra*.

v)   Context is everything: The repetition of certain offences may be quite troubling

As noted earlier, a significant gap in the history of offending is a mitigating feature to the extent that it demonstrates that an offender is capable of ongoing pro-social behaviour such that an unfortunate blemish ought to be discounted, if possible, in light of the circumstances of the offence. Nevertheless, as in all things, context is a crucial issue. Thus, an offender who commits murder 25 years apart will receive very credit while another who is involved in minor mischief every six or seven years will not be dealt with harshly, all other things being equal.

In this respect, note the reference to the gap in the offender's record at para. 8 and 9 of *R. v. Bajada* (2003), [2003] O.J. No. 721, 2003 CarswellOnt 617, 169 O.A.C. 226, 173 C.C.C. (3d) 255 (C.A.). Nevertheless, a six-year term for possession of cocaine for the purpose of trafficking was imposed, in light of the serious aggravating elements associated with the offence. The presence of a recent entry on the record would have been aggravating, but that is a different matter than indicating that the absence of a recent entry is mitigating. It may be given favourable consideration, all other things being equal.

A further example of the passage of time not being given much mitigating weight is seen in *R. v. Dhesi* (2001), [2001] O.J. No. 1343, 10 M.V.R. (4th) 26, 143 O.A.C. 114, 2001 CarswellOnt 1182 (C.A.). The

Court of Appeal took into account a 1977 conviction for impaired operation.

An earlier case of note is that of *R. v. Kehoe* (March 15, 1965), Doc. Toronto 40/65, [1965] O.J. No. 152 (C.A.), in which an eight-month jail term was selected. The Court found it to be a vicious assault by an offender convicted in 1940 for a similar offence and in 1962 of assault and common assault. See para. 1. In light of the fact that the trial judge gave serious consideration to the question of sentence, the appellate tribunal refused to intervene. See also page 328 of *R. v. Rodway* (1964), 44 C.R. 327, 1964 CarswellMan 2 (Q.B.).

vi)   A "gap" may be in evidence, but severity is still justified

As a related principle, although the gap in the offender's record may justify the sentencing court in ignoring the prior entry or entries, it may nevertheless be appropriate for severity to dictate the selection of the sentence in light of the aggravating elements at play. In other words, the decision to assign no weight to distant convictions may not result in a favourable sentence as seen in *R. v. Barry* (November 20, 1969), MacKay, Kelly and Evans JJ.A., [1969] O.J. No. 722 (C.A.).

The Court noted at para. 4 that "...he has some previous minor convictions for theft and breaking and entering, but they were over 15 years ago and we do not take them into consideration as there have been no offences committed in the intervening period." Nevertheless, it set aside the six-month definite and six-month indefinite term, noting that he was in possession of liquor from a truck that had been hijacked, containing at least $38,000 worth of alcohol. He received a two year less one day determinate term, followed by 18 months indeterminate.

Consider as well *R. v. Wright*, [2002] A.J. No. 892, 303 A.R. 371, 273 W.A.C. 371, 2002 CarswellAlta 874, 2002 ABCA 170 (C.A.), at para. 4. Although a ten-year gap in the offender's record was underlined, it could not assist greatly in light of the quite serious offence involving planning, racial overtones, and the extreme degree of violence justifying a 12-year term.

Many examples are found of a "gap" leading to no more than a favourable comment by the sentencing court, a recognition if you wish of some ability to function in organized society, but an unwillingness so to do. For example, para. 29 of *R. v. Hewlett*, [2002] A.J. No. 960,

167 C.C.C. (3d) 425, 321 A.R. 165, 281 W.A.C. 165, 2002 CarswellAlta 942, 2002 ABCA 179 (C.A.) reads: "On the mitigation side, it does appear that in recent years, Hewlett was trying to turn his life around. He had married; he was attending a community college; and there appears to have been some gap in his criminal activity." A further example is that of *R. v. Stewart*, [2002] B.C.J. No. 1896, 174 B.C.A.C. 6, 2002 CarswellBC 1965, 2002 BCCA 463, 286 W.A.C. 6 (C.A.), at para. 11. A further example is seen in *R. v. Noble* (1988), [1988] A.J. No. 349, 86 A.R. 319, 1988 CarswellAlta 498 (C.A.) where the Court noted that the offender's record included a "large gap". See para. 3. Although this factor was worthy of recognition, it could not temper the reach of severity in light of the violent nature of the offences.

Finally, note that *R. v. Blackbird* (1993), [1993] M.J. No. 332, 88 Man. R. (2d) 31, 51 W.A.C. 31, 1993 CarswellMan 258 (C.A.) sets out at paras 4-5 that a lengthy related record generally denies an accused the right to any leniency but that the time gap in this case entitles him to at least a modicum of leniency.

vii)   Focusing on the presence of a "gap" should not trump the evaluation of the seriousness of the prior record

As a matter of advocacy, it may be opportune to draw the attention of the Court to the limited extent or importance of the record prior to seeking to underline the presence of any suggested gap. Common sense suggests that minor shoplifting offences do not constitute evidence of serious misconduct and this submission may be as telling, if not more, than the related contention that the gap in time speaks volumes about attempts at reformation.

In this respect, note the minority opinion of Brooke J.A. in *R. v. Gallizzi* (November 18, 1969), MacKay, Evans and Brooke JJ.A., [1969] O.J. No. 710 (C.A.). His Lordship would have reduced a 12-year term to eight years in the case of a serious extortion, to reflect the absence of any record, save an offence of carrying a weapon some years ago, apparently a pocket knife, for which a very small fine was imposed.

In the same vein, *R. v. Graveline* (1958), [1958] O.J. No. 79, 1958 CarswellOnt 6, 27 C.R. 287, 120 C.C.C. 367 (C.A.) provides some insight into the significance of any gaps respecting serious entries in the offender's record. Paragraph 12 sets out that the offender

...has a record dating back to 1934, but the last particularly serious offence of which he was convicted was in 1947. Since then he has had three convictions, one keeping liquor for sale in 1948, another for causing a disturbance in 1955, and another for driving a motor vehicle while disqualified, in 1956. It would appear that he has been fairly regularly employed at one of the motor car manufacturing plants in Windsor, and having regard to his record prior to 1948 it would appear that since then he has been making some effort to stay out of trouble, or at least he has not been in as much trouble since then. . .

Note the interesting nuance advanced by defence counsel in *R. v. McDonald* (1997), [1997] A.J. No. 960, 208 A.R. 348, 30 M.V.R. (3d) 178, 1997 CarswellAlta 867 (Prov. Ct.), at para. 10 to the effect that consideration must be given to the gap as between convictions and the period between sentences of imprisonment. The Court did not comment directly on this submission. It may be a useful submission on occasion to support the view that the prior offences were not too serious and that the only entries on the record that are to be evaluated in fixing the "gap" are those resulting in custody.

viii) Has the offender shown that the "gap" demonstrates the assimilation of pro-social values?

In the ultimate analysis, a more favourable outcome in sentencing may be predicted in cases in which it can be shown that the offender has assimilated pro-social values but that the events surrounding the commission of the offence obliterated that understanding of right and wrong. Viewed from the opposite perspective, if Crown counsel can demonstrate that the absence of a gap in the accused's criminal record suggests that s/he has not gained much insight into appropriate behaviour, then leniency is less likely to be the animating principle. See *R. v. Remillard* (1998), [1998] A.J. No. 701, 222 A.R. 177, 1998 CarswellAlta 572 (Prov. Ct.).

In this context, it will be instructive to contrast the majority and minority opinions found in *R. v. Smallboy* (1997), [1997] A.J. No. 312, 196 A.R. 231, 141 W.A.C. 231, 1997 CarswellAlta 309 (C.A.). At para. 10, Fraser C.J.A. remarked in dissent: "I think it is very important to note that there was a gap of approximately five years during which time he was not involved in any offences. It is true that for some period of that time he was in prison, but that only accounts for approximately one of the five years. Her Ladyship went on to remark that once he was released from prison on mandatory supervision, he started up his own business and, by all accounts, he was a productive member of society, operating a business.

By contrast, the majority observed at para. 2 that "there had been some gap. Before the gap, the accused, unfortunately, had a long record, the great majority of it for similar matters, and the accused had had two years' jail for driving while impaired on a previous occasion." Further, note the comments consigned at para. 3: "The accused is not very young anymore, and he doesn't appear to have had much insight into his problems until very very recently. Now, by the time of sentencing, we are told that he realizes that his problem isn't driving at all, his problem is drinking. Unfortunately, until very recently he hasn't had that insight and during the five-year gap that I mentioned, it is not suggested that he wasn't drinking, it was just that he wasn't driving." In substance, the majority focused not on the gap in offending, but on the absence of a gap in terms of pro-social conduct.

The next decision also makes plain that the gap was entitled to little favourable weight as it did not demonstrate any true resolve to act responsibly. Thus, para. 24 of *R. v. Galbraith* (1997), [1997] A.J. No. 744, 1997 CarswellAlta 626 (Prov. Ct.) sets out that "At the time of this offence, the accused had one prior conviction for a similar offence and a lengthy criminal record, dating from 1976 on a fairly continuous basis right throughout to 1996. There is a three-year gap in his record between the years 1987 to 1990, but in general, his history is one of continued involvement in crime."

Note the guidance of the British Columbia Court of Appeal on the "assimilation element" of the "gap" principle in *R. v. Mitzel*, [2002] B.C.J. No. 1176, 171 B.C.A.C. 200, 2002 CarswellBC 1215, 2002 BCCA 333, 280 W.A.C. 200 (C.A.). As noted at para. 8:

> It is, in my view, not strictly so that the appellant "cannot take any benefit" from the gap in these circumstances, because the entire record was before the Court and the appellant's capacity to be conviction-free for a substantial period of time is a positive feature of his profile. However, that statement in itself would not persuade me that an error of principle was demonstrated by the sentencing judge as the comment simply may reflect the trial judge's view that little weight should be given to the gap, in circumstances in which the offence was committed while on bail.

By way of background, note that the offender has a significant criminal record for a young man of 26, but the record, except for these matters on which he was sentenced, is rather dated in the context of his years. Refer to para. 4. In effect, there was a five-year gap.

Of note, para. 4 also records that between the present offence and his previous last offence, he addressed his substance abuse problem, which had at least partly figured in his offences and in order to avoid falling into bad habits with associates in his home town he had moved away and had sought to reside independently. His source of income was a disability pension. The Court was told that the appellant committed the offences when he was unable to manage on his income and that they were not caused by back-sliding on his substance abuse issues.

Hence, if we stand the holding on its head, but for the gap in the record and the demonstration of an ability to attack with success the causes of criminality, a far more severe sentence might have been selected. A related judgment is that of *R. v. Stewart*, [2002] B.C.J. No. 1896, 174 B.C.A.C. 6, 2002 CarswellBC 1965, 2002 BCCA 463, 286 W.A.C. 6 (C.A.). Para. 11 is instructive in pointing out a gap in the appellant's record from 1991 to 1998. "During part of that time he worked as a fisherman out of Prince Rupert and apparently dealt with his drug problem. However, he fell back into his addiction and used cocaine and heroin. He has also had a problem with the abuse of alcohol.

ix) The extreme position: Any "gap" may be seized upon as a sign of possible reformation

At times, the principle is "stretched" somewhat in order to accentuate the positive feature of some trouble-free period of time, albeit a short period, but one that permits some hope of future rehabilitation against a rather bleak background of criminal infractions. In few words, any gap is worthy of credit.

For example, in *R. v. K. (H.M.)*, [2001] A.J. No. 1176, 297 A.R. 264, 2001 CarswellAlta 1223, 2001 ABPC 163 (Prov. Ct.), the Court took a sympathetic approach, measuring the gap against the otherwise unbroken period of wrongdoing. As we see at para. 27:

> The accused's record severely limits the ability of the Court to exercise any degree of leniency in the sense of imposing a sentence which does not contemplate imprisonment. In August of

1998, this accused received 15 months' incarceration for break and enter. The Crown argues that he should receive more this time. Since the date of his last conviction for break and enter, until the date of this offence, he has managed to stay out of trouble, except for a conviction for mischief which occurred in January of 2001. I recognize that his actual incarceration would have played a significant role in keeping him crime free during that two and one-half year period; although that does not explain entirely his good behaviour during that period. Indeed, given his past history, this time period with no criminal activity represents a significant gap for this particular man. He appears to have made a significant effort to remain crime free, although ultimately the factors that have led him to crime in the first place as discussed in the psychological assessment without being addressed in any way, led him back to criminal activity such as is represented before the court at this time.

The trial judge added, at para. 31: ". . .it is clear that he has the ability to avoid criminal activity for periods of time as shown by the gap between his last conviction for break and enter in 1998 and his most recent criminal activity in January of 2001. I believe that he falls back into criminal activity as a consequence of his many problems, including his lack of education, childhood abuse issues and substance abuse."

x)   A "gap" and achieving "first offender" status once again

In *R. v. Tustin* (November 5, 1971), Kelly, Jessup, Brooke JJ.A., [1971] O.J. No. 837 (C.A.), at para. 3, we read, "We do not disagree with [the offender] when he says that on account of the length of period since [he] achieved his record that he should be treated as a first offender and we would, therefore, not distinguish between him and his co-accused." No details as to length of time involved.

Once again, it is a factor that may or may not be decisive, or even influential. Note the reference to the gap in the offender's record at para. 8 and 9 of *R. v. Bajada* (2003), [2003] O.J. No. 721, 169 O.A.C. 226, 173 C.C.C. (3d) 255, 2003 CarswellOnt 617 (C.A.). Nevertheless, a six-year term for possession of cocaine for the purpose of trafficking was imposed. In effect, the trial judge stated no matter how long the gap was the appellant was not entitled to better treatment than a first offender.

xi) The "gap" principle and offences of violence

In *R. v. Lockyer*, [2000] N.J. No. 306, 195 Nfld. & P.E.I.R. 1, 586 A.P.R.
1, 2000 CarswellNfld 311, 2000 NFCA 59 (C.A.), leave to appeal refused (2001), 2001 CarswellNfld 114, 2001 CarswellNfld 115, 270 N.R.
192 (note), 204 Nfld. & P.E.I.R. 180 (note), 614 A.P.R. 180 (note)
(S.C.C.), the dissenting opinion of Marshall J.A. includes these observations, at para. 143:

> As para. 81 recounts, in his sentencing disposition the judge
> proceeded on the footing that the gap principle either did not apply,
> or had diminished effect. Counsel challenges this, contending the
> approximate 13 years interval between his client's attempted mur-
> der of his first wife [and the present conviction for manslaughter]
> ought to have been taken into account in assessing the sentence
> for the manslaughter. In this argument, counsel seeks to weaken
> the grounds for holding the killing of Mrs. Coady was "part of a
> pattern of violent behaviour which threatens the physical safety
> of others", thereby bringing the sentencing of Mr. Lockyer within
> the ambit of that justification for life imprisonment enunciated in
> *Horvath*. Counsel maintains the facts just do not fit with a large
> pattern of violent behaviour, and that the violence relied upon must
> be closer together in time.

Marshall J.A. added, at para. 144: "Agreement cannot be lent to counsel's position. In the first place, it seems reasonable to view the gap
principle as having diminishing marginal utility where crimes of personal
violence, as contrasted with offences against property, are concerned."

Of interest, the minority opinion stood the gap argument on its head,
as noted below:

> More importantly, however, in the circumstances of this case,
> it would appear that the long period between the attempted murder
> and the killing of Mrs. Coady should redound as an aggravating,
> rather than mitigating, factor in fixing a fit sentence for the man-
> slaughter of Mrs. Coady. This is because the fact that 13 years
> expired between the shooting of Mr. Lockyer's first wife in her
> chest and the dropping of Mrs. Coady over the bridge to her death
> should, in itself, be of real concern in addressing the violent pro-
> pensities of this man. It, and his serious assault upon his second
> wife which occurred in relative proximity to Mrs. Coady's demise,
> stand as evidence that his capacity for extreme violence had not

abated over the years, and legitimately heightens apprehension over him representing a real and continuing danger to the public.

Noteworthy as well are the observations found at para. 178:

> The pattern manifested in his crimes on those three women was not broken by the 13-year lapse between the attempted murder by Mr. Lockyer of his first wife and his last two offences. Nor may its significance be considered diminished by the span. To the contrary, the gap accentuates the danger as it witnesses a long-standing proclivity for violence that had not subsided over the years. There is no room to gainsay that the judge at first instance was sentencing a man with a disturbing history of serious violence.

xii)   May a "gap" be seen as aggravating?

On occasion, it may be asked whether evidence of a gap is not somehow construed as slightly aggravating in that although the offender is seen as having been capable of great progress, the subsequent "slide backwards" may be viewed quite harshly. Consider the example found in *R. v. Stewart*, [2002] B.C.J. No. 1896, 2002 CarswellBC 1965, 2002 BCCA 463, 174 B.C.A.C. 6, 286 W.A.C. 6 (C.A.), at para. 11. "The sentencing judge noted a gap in the appellant's record from 1991 to 1998. During part of that time he worked as a fisherman out of Prince Rupert and apparently dealt with his drug problem. However, he fell back into his addiction and used cocaine and heroin. He has also had a problem with the abuse of alcohol." May it be argued that there is a fear that somehow the offender's inability to stay out of difficulties will be assessed far too severely?

xiii)   The obvious question: How lengthy must the gap be to garner mitigating weight?

A)   Older cases suggest that a quite lengthy period is required

It may be of assistance to begin by considering an extreme (and quite dated) precedent. At page 358 of *R. v. Comeau* (1912), 19 C.C.C. 350, 1912 CarswellNS 98, 46 N.S.R. 450, 5 D.L.R. 250 (C.A.), a case touching upon previous chaste character, we read, "...a young girl who goes wrong, quickly repents and is absolutely virtuous for the next 20 years...

[might be considered in a non-negative light]." One hopes that does not indicate that the courts were then requiring offenders to "go clean" for 20 years prior to acquiring a good character once again.

Noteworthy as well is the well-known cases of *R. v. Bannerman* (1966), 55 W.W.R. 257, 48 C.R. 110, 1966 CarswellMan 9 (C.A.), affirmed (1966), 57 W.W.R. 736, 50 C.R. 76, 1966 CarswellMan 53, [1966] S.C.R. v. The dissent observed that the trial judge erred in concluding that the offender had previously been convicted of a crime of violence. It was in fact a conviction for causing a disturbance when he was 17 and in the Air Force, for which he received a fine of $15.00. Schultz J.A. noted that the conviction was 12 years old and it should not have had any bearing on the case.

Note as well *R. v. Huywan* (March 17, 1965), Roach, MacKay and Wells JJ.A., [1965] O.J. No. 151 (C.A.). The offender was sentenced at trial to two years for what is known as "high-grading", that is to say he was involved in stealing ore from the mine where he was employed. At para. 3, the Court noted that the offender was 45, married, with two grown up children. He is a miner and was a shift boss at the relevant time. His record was described as serious from 1939 to 1944 but he enjoyed a gap of 11 years until a theft in 1955, resulting in a six-month term. Thereafter, no difficulties until the serious offence of theft.

B) A lesser relative period for youthful offenders

The trend of the cases suggests that the calculation of the length of time constituting the "gap" might be more favourable in the case of younger offenders than in other cases, in keeping with the other mitigating elements in such cases, notably maturity. Stated otherwise, a period of success totalling two years might not impress a sentencing court addressing the situation of a middle-aged individual but it might sway a court in the case of a 20-year-old, especially if other elements are present.

In this vein, *R. v. Murray* (1960), 128 C.C.C. 357, 32 W.W.R. 321, 1960 CarswellSask 30 (C.A.) provides an example of leniency being granted due to a number of factors: the offender's youth, the gap in his record, his employment, his marriage and family responsibilities, and his having desisted from the offence prior to any discovery.

> *C)   A lesser period may be found suitable if other mitigating elements are present*

As noted immediately above in the case of *R. v. Murray* (1960), 128 C.C.C. 357, 32 W.W.R. 321, 1960 CarswellSask 30 (C.A.), leniency may be more easily achieved if the gap, such as it is, is advanced against a background of favourable elements such as the offender's youth, employment, family responsibilities, and a decision to desist from wrongdoing prior to any discovery.

Indeed, on occasion, sentencing courts will seize on some indication of reformation, however slight, to justify leniency. In the case of *R. v. McKenzie* (1960), 128 C.C.C. 92, 1960 CarswellSask 8, 31 W.W.R. 337, 33 C.R. 361 (C.A.), the Court remarked that "From all the evidence it is difficult to assign a reason for his entry into crime so soon after his release but it may have been caused by his association, not only with . . . but with the several others who were seen in his company, all of whom had substantial criminal records." See pages 102-103 [C.C.C.].

R. v. Kirkland (1956), [1957] S.C.R. 3, 117 C.C.C. 1, 1956 CarswellOnt 36, 25 C.R. 101 records these comments, at page 7 [C.C.C.]: ". . . there is no evidence that during the six months following his release from the penitentiary in April 1952 the appellant had done anything unlawful or dishonest. Such evidence as there is goes to show that he was trying to obtain work, albeit without much success, and was doing such work as he was able to get." In other words, even six months without offending was sufficient to garner some credit.

> *D)   A general review*

R. v. Verral, [2003] A.J. No. 749, 2003 CarswellAlta 824, 330 A.R. 171, 299 W.A.C. 171, 2003 ABCA 184 (C.A.) includes these remarks, at para. 5: "The sentencing judge referred to a lengthy criminal record of the appellant, acknowledging that the vast majority of the offences occurred between 1975 and 1988, followed by a significant gap until 1998 when his driving related offences occurred. . .".

In the case of *R. v. C. (A.C.)*, 272 A.R. 130, 2000 CarswellAlta 1008, [2000] A.J. No. 1100, 2000 ABQB 654 (Q.B.), the Court characterized as "considerable" the gap. Refer to para. 8. It spanned from 1987 to February, 1995. *R. v. Colbourne*, [2002] A.J. No. 1525, 2002 CarswellAlta 1602, 2002 ABPC 141 (Prov. Ct.), at para. 15, consigns the remarks of the trial judge that ". . . there is a substantial gap of some eight years in his record prior to his most recent conviction in 2002."

R. v. Makinaw, [2002] A.J. No. 1529, 2002 CarswellAlta 1577, 331 A.R. 179, 2002 ABPC 193 (Prov. Ct.) records the observation that "The accused also has a short and largely unrelated record. There is a gap of over six years since his last conviction." See para. 8.

In her dissenting opinion, Fraser C.J.A. remarked at para. 10 of *R. v. Smallboy* (1997), [1997] A.J. No. 312, 196 A.R. 231, 141 W.A.C. 231, 1997 CarswellAlta 309 (C.A.), "In reviewing Mr. Smallboy's record, I think it is very important to note that there was a gap of approximately five years during which time he was not involved in any offences. It is true that for some period of that time he was in prison, but that only accounts for approximately one of the five years. Her Ladyship went on to remark that once he was released from prison on mandatory supervision, he started up his own business and, by all accounts, he was a productive member of society, operating a business.

By contrast, the majority observed that "In this case there was a gap of some years before the appellant was again detected in care and control of his motor vehicle while he had alcohol in his system of over .08." See para. 1. Of note, para. 2 records these observations: "Now, I mentioned that there had been some gap. Before the gap, the accused, unfortunately, had a long record, the great majority of it for similar matters, and the accused had had two years' jail for driving while impaired on a previous occasion."

Finally, note the comments consigned at para. 3: "The accused is not very young anymore, and he doesn't appear to have had much insight into his problems until very very recently. Now, by the time of sentencing, we are told that he realizes that his problem isn't driving at all, his problem is drinking. Unfortunately, until very recently he hasn't had that insight and during the five-year gap that I mentioned, it is not suggested that he wasn't drinking, it was just that he wasn't driving."

A further example of some minor credit being assigned for a five-year gap is seen in *R. v. Mitzel*, [2002] B.C.J. No. 1176, 171 B.C.A.C. 200, 2002 CarswellBC 1215, 2002 BCCA 333, 280 W.A.C. 200 (C.A.), at para. 4 and para. 8.

Note the observations of Fraser C.J.A. at para. 3 of *R. v. D. (M.J.)* (1998), [1998] A.J. No. 1352, 1998 CarswellAlta 1124 (C.A.) "we are also of the view that the background context, coupled with Mr. Dutchek's four-year gap in his criminal record, and his recent work record (which has been by all accounts a very good one) make it appropriate for us to recommend that Mr. Dutchek be considered for early parole and we so recommend."

Note that in *R. v. B. (R.I.)*, 2001 ABPC 178, 2001 CarswellAlta 1340 (Prov. Ct.), the Court remarked at para. 37, in the context of a bail hearing: "Again based upon an analysis of R. I.B.'s record, I am struck by the three-year gap from his last conviction to these alleged offences. Given that he was a regular and repeat performer before then, I believe some comfort can be put on this gap."

In *R. v. Andre*, [2000] N.W.T.J. No. 43, 2000 CarswellNWT 38, 2000 NWTCA 4 (C.A.), it was observed at para. 11 that the prior record is horrendous and since 1976, "about the only gap of significance has been 1992, 1993, and part of 1994".

Counsel should be vigilant in reviewing the record to ascertain when the offences took place, not merely when the convictions were recorded as the delays in prosecution (including detection) might result in distorting the actual order of wrongdoing. For example, in *R. v. M. (T.E.)*, (*sub nom.* R. v. McDonnell) [1997] 1 S.C.R. 948, (*sub nom.* R. v. McDonnell) [1997] S.C.J. No. 42, (*sub nom.* R. v. McDonnell) 145 D.L.R. (4th) 577, (*sub nom.* R. v. McDonnell) 210 N.R. 241, [1997] 7 W.W.R. 44, 49 Alta. L.R. (3d) 111, (*sub nom.* R. v. McDonnell) 196 A.R. 321, (*sub nom.* R. v. McDonnell) 114 C.C.C. (3d) 436, 6 C.R. (5th) 231, 1997 CarswellAlta 213, 1997 CarswellAlta 214, (*sub nom.* R. v. McDonnell) 141 W.A.C. 321, (*sub nom.* R. v. McDonnell) 43 C.R.R. (2d) 189, we read at para. 12: "The Court held that the gap in time between the two incidents was not a mitigating factor, nor was this a case where concurrent sentences were appropriate." The gap in time was of seven years. This conclusion may reflect the fact that the offender had not been sentenced for the first offence prior to committing the second.

xiv) The Court may credit more than one "gap":

A) In general

Note the interesting remarks consigned at page 336 [C.C.C.] of *Paulk, Re* (1955), 111 C.C.C. 333, 1955 CarswellSask 10, 21 C.R. 40, 14 W.W.R. 693 (C.A.): "...there was a period between early in 1942 and August 31, 1946, when he was not convicted of any offence and another period between the middle of the year 1948 and February, 1953, when no conviction was recorded against him. During these periods the accused must have succeeded, to some extent, in rehabilitation."

Counsel's argument must therefore be that if there was some success in the past, it may be renewed in the future if the precise reason for the "slip" may be identified, be it poor associations, substance abuse, loss of employment, etc. Refer in particular to *R. v. K. (H.M.)*, [2001] A.J. No. 1176, 297 A.R. 264, 2001 CarswellAlta 1223, 2001 ABPC 163 (Prov. Ct.), at para. 27 and 31.

> He appears to have made a significant effort to remain crime free, although ultimately the factors that have led him to crime in the first place as discussed in the psychological assessment without being addressed in any way, led him back to criminal activity such as is represented before the Court at this time. . .

> . . .it is clear that he has the ability to avoid criminal activity for periods of time as shown by the gap between his last conviction for break and enter in 1998 and his most recent criminal activity in January of 2001. I believe that he falls back into criminal activity as a consequence of his many problems, including his lack of education, childhood abuse issues and substance abuse.

B)   With reference to particular offences

In the case of *R. v. Casey* (1997), [1997] A.J. No. 1040, 214 A.R. 295, 1997 CarswellAlta 1169 (Q.B.), the trial judge juxtaposes the fact of multiple entries on the criminal record with, on the one hand, gaps, and the particular nature of the wrongdoing, on the other. As we read at para. 25,

> The accused's criminal antecedents date back to 1949 when he was given a six-month suspended sentence for possession of a sawed-off rifle. His record contains several entries for property and drug offences prior to 1976 when he was released on mandatory supervision. Thereafter, following a gap of some four and a half years, he was fined in 1981 and again in 1982 of driving over .08. Following a gap of some seven years, he was fined in 1989 for another driving over .08 offence. One offence of violence appears on his record and dates back some 28 years to 1969, namely assault causing bodily harm for which he received a $50 fine. His record mainly relates to substance and alcohol abuse. It is noted that he was offence-free for approximately seven years before this offence occurred.

By carefully distinguishing between the periods of non-offending and the nature of the offences, it is possible to create multiple gaps — both absolute ones and relative ones, touching upon the nature of the offences. This type of success was in evidence at para. 2 of *R. v. Grunerud*, [2000] A.J. No. 282, 2000 CarswellAlta 224, 2000 ABCA 87 (C.A.). It records the following comments: "Given the efforts to date the appellant has made in rehabilitating himself, we reduce the sentence to one day in jail . . . In coming to this decision, we are mindful that there is a gap of several years in the appellant's record for violence-related offences."

xv)   Gaps created by prosecutorial policy

On occasion, counsel must be alert to the significance of gaps that are given added weight by reason of prosecutorial policy. For example, the Attorney General of Ontario encourages prosecutors to consider the wisdom of filing a notice of increased penalty in the case of an offender whose prior impaired conviction occurred over five years earlier.

For the sake of completeness, note *Merritt v. Headon* (1926), 47 C.C.C. 74, 1926 CarswellSask 107, [1927] 1 W.W.R. 53, 21 Sask. L.R. 237, [1927] 1 D.L.R. 940 (K.B. [In Chambers]). The offender argued that his prior liquor offence ought not to have been counted as it occurred over six months prior the subsequent offence. This had been the holding in a Manitoba judgment, *R. v. McIlwain*, 46 C.C.C. 76, 1926 CarswellMan 50, [1926] 2 W.W.R. 721 (Co. Ct.). MacKenzie J. rejected this submission, finding no support for it in the provincial legislation. His Lordship imposed the minimum fine of $250.00. In other words, there is no statutorily defined gap period.

In the case of *R. v. Abbott* (1996), [1996] A.J. No. 243, 182 A.R. 149, 1996 CarswellAlta 212 (Prov. Ct.), it was remarked that "Defence counsel raises what he calls the 'gap principle' in sentencing and says that the prior convictions are 10 and 11 years old. That s. 255(1)(a)(iii) does not limit the time within which the previous convictions must have occurred and that these provisions having been in the Criminal Code since 1969 one could theoretically be facing a minimum sentence of 90 days even where the previous convictions were imposed 25 years ago, unless he could obtain relief under s. 24(1) of the Charter." The Court was of the view that nothing prevented taking into account such dated convictions, but that the Charter might operate to stay automatic jail sentences. . .

xvi)   Gaps created by imprisonment?

Johnstone J. was not prepared to countenance a submission to the effect that any "gap" arose as a result of imprisonment in *R. v. Kubbernus* (2000), [2000] A.J. No. 1054, 272 A.R. 99, 2000 CarswellAlta 978 (Q.B.). Para. 36 records that

> This concept also relates to restraint in that it acknowledges that a person who has rectified past behaviour should also be considered as having better prospects for individual deterrence and rehabilitation. There is no basis for making any such finding here. *To suggest that because this offender has a gap in his criminal record because he had been incarcerated for over four and one-half years is oblivious to the lack of proof that the offender has behaved while in custody and more importantly turned his life around.* The relevance of such a gap in his record fades when it is apparent that the offender has simply resumed a criminal lifestyle after what appeared at first blush to be a period of harmony in the law. . . [emphasis supplied]

The Court added that "This offender re-offended twice while on parole, choosing, it is apparent, to resume a life of crime and persist therefore in it. Rather than embarking upon a lifestyle of crime avoidance, his propensity was toward a continuation of a life of crime. As a result he can no longer argue that he had a period of reformation." See para. 37

On the other hand, however, some credit was assigned for a period of confinement in *R. v. K. (H.M.)*, [2001] A.J. No. 1176, 297 A.R. 264, 2001 CarswellAlta 1223, 2001 ABPC 163 (Prov. Ct.), at para. 27:

> Since the date of his last conviction for break and enter, until the date of this offence, he has managed to stay out of trouble, except for a conviction for mischief which occurred in January of 2001. I recognize that his actual incarceration would have played a significant role in keeping him crime free during that two and one-half year period; although that does not explain entirely his good behaviour during that period. Indeed, given his past history, this time period with no criminal activity represents a significant gap for this particular man. He appears to have made a significant effort to remain crime free . . .

Note as well that in her dissenting opinion, Fraser C.J.A. remarked at para. 10 of *R. v. Smallboy* (1997), [1997] A.J. No. 312, 196 A.R. 231,

141 W.A.C. 231, 1997 CarswellAlta 309 (C.A.), "In reviewing Mr. Small-boy's record, I think it is very important to note that there was a gap of approximately five years during which time he was not involved in any offences. It is true that for some period of that time he was in prison, but that only accounts for approximately one of the five years."

xvii)   Gaps followed by a serious period of offending

As a general rule, little credit is assigned to a "gap" in the history of an offender if such a period of demonstrated pro-social behaviour is followed by a significant period of anti-social activity. This perspective on sentencing was expressed in this fashion at para. 15 of *R. v. Spinder*, [2003] B.C.J. No. 1485, 2003 CarswellBC 1569, 184 B.C.A.C. 145, 302 W.A.C. 145, 2003 BCCA 373 (C.A.): "Can it then be said that it was excessive for the crime in question? Appellant's counsel say it is because it fails to recognize a 'gap' in the appellant's criminal record and it fails to pay homage to the 'step-up' principle. In my opinion, neither of these submissions are soundly based. The so-called 'gap' is but a part of the criminal history and, in any event, the gap was followed by a significant pace of criminal behaviour."

A related judgment is that of *R. v. Stewart*, [2002] B.C.J. No. 1896, 174 B.C.A.C. 6, 2002 CarswellBC 1965, 2002 BCCA 463, 286 W.A.C. 6 (C.A.). Para. 11 is instructive in pointing out a gap in the appellant's record from 1991 to 1998. "During part of that time he worked as a fisherman out of Prince Rupert and apparently dealt with his drug problem. However, he fell back into his addiction and used cocaine and heroin. He has also had a problem with the abuse of alcohol.

xviii)   The influence of a pre-sentence report

In *R. v. Atkinson* (January 13, 1966), Doc. Toronto 396/65, [1966] O.J. No. 15 (C.A.), McLennan J.A. noted that "[t]he probation report ... indicates that in spite of this lengthy criminal record, it would appear that the prisoner has made an effort to remain free of difficulty during the past four years ... he appears to be concerned about his wife, who is in ill health...". See para. 2 and the next, where the Court recorded that "... the prisoner has made an effort in the past four years to live a law-abiding life and support his family...". Nevertheless, his sentence was not reduced. The gap serves to make plain that there is no reason for him to engage in criminal behaviour. At other times, it permits the focus of the enquiry to be drawn to the reason why the offender ceased to be law abiding. See also *R. v. Fernandes* (May 11, 1966), MacKay,

Schroeder and McLennan JJ.A., [1966] O.J. No. 291 (C.A.), at para. 2.

xix)   The impact of a "gap" between as yet unprosecuted offences: The "spree" principle

Some valuable guidance is found in *R. v. Mahamud*, [2001] B.C.J. No. 1985, 2001 CarswellBC 2044, 2001 BCCA 558 (C.A.) on the question of the time period separating two or more offences that are all committed prior to the first arrest. In effect, how does the "spree" principle apply, if at all? The Court of Appeal expressed the issue at para. 4-5 by noting that allowance is at times made in the case of an offender who commits a number of offences within a brief time period that may be characterized as a time of weakness or a troubled period. However, if the gap between the offences is significant, than it is expected that the offender's moral compass will be triggered and the ability to distinguish right from wrong will come into play. Stated otherwise, the passage of sufficient time after a first offence for one's conscience to start to operate makes a further offence an aggravating element.

xx)   Expert evidence and "gaps" in the offender's record

Note that in *R. v. McDowell*, [2002] A.J. No. 1565, 2002 CarswellAlta 1646, 2002 ABPC 199 (Prov. Ct.), the Court considered the impact of a gap between offences in the formation of an expert opinion on the risk profile that may be drawn of an offender.

xxi)   Summary for advocates

Whenever possible, it appears that sentencing Courts will seize upon a "gap" in the history of an offender to justify leniency if it can be shown to be an indication of an ability to "go straight". Consider the degree of moral blame attached to the offence described in *R. v. White* (March 17, 1970), Aylesworth, MacKay and Kelly JJ.A., [1970] O.J. No. 212 (C.A.). The offender, 40 years of age, "shamefully defrauded an elderly lady" out of $83.00. The Court took pains to point out the particularly serious nature of the wrongdoing, having to do with preying upon the old, the infirm and the like, making reference to *R. v. Major* (1966), 48 C.R. 296, 1966 CarswellOnt 17 (C.A.). Refer to para. 2. It added that unlike the *Major* case, this was an isolated instance.

Nevertheless, it highlighted in para. 1 that he had not committed an offence for seven years "and one must assume was a proper citizen".

It then made plain at para. 2 that he "has demonstrated his ability to go straight, as it were, for a great length of time considering his previous record and his previous inclinations as indicated by that record." He received a three-month sentence and probation for one year. In sum, the Court's interference was premised upon the special circumstances and the overstressing of the deterrent aspect in sentencing in light of the unusual facts.

At the end of the day, the "gap" principle is a well-recognized mitigating element in sentencing in that it is capable of demonstrating that an offender has succeeded in avoiding misconduct for a significant period of time. In such cases, defence counsel must seek to demonstrate that pro-social attitudes have been assimilated and that the misconduct can be characterized fairly as "isolated, "out-of-character" or "exceptional". How long is long enough to justify such a qualifier is a difficult question, but it should be asserted that all other things being equal, restraint in the selection of incarceration may be wise in light of the success at "going straight".

g)   Behaviour and the trivial nature of the wrongdoing:

i)   The legislative background

It may be of assistance for counsel in framing submissions in what may be fairly described as "trivial offences" to consider referring to the legislative history of the sentencing provisions found in the Criminal Code. For example, at para. 10, page 230 of *R. v. Young* (1901), [1901] O.J. No. 198, 2 O.L.R. 228, 4 C.C.C. 580 (C.A.), the Court remarked, ". . . the Criminal Code, sec. 971, 55-56 Vict. Ch. 29(1), provides that having regard to the trivial nature of the offence and any extenuating circumstances, the Court may, instead of sentencing the offender at once to any punishment, 'direct that he be released on his entering into a recognizance with or without sureties, and during such period as the Court directs, to appear and receive judgment when called upon, and in the meantime to keep the peace and be of good behaviour.'"

The intriguing fact is that the prosecutor moved for sentence to be imposed 14 years later "because it is alleged he has broken a condition of his recognizance by not being of good behaviour [by defaming the prosecutor]". See para 13, page 230. He was convicted of libel on April 28, 1887, and the motion was decided on July 7, 1901. The Court left the matter to the civil courts, but without commenting on the maximum period for return of the offender to receive judgment.

R. v. Webb, 62 C.C.C. 279, 1933 CarswellSask 59, [1933] 3 W.W.R. 431 (C.A.) provides a useful historical illustration of the Court of Appeal intervening in order to reduce a penitentiary-length sentence meted out in the case of a repeat offender guilty of a trivial crime. The offender was guilty of stealing a coat worth $15.00 and Haultain C.J.S. noted that he was then sentenced to two years and three months in the Prince Albert Penitentiary. His Lordship then remarked, "[a] large number of previous convictions were proved against the appellant, the majority of which, however, were for vagrancy or being drunk and disorderly. The fact that the appellant has committed other offences is not, in the opinion of the Court, sufficient reason for imposing a term in the penitentiary for the comparatively trivial offence in the present case." Refer to page 279 [C.C.C.].

The Court of Appeal later noted the case of *R. v. Taylor* (1924), 18 Cr. App. R. 143, the same learned Judge instructed us as follows:

> The appellant pleaded guilty to the charge of stealing a woman's coat from a lobby leading to the office where she was employed. He is 35 years old, and he had previously been convicted on 20 occasions. The last sentence he served was one of 18 months' imprisonment, from which he was released in October, 1923. He was out of prison for nine months before the commission of the present crime. It has been said over and over again in this Court that the mere fact that a man has been convicted many times is not in itself sufficient reason for passing a heavy sentence on him for an offence which is trivial in itself. The Court is satisfied that the proper sentence here is one of twelve months' imprisonment with hard labour.

ii)   Behaviour and silly offences

It is suggested that the proportionality principle serves to temper the reach of general and specific deterrence in cases of trivial offences, even though committed by offenders with lengthy records. One example arises in *R. v. Moore* (May 5, 1970), Aylesworth, McGillivray and Jessup JJ.A., [1970] O.J. No. 328 (C.A.). Paragraph 1 sets out the holding "We think there is a grave error in principle indicated in a sentence of two years [for] a shoplifting episode of $9.93. In our view a sentence commensurate with the crime, even with the background of the accused, is a sentence of three months in jail." The record was not disclosed in the brief report.

If counsel is able to characterize the offence as being silly in nature, then great success in sentencing may be achieved. For example, Gale C.J.O. reduced substantially a jail term meted out to a mature first offender, but did not go so far as to declare that a suspended sentence was appropriate in *R. v. McKimm* (1969), [1970] 1 C.C.C. 340, [1970] 1 O.R. 819, 1969 CarswellOnt 925 (C.A.). The Court was critical of the decision of the trial judge to impose concurrent terms of 18 months for break and enter and theft and theft of automobile.

The offender was not involved in the

> . . . usual breaking and entering case nor the usual theft of a truck. It was a silly act by an intoxicated man who theretofore had lived an exemplary life. That it was a silly act is pointed up by the sequence of events: the accused, wearing his employee's uniform. . .in an intoxicated condition, broke into the accused's employer's plant late in the evening and [stole goods] then, after driving away the truck in question which in fact was the truck that he drove regularly in his employment, and upon being advised that the police were looking for him, he telephoned the police and surrendered himself. At all times he co-operated with the police and when it was all over and the enormity of what he had done came home, he was genuinely remorseful and disgusted with his performance.

Subsequently, the Court repeated that this was not the usual breaking and entering or theft case one sees constantly in the courts. See page 341 [C.C.C.].

h)   Behaviour and delay in sentencing

The impact of delay in sentencing may not be seen, at first blush, as a factor that involves moral blame but in the ultimate analysis, how an offender reacts to the criminal process and, on occasion, to the sentence itself, reveals much about the willingness to make amends. In one respect, it will profit the advocate to focus the Court's attention on the offender who takes advantage of appellate or other delays to "turn over a new leaf". For example, in *R. v. Echegoyen* (2001), [2001] O.J. No. 1021, 143 O.A.C. 147, 2001 CarswellOnt 827 (C.A.), the Court granted a measure of leniency, chiefly on the grounds that "Four years have passed since the commission of this offence and, except for a breach of recognizance, the appellant has conducted himself as a responsible citizen and a good parent. He has served seven and one-half weeks of the sentence." See para. 9. Hence, "[i]n the circumstances, it is in the public interest to reduce the sentence to time served." Refer to para. 10.

Note as well *R. v. Hayes* (2001), [2001] O.J. No. 684, 142 O.A.C. 57, 2001 CarswellOnt 534 (C.A.). Para. 2 sets out that "There are unusual aspects to this case. The appellant has been on bail for a total of almost four years. In that time, she has severed her relationship with the motorcycle gang, abstained from the use of drugs, served a six-month sentence for the Orillia offence and three months of the sentence imposed by the trial judge in this case. All indications are that the appellant is fully rehabilitated."

R. v. Hadida (2001), [2001] O.J. No. 843, 2001 CarswellOnt 652 (C.A.) contains these observations at para. 2: "...over four years have passed since the offence was committed and 18 months have passed since the imposition of the sentence." Reference is also made to *R. v. Dumont* (2001), [2001] O.J. No. 564, 141 O.A.C. 324, 2001 CarswellOnt 473 (C.A.). The offence involved the female accused pointing a firearm without lawful excuse at her two children on one occasion approximately 19 years ago, sometime between January of 1979 and December of 1981. At para. 35, Mr. Justice Labrosse remarked: "The requirements of s. 742 of the Criminal Code are satisfied ... the appellant has no criminal record and the Court was dealing with an event that had occurred a long time ago." The Court imposed a curfew from 10:00 p.m. to 7:00 a.m. for the duration of the 12-month period of detention. See also *R. v. Francis* (2000), [2000] O.J. No. 5043, 139 O.A.C. 385, 2000 CarswellOnt 4881 (C.A.).

i)   Behaviour and the escalation of violence: An aggravating factor as it marks poor behaviour with a high degree of moral blame

Having reviewed at length the favourable element of a lengthy period without offending, it will be of assistance to consider the contrary scenario.

In this respect, note that in *R. v. Bates* (2000), [2000] O.J. No. 2558, 134 O.A.C. 156, 146 C.C.C. (3d) 321, 35 C.R. (5th) 327, 2000

CarswellOnt 2360 (C.A.), there were serious aggravating factors that characterized the respondent's behaviour. These included an escalating pattern of harassment over three months including the assault, unauthorized entry of the complainant's home while the family was out, telephone calls, physical approaches, lying in wait, threats involving profanity, predatory following, harassing friends of the complainant and the final threat of homicide and suicide with a realistic-looking weapon." Refer to para. 47.

R. v. Ward, at para. 2, makes plain that repeated instances of violence directed at the same victim will be the subject of a severe response by the courts. See also *R. v. Patenaude* (2000), [2000] O.J. No. 3035, 2000 CarswellOnt 2862 (C.A.), at para. 4.

R. v. Valle-Quintero (2002), [2002] O.J. No. 4107, 2002 CarswellOnt 3583, 169 C.C.C. (3d) 140, 165 O.A.C. 275 (C.A.) emphasizes one element of the many aggravating factors: the breach of the court order requiring the offender to not have contact with the victim. As noted, he breached the order by attempting to kill her!

Para. 71 records the following comments in this respect:

> The fact that the attempted murder occurred while the appellant was on bail, on terms designed to protect the complainant, was but one relevant factor which the trial judge could, and did, consider in fashioning a proper sentence. It formed part of the overall context in which the offence occurred and bore directly on the circumstances of the appellant relevant to sentencing. Here, the sentence imposed by the trial judge was not directed only or primarily at that aspect of the appellant's misconduct. Rather, the trial judge considered the need for specific and general deterrence and fashioned a lengthy sentence of imprisonment to denounce all of the appellant's conduct. In *R. v. Bates*, [2000] O.J. No. 2558, 134 O.A.C. 156 (C.A.), this Court emphasized how critical it is that offenders not breach court orders or their undertakings to the Court while on release.

Understandably, little leniency was in evidence, in keeping with the elevated moral blameworthiness associated with the grave misconduct.

j) Behaviour while on parole

The Court of Appeal considered the offender's progress while serving day parole in the case of *R. v. Corpus* (2000), [2000] O.J. No. 549, 2000 CarswellOnt 497, 130 O.A.C. 84 (C.A.) at paras. 10-11.

The same negative conclusions open to a sentencing court when informed of an offender's poor response to probation will be drawn when faced with a negative response to parole. For example, see *R. v. Lauzon* (2000), [2000] O.J. No. 3940, 137 O.A.C. 153, 2000 CarswellOnt 3837 (C.A.), leave to appeal refused (2001), 2001 CarswellOnt 3170, 2001 CarswellOnt 3171, 276 N.R. 397 (note), 155 O.A.C. 199 (note) (S.C.C.), at para. 18.

k)   Behaviour while on probation

A poor prior response to probation may be devastating. In *R. v. M. (T.)* (2000), [2000] O.J. No. 2619, 133 O.A.C. 169, 2000 CarswellOnt 2188 (C.A.), this was cited as one of many reasons disentitling a youthful offender to leniency. See para. 10. In *R. v. Mankoo* (2000), [2000] O.J. No. 1869, 132 O.A.C. 270, 2000 CarswellOnt 1874 (C.A.), it was noted that the offender was on probation when he committed serious counterfeiting offences. This was a factor that influenced the refusal of a community-based disposition. *R. v. Ward* (2000), [2000] O.J. No. 301, 2000 CarswellOnt 323 (C.A.) also demonstrates that aggravating weight will be assigned to an offence committed while subject to probation. See para. 2 and para. 12 of *R. v. Pupovic* (2000), [2000] O.J. No. 4427, 138 O.A.C. 193, 2000 CarswellOnt 4112 (C.A.), leave to appeal refused (2001), 2001 CarswellOnt 872, 2001 CarswellOnt 873, 271 N.R. 192 (note), 149 O.A.C. 199 (note) (S.C.C.).

In the case of *R. v. Howlett* (2002), [2002] O.J. No. 3525, 2002 CarswellOnt 2977, 163 O.A.C. 48 (C.A.), a prosecution for driving while disqualified, the Court noted at para. 2 that "[t]he appellant was stopped by the police on January 17, 2002 for a traffic violation. He could not provide a driver's licence and gave a false name. Further investigation revealed his true identity and the fact that he was prohibited from driving under a number of suspensions, the most recent being a court-imposed prohibition for three years commencing on April 28, 2000." At para. 7, we read the comment that the sentencing judge stated that the offence was aggravated by the fact that the appellant had provided a false name on apprehension. Nothing suggests that the Court of Appeal disagreed with this view, to the contrary...

l)   Behaviour and the impact of provocation

R. v. Benjamin (2002), [2002] O.J. No. 3563, 2002 CarswellOnt 3118 (C.A.), provides an illustration of the mitigating effect of provocation in a case of assaultive behaviour. As set out at para. 2, the trial judge's failure to take provocation into account resulted in an error in principle. Accordingly, the Court reduced the four-year term to one of three years. What this simple example underscores is that the degree of moral blame is attenuated in the case of an offender who did not seek out a violent encounter, but who could not walk away from one when it was encountered.

Provocation is an excellent example of an outside "force" that manifests itself to lessen the moral blameworthiness that may be associated with the offence. In a real sense, it may explain why the offender acted in such an uncharacteristic fashion, or the reason for such an "isolated" offence.

Of course, the degree of provocation may not serve to reduce the moral obloquy to any appreciable degree. In the case of *R. v. Clarke* (2003), [2003] O.J. No. 1966, 2003 CarswellOnt 1922, 172 O.A.C. 133 (C.A.), a 47-year-old intoxicated, emaciated and frail man who suffered from numerous health problems was stabbed seven times in his own home and killed by his friend and neighbour. The Court of Appeal observed that there was some provocation, as we read at para. 4. Para. 7(i) contains the observation that among the aggravating factors was that "the appellant characterized himself as flying into 'pure rage' against a friend who had only slightly provoked him...".

Further, para. 6 reports that "[i]n our view, the trial judge was also in error in stating that 'provocation cannot mitigate a sentence in a case like this.' In *R. v. Stone*, [1999] 2 S.C.R. 290 at para. 237, Bastarache J. for the Court, held that, '[t]he argument that the provocation factor was spent because it had already served to reduce the legal character of the crime overlooks the purpose of s. 232 and therefore must fail.' Thus, provocation is one of the many factors to be considered when assessing the appropriate sentence. In this case, it deserved some modest consideration."

In the case of *R. v. P. (L.)* (2003), [2003] O.J. No. 251, 2003 CarswellOnt 193, 168 O.A.C. 170, 172 C.C.C. (3d) 195 (C.A.) para. 23 includes these observations: "The serious consequences of this offence for J. cannot be overstated. The trial judge properly gave these consequences significant weight in determining the appropriate disposition." See para. 24. Having so found, it went on to conclude that "We are satisfied, however, that the trial judge erred in finding that the injuries actually suffered by J. were reasonably foreseeable at the time of the assault. The evidence of the experts suggests that the tragic consequences were far from foreseeable." In addition, the trial judge erred

in principle in failing to give sufficient weight to the circumstances surrounding the assault.

As we read at para. 25:

> On his findings, the confrontation between the appellants and
> J. was precipitated by the appellants' reasonable and genuine
> belief that J. was responsible for the disgusting racial graffiti which
> was appearing in the neighbourhood. Also on his findings, the
> appellants did not seek out J. intending to assault him. The vio-
> lence which occurred at the time of the confrontation was spon-
> taneous and very brief. The facts of this case, while no doubt
> serious, are clearly less serious than those outlined in *R. v. R.R.O.*,
> [1997] O.J. No. 341 (C.A.), where this Court upheld the disposition
> of one year secure custody for aggravated assault.

Turning to the question of the appropriate disposition, the Court held
that "despite R.B.'s positive antecedence and his favourable prospects,
we are satisfied that a significant period of secure custody is required
to adequately reflect the seriousness of this offence." Mitigating weight
was placed on the fact that he has been under a form of house arrest
since July 1999, that he has been on bail pending appeal on very strict
terms including house arrest since March 2001, and that the appeal
should have been heard long ago through no fault of his. "The fresh
evidence also indicates that the offence and its aftermath have had
extraordinary adverse ramifications for R.B. and the rest of his family.
R.B. is now 20 years old. It is fair to say that he is far removed from
the young man who committed this heinous offence." See para. 26. In
the result, a six-month closed custody term was selected, followed by
probation for one year.

The lack of provocation is also a factor to be assessed. Refer to *R. v.
Ahmed-Saidi* (2001), [2001] O.J. No. 242, 140 O.A.C. 346, 2001
CarswellOnt 184 (C.A.), at para. 10.

By contrast, in *R. v. L. (B.R.)* (May 3, 2000), Doc. C32462, [2000] O.J.
No. 3370 (C.A.) the Court of Appeal reduced a three-year sentence for
a violent offence involving an intimate partner, not otherwise described,
chiefly on the grounds of the young age of the offender, his remorse,
and the absence of a record. Notable as well is the fact that the offence
took place in the midst of an argument between the offender and the
complainant, immediately after the complainant struck the former. There
was no time for planning. It is the offender's refusal or inability to check

the criminal tendency during the planning stage that is of concern. Refer to para. 3.

m) Callous behaviour

A further aggravating element of behaviour is callousness. In *R. v. Burke* (2001), [2001] O.J. No. 1119, 143 O.A.C. 286, 2001 CarswellOnt 929, 41 C.R. (5th) 134, 153 C.C.C. (3d) 97, 53 O.R. (3d) 600, 61 O.R. (3d) 256 (note) (C.A.), reversed 2002 CarswellOnt 1970, 2002 CarswellOnt 1971, 2002 SCC 55, 164 C.C.C. (3d) 385, 213 D.L.R. (4th) 234, 2 C.R. (6th) 1, 290 N.R. 71, 160 O.A.C. 271, [2002] 2 S.C.R. 857, the offender fired five times and struck the victim three times, a deliberate act that was planned. Indeed, the trial judge found that after the victim was shot, he moved towards him and aimed again, and pulled the trigger a number of times. "But for the fact that the gun had already been emptied of bullets, I have no doubt that the accused would have faced a charge of first degree murder." See para. 52.

Reference is also made to *R. v. Sturge* (2001), [2001] O.J. No. 3923, 2001 CarswellOnt 3691, 17 M.V.R. (4th) 272 (C.A.). The offender twice involved himself in police chases injuring police officers on both occasions. See para. 5 and 6. He showed no regard for their safety.

n) Behaviour behind the wheel

R. v. Mascarenhas (2002), [2002] O.J. No. 2989, 2002 CarswellOnt 2517, 60 O.R. (3d) 465, 162 O.A.C. 331, 29 M.V.R. (4th) 1 (C.A.) illustrates rather ably the horror of the offender whose behaviour, if unchecked, leads to tragedy. The Court of Appeal took pains to demonstrate that it was concerned with a sentence appeal as against a total term of 12 years [reduced to 10.5 by reason of pre-trial credit] in circumstances that included blood-alcohol readings above 338 milligrams, the inability to control a vehicle such that it struck down two people walking on a roadside path, the further inability to control the vehicle after the fatal collision, not to mention a horrendous drinking and driving record and bail conditions prohibiting both drinking and driving. Very little could be said in mitigation, save for guilty pleas at various stages of the proceedings, and some efforts to overcome alcoholism.

o) Behaviour and planning

It is an aggravating factor that offender has a related record, as made plain in *R. v. Baxter* (2002), [2002] O.J. No. 3565, 2002 CarswellOnt

3120 (C.A.). A 12-month sentence was within the appropriate range for a second offence of making a threat to the same victim. Of note, the threat was detailed and serious and was not a spontaneous offence due to a chance event or meeting.

Generally speaking, planning is an aggravating element in that the courts conclude that the time between the planning and the commission did not serve to bring the offender to his or her senses. See *R. v. Burke* (2001), [2001] O.J. No. 1119, 143 O.A.C. 286, 2001 CarswellOnt 929, 41 C.R. (5th) 134, 153 C.C.C. (3d) 97, 53 O.R. (3d) 600, 61 O.R. (3d) 256 (note) (C.A.), reversed 2002 CarswellOnt 1970, 2002 CarswellOnt 1971, 2002 SCC 55, 164 C.C.C. (3d) 385, 213 D.L.R. (4th) 234, 2 C.R. (6th) 1, 290 N.R. 71, 160 O.A.C. 271, [2002] 2 S.C.R. 857, in which the offender planned to shoot his victim over a drug debt. See para. 51. Note that any opportunity to demonstrate the absence of planning should be exploited, as in the case of *R. v. Wang* (2001), [2001] O.J. No. 1491, 144 O.A.C. 115, 153 C.C.C. (3d) 321, 2001 CarswellOnt 1321 (C.A.), additional reasons at (2001), [2001] O.J. No. 1961, 2001 CarswellOnt 1773 (C.A.). The Court of Appeal observed that an accomplice testified that Wang had not taken part in planning the home invasions. See para. 65.

By contrast, when the offence is unsophisticated, demonstrating no planning, it is noted by the sentencing court. See para. 4 of *R. v. Sturge* (2001), [2001] O.J. No. 3923, 2001 CarswellOnt 3691, 17 M.V.R. (4th) 272 (C.A.).

That an offence is well planned is often quite aggravating in that it suggests that the offender's moral compass is non existent, and only a significant attribution of correctional resources will remedy this situation. For example, in *R. v. Wilson* (2003), [2003] O.J. No. 1047, 2003 CarswellOnt 993, 174 C.C.C. (3d) 255, 170 O.A.C. 128 (C.A.), para. 8 records that the quantum of the fraud reached close to $900,000. "The fraud was systematic and well planned, taking place over four years and involving several participants."

Stated otherwise, an offender who never listens to his/her conscience is far more likely to commit a further offence of a like nature in the future, and this anticipated threat to the community must be addressed. Having said that, counsel might wish to point out that it is unlikely that s/he will be in a similar position of trust in the future.

Hence, unlike an offence that is rooted in an event that springs forth due to chance, a planned offence may demonstrate an elevated degree of moral blameworthy conduct. Thus, in *R. v. Pasdari* (2003), [2003] O.J. No. 319, 2003 CarswellOnt 452 (C.A.), Rosenberg J.A. remarked as follows, at para. 1:

> We agree with the trial judge that deterrence and denunciation were the paramount consideration in this case. This was a well-planned offence in which the appellant intended to take his daughter to Iran. In the course of his planning for the offence the appellant emptied various joint bank accounts, saving accounts and his RRSP. He took all of the child's clothing and toys. But for his wife's quick action it is simply uncertain when he might have returned to Canada with the child. The offence has here a serious impact on his wife.

R. v. K. (D.) (2003), [2003] O.J. No. 562, 2003 CarswellOnt 542, 169 O.A.C. 97 (C.A.) emphasizes that it is a serious aggravating element to commit "a horrific series of sexual assaults with various weapons over a protracted period." See para. 3. The victim was the then wife of the offender and she was assaulted five times over 12 years, twice with a gun, once with a hatchet and three times with knives. There were death threats and once she was forced, with a knife pointed at her, to fellate the offender. Para. 3 concludes that "...the offences reveal cruel, dehumanizing treatment ... and conduct designed ... to demean, terrorize, humiliate and subjugate [the victim]."

As noted at para. 7, "[t]he admitted offences are horrendous in nature. They arose from a domestic relationship. They were carried out in a brutal and horrifying manner over a lengthy time. Thus, they were not isolated occurrences. The victim impact statement ... confirms the profoundly scaring and continuing aftermath of the assaults. Several of the offences showed clear hallmarks of planning and deliberation. Two of the offences were committed while the appellant's two young children were at home. Although [he] pleaded guilty to the offences, the record reveals no evidence of remorse. Indeed, on the record before us, the prospects for [rehabilitation] are highly speculative."

In *R. v. Dewald* (2001), [2001] O.J. No. 1716, 144 O.A.C. 352, 54 O.R. (3d) 1, 156 C.C.C. (3d) 405, 2001 CarswellOnt 1551 (C.A.), the offender killed his children in breach of the most sacred trust resulting in a worst offence, leaving aside the planning and motive elements. At the end of the day, a father who drowned his two children was sentenced to 17 years without parole eligibility, down from the 23 years imposed at trial.

Significant elements of planning and deliberation are viewed as aggravating as these elements make plain that the offender lacked the conscience necessary to arrest him or her from going ahead with the offence. See *R. v. Forrest* (2000), [2000] O.J. No. 755, 130 O.A.C. 86, 2000 CarswellOnt 667 (C.A.) at para. 3. It is the same type of concern in the case of repeated sexual violence: the offender's inability to stop augurs poorly for future rehabilitation. See the dissent in *R. v. W. (A.G.)* (2000), [2000] O.J. No. 398, 130 O.A.C. 78, 2000 CarswellOnt 358 (C.A.) at paras. 8-9.

By contrast, in *R. v. L. (B.R.)* (May 3, 2000), Doc. Toronto C32462, [2000] O.J. No. 3370 (C.A.) the Court of Appeal reduced a three-year sentence for a violent offence involving an intimate partner, not otherwise described, chiefly on the grounds of the young age of the offender, his remorse, and the absence of a record. Notable as well is the fact that the offence took place in the midst of an argument between the offender and the complainant, immediately after the complainant struck the former. There was no time for planning. It is the offender's refusal or inability to check the criminal tendency during the planning stage that is of concern. Refer to para. 3.

Note also that in *R. v. Pupovic* (2000), [2000] O.J. No. 4427, 138 O.A.C. 193, 2000 CarswellOnt 4112 (C.A.), leave to appeal refused (2001), 2001 CarswellOnt 872, 2001 CarswellOnt 873, 271 N.R. 192 (note), 149 O.A.C. 199 (note) (S.C.C.), the Court of Appeal agreed that there had been planning to tie up one victim, but that it was not correct to conclude that any plan existed to kidnap her and another. See para. 12. See also para. 7 of *R. v. Garrod* (2000), [2000] O.J. No. 3636, 2000 CarswellOnt 3425 (C.A.).

4.   AN EXAMINATION OF THE OFFENDER'S ATTITUDE AND MORAL BLAMEWORTHINESS:

a)   Introduction

Does the offender's attitude suggest a potential for rehabilitation? That is the ultimate question to be answered by the Court and for which the assistance of counsel may be decisive. To repeat, it is the duty of counsel to marshal all information that will permit the Court to find that the offender is a good if not an excellent candidate for rehabilitation. In the absence of such information, the Court may select a denunciatory sentence as in the case of *R. v. M. (T.)* (2000), [2000] O.J. No. 2619, 133 O.A.C. 169, 2000 CarswellOnt 2188 (C.A.).

Counsel has a duty to point out to clients in the most forceful terms that their attitude post-offence will be scrutinized and that they must avoid the type of report recorded at para. 10: "...he declared he had no interest in academic work and no motivation to pursue it. Nor had he seen any psychiatrists or psychologists, saying he would rather play cards. He had previously responded poorly to probation, showing little inclination to change his ways or improve his situation." Worse yet, the Court received no information on his progress, if any, post-sentencing. This was cited as a factor militating against leniency in the case of *R. v. Lewis* (2000), [2000] O.J. No. 2245, 133 O.A.C. 172, 2000 CarswellOnt 2094 (C.A.) at para. 10.

In *R. v. Fudge* (2000), [2000] O.J. No. 2780, 2000 CarswellOnt 2628 (C.A.), the Court of Appeal emphasized in the first paragraph that the offender committed a crime of violence, having accumulated a record for crimes of violence, making her a significant danger to the community and to herself, not just by her prior conduct but also by reason of her addictions and her mental state. In sum, she was a real risk to the safety of the community.

Nevertheless, great leniency was shown to her by reason of the fact in the two years between the commission of the offence and the imposition of sentence, she turned her life around. "She is in a positive relationship with her husband, has developed a strong support network in the community and has remained drug and alcohol free. She has continued her progress since this sentence was imposed some six months ago." Refer to para. 2.

The Court of Appeal accepted that the trial judge had selected appropriate terms of a conditional sentence to guard against a return to her prior lifestyle. "She crafted a conditional sentence which was directed very much to the specific situation and concerns raised by this particular offender. The terms imposed by the trial judge also contain a significant punitive component." Refer to para. 4. It did not interfere with the sentence.

b)   Examples of a positive attitude:

i)   A positive attitude as shown by an apology

In *R. v. S. (D.C.)* (2000), [2000] O.J. No. 885, 47 O.R. (3d) 612, 131 O.A.C. 396, 2000 CarswellOnt 840 (C.A.) the offender apologized to both of his victims by means of a letter. See para. 8. This genuine expression of remorse was given great weight by the Court of Appeal, as noted at para. 13.

ii) A positive attitude as shown by co-operation with the police

In the somewhat unusual case of *R. v. MacDougall* (1995), [1995] M.J. No. 531, 107 Man. R. (2d) 236, 109 W.A.C. 236, 1995 CarswellMan 459 (C.A.) the offender was led by her son to attempt to smuggle narcotics into the jail in which he was detained. At para. 3, the Court noted: "The accused co-operated with police authorities and entered a plea of guilty. A pre-sentence report indicates that the accused realizes the gravity of her actions.

One signal element in the assignment of mitigating weight to the scale involving offenders is the degree to which co-operation is shown to the work of the authorities. In this respect, *R. v. H. (C.N.)* (2002), [2002] O.J. No. 4918, 2002 CarswellOnt 4327, 170 C.C.C. (3d) 253, 62 O.R. (3d) 564, 167 O.A.C. 292, 9 C.R. (6th) 103 (C.A.) includes a useful review of the mitigating factor of co-operating with the police. The background finding was the offender had co-operated but this was disparaged by the Crown on the basis that the co-operation was minimal and it should be disregarded since it proved of no practical use to the police.

Justice Rosenberg made plain at para. 39 that the trial judge found that the offender voluntarily provided all of the information that he had including names, telephone numbers and photographs. He also found that the information, if acted upon, might have led to the arrest and prosecution of principals in the cocaine importation venture. He also found that the police were only mildly interested in the information and took few investigative steps. To be balanced, it must also be noted that the offender's co-operation with the authorities ended on the night of his arrest as he did not seek out the police to provide further information.

The Court observed "...that co-operation with the police is a substantial mitigating factor where the accused has provided extensive information that has led to the prosecution of others for serious offences." See para. 40. However, it was held that it would be too narrow a test to require that the information or assistance must be of practical use in the sense that it can be acted upon. Rosenberg J.A. preferred the somewhat broader view taken by the majority in *R. v. Cartwright* (1989), 17 N.S.W.L.R. 243 (C.A.) at 252-53:

In order to ensure that such encouragement is given, the appropriate reward for providing assistance should be granted whatever the offender's motive may have been in giving it, be it genuine remorse (or contrition) or simply self-interest. What is to be encouraged is a full and frank co-operation on the part of the offender, whatever be his motive. The extent of the discount will depend to a large extent upon the willingness with which the disclosure is made. The offender will not receive any discount at all where he tailors his disclosure so as to reveal only the information which he knows is already in the possession of the authorities. The discount will rarely be substantial unless the offender discloses everything which he knows. To this extent, the inquiry is into the subjective nature of the offender's co-operation. If, of course, the motive with which the information is given is one of genuine remorse or contrition on the part of the offender, that is a circumstance which may well warrant even greater leniency being extended to him, but that is because of normal sentencing principles and practice. The contrition is not a necessary ingredient which must be shown in order to obtain the discount for giving assistance to the authorities.

Again, in order to ensure that such encouragement is given, the reward for providing assistance should be granted if the offender has genuinely co-operated with the authorities whether or not the information supplied objectively turns out in fact to have been effective. The information which he gives must be such as could significantly assist the authorities. The information must, of course, be true; a false disclosure attracts no discount at all. What is relevant here is the potential of the information to assist the authorities, as comprehended by the offender himself. . .

Among the policy considerations the Court pointed to at para. 43 as justifying leniency are a number of elements rooted in moral considerations, notably

3) The speedy proffering of information is encouraged by those who have it as part and parcel of their acceptance of responsibility for the matters with which they are charged;

6) A sentence for an offender who has helped the police may be one of intense severity in prison on account of such matters as fear of reprisals or removal to a prison far from family. . .

10) Where an informer's identity is known, that person's days of living by crime are probably at an end. . .

The Court emphasized the point that it is not necessary that the police enjoy success based on the co-operation by pointing out that in the *Madden* case the appellant had participated in a controlled delivery that failed through no fault of the appellant, but credit was extended nevertheless. Hence, para. 45 records the view:

...this Court is entitled to consider the respondent's co-operation as an extenuating circumstance that would permit a sentence outside the six to eight year *Cunningham* range. That said, in my view, the reduction for that factor should be modest in this case, something in the range of one year. The respondent provided information most of which, with very little effort, the police could have obtained themselves by searching the respondent's belongings. The degree of co-operation was far different than the assistance provided in the John Doe case. . .

In *R. v. Shakes* (2001), [2001] O.J. No. 870, 2001 CarswellOnt 658 (C.A.) the Court's oral endorsement emphasized the offender's "quite extraordinary co-operation with the police." See para. 1. The Court also noted the significant rehabilitation. Hence, the 20-month sentence was converted to a conditional one.

Note in passing the four-year term, in addition to almost two years in pre-trial custody, meted out to an offender who was guilty of manslaughter in *R. v. Biscombe* (2001), [2001] O.J. No. 4221, 2001 CarswellOnt 3788, 151 O.A.C. 233 (C.A.), at para. 2. Notable is the fact that he testified for the Crown.

Refer to *R. v. S. (M.)* (2001), [2001] O.J. No. 211, 140 O.A.C. 306, 2001 CarswellOnt 175 (C.A.). See also *R. v. Burke* (2001), [2001] O.J. No. 1119, 143 O.A.C. 286, 2001 CarswellOnt 929, 41 C.R. (5th) 134, 153 C.C.C. (3d) 97, 53 O.R. (3d) 600, 61 O.R. (3d) 256 (note) (C.A.), reversed 2002 CarswellOnt 1970, 2002 CarswellOnt 1971, 2002 SCC 55, 164 C.C.C. (3d) 385, 213 D.L.R. (4th) 234, 2 C.R. (6th) 1, 290 N.R. 71, 160 O.A.C. 271, [2002] 2 S.C.R. 857, in which he surrendered to authorities after being found not guilty at trial. See para. 51. Lastly, *R. v. Swaby* (2001), [2001] O.J. No. 2390, 155 C.C.C. (3d) 235, 54 O.R. (3d) 577, 147 O.A.C. 83, 44 C.R. (5th) 1, 2001 CarswellOnt 2160 (C.A.) may also be read as demonstrating that co-operation with the authorities will result in a lenient sentence. As shown at para. 2, an accused who had a significant criminal record and who was the subject of immigration proceedings pleaded guilty to possession of a handgun, and received a sentence of time served, being 42 days. He was the main Crown witness against Mr. Swaby. The latter received a six-month sentence for being an occupant of a motor vehicle knowing there was present a restricted weapon for which no occupant held a permit. In dissent, the majority ordering a new trial, MacPherson J.A. opined that he would not have allowed the sentence appeal.

The Ontario Court of Appeal appears to have held that the refusal of an offender to implicate others is not to be held to be an aggravating factor. In *R. v. Kaup* (2000), [2000] O.J. No. 120, 128 O.A.C. 301, 2000 CarswellOnt 93 (C.A.), the Court remarked that "The appellant refused to assist the police by helping to identify [the co-accused] because he feared that he would suffer reprisals in the correctional system if he did so. The trial judge treated this as an aggravating factor in some of his comments during the course of the hearing and in his reasons for sentence." Refer to para. 2. The Court of Appeal did not endorse these observations and had it wished to hold that this counts within the general rubric of lack of co-operation with the authorities, it could easily have done so. See also *R. v. Price* (2000), [2000] O.J. No. 886, 144 C.C.C. (3d) 343, 33 C.R. (5th) 278, 2000 CarswellOnt 837, 72 C.R.R. (2d) 228, 140 O.A.C. 67 (C.A.) at para. 56.

iii)   The desire to reform shows a positive attitude

As a general rule, it is mitigating that evidence of an anti-social attitude was brief and has been corrected by means of self-rehabilitation. *R. v. Vandervoort* (2002), [2002] O.J. No. 3471, 2002 CarswellOnt 2912 (C.A.), provides an example of a conditional sentence being substituted for a jail sentence in circumstances in which the Court of Appeal concluded that although "[t]he offence was serious and clearly called for a custodial disposition", the progress shown by the youthful adult offender would be compromised by a period of imprisonment. Refer to paras. 1 and 4.

Of primary importance to the Court's determination that leniency was appropriate was the threshold finding that "[t]his young person fell off the rails for a short period of time but had fully rehabilitated herself by the time of sentencing. She had returned to live with her family, resumed her schooling, was employed part-time, become involved in community work including counselling troubled youth." See para. 2. Paragraph 4 makes plain how that "[t]o send this young person to jail would under-

mine the outstanding effort she had made to straighten out her life."
Accordingly, the appellate tribunal disagreed with the emphasis placed
by the trial judge on denunciation. In the result, the sentence was varied
to a conditional sentence of nine months on the statutory conditions
and in addition house arrest as suggested by counsel for the appellant,
plus community service for 100 hours. She was ordered to reside with
her parents, maintain employment or attend school and abstain from
drugs.

iv) The impact of a favourable pre-sentence report in demonstrating a positive attitude

As a self-evident proposition, this is a mitigating factor in sentencing.
An example of the application of this principle is seen in *R. v. Kerr*
(2001), [2001] O.J. No. 5085, 2001 CarswellOnt 4473, 153 O.A.C. 159
(C.A.), at para. 6. The evidence before the sentencing judge included
a pre-sentence report, and a letter and testimony from Dr. Jollymore,
who had treated the appellant for his heroin addiction since November
6, 1999. "The pre-sentence report indicated that the appellant was a
suitable candidate for community supervision. According to the report,
the appellant: had no previous criminal record; was co-operative and
appeared to appreciate the seriousness of his situation; had "fallen
victim to drug addiction" but was willing to accept responsibility for his
offences; had a caring and supportive upbringing and family; lived with
his parents, who supported his intention to remain there; had friends
who were of good character and had no criminal record; was working
full-time in his father's home improvement/renovation business; and
was "academically capable" and "talented at art."

What of a negative pre-sentence report? A possible answer is seen in
R. v. Bayani (2003), [2003] O.J. No. 2437, 2003 CarswellOnt 2316, 173
O.A.C. 36 (C.A.). As we read at para. 4, ". . . the pre-sentence report
was very negative, the respondent being described as being at risk for
offending with violence and as not being amenable to counselling or
community service. In addition, he expressed no remorse for his misconduct."

A further example, touching upon a youthful offender, is derived from
para. 1 of *R. v. A. (J.R.)* (2003), [2003] O.J. No. 999, 2003 CarswellOnt
913 (C.A.): "We are unable to state that the disposition did not represent
a fit sentence, although perhaps at the high end. The appellant had a
poor Youth court record, committed the offence herein while on probation and is faced on his appeal with a negative pre-disposition report."

It would be tedious to list a number of cases in which reference is made to pre-sentence reports commenting on the offender's inability to accept responsibility for any wrongdoing. Suffice it to note that in *R. v. Glassford* (1988), [1988] O.J. No. 359, 27 O.A.C. 194, 1988 CarswellOnt 59, 63 C.R. (3d) 209, 42 C.C.C. (3d) 259 (C.A.), at page 12, one reads: "There is some evidence that the subject may experience a problem with alcohol and drugs, although the subject believes his use of both alcohol and drugs is non-problematic. Sources also indicate the subject has a volatile temper which he has difficulty controlling. He does not respond well to discipline and when confronted with his undesirable behaviour becomes hostile and aggressive. He appears to be an immature individual who finds it difficult to accept accountability for his actions."

c) Attitude and remorse:

i) The impact of remorse in sentencing

In *R. v. Eakin* (2000), [2000] O.J. No. 1670, 132 O.A.C. 164, 2000 CarswellOnt 1650, 74 C.R.R. (2d) 307 (C.A.), leave to appeal refused (2001), 2001 CarswellOnt 1803, 2001 CarswellOnt 1804, 82 C.R.R. (2d) 188 (note), 272 N.R. 193 (note), 150 O.A.C. 199 (note) (S.C.C.), it was observed at para. 20 that "...it is submitted that the trial judge erred in considering the appellant's failure to accept responsibility as an important factor in determining both that he was a dangerous offender and that an indeterminate sentence was appropriate as opposed to a definite period of incarceration." At the next paragraph, the Court responded: "Counsel for the appellant is quite correct in stating that an offender's decision to plead not guilty and defend the matter cannot be considered as an aggravating factor in sentencing." It held, however, that the trial judge did not treat the failure to acknowledge responsibility as an aggravating factor. It did conclude that the lack of remorse had an important bearing on the psychiatric opinions of the experts called by both the Crown and the defence as it was relevant to the offender's present and future dangerousness to the public and to his prospects for treatment.

Further, in *R. v. Syed* (2000), [2000] O.J. No. 3535, 22 C.C.L.I. (3d) 163, 2000 CarswellOnt 3291 (C.A.), it was acknowledged that the trial judge erred in principle in holding that the absence of remorse was an aggravating factor. See para. 14.

In the case of repeat offenders, however, it is becomes more difficult to accept the presence of remorse; in other words, as the record of offending increases, it becomes more difficult to accept that non-custodial sentences will permit the necessary introspection and maturation to occur.

Lack of remorse, as found by the trial judge, influenced the decision not to grant a conditional sentence in *R. v. Krushel* (2000), [2000] O.J. No. 302, 130 O.A.C. 160, 31 C.R. (5th) 295, 2000 CarswellOnt 325, 142 C.C.C. (3d) 1 (C.A.), leave to appeal refused (2002), 2002 CarswellOnt 4384, 2002 CarswellOnt 4385, (*sub nom.* R. v. Grey) [2002] S.C.C.A. No. 293, 307 N.R. 200 (note) (S.C.C.). Refer to paras. 31-32. In *R. v. Pavich* (2000), [2000] O.J. No. 4209, 2000 CarswellOnt 4116, 138 O.A.C. 349 (C.A.), the Court of Appeal commented that "The trial judge appeared offended at the lack of remorse exhibited by the appellant. Indeed, while she was awash in self-pity at being caught, she expressed almost no concern for what she had inflicted on her employer. In the circumstances, we are concerned that the trial judge treated her absence of remorse as an aggravating factor rather than stating that it was not a mitigating one and he erred in so doing. In our view, an appropriate sentence would be 12 months to be served in prison." Refer to para. 5.

The bookkeeper to a law firm, who was paid $85,000 a year, "...pleaded guilty to misappropriating $204,238.30 from her employer over a period of some three years [involving 180 separate transactions]. Para. 2 records, "The circumstances that support the sentence are that the appellant's offence constituted a significant breach of trust. She exploited her position as an office manager of a small three-partner law firm. It lost a substantial amount of money and endured significant hardship as a result of the offence. None of the funds have been recovered and no restitution has been made. This misappropriation was not an isolated affair. It was extensive and consisted of two separate schemes carried out simultaneously over a three-year period and involved over 180 separate transactions."

Disclosure by an offender of the commission of wrongdoing not previously made known to the authorities by a victim is a mitigating factor as it indicates tremendous remorse and a resolve to act responsibly. See *R. v. S. (D.)* (2000), [2000] O.J. No. 2611, 2000 CarswellOnt 2486 (C.A.), at para. 3. It may not be sufficient, however, to avoid the selection of a jail sentence.

R. v. Krushel (2000), [2000] O.J. No. 302, 130 O.A.C. 160, 31 C.R. (5th) 295, 2000 CarswellOnt 325, 142 C.C.C. (3d) 1 (C.A.), leave to appeal refused (2002), 2002 CarswellOnt 4384, 2002 CarswellOnt

4385, (*sub nom.* R. v. Grey) [2002] S.C.C.A. No. 293, 307 N.R. 200 (note) (S.C.C.), at para. 31, provides an example of the Court of Appeal upholding a trial judge's conclusion that a conditional sentence would not be appropriate to sanction an offence of criminal harassment. Although a first time offender, he demonstrated no remorse and the conduct spanned a number of years including a period of time during which he was subject to a peace bond. It had a dramatic effect on the lives of the victim and his children.

That the absence of remorse is a negative factor in the selection of a sentence is borne out by the following case. It signals a lack of insight and does not suggest future rehabilitation. See *R. v. Lauzon* (2000), [2000] O.J. No. 3940, 137 O.A.C. 153, 2000 CarswellOnt 3837 (C.A.), leave to appeal refused (2001), 2001 CarswellOnt 3170, 2001 CarswellOnt 3171, 276 N.R. 397 (note), 155 O.A.C. 199 (note) (S.C.C.), at para. 18.

In *R. v. S. (D.C.)* (2000), [2000] O.J. No. 885, 47 O.R. (3d) 612, 131 O.A.C. 396, 2000 CarswellOnt 840 (C.A.), the offender apologized to both of his victims by means of a letter. See para. 8. This genuine expression of remorse was given great weight by the Court of Appeal, as noted at para. 13. In *R. v. L. (B.R.)* (May 3, 2000), Doc. Toronto C32462, [2000] O.J. No. 3370 (C.A.), the Court of Appeal reduced a three-year sentence for a violent offence involving an intimate partner, not otherwise described, chiefly on the grounds of the young age of the offender, his remorse, and the absence of a record. See also paras. 22-24 of *R. v. Godfree* (2000), [2000] O.J. No. 3409, 2000 CarswellOnt 3316, 136 O.A.C. 49, 7 M.V.R. (4th) 60 (C.A.).

In *R. v. Heaslip* (2001), [2001] O.J. No. 1043, 10 M.V.R. (4th) 220, 144 O.A.C. 107, 2001 CarswellOnt 850 (C.A.), the offender pleaded guilty to two counts of impaired driving causing death and one count of impaired operation of a motor vehicle causing bodily harm. At para. 10, the Court emphasized the fact that "the respondent was remorseful." Refer to *R. v. S. (M.)* (2001), 140 O.A.C. 306, [2001] O.J. No. 211, 2001 CarswellOnt 175 (C.A.). Indeed, para. 4 speaks of genuine remorse. See also *R. v. Francis* (2000), [2000] O.J. No. 5043, 139 O.A.C. 385, 2000 CarswellOnt 4881 (C.A.).

But see *R. v. Burke* (2001), [2001] O.J. No. 1119, 143 O.A.C. 286, 2001 CarswellOnt 929, 41 C.R. (5th) 134, 153 C.C.C. (3d) 97, 53 O.R. (3d) 600, 61 O.R. (3d) 256 (note) (C.A.), reversed 2002 CarswellOnt 1970, 2002 CarswellOnt 1971, 2002 SCC 55, 164 C.C.C. (3d) 385, 213 D.L.R. (4th) 234, 2 C.R. (6th) 1, 290 N.R. 71, 160 O.A.C. 271, [2002]

2 S.C.R. 857, in which the trial judge noted the aggravating circumstance that the weapon, a revolver, was never recovered. See para. 49. Presumably, the concern is that it will be used again to harm someone and that a remorseful person would have turned it in.

Although not described as remorse in the report of *R. v. Sturge* (2001), [2001] O.J. No. 3923, 2001 CarswellOnt 3691, 17 M.V.R. (4th) 272 (C.A.) it is noteworthy that the offender pleaded guilty at the first opportunity to a number of serious offences and that he "readily acknowledged responsibility for the robberies when arrested." See para. 4.

ii)   Lack of remorse as an indication of recidivism

A prized illustration of the degree to which sentencing courts will place an offender high on the scale in cases of lack of remorse is seen in *R. v. Valle-Quintero* (2002), [2002] O.J. No. 4107, 2002 CarswellOnt 3583, 169 C.C.C. (3d) 140, 165 O.A.C. 275 (C.A.). In sum, the fear of the Court was that the offender would once again try to kill the victim unless he was locked away for such a significant period of time that he would either obtain the assistance he required, or detest the prison experience to such an extent that he would leave her alone. Para. 73 sets out an example of the "credibility" analysis that a trial judge may engage in to conclude that the offender's claimed remorse is not sincere. Although the lack of remorse is not an aggravating factor, the presence of remorse is clearly mitigating and there is a significant impact to a finding that no remorse is evident. In this respect, note that the pre-sentence report was relied upon for this conclusion.

iii)   Lack of remorse as an indication of a lack of potential for reform

R. v. D'Amour (2002), [2002] O.J. No. 3103, 2002 CarswellOnt 2603, 166 C.C.C. (3d) 477, 4 C.R. (6th) 275, 163 O.A.C. 164, 96 C.R.R. (2d) 315 (C.A.) is the only decision of the Court of Appeal for Ontario that I am familiar with that appears to uphold a trial judge's decision to impose a short, sharp period of imprisonment for a first offender guilty of a non-violent offence. The offender was in receipt of benefits pursuant to the General Welfare Assistance Act and failed to report employment income to such an extent that she received $14,636.98 over a two-year period for which she was not entitled. The trial judge declined defence counsel's submission that she be permitted to serve her sentence of detention within the community, selecting instead a 90-day jail term, to be served intermittently.

At para. 67, we read that the motivation for the offence was to permit this single parent to fund her 20-year-old daughter's attendance at a professional dance school in Germany. Further, that she testified that she would renew her activities in the future should it prove necessary. Thus, in light of the systematic nature of the wrongdoing, the substantial amount of money obtained, the motivation identified, and the "open and unrepentant disrespect for the law", as set out at para. 70, the primacy in sentencing was assigned to specific deterrence. Although sight was not lost of her industry in general, and her difficult situation, it was her attitude that required correction by means of a period of detention.

At bottom, it must be understood that a jail term was selected even though she was no danger to the community as she could be trusted to attend at the place of confinement every weekend. Nevertheless, a period of imprisonment was required to emphasize the seriousness of her misconduct: "There is no basis upon which this Court can interfere with [the trial judge's] conclusion that a short period of intermittent incarceration was necessary."

In *R. v. Condo* (March 27, 1981), Howland C.J.O., Jessup and Martin JJ.A., [1981] O.J. No. 35 (C.A.) the Court remarked that a 16-year-old guilty of participating in a serious robbery had known a deprived childhood and the pre-sentence report respecting him was generally unfavourable. "It indicated he was physically aggressive to perceived threats and defiant towards those in authority. He had also had a heavy involvement with drugs." In such a case, it is doubtful that the mere fact that he was before a court would serve to impress upon him the seriousness of his misbehaviour. In many such instances, firmness if not severity might be indicated in order to address this concern.

d)   Attitude as reflected by breach of court orders

As we have seen, credit is assigned to those offenders who co-operate with the authorities by confessing, by offering to return stolen goods, by making apologies, by advancing early guilty pleas. It stands to reason that no such credit is available in the case of those who breach court orders such as probation, bail and prohibition orders as they demonstrate a poor attitude, not conducive to reformation.

In *R. v. Stewart* (2002), [2002] O.J. No. 3391, 2002 CarswellOnt 2872, 163 O.A.C. 391 (C.A.), we are provided with the following illustration, at para. 10:

With respect to sentence, the appellant's sentence is effectively equivalent to nine years and nine months. The appellant submits that the disparity between his sentence and that of the co-accused, Tim Lindsay, who received a sentence of three years in addition to 15 months' pre-trial custody is an error in principle. Mr. Lindsay pled guilty in separate proceedings to a lesser number of charges. We do not agree that the sentence is an error in principle. The appellant instigated the assault. Unlike Mr. Lindsay, he was on probation at the time of the offences and on bail. Allowing double credit for pre-trial custody in these circumstances was not required.

e) Attitude and test cases

Counsel must distinguish between test cases initiated by defendants and those that result from a newly proclaimed offence. In the latter case, the publicity and public discussion generated from the prosecution furthers the goal of educating the community, or the particular group within the community, as to the prohibition that now is in effect respect conduct that was previously legal. In such cases, the penalty need not be too severe to further this goal. In addition, it strikes at the principle of restraint to impose a severe sanction in a case in which the moral blameworthiness of the conduct may be far from elevated, in light of the ignorance attaching to the proscription surrounding the misconduct. For example, in *R. v. Harkness* (1905), 10 O.L.R. 555, 10 C.C.C. 199 (C.A.), Osler J.A. noted that leniency should be permitted in sentencing, as it was the first prosecution under a new provision of the Code and thus, it seems to have been a test case. See para. 31, page 566.

f) Attitude and religious scruples

In *R. v. Lewis* (1903), [1903] O.J. No. 123, 6 O.L.R. 132, 7 C.C.C. 261 (C.A.), a prosecution involving parents who refused to provide medical treatment by reason of religious belief, Moss C.J.O. remarked at para. 23, page 267 [C.C.C.], "In one form or another it has been frequently said by able judges, and it cannot be too widely known or too often repeated, that where an offence consists of a positive act, which is knowingly done, the offender cannot escape punishment because he holds a belief which impels him to think that the law which he has broken ought not to exist or ought never to have been made."

g)   An examination of the offender's willingness to make amends and moral blameworthiness:

i)   Introduction

The willingness to make amends is a significant element in the evaluation of the moral blameworthiness associated with criminal misconduct. Even though one cannot "undo the harm done", one may ring the doorbell and apologize in the case of a trivial mischief, or contact the police and admit significant sexual violence as did the offender in *R. v. H. (D.A.)* (2003), [2003] O.J. No. 143, 2003 CarswellOnt 148, 171 C.C.C. (3d) 309, 168 O.A.C. 176, 10 C.R. (6th) 109 (C.A.) as set out at para. 42.

A further example is taken from *R. v. Gottli* (1997), [1997] M.J. No. 361, 119 Man. R. (2d) 171, 1997 CarswellMan 359 (Q.B.), at para. 26: "In my view, there can be cases where a lawyer who commits criminal breach of trust will properly receive a conditional sentence, particularly if he/she makes restitution and brings the matter to the light of the authorities before a Law Society audit discovers the matter." Unfortunately for him, the offender did not do so, going so far as to mislead investigators.

In the case of *R. v. Barton* (2002), [2002] O.J. No. 4105, 2002 CarswellOnt 3584, 165 O.A.C. 294 (C.A.), the offender argued that the trial judge had failed to place sufficient weight on his prospects for rehabilitation. Mr. Barton had received a global sentence of 32 months imprisonment after credit of 40 months for time spent in pre-trial custody after pleading guilty to one count each of sexual assault, unlawful confinement and breach of recognizance of bail.

As set out at para. 11, the Court of Appeal remarked that the trial judge's reasons indicate that he took into account the appellant's prospects for rehabilitation and noted, in this case, that some counselling for alcohol or substance abuse would be necessary. He was consuming alcohol and marijuana on the day in question, contrary to his bail terms. The trial judge also stated that he took into account the appellant's psychiatric evaluations which confirmed that the appellant abused alcohol "quite significantly" and that he admitted drinking "too much alcohol, consisting from 6 to 18 beers just about every day." Those evaluations further stated that future abstinence from alcohol would lessen the risk of re-offending.

The Court concluded, "[a]ccordingly, by considering the contents of those evaluations, the trial judge was alive to the fact that treatment of the appellant for his substance abuse problem could contribute to his rehabilitation. The weight to be assigned to that fact was a matter for the trial judge to decide."

All of which is to say that in placing the offender's willingness to make amends on the scale of offending, the desire to reform and the ability to reform are both to be evaluated, but no magic formula is known that guarantees leniency if the prospects for rehabilitation are good or that warrants severity if they are not. Each offender falls to be evaluated in a global fashion but this factor, the willingness to make amends, may well be decisive.

ii) The presence of a support network as it influences the ability to make amends

In *R. v. Fudge* (2000), [2000] O.J. No. 2780, 2000 CarswellOnt 2628 (C.A.), the Court of Appeal emphasized in the first paragraph that the offender committed a crime of violence, having accumulated a record for crimes of violence, making her a significant danger to the community and to herself, not just by her prior conduct but also by reason of her addictions and her mental state. In sum, she was a real risk to the safety of the community.

Nevertheless, great leniency was shown to her by reason of the fact in the two years between the commission of the offence and the imposition of sentence, she turned her life around. "She is in a positive relationship with her husband, has developed a strong support network in the community and has remained drug and alcohol free. She has continued her progress since this sentence was imposed some six months ago." Refer to para. 2.

The Court of Appeal accepted that the trial judge had selected appropriate terms of a conditional sentence to guard against a return to her prior lifestyle. "She crafted a conditional sentence which was directed very much to the specific situation and concerns raised by this particular offender. The terms imposed by the trial judge also contain a significant punitive component." Refer to para. 4. It did not interfere with the sentence.

Strong family support, as noted in many cases such as *R. v. Nelles* (2000), [2000] O.J. No. 3034, 135 O.A.C. 265, 2000 CarswellOnt 2861

(C.A.) at para. 4, is a factor that tends to relieve the Court from having to impose a severe (or more severe) sentence on the grounds that the offender is less likely to re-offend if he or she has a support network. See *R. v. Godfree* (2000), [2000] O.J. No. 3409, 2000 CarswellOnt 3316, 136 O.A.C. 49, 7 M.V.R. (4th) 60 (C.A.) at paras. 22-24.

Of course, as submitted by the Crown successfully in *R. v. Dharamdeo* (2000), [2000] O.J. No. 4546, 139 O.A.C. 137, 149 C.C.C. (3d) 489, 6 M.V.R. (4th) 175, 2000 CarswellOnt 4575 (C.A.), at para. 20, the danger to the community of further offences may not in any way be ameliorated by releasing him to the care of his parents who had demonstrated a history of being completely unable to control him or effect any change in his behaviour.

In *R. v. Kaup* (2000), [2000] O.J. No. 120, 128 O.A.C. 301, 2000 CarswellOnt 93 (C.A.) the judgment begins by setting out that "The youthful appellant, who was only 18.5 years old at the time of the offence, has no criminal record. He has lived a nonviolent, productive life and has lived at home with a stable and supportive family. He pleaded guilty to the offence and his post-apprehension conduct indicated significant remorse." See p. 301, para. 1. In such cases, it would be useful to have the probation officer meet with the parents and other relatives in advance, and to have each one present. At p. 302, para. 3, we note that he is to live with his parents under a strict curfew. Accordingly, nothing prevents you from having a video of the room, the house, the preventive arrangements.

Para. 42 of *R. v. H. (D.A.)* (2003), [2003] O.J. No. 143, 2003 CarswellOnt 148, 171 C.C.C. (3d) 309, 168 O.A.C. 176, 10 C.R. (6th) 109 (C.A.) emphasizes the support system the offender enjoys, making reference to the following:

> Earlier interventions at the time his relatives sexually assaulted him and when he assaulted his common-law wife had not met with much success. The difference now seems to be that it is the respondent who is motivated to try to recover from the years of abuse and alcoholism. In this, as I have said, he has the support of a number of community-based resources. He had a Grade 5 education. He is now taking courses to upgrade his education at Confederation College. He has completed one course and is now taking a literacy and basic skills course. He has taken steps to deal with the sexual problems at Lakehead Psychiatric Hospital. He has continued to see the psychologist to whom he made the initial disclosure. He is abstaining from the consumption of alcohol

and drugs. Finally, and significantly, the respondent has the support of his common-law spouse. She is hopeful that in time she and the respondent will be able to re-establish their family unit.

All of which to say, lengthy stable relationships are mitigating and anything that promotes them is to be fostered. As a general rule, defence counsel will enjoy some success if they are able to point to evidence of some form of long term stable relationship that will serve to anchor the offender, now that the wrongdoing has disclosed a susceptibility to stress, to alcohol abuse, to addictive gambling, etc. In addition, the presence of this form of baseline support is often seen as a motivating factor, as the offender has jeopardized this situation and may be well disposed to undertake whatever is necessary not to further imperil the relationship, be it a romantic one, one based on employment, or friendship, etc.

A long-term stable marriage as a rehabilitative element was in evidence in *R. v. Nikitin* (2003), [2003] O.J. No. 2505, 2003 CarswellOnt 2360, 176 C.C.C. (3d) 225, 38 M.V.R. (4th) 223, 173 O.A.C. 164 (C.A.). In fact, leaving aside the mitigating element as such, from the offender's perspective, the fact remains that defence counsel may be successful in emphasizing the secondary harm that might befall vulnerable family members should certain punitive elements in sentencing be selected.

Although the selection of this theme under this rubric may be somewhat arbitrary, for present purposes, it is thought wise to consider all support networks under the heading of an offender's willingness to make amends. Most will agree that it is often by reason of a lack of an effective familial and social network that offenders "get into trouble", and it is often only with the assistance of such a network that reformation is possible.

In this respect, note *R. v. S. (J.)* (1986), [1986] M.J. No. 168, 39 Man. R. (2d) 234, 1986 CarswellMan 173 (C.A.), which provides a comparatively rare example of a pre-sentence report setting out a probation officer's opinion of the offender's poor sense of right and wrong; his moral values if you wish. At page 5 (Q.L.), the case report includes the comment that "The respondent is described in the pre-sentence report as an unsophisticated individual who has had difficulty in accepting that his behaviour in this matter was immoral. In the pre-sentence report, it is stated that the respondent came from a rather deprived background and that he has only begun to recognize that he is an offender." He committed numerous sexual offences against his teenage daughter over a period of three years.

Offenders who hail from what has been described by Martin, J.A. as an "impeccable background", as seen at p. 373, para. 3. of *R. v. Boyd* (1979), 47 C.C.C. (2d) 369, 1979 CarswellOnt 1334 (C.A.), enjoy a considerable advantage over those who do not. Nevertheless, what must be considered is the desire to make amends, not necessarily the means, although the means cannot be overlooked for obvious reasons. The rationale that counsel may wish to exploit is assimilated to prizes for the "most improved" student or athlete: What matters is the effort, not simply the final standing.

A question that counsel must consider is whether the willingness to make amends be discounted if little "pain" is experienced. It should be understood that on occasion, an offender who hails from a fortunate background may be seen in a less favourable position from the perspective of moral fault. In fact, it is suggested that on occasion, some aggravating weight is assigned to those who had exploit their position. In *R. v. Gray* (1995), 76 O.A.C. 387, 1995 CarswellOnt 1744, 95 D.T.C. 5262 (C.A.), leave to appeal refused (1995), 193 N.R. 239 (note), 89 O.A.C. 79 (note) (S.C.C.), for example, para. 33 reads: "Both appellants have impressive and respectable backgrounds, which is generally the case with persons who are capable of attracting substantial loans from the government agency for a sophisticated business purpose."

Not only did these backgrounds permit the facilitation of the commission of the offence(s), but they make it easier to satisfy fines, etc. In such cases, the controversial question is whether Courts should add a measure of punishment to balance the scales. The contending argument is that to fail to do so results in little effective punishment and no deterrent; on the other hand, to treat similarly situated offenders differently based on their background may be to introduce an element of discrimination.

In this respect, Judge Loranger commented in *R. v. Littler* (1972), 13 C.C.C. (2d) 530, 41 D.L.R. (3d) 523 (Que. C.S.P.), varied (1974), 27 C.C.C. (2d) 216, 65 D.L.R. (3d) 443 (Que. C.A.) that the accused, guilty of a million dollar fraud, enjoyed good community standing and was active in charitable and church activities. Refer to page 553. See also *R. v. Shanower*, 8 C.C.C. (2d) 527, 1972 CarswellOnt 914, [1972] 3 O.R. 722 (C.A.), at p. 529.

iii)   Support from the victim

R. v. Valle-Quintero (2002), [2002] O.J. No. 4107, 2002 CarswellOnt 3583, [2002] O.J. No. 4107, 169 C.C.C. (3d) 140, 165 O.A.C. 275 (C.A.)

provides valuable instruction on the dynamics at play when a victim files or advances what amounts to a favourable victim impact statement. As set out at para. 66, "[b]y the time of the appellant's sentencing hearing, the complainant had experienced a change of heart regarding the appellant and was visiting him in jail on a frequent basis. She testified at the sentencing hearing that she had not suffered any psychological problems arising from the incident in question and urged that the appellant receive the "most minimum sentence." The trial judge discounted these observations on the grounds that she had been manipulated by the offender who continued to exercise control over her. Accordingly, it was open to the trial judge to conclude that she had been traumatized by the incident and that she would not be able to put this behind her.

On the other hand, nothing was said by the Court of Appeal to suggest that a true statement of support by the victim, made without any hint of lingering intimidation or coercion, could not be considered favourably as an indication of support for an offender desirous of making amends.

iv)   Support from the offender's family

As noted, it is always apposite to consider the favourable weight assigned to those who enjoy a positive support network. This factor was emphasized by Abella J.A. at para. 2 of *R. v. Kerr* (2001), [2001] O.J. No. 5085, 2001 CarswellOnt 4473, 153 O.A.C. 159 (C.A.): "[t]he appellant was 27 years old at the time of sentencing and the youngest of three children in a close-knit family. He has a stable and close relationship with his parents and two sisters. He has no criminal record, and his family indicates that he has never been violent or verbally abusive." Of interest, the Court did not focus on his family's inability to control his on-going drug abuse, or his participation in the serious instances of trafficking. The focus of the Court was limited to the support and encouragement he would receive in the future and, indirectly, to the belief that they would enforce whatever conditions were in place. See also para. 18 of *R. v. Cohen* (2001), [2001] O.J. No. 1606, 144 O.A.C. 340, 2001 CarswellOnt 1440 (C.A.).

v)   Family support and a desire to reform

In those rare instances in which it is appropriate, sentencing courts welcome the type of observation found in *R. v. King* (1990), [1990] M.J. No. 414, 66 Man. R. (2d) 130, 1990 CarswellMan 150 (C.A.), leave to appeal refused (1991), 73 Man. R. (2d) 237 (note), 130 N.R. 319 (note) (S.C.C.), at page 5:

> The accused's involvement in this crime appears to have brought him to his senses. The pre-sentence report indicates that he ceased all involvement with alcohol immediately, and sought assistance within Alcoholics Anonymous. He has disassociated with those who might lead him astray. He has mended his relationships within his own family, the members of which appear to be responsible and supportive. He had a stable relationship with a young woman prior to this offence, and that relationship has weathered the storm of this particular incident.

vi)   Early attempts to repay for the damage or the loss

In cases of restitution, some credit in sentencing should be granted as it demonstrates pro-social values and a resolve to repair the harm done. Note that the trial judge erred in failing to credit the restitution made by the offenders in *R. v. Chavali* (2002), [2002] O.J. No. 3788, 2002 CarswellOnt 3335 (C.A.), leave to appeal refused (2003), 2003 CarswellOnt 1059, 2003 CarswellOnt 1060 (S.C.C.). However, as made plain at para. 4, this error did not affect the sentence.

By way of contrast, it may be that though there has been early restitution, little credit may be assigned if it is considered that much more might have been done to assist the victim(s). In this respect, note *R. v. Torchia* (2002), [2002] O.J. No. 3075, 2002 CarswellOnt 2586 (C.A.), at para. 7. It is often a question of degree.

vii)   The lack of a resolve to "make amends" is not aggravating, but it is not mitigating

The Court of Appeal quoted without any obvious disapproval the following passage from the pre-sentence report in *R. v. Valle-Quintero* (2002), [2002] O.J. No. 4107, 2002 CarswellOnt 3583, 169 C.C.C. (3d) 140, 165 O.A.C. 275 (C.A.): "It is the opinion of the writer that the subject is a manipulative, violent and duplicitous individual who does not possess the capacity or the desire to understand either the gravity or potential consequences of his actions." Refer to para. 67. The instruction to be drawn from this passage is that although no aggravation arises from a lack of desire to reform, no mitigation is available either. The lack of remorse does not result in a worse sentence.

Aggravation may arise if the offender is seen as a threat to re-offend, however. In this respect, note that the Court of Appeal quoted briefly at para. 73 from post-conviction materials setting out that the offender posed a great risk to re-offend, chiefly by reason of his lack of remorse and lack of insight into his actions.

In this respect, *R. v. Cheddesingh* (2002), [2002] O.J. No. 3176, 2002 CarswellOnt 2660, 162 O.A.C. 151, 60 O.R. (3d) 721, 168 C.C.C. (3d) 310 (C.A.), leave to appeal allowed (2003), [2003] S.C.C.A. No. 112, 2003 CarswellOnt 3302, 2003 CarswellOnt 3303 (S.C.C.) is of particular assistance. In Cheddesingh, the Court of Appeal had no difficulty in identifying the extensive psychiatric and psychological evidence in support of the trial judge's conclusion that made it plain that the offender would present evidence of dangerousness well after the normal period of parole ineligibility. Refer in particular to para. 24 and the discussion respecting the offender's borderline personality disorder and his anti-social personality disorder at paras. 25-32. The Court had little difficulty in finding that "recidivism was a virtual certainty if release occurred in the near future." See para. 32. Accordingly, the trial judge's order that parole be delayed was upheld, but the period was fixed at ten years, not the eight-year term mistakenly selected at trial.

viii)   The offender has vowed to reform

The British Columbia Court of Appeal dealt with the sentence appeal of a former priest who pleaded guilty to five indecent assaults for which a total three-year sentence was meted out. Of note, in the course of pre-charge therapy, the offender "... had pledged himself never to be alone with children and to avoid close friendships with persons who have young children". See *R. v. Blancard* (1992), 12 B.C.A.C. 90, 23 W.A.C. 90, 1992 CarswellBC 980, [1992] B.C.J. No. 762 (C.A.), at p. 95, para. 28. The Court allowed his appeal and reduced the prison term to a total of 12 months, to be followed by two years of probation including conditions "... that he will not be in the company of any child under the age of 13 unless accompanied by another adult" (p. 95, para. 28).

Note as well *R. v. Reid* (1993), [1993] M.J. No. 426, 88 Man. R. (2d) 113, 51 W.A.C. 113, 1993 CarswellMan 234 (C.A.). One reads at para. 3: "We are of the view that sentences totalling four years were too high for the circumstances of this offender and of these offences. The accused had no prior record at the time of these offences. His pre-sentence report and supporting letters report favourably on his character, his employment history and his prospects for the future."

The lesson to be drawn is that a resolve to act responsibly that is put forth with some circumstantial guarantee of success may be welcomed by the Court. Thus, an offender who is fighting alcoholism and who enlists a score of supporters to help him remain sober will be given more credence than one who neither verbalises reform, nor takes the trouble to seek out assistance.

ix)　Making amends as opposed to being ordered to perform community service work or pay restitution

It must be emphasized that little credit is assigned to one who has to wait to be ordered to perform community service work or to pay restitution. In few words, it doesn't show a willingness to make amends. In this respect, it must also be noted that it is controversial whether there is any penalty in performing work one would have done is any event. For example, the offender who has coached soccer for years is not making a greater contribution to the community by serving community service hours in that capacity. And, by parity of reasoning, a person who repays what was stolen or damaged has done little by way of restorative justice.

In this respect, note *R. v. Foley* (1982), 2 C.C.C. (3d) 570, 1982 CarswellBC 800 (C.A.) in which an offender was ordered to perform 1,000 hours of work as part of a community grounded sentence. The offender was convicted of trafficking in narcotics. As part of his sentence, he was required to perform a work of art. As set out in the judgment, "... It was not just community service. [Foley] is an artist and the trial judge directed that the 1,000 hours be employed in creating a work of art for Vancouver". See page 571. In the event, he was required to sculpt a work of art for the benefit of the children's zoo of the City. As held by Seaton, J.A., certain concerns arise in the case of court-ordered performance of such a task, as opposed to the execution of a set number of hours. The following passages are reported at page 571:

> The community service officer pointed out that while community service work is usually imposed by a certain number of hours, it is sometimes done by requiring that a certain task be performed, and he suggests that in this case it would be appropriate to have the task of preparing a sculpture to the satisfaction and under the direction of [an official of the zoo]

> . . .

The next problem is that the order made no provision to cover the cost of the materials ... If the respondent was required to bear the cost of the sculpture, that will be a monetary penalty imposed by the court which will go a long way to satisfy the need for punishment.

The Court was concerned that this form of order would discriminate against those lacking in any special talents, as noted at page 571, but this concern was set aside.

Further, and more importantly for present purposes, the Crown argued that the trial judge failed to assign sufficient weight to the principle of general deterrence. Mr. Justice Seaton observed that the prosecution had advanced the belief that "... *to require that [a person] spend 1,000 hours doing what he likes doing is no penalty at all*". [Emphasis added] See page 571 again. He further remarked, as a matter of first impression, that he was inclined to agree with the prosecution in this respect but did conclude that "In a case such as this I think it important that there be punishment, that punishment be seen by others who know of the circumstances and that it be seen by the respondent himself". Refer again to page 571.

In the result, the British Columbia Court of Appeal concluded that the community service order was insufficient by itself to address properly all sentencing issues. Therefore, Foley was ordered to forfeit any right to seek reimbursement or recovery of the sum of $4,394 seized from him at the time of arrest. As well, the sculpting costs, assessed at no less than $2,000 were also ordered to be borne by him.

4

Mitigating and Aggravating Principles and Circumstances

1. THE GUILTY AND NOT GUILTY PLEAS:

a) Introduction

As is well known, one of the most powerful mitigating factors in sentencing is the decision of an offender to advance a guilty plea to the accusation(s), as this is often interpreted as an indication of remorse and a first step towards rehabilitation. In addition, an offender who pleads guilty may be well placed to point to other mitigating features such as sparing the victim the anguish of testimony, enhancing the opportunity for the victim and the community to arrive at some form of closure, as well as saving valuable court time and the costs associated with the prosecution.

It is also well known that a guilty plea may be entitled to less consideration and, at times, to no consideration, by reason of such varied factors as the conduct of the defence, the nature of the evidence available to sustain the prosecution, the timing of the guilty plea, to name but three.

And what of a not guilty plea? It is often suggested that a not guilty plea is an aggravating factor in sentencing as it demonstrates a lack of remorse among other negative facts. As will be discussed, however, this view should be contested as it ill-serves the presumption of innocence and the right to silence.

In the result, the question of the mitigating weight to be assigned to an offender who pleads guilty, or who does not, is quite controversial. In this section, the purpose pursued is to attempt to identify all of the animating principles, both mitigating and aggravating, that arise when an accused person elects to plead guilty, or to plead not guilty. The organization of all of these disparate principles within a series of thematic outlines will serve to orient counsel in the preparation of their submissions when seeking to defend, (or contest, as the case may be), the allocation of favourable or unfavourable weight resulting from the decision to plead guilty or not guilty.

To facilitate the review, the discussion is organized into three main topics:

1) The mitigation, if any, inherent in the guilty plea at various stages of the trial;

2) The mitigation, if any, that may be assigned to an offender who pleads guilty when conviction appears to be inevitable; and

3) The mitigation, if any, arising as a result of a not guilty plea.

b) The mitigation, if any, inherent in the guilty plea at various stages of the trial

In this first part of the discussion, brief attention is drawn to the fundamental issue whether mitigation must arise from the very fact of entering a guilty plea. More to the point, is remorse inherent in a guilty plea? By reason of the well-known cases in this respect, it is not necessary to delve too deeply into this aspect of the issues. Thereafter, the numerous sub-issues that arise out of the timing, scope and nature of the guilty plea fall to be examined. The discussion will then focus on concerns associated with the secondary advantages conferred on victims, on the one hand, and on the administration of justice, on the other, when an accused person elects to plead guilty.

c) The guilty plea: Is it always mitigating?

i) As a general rule, mitigation is awarded to an offender who pleads guilty, irrespective of remorse

Although many cases could be advanced in support of the proposition that an offender who pleads guilty to an accusation is entitled at the outset to be considered as a serious candidate for rehabilitation by reason of this positive action which should be presumed to be an indication of remorse, and of a resolve to act responsibly in the future, reference to one case will suffice at this stage. In *R. v. Faulds* (1994), [1994] O.J. No. 2145, 20 O.R. (3d) 13, 79 O.A.C. 313, 1994 CarswellOnt

147 (C.A.), the Court of Appeal provides useful instruction at para. 14, p. 17 [O.R.] respecting the weight to be assigned to a guilty plea:

> The effect of a guilty plea in setting the appropriate sentence will vary with the circumstances of each case. In some cases, a guilty plea is a demonstration of remorse and a positive first step towards rehabilitation. In other cases, a guilty plea is simply a recognition of the inevitable...

This presumption of remorse accompanying a guilty plea is consonant with first principles as it should serve to make plain an understanding by the offender of having wronged, of the moral blame associated with the misconduct, and of the need for some form of sanction that is invited to be applied by the very act of acknowledging guilt. As will be seen repeatedly throughout the following pages, however, this presumption is subject to be discounted, if not wholly displaced, upon a closer examination of the offender and of the circumstances of the offence and of the proceedings. A simple example is encountered at para. 7 of *R. v. K. (D.)* (2003), [2003] O.J. No. 562, 2003 CarswellOnt 542, 169 O.A.C. 97 (C.A.) suggesting that the lack of remorse depreciates the guilty plea.

By way of further introductory comment, reference is made to *R. v. P. (C.A.),* [2000] O.J. No. 1249, [2000] O.T.C. 309, 2000 CarswellOnt 2938 (S.C.J.), at para. 28: "It has been observed in previous cases that a guilty plea is always a mitigating factor, although the amount of credit to be afforded to the guilty plea can vary in the circumstances."

By contrast, *R. v. M. (C.B.)* (1992), [1992] P.E.I.J. No. 40, 99 Nfld. & P.E.I.R. 280, 315 A.P.R. 280, 1992 CarswellPEI 134 (C.A.) concludes with the observation: "A guilty plea does not automatically entitle an accused to a reduction of sentence. The circumstances surrounding the offence must be taken into consideration and the final result is in the discretion of the sentencing judge."

It will be useful to interject that an offender whose counsel is successful in characterizing as remorseful, or "truly remorseful" as seen in *R. v. Power* (2003), [2003] O.J. No. 2414, 2003 CarswellOnt 2764, 176 C.C.C. (3d) 209, 174 O.A.C. 222 (C.A.), at para. 9, is much further from the jailhouse doors than one whose counsel is not so successful. Why? Simply because a remorseful individual is one more likely to be insightful respecting the harm caused and thus least likely to require a full measure of correctional resources and, in addition, one who has shown an understanding of pro-social values such that there is in operation a "moral compass" that can be expected to provide a greater degree of direction in futures instances of stress or temptation.

Can it be doubted that the offender who accepts responsibility demonstrates a pro-social attitude inconsistent, to a greater or lesser degree, with elevated moral blameworthiness? See *R. v. Doerksen* (1990), [1990] M.J. No. 2, 62 Man. R. (2d) 259, 1990 CarswellMan 2, 19 M.V.R. (2d) 16, 53 C.C.C. (3d) 509 (C.A.) and the comment: "Also put forward in mitigation was the accused's genuine remorse and the lesson taught him by the incident. He told the probation officer who prepared the pre-sentence report that it was folly to guess one's blood alcohol level as he had done. He has voluntarily attended group meetings of Alcoholics Anonymous to give his testimony as to the wisdom of the exhortation: 'If you drink, don't drive.'" Refer to page 9 (Q.L.). This is different, it is suggested, from remorse and deserves greater weight in mitigation. Refer as well to *R. v. Beaulieu* (1997), [1997] M.J. No. 369, 118 Man. R. (2d) 148, 149 W.A.C. 148, 1997 CarswellMan 337 (C.A.), at para. 3.

In the final analysis, the greater the evidence of moral blameworthy conduct up to and including the selection of the plea, the lesser is the likelihood of leniency. Conversely, the greater the evidence that counsel can marshal of conduct indicating a sense of right and wrong, the greater the likelihood of mitigation operating in the selection of the fit and proper sentence.

Notwithstanding the foregoing, the guilty plea stands on no different footing from any mitigating feature. At the end of the day, it may not be sufficient to block the reach of denunciation and general deterrence, although it can blunt the assignment of aggravating weight in any number of instances. In this vein, regard must be had for *R. v. Wilson* (2003), [2003] O.J. No. 1047, 2003 CarswellOnt 993, 174 C.C.C. (3d) 255, 170 O.A.C. 128 (C.A.). In particular, refer to para. 4 where we read: "We accept the Crown's submissions that (1) the trial judge over-emphasized the significance of the respondent's guilty plea...".

> **ii) As a general rule, greater mitigating weight is assigned to a guilty plea advanced at an early stage of the proceedings**

It is suggested that the guilty plea is the foremost vehicle to transport the offender away from the jailhouse and away from severe sanctions, all other things being equal. No other action best demonstrates remorse and a resolve to act responsibly. As a matter of logic, therefore, the earlier the guilty plea, the greater the likelihood that the sentencing court will see it as a true indication of remorse and acceptance of responsibility.

In this respect, reference is made to *R. v. Gillan* (2003), [2003] O.J. No. 2315, 2003 CarswellOnt 2364 (C.A.). Para. 3 underlines that the trial judge "was entitled to take the timing of the guilty plea into account in assessing its mitigation value. He did no more."

The question of the timing is a particularly controversial question, however, and it may be of assistance to examine the various issues in a thematic fashion, in accordance with the various potential stages of a trial.

d) The early guilty plea:

R. v. P. (C.A.), [2000] O.J. No. 1249, [2000] O.T.C. 309, 2000 CarswellOnt 2938 (S.C.J.) instructs us at para. 28 that "a fairly prompt guilty plea such as to spare the complainant from having to testify in court or to relive the matter over a prolonged period of time is deserving of extra weight."

Consider as well an example of a guilty plea offered on the day the charges were presented. In *R. v. Koppang*, [2002] A.J. No. 1519, 317 A.R. 234, 284 W.A.C. 234, 2002 CarswellAlta 1584, 2002 ABCA 295 (C.A.), para. 11 sets out that ". . . the trial judge does not give any credit for the early guilty plea with respect to the two indictment charges that initiated from the events occurring that day. In fact, those charges were laid immediately and the appellant entered his plea the same day."

Note as well the repeated references to an early guilty plea in *R. v. P. (D.J.)* (1997), [1997] A.J. No. 737, 200 A.R. 308, 146 W.A.C. 308, 1997 CarswellAlta 622 (C.A.) at paras. 3 and 8: "He admitted the offence, and pled guilty at the first possible occasion, his very first appearance in Court" and "However, there was a very prompt guilty plea. . ." A further example is seen in *R. v. Rockey* (2001), [2001] O.J. No. 1672, 2001 CarswellOnt 1447 (C.A.), the Court's oral endorsement noted that the offences were very serious, and that the offender had a lengthy youth record, but emphasized his early guilty plea, that he is still quite young, and that he suffered terrible abuse as a child.

Two further examples for counsel to cite arise in the cases of *R. v. Cerasuolo* (2001), [2001] O.J. No. 359, 151 C.C.C. (3d) 445, 140 O.A.C.

114, 2001 CarswellOnt 323 (C.A.) and *R. v. Sturge* (2001), [2001] O.J. No. 3923, 2001 CarswellOnt 3691, 17 M.V.R. (4th) 272 (C.A.). In the former, importance was assigned to the early resolution of the proceedings, thus sparing the complainant from the need to testify. In the latter, para. 4 reads: "He pled guilty at the first opportunity...".

By way of contrast, a guilty plea that is not advanced early on in the proceedings may not be entitled to too much by way of mitigating weight. Thus, in *R. v. Mallea* (1998), [1998] A.J. No. 1033, 228 A.R. 167, 188 W.A.C. 167, 1998 CarswellAlta 872 (C.A.), para. 6 points out that "The sentencing judge also overemphasized the affect of a guilty plea. As counsel for the respondent acknowledged at the sentencing hearing the plea was not early."

Counsel are encouraged to communicate to the prosecution as early in the process as possible the instructions to enter a guilty plea in sensitive cases such as home invasions, sexual assaults, motor vehicle fatalities, etc., in order to be better able to argue subsequently that every effort was made to spare the victim(s) any additional hardship and anxiety.

i) An early guilty plea after an early admission of responsibility

If an early guilty appears to qualify for the typical presumption identified earlier, and for additional credit due to its favourable timing, then it stands to reason that an offender who not only pleads guilty at the outset, but does so after having done some other early act indicating remorse and a resolve to act responsibly will be deserving of even more enhanced credit. In this respect, consider *R. v. P. (R.B.)* (1998), [1998] M.J. No. 473, 131 Man. R. (2d) 121, 187 W.A.C. 121, 1998 CarswellMan 471 (C.A.), at para. 9: "The custodial period was reduced because of the unsophisticated nature of the offences and the offender, his immediate admission of responsibility to the police, his early entry of guilty pleas, his relative youth, and the fact that this is his first period of imprisonment."

In this respect, it is difficult to imagine a more advantageous position for defence counsel in sentencing than what was in evidence in *R. v. Blind*, [2000] S.J. No. 732, 200 Sask. R. 14, 2000 CarswellSask 727, 2000 SKQB 536 (Q.B.). As noted at para. 34, the trial judge took into account as mitigating factors "Acknowledgement of his crime and his responsibility. Donald Blind immediately acknowledged his responsibility for his actions. As soon as he knew someone had been hit he made arrangements to go to the police station to turn himself in. He verbally acknowledged his responsibility for his crime and his sorrow at its result at the first opportunity. This has culminated in his plea of guilty to the charge of manslaughter and his apology in Court to the family. . .".

To repeat, not only did the offender plead guilty at an early opportunity, but he did so after turning himself over to the authorities and co-operating fully with their investigation, and implicating himself in the wrongdoing for which he pleaded guilty.

Finally, note that *R. v. H. (D.A.)* (2003), [2003] O.J. No. 143, 2003 CarswellOnt 148, 171 C.C.C. (3d) 309, 168 O.A.C. 176, 10 C.R. (6th) 109 (C.A.) records these comments at para. 37: "...the respondent was fully co-operative with the police, provided a videotaped statement to them and, of course, pleaded guilty."

ii)   The early guilty plea and apology

Not unlike the situation of an early guilty plea accompanied by an acknowledgement of responsibility, an offender who advances an apology early on in the proceedings is entitled to more favourable consideration. One example is drawn from *R. v. Koppang*, [2002] A.J. No. 1519, 317 A.R. 234, 284 W.A.C. 234, 2002 CarswellAlta 1584, 2002 ABCA 295 (C.A.), at para. 19: "From a mitigation point of view, there must be some acknowledgment of the early apology and guilty plea."

e)   The not so early plea:

i)   Introduction

What credit may be assigned to late guilty pleas? As a general rule, the sentencing courts will examine the conduct of the defence in assessing the credit to be assigned to a late guilty plea and, in particular, will be reluctant to award much by way of mitigating weight to guilty pleas that do not result in sparing witnesses from having to testify or that fail to save court time that might be utilized for other pressing matters.

This critical attitude is reflected in the extreme example that follows, selected for emphasis. Para. 18 of *R. v. Randhile* (1997), [1997] A.J.

No. 1238, 209 A.R. 209, 160 W.A.C. 209, 121 C.C.C. (3d) 565, 1997 CarswellAlta 1058 (C.A.) records how:

> Both appellants argued that the pleas came as soon as possible. Counsel spoke of negotiations in progress, the youth of the appellants, and the link between their legal positions as reasons why the pleas could not have come any earlier. In rejecting any credit for what the judge called a "so-called early guilty plea" the sentencing judge referred to the challenge to the entire panel, the 16 witnesses called, 12 exhibits entered and the four days of trial. The basis for an early guilty plea being a mitigating factor is the cost saving to the system and the relief to witnesses of not having to testify. The pleas in this case could not be said to have done either. The pleas here might have been "early" as far as the appellants were concerned but they were not "early" as far as the administration of justice or the witnesses were concerned. For example, Mr. . . . who was present during the killing, was not spared the requirement of testifying. We cannot see any error in the sentencing judge giving no credit for an early guilty plea.

Counsel must understand that it is possible to avoid such negative results by means of certain procedural steps, notably the establishment of sound lines of communication with the prosecution, the police and, on occasion, the victim(s). For example, it may be useful to point out to the Court that counsel agreed as a result of pre-trial discussions that a guilty plea would be advanced if a step undertaken by the defence was not successful, such as a Charter motion, or a submission that a statement is not voluntary. In such circumstances, it seems consonant with the proper administration of justice to award credit. In support, reference is made to para. 5 of *R. v. Drisdelle* (2002), [2002] O.J. No. 3901, 2002 CarswellOnt 3384, 165 O.A.C. 107 (C.A.). The majority opinion sets out the interesting comment that "[f]ollowing an extended period of pre-trials, the appellant pleaded guilty to both robbery charges." It seems that no loss of credit resulted from the lack of an early guilty plea, in keeping with the sophisticated procedures for resolution discussions, pre-trial conferences, etc. The minority judgment did not advance any comments in this respect.

In addition, the notice given by the defence may be quite critical in this assessment. In many cases, a delayed plea to permit the completion of a work contract, or a school semester, will not deprive an offender of appropriate credit if the Crown has been alerted to the precise intentions that are to be followed. In such a case, the victim is informed of the resolution, no trial time is reserved, etc.

In this respect, note the negative situation that arises owing to the lack of effective communication as illustrated in *R. v. Stang*, [2001] A.J. No. 1689, 299 A.R. 174, 266 W.A.C. 174, 2001 CarswellAlta 1717, 2002 ABCA 15 (C.A.), at para. 1. The guilty plea occurred on the date of trial and the Crown was not notified of the change of plea.

Thus, the need for counsel for the defence to inform the Court of the accused's intentions as soon as possible and as early on in the proceedings is of paramount importance in the circumstances. An example taken from *R. v. Venn*, [2002] A.J. No. 492, 299 A.R. 328, 266 W.A.C. 328, 2002 CarswellAlta 516, 2002 ABCA 92 (C.A.), leave to appeal refused (2003), 2003 CarswellAlta 76, 2003 CarswellAlta 77, [2002] S.C.C.A. No. 244, 310 N.R. 399 (note), 327 A.R. 344 (note), 296 W.A.C. 344 (note) (S.C.C.) is instructive. It was argued that the sentencing judge erred in failing to consider an early admission of guilt as a mitigating factor. More to the point, it was submitted that "At trial, the break and enter was admitted by the appellant and the only issue was whether it was committed with an intent to commit a sexual offence. That issue was resolved in favour of the appellant. It is argued that this circumstance is akin to a guilty plea, and should have been considered as a mitigating factor." See para. 23.

The Court found, however, that this had not been communicated clearly to the trial judge. It is not clear what credit, if any, might have been granted had the facts been otherwise but it appears obvious that it would be open to award some credit in light of the savings in court time, and the responsible attitude shown by the limited concession.

The discussion will now focus attention on the particular issues associated with guilty pleas at various precise stages. The duty cast upon defence counsel is to "justify", if you will, the delays at each of these stages.

ii)   The credit to be assigned to a guilty plea after multiple court appearances but before a trial date

R. v. Phun (1997), [1997] A.J. No. 1142, 56 Alta. L.R. (3d) 266, 209 A.R. 266, 120 C.C.C. (3d) 560, 160 W.A.C. 266, 1997 CarswellAlta 985 (C.A.) makes plain that less weight may be assigned to a guilty plea entered ". . . over three years after the charges were laid and after numerous court appearances." See para. 38. Nevertheless, the fact of a guilty plea must be emphasized. In such a situation, attention should be drawn to newly discovered information not previously disclosed, a newly released judgment foreclosing an anticipated defence, or, if nothing else, that the change of heart demonstrates a desire to pursue rehabilitation, albeit somewhat later than was otherwise possible. After all, the defendant is presumed innocent.

iii) The credit to be assigned to a guilty plea after the preliminary hearing

Note the guidance found at para. 72 of *R. v. Ralph* (1993), [1993] N.J. No. 46, 105 Nfld. & P.E.I.R. 220, 331 A.P.R. 220, 1993 CarswellNfld 256 (C.A.): "The respondent's guilty plea came after the preliminary inquiry and is therefore less of a factor than if it had come earlier."

Noteworthy as well is the instruction found at para. 9 of *R. v. Melanson* (1998), [1998] N.B.J. No. 140, 199 N.B.R. (2d) 338, 1998 CarswellNB 137, 510 A.P.R. 338 (C.A.): "The plea of guilty following the preliminary hearing is a matter that may be taken into account as a mitigating factor. A plea of guilty before the preliminary hearing rather than after may be considered a degree more positive since it may show a greater measure of consideration for the victim. On the other hand, the evidence may be so overwhelming that the guilty plea is only a reflection of reality."

Again, counsel must assert the primacy to be assigned to a guilty plea, as it does spare further testimony and court time, then attempt to point out any relevant explanation as noted earlier such as new evidence, changes in the law, etc.

iv) The credit to be assigned to a guilty plea on the day of trial

As a general statement, the guilty plea on the day of trial, to the original charge(s), is deserving of credit for it demonstrates, albeit belatedly, some remorse and a resolve to accept responsibility, and it furthers the community interest in sparing the complainant(s) from having to testify and permits the court time to be diverted to other pressing cases.

In certain instances, greater credit is available by reason of communication to the prosecution in advance, to foster the interests of the witness or witnesses and to allow greater marshalling of court resources. For example, *R. v. P. (C.A.)*, [2000] O.J. No. 1249, [2000] O.T.C. 309, 2000 CarswellOnt 2938 (S.C.J.) records at para. 28 that "Here the plea of guilty was entered on the date set for trial in this

Court, albeit the Court had been pre-alerted to the fact that it would be a plea." The Court did not advance any further guidance on this point, having discounted the guilty plea somewhat by reason of the strong evidence. See para. 29.

v) The credit to be assigned to a guilty plea after the start of the trial

An excellent example of the type of issues confronting counsel and the Court in a situation of a late guilty plea, after many days of trial, arose in *R. v. Khamphila* (1998), 71 O.T.C. 241, 1998 CarswellOnt 3250 (Gen. Div.). Of note, on the 12th day of a jury trial, and just as the Crown was to introduce D.N.A. evidence, the offender, through his counsel, indicated an intention to offer a guilty plea to both counts alleging violent offences. At para. 36, the report sets out that "The remorse issue is unclear. In certain circumstances, a guilty plea may indicate remorse." The Court also remarked that ". . .The guilty plea acknowledging the wrongdoing is, in some measure, a mitigating circumstance, even at this late date, notwithstanding that, both complainants had been required to testify." See para. 42 and the comments at para. 43 to the effect that "The Martin Report does refer to the guilty plea being a mitigating circumstance, particularly, where it's made at an early stage."

In other words, counsel must stress the fact that a guilty plea, at any time, is worthy of some credit for the general reasons mentioned repeatedly thus far. Again, it is a question of balancing. In this respect, note the strong language selected by the Alberta Court of Appeal in *R. v. Zerb* (1996), [1996] A.J. No. 637, 187 A.R. 36, 127 W.A.C. 36, 1996 CarswellAlta 607 (C.A.) at para. 4: "The appellant argues that the trial judge did not take into consideration sufficiently the factor of the remorse of the appellant. Our answer is that a guilty plea at trial, where the Crown witnesses have been called, demonstrates less remorse than a guilty plea at the outset prior to the calling of any witnesses." Notice also *R. v. R. (D.)* (2003), [2003] O.J. No. 561, 2003 CarswellOnt 543, 169 O.A.C. 55 (C.A.). In particular, para. 5 records that although he entered guilty pleas, "he did not do so until after his daughter had been required to testify at a preliminary inquiry."

At the end of the day, any efforts by the prosecution to assert a principle according to which no credit may be assigned after the start of the trial should be resisted by reference to the more nuanced position set out herein.

vi) The credit that arises in the case of a late guilty plea after an adverse ruling

Note the interesting situation discussed in *R. v. Granston* (2000), [2000] O.J. No. 2437, 134 O.A.C. 87, 146 C.C.C. (3d) 411, 2000 CarswellOnt 2256, 77 C.R.R. (2d) 131 (C.A.). In essence, the accused pleaded guilty after an adverse ruling on an application to exclude evidence. Refer to para. 2. The trial judge did assign mitigating weight to this plea, by light of the serious Charter issues to be litigated. See para. 4. The difficulty is that the accused then sought to appeal the ruling, and was met with the response that their had been a voluntary guilty plea. In the circumstances, it might be preferable to simply plead not guilty and to indicate that no contest of the Crown's case will involve any issue but the defined issue as disclosed to the prosecution and to the Court during the pretrial. In many cases, this will save court time, not be inconsistent with a sense of responsibility, and is consonant with the presumption of innocence.

vii) The credit that arises in the case of a late guilty plea to a lesser offence

The case of *R. v. Zimmer* (1991), [1991] S.J. No. 84, 63 C.C.C. (3d) 61, 89 Sask. R. 281, 1991 CarswellSask 269 (C.A.) is quite instructive in pointing out that significant credit may arise in the case of a late guilty plea to a lesser offence, with the agreement of the prosecution. In sum, the defendant was justified in pleading not guilty for the Crown has acknowledged the absence of proof, and is entitled to the credit assigned to an early guilty for entering such a plea as soon as the new information or charge is advanced.

Of course, care must be shown to ensure that all credit is assigned. An example of the possible difficulties is seen in *Zimmer*. Mr. Zimmer was charged with the second-degree murder of his female partner. At trial, he agreed to plead guilty to manslaughter, with the consent of the Crown. Nevertheless, the prosecution appeared to be submitting that the sentence should reflect the legal and factual underpinnings of murder. As noted at para. 8, page 64 [C.C.C.], "What counsel was saying to the trial judge, therefore, was that the Crown would probably have been unable to prove the intention contemplated by s. 229(a)(i) or the intention, knowledge, and recklessness required of s. 229(a)(ii) [by reason of gross intoxication]. Having regard for that, and in light of the plea which was accepted in consequence, the death had to be taken as both unintended and unforeseen by the appellant."

The Court of Appeal went on to note that "What was being suggested by all this? Was it being said in effect that this was a murder which could not be proved, or that the mental element for murder was present in some, though not complete, degree? If so the submission was mis-conceived. I repeat, the death had to be taken as unintended and unforeseen by the appellant, and in that sense the offence was far removed from murder." Refer to para. 13, page 65 [C.C.C.].

For present purposes, what is to be underlined is that although the offender did not plead guilty to the charge of second degree murder, whether early on in the proceedings or at all, nothing untoward should result from that decision as the trial concluded with that accusation being withdrawn. In few words, he was not guilty of that offence. There-fore, he was entitled to contest the prosecution, not merely because it is the undoubted right of any accused, but for the unanswerable reason that the prosecution acknowledged that it could not be shown that he was guilty of the offence charged. No lack of credit could possibly arise from this scenario. In the result, the correct evaluation of the situation would see counsel stress that Mr. Zimmer entered a guilty plea at the first opportunity to the accusation of manslaughter. He was entitled to full credit for this early acknowledgement of guilt.

Counsel must be mindful of *R. v. McDow* (1996), 147 N.S.R. (2d) 343, 426 A.P.R. 343, [1996] N.S.J. No. 52, 1996 CarswellNS 60 (C.A.), at para. 90: "The plea of guilty is consistent with remorse and has saved the community the expense of a trial. The extent to which it should be taken into account in determining a reduction in the length of sentence is somewhat modified when one considers the plea of guilty to a lesser charge was not entered until the night before the trial was to com-mence." With respect, if the accused was not convicted of the more serious charge, then s/he was justified in pleading not guilty as s/he was found not guilty. However, if the accused refused earlier offers to plead guilty to the lesser charge, than it may be appropriate to discount the guilty plea to some extent.

In the result and as a practical matter, counsel would be in a far more advantageous position at the sentence hearing if it could be shown that the accused had always been prepared to plead guilty to this reduced charge and that the decision of the prosecutor to refuse this plea led to the necessity of the preliminary inquiry and the scheduling of the trial, with the consequent anguish for the family and friends of the victim, the attendant expenses, and the other consequences that flow from the trial process.

viii) The credit that arises in the case of a late guilty plea in situations in which the prosecution withdraws one or more of the accusations

The guidance put forth by the Alberta Court of Appeal in *R. v. Hindes* (2000), [2000] A.J. No. 808, 84 Alta. L.R. (3d) 78, 261 A.R. 108, 225 W.A.C. 108, 4 M.V.R. (4th) 141, 2000 CarswellAlta 682 (C.A.) is quite compelling. As we read at para. 28,

> We also have some concerns about the sentencing judge's approach to the guilty plea in this case. It appears that the sentencing judge minimized the credit for the guilty plea because the plea was entered after the preliminary inquiry and just three weeks before trial. Sentencing judges frequently refuse, quite properly, to give full credit for a guilty plea where it comes late in the process, after the preliminary and just before trial. However, the date on which the accused first had the opportunity to enter a guilty plea to the offences is material. Counsel advises that the first time Mrs. Hindes was afforded the opportunity to plead to just these offences, she did so. *She had been facing some seven charges previously and cannot be faulted for failing to enter a guilty plea to some if she was going to be forced to trial on the others.* Thus, before the credit for a guilty plea is minimized, the sentencing judge should consider whether there was a significant change in the charges. Here they changed materially, and credit should not have been minimized. [emphasis supplied]

ix) The credit to be assigned in cases of some guilty and some not guilty pleas:

At times, the effect of a guilty plea may be difficult to evaluate. For example, in *R. v. Bates* (2000), [2000] O.J. No. 2558, 134 O.A.C. 156, 146 C.C.C. (3d) 321, 35 C.R. (5th) 327, 2000 CarswellOnt 2360 (C.A.), the offender pleaded guilty to some charges, but defended others and was found not guilty on certain counts. The Court of Appeal found that "The guilty pleas are a factor which stands in his favour on sentencing even though the victims were required to testify at trial." Refer to para. 43.

A) The guilty plea and calling the victim(s) to testify at the sentence hearing

Reference to *R. v. Packwood* (1993), [1993] B.C.J. No. 1628, 31 B.C.A.C. 155, 50 W.A.C. 155, 1993 CarswellBC 1045 (C.A.) illustrates one difficulty associated with assigning credit for guilty pleas: the situation in which the victim must testify notwithstanding the guilty plea. As we see at para. 15, "In some cases the entry of a guilty plea obviates the necessity of a complainant having to testify. That is sometimes a mitigating circumstance, particularly in sexual assault type cases, and in cases involving young complainants. But in this case Ms. . . . was called upon to testify at the sentencing proceedings and was cross-examined by counsel for the appellant."

Note as well para. 18 of *R. v. M. (C.B.)* (1992), [1992] P.E.I.J. No. 40, 99 Nfld. & P.E.I.R. 280, 315 A.P.R. 280, 1992 CarswellPEI 134 (C.A.): "It will be instructive to observe that the trial judge did not grant this discount, in light of the circumstances, as a matter of discretion. In particular, it was noted that the guilty plea was only entered after the complainant had testified at both the preliminary hearing and the trial. Moreover, the complainant was then required to testify at the sentence hearing respecting the frequency and nature of the offence."

Accordingly, although trial time may have been avoided in such cases, it is debatable how much remorse is in evidence and how much the complainant was spared from having to testify.

B) The lack of remorse and a guilty plea

Notwithstanding the foregoing, it must be emphasized that the lack of remorse depreciates the guilty plea, as noted at para. 7 of *R. v. K. (D.)* (2003), [2003] O.J. No. 562, 2003 CarswellOnt 542, 169 O.A.C. 97 (C.A.). Further, counsel must be wary of the attitude of an offender that may fairly be said to communicate a desire to commit the offence again. One striking example is found in *R. v. Burke* (May 3, 1989), Doc. 82/89, [1989] M.J. No. 226 (C.A.). The accused, a 27-year-old first offender, pleaded guilty to having committed a particularly violent and brutal assault, upon a long-time acquaintance of the accused. As set out at page 2 (Q.L.):

> The pre-sentence report and the psychiatric assessment point to characteristics of the accused which we consider to be unsettling and disturbing. The probation officer noted in his report: "There was little evidence of genuine remourse [sic] or empathy for the victim."

. . .

If asked if he would react similarly in this type of situation in the future he indicated he would beat the complainant but not as badly. Mr. Burke went on to state that he knows his personal values are such that others may disagree with them, explaining that if someone violates his rights that individual forfeits his. He added that if someone would push him in the future, he may react the same way.

C) The guilty plea and a discount based on a fixed percentage

Certain cases support the granting of a discount for a guilty plea that is in accord with a fixed mathematical formula, in accordance with the English practice it seems. For example, MacDonald C.J.T.D. observed in *R. v. S. (C.J.)* (1994), [1994] P.E.I.J. No. 53, 120 Nfld. & P.E.I.R. 70, 373 A.P.R. 70, 1994 CarswellPEI 100 (T.D.), at para. 41: "Previously I have stated a sentence could be reduced by one-quarter to one-third for a guilty plea. . .".

Note as well the instruction found at para. 16-18 of *R. v. M. (C.B.)* (1992), [1992] P.E.I.J. No. 40, 99 Nfld. & P.E.I.R. 280, 315 A.P.R. 280, 1992 CarswellPEI 134 (C.A.):

> [16] The appellant submits that he should have received a reduction in sentence as a result of his early guilty plea. He relies on the decision of this Court in *R. v. Bruce* (1982), 35 Nfld. & P.E.I.R. 530, 99 A.P.R. 530 and in the decision of Chief Justice MacDonald of the Prince Edward Island Supreme Court Trial Division in *R. v. S. S.*, [1990] P.E.I.J. No. 84, [1990] 1 P.E.I.R. E7, 84 Nfld. & P.E.I.R. 102, 262 A.P.R. 102, for the proposition that he should have received a reduction in sentence of one-quarter to one-third of the sentence which would have been imposed if there had been a contest.

> [17] Chief Justice MacDonald states in the S.S. case at p. E7-5, p. 104:

> "A discount of one-quarter to one-third of an undiscounted sentence would appear to be appropriate if there are no other mitigating circumstances."

> [18] The trial judge refers to the remarks of Chief Justice Mac-Donald in the S.S. case and also refers to the statement of this

Court in *R. v. Lyons*, [1991] P.E.I.J. No. 10, [1991] 1 P.E.I.R. A2, 89 Nfld. & P.E.I.R. 33, 278 A.P.R. 33, where Mr. Justice McMahon states at pp. A2-2 to A2-3:

"The first mitigating factor considered was the guilty plea (after a preliminary hearing), which the trial judge figured would justify a discount of between one-quarter and one-third of the sentence imposed if there had been a trial. No doubt a guilty plea is to be considered as a factor in the sentencing process but I would not agree that it would justify a one-quarter to one-third reduction in sentence, at least not in all cases."

It will be instructive to observe that the trial judge did not grant this discount, in light of the circumstances, as a matter of discretion. In particular, it was noted that the guilty plea was only entered after the complainant had testified at both the preliminary hearing and the trial. Moreover, the complainant was then required to testify at the sentence hearing respecting the frequency and nature of the offence.

With reference to the English practice, it will be instructive to note *R. v. Hernandez* (1990), [1990] N.B.J. No. 557, 108 N.B.R. (2d) 245, 269 A.P.R. 245, 57 C.C.C. (3d) 477, 1990 CarswellNB 556 (C.A.), at para. 15, pages 481-482 [C.C.C.]:

The appellants also submit that their sentences should be reduced because their plea of guilty saved the state much time and expense. A guilty plea may be, and usually is, taken into account as a mitigating factor. Again, the circumstances surrounding the offence must be taken into account because in Canada, unlike England, there is no automatic entitlement to a reduction of sentence upon a guilty plea.

The English practice was described as "entirely pragmatic" by McEachern, C.J.B.C. in *MacMillan Bloedel Ltd. v. Simpson*, [1994] B.C.J. No. 268, (*sub nom.* MacMillan Bloedel Ltd. v. Brown) 44 B.C.A.C. 241, (*sub nom.* MacMillan Bloedel Ltd. v. Brown) 71 W.A.C. 241, [1994] 7 W.W.R. 259, 92 B.C.L.R. (2d) 1, 88 C.C.C. (3d) 148, 1994 CarswellBC 218 (C.A.). It will be of assistance to cite in full His Lordship's guidance, as recorded at para. 56:

This question [surrounding the weight to be given to guilty pleas] has troubled judges and legal writers for some time. An entirely pragmatic practice has developed in England, where it is now well settled that a plea of guilty will usually result in a reduction of from one-quarter to one-third of the sentence that would otherwise be imposed; see *R. v. Layte* (1983), 38 C.R. (3d) 204 (Ont. Co. Ct.), where most of the jurisprudence on this question is discussed. The rationale for the English practice has been described in a number of cases. In *R. v. Davis* (1980), 2 Cr. App. Rep. (S.) 168 (C.A.), the Court referred to the fact that some accused waste much public time and money and added that:

"They should be encouraged to stop these sort of tactics. In this case they did not try to hoodwink the Court in any way. They did not try to cause as much trouble as they could."

D)   The guilty plea and a discount based on a fixed formula

Although very little authority is known on this point, the Newfoundland Court of Appeal did not criticize the trial judge's suggestion that it would be proper, in the future, to reduce a sentence for manslaughter by one year, to reflect the guilty plea, in conformity with a fixed formula. Refer to paras. 6 and 7 of *R. v. Kittle* (1996), [1996] N.J. No. 177, 142 Nfld. & P.E.I.R. 87, 445 A.P.R. 87, 1996 CarswellNfld 329 (C.A.).

E)   The guilty plea and the waiver of the chance of being acquitted

R. v. Finley (1998), [1998] O.J. No. 974, 54 O.T.C. 36, 1998 CarswellOnt 1110 (Gen. Div.) provides valuable instruction on the significance of a guilty plea in the face of a prosecution that is at the antipodes of "caught red-handed" situation. Although the passages to be quoted are lengthy, the guidance set out therein is of such importance as to warrant repetition in full:

[11] I will say, as well, that I give you extra credit for your pleas of guilty in this case because of the particular difficulties touched upon by counsel in mounting a successful prosecution for what we sometimes now call "historic sexual assaults". Such cases are difficult to prosecute. They are also difficult to defend for many of the same reasons because of the flawed memories affected by the passage of time, because of missing evidence and ultimately the absence of corroboration for the testimony of the victims or for the defendant. The Court is mindful of the onus, as always, on the Crown to prove guilt beyond a reasonable doubt. It is not unusual, particularly in cases involving historic sexual assault, that

the Court believes the evidence given by a complainant but must in the final analysis have some reasonable doubt based on a sworn denial by the accused when there is no supporting evidence, corroborative evidence, for one side or the other. Such a result is often unsatisfying but is unavoidable. Indeed, the absence of evidence in order to permit an accused to prepare and present full answer and defence may, on occasion result in the granting of a judicial stay.

[12] Otherwise expressed. . . you had a chance of acquittal based upon what would have been, I know, the competent and thorough defence that would have been put forward . . . You have given up that opportunity, you have waived that defence, you have given up the chance of being acquitted on these charges and for that you deserve full credit.

Hence, whatever may be the correct legal position in a situation in which there is no hope of acquittal, a guilty plea advanced in a case in which there is a chance of being found not guilty is deserving of full credit.

F) The not guilty plea that is tantamount to a guilty plea

On occasion, accused individuals will plead not guilty (or refused to enter a plea), to then admit all of the facts giving rise to the prosecution, with the result that the Court registers a finding of guilt without any witnesses having to testify, and with very little demand being made on the limited resources of the administration of justice. This type of situation often arises in cases in which civil litigation is undertaken or may be expected to and the offender wishes to avoid an admission that might be raised in the litigation.

In such cases, counsel might wish to point to the guidance advanced in *R. v. T. (G.)* (1997), [1997] O.J. No. 3873, 41 O.T.C. 63, 1997 CarswellOnt 3962 (Gen. Div.). As noted at para. 2, the accused entered a plea of not guilty to charges of sexual assault and touching for a sexual purpose "but did not contest the evidence that the Crown read in as its case and conceded that the Crown would be able to establish the facts as read in." Belleghem J. held that this procedure is tantamount to the "nolo contendere" procedure used in the United States in matters in which a finding of guilt is not contested for sentencing purposes and "is tantamount to a plea of guilty and the accused is entitled, to the extent that the process is consistent with a plea of guilt, to the considerations that would flow from such a plea."

In reaching this conclusion, the Court rejected the submission of the prosecution that unless or until the accused acknowledges and accepts the wrongful behaviour which he concedes the Crown could establish, he would not be a suitable prospect for rehabilitation. Refer to para. 5. While the argument was found to be attractive, the conclusion of the Court was that the process employed was sufficient to entitle the accused to whatever degree of mitigation may flow from a finding of remorse. Indeed, para. 36 records the view of the Court that this process did not in any way diminish the entitlement of the accused to the benefit of the mitigation that is inherent in a display of remorse.

Irrespective of the analysis advanced for consideration by the sentencing court, counsel must strive to obtain what Hill J. described as "real consideration for his [or her] pleas of guilt." See *R. v. Miller* (1997), [1997] O.J. No. 3911, 40 O.T.C. 17, 1997 CarswellOnt 3524 (Gen. Div.), at para. 44.

G) The guilty plea and affirming the truth of the victim's complaint

In closing this section, it is useful to underscore how a guilty plea serves to bring closure and to validate the complaint, for the victim may be faced with pressure from friends and family of the defendant to "recant", to use a polite word. One of the interesting points raised by Reilly J. in *R. v. Finley* (1998), [1998] O.J. No. 974, 54 O.T.C. 36, 1998 CarswellOnt 1110 (Gen. Div.) concerns the validation of a victim's complaint as a result of a guilty plea. As set forcefully out at para. 10:

> Of greatest importance, your pleas of guilty I would hope, even more than a finding of guilt registered by a judge or a jury, is a direct acknowledgement from you, the perpetrator, to these women that they were telling the truth. The truth that they were abused by you so many years ago. That will, hopefully, be a significant, positive factor in the continuing healing process in being able, hopefully, some day, if not as yet, to finally put these terrible events behind them. In other words, it is not simply a third person, a judge or jury, who has weighed the evidence and found your guilt established beyond a reasonable doubt. You have acknowledged your guilt to these women and to the world. Finally their position has been fully justified.

H) The guilty plea and societal interests

To date, the discussion has largely focused on the advantages that an offender may derive from advancing a guilty plea, and in doing so at an early point in the proceedings. At this stage, it will be useful to remind counsel of the twin societal interests at play in assigning credit for guilty pleas: 1) the sparing of the victim(s) and the witnesses from having to testify and 2) the reduced demands on the scarce resource of court time.

I) Credit for sparing victims and other witnesses from the ordeal of testifying

One of the first and foremost authorities in respect to the broadening of the "values" assigned to guilty pleas is *R. v. Sandercock* (1985), [1985] A.J. No. 817, [1986] 1 W.W.R. 291, 40 Alta. L.R. (2d) 265, 62 A.R. 382, 22 C.C.C. (3d) 79, 48 C.R. (3d) 154, 1985 CarswellAlta 190 (C.A.), at para. 23: "In recent years, great emphasis has been put on a prompt guilty plea as a special and major mitigating factor. It used to be said that this was relevant only to show remorse. Aside entirely from any remorse, however, an accused should receive substantial recognition either for sparing the victim the need to testify or to wait to testify, or for waiving some of his constitutional rights in deference to expeditious justice." In this respect, note that the expression "strain of the trial" was selected in *R. v. Sajna* (1991), [1991] B.C.J. No. 3688, 9 B.C.A.C. 233, 19 W.A.C. 233, 1991 CarswellBC 977 (C.A.), at para. 13.

In *R. v. Finley* (1998), [1998] O.J. No. 974, 54 O.T.C. 36, 1998 CarswellOnt 1110 (Gen. Div.), a passage at para. 10 captures the rationale that justifies, in part, the credit to be assigned to a guilty plea: sparing the victims(s) the anguish of having to testify and to re-live the traumatic events. As we read,

> . . . The avoidance of the trauma that a contested trial would have unquestionably have had upon some of these women is of greater significance. I suspect the opportunity to finally face you in open court and to tell their story may have been, for some of the women, cathartic, a final release, their chance to be heard in open court under oath. However, even in those circumstances it would not have been a comfortable experience. . . ..

As a matter of common sense and practical experience, greater credit is to be assigned in cases in which sensitive trials are avoided or vulnerable witnesses are spared testimony. Less credit is available in cases in which a brief trial for shoplifting is avoided, or which spares a veteran police officer from testifying as to an impaired operation investigation.

This instruction was expressed quite ably by MacDonald C.J.T.D. in *R. v. S. (C.J.)* (1994), [1994] P.E.I.J. No. 53, 120 Nfld & P.E.I.R. 70, 373 A.P.R. 70, 1994 CarswellPEI 100 (T.D.), at para. 41: ". . . a major mitigating factor is a guilty plea. This is especially so in a case involving sexual assault as the victim is much more emotionally involved in the case than, for example, a victim in a theft case." The Court added that "The emotional trauma suffered by S.G.S. in giving evidence was extremely painful to witness. Similarly, J.A.A. and B.H.K. suffered while giving testimony."

Note as well the observations in *R. v. Ralph* (1993), [1993] N.J. No. 46, 105 Nfld. & P.E.I.R. 220, 331 A.P.R. 220, 1993 CarswellNfld 256 (C.A.), at para. 71: "A guilty plea generally acts as a mitigating factor particularly in sentencing offences where the victims are spared the agony of giving evidence of a distasteful episode in their lives."

R. c. Parent, [2001] N.B.J. No. 191, 236 N.B.R. (2d) 370, 611 A.P.R. 370, 2001 CarswellNB 189, 2001 NBCA 60 (C.A.) is also apposite. Para. 15 underlines: "I believe that Mr. Parent's guilty plea is a particularly mitigating factor in this case given the large number of charges and victims, who would have undoubtedly been significantly disrupted by the preliminary inquiry and the trial."

By parity of reasoning, where the victim does not appear to be either vulnerable, or unwilling to testify, or will not be required at trial, then credit (or more appropriately, enhanced credit) may be denied. An example is seen in *R. v. Tkachuk*, [2001] A.J. No. 1277, 159 C.C.C. (3d) 434, 17 M.V.R. (4th) 4, 293 A.R. 171, 257 W.A.C. 171, 2001 CarswellAlta 1318, 2001 ABCA 243 (C.A.). Para. 21 sets out instruction under the heading "the appellant was entering a guilty plea eliminating the necessity of the victim having to testify."

> This is an appropriate consideration in cases where the victim has been subject to trauma or violence, particularly in cases of sexual assault. Here, however, Mrs. . . . victim impact statement clearly states that she is outraged at the horrible changes to her life, and would gladly have testified. If that impression is wrong, it seems that Mr. . . ., who was a passenger in the vehicle, could have provided the same evidence as his wife. That assumes the

evidence of the . . . was even necessary. It appears that the appellant's confession to the police 11 days after the incident, which he admits was voluntary, and the evidence at the scene may well have been sufficient to secure a conviction.

J) The issue of guilty pleas and the savings to the administration of justice in money terms

I wish to remind counsel again of the instruction found in *R. v. Sandercock* (1985), [1985] A.J. No. 817, [1986] 1 W.W.R. 291, 40 Alta. L.R. (2d) 265, 62 A.R. 382, 22 C.C.C. (3d) 79, 48 C.R. (3d) 154, 1985 CarswellAlta 190 (C.A.), at para. 23: "In recent years, great emphasis has been put on a prompt guilty plea as a special and major mitigating factor. It used to be said that this was relevant only to show remorse. Aside entirely from any remorse, however, an accused should receive substantial recognition either for sparing the victim the need to testify or to wait to testify, or for waiving some of his constitutional rights in deference to expeditious justice."

Consider as well the direct attention given to the issue of guilty pleas and the cost of the administration of justice in *R. v. Diez* (1998), [1998] O.J. No. 3962, 77 O.T.C. 66, 1998 CarswellOnt 3851 (Gen. Div.), at para. 8:

> In mitigation I cannot stress enough the effect of the accused's plea of guilty. The fact he has saved an over-burdened court system time, money and space. In consideration of the aggravating features of the offence the amount of money certainly is one of those.

Emphasis must be placed not only on the question of money, but on the related issues of cost and space.

It will also be of assistance to refer to para. 95 of *R. v. Spellacy* (1995), [1995] N.J. No. 215, 131 Nfld. & P.E.I.R. 127, 408 A.P.R. 127, 1995 CarswellNfld 297 (C.A.): "The cost of the trial is not to be considered in the imposition of sentence...".

R. c. Parent, [2001] N.B.J. No. 191, 236 N.B.R. (2d) 370, 611 A.P.R. 370, 2001 CarswellNB 189, 2001 NBCA 60 (C.A.) is also apposite. Para. 14 highlights the instruction in *R. v. J. (R.K.)* (1998), [1998] N.B.J. No. 483, 207 N.B.R. (2d) 24, 1998 CarswellNB 448, 529 A.P.R. 24 (C.A.) consigned at para. 24 to the effect that "In most cases, a plea of guilty is a powerful mitigating factor. The reasons for this are well known. First, such a plea quite properly reduces the punishment which otherwise would be meted out because it saves precious time and scarce resources. . .."

The final word is taken from Chief Justice McEachern's instructive judgment in *MacMillan Bloedel Ltd. v. Simpson*, [1994] B.C.J. No. 268, (*sub nom.* MacMillan Bloedel Ltd. v. Brown) 44 B.C.A.C. 241, (*sub nom.* MacMillan Bloedel Ltd. v. Brown) 71 W.A.C. 241, [1994] 7 W.W.R. 259, 92 B.C.L.R. (2d) 1, 88 C.C.C. (3d) 148, 1994 CarswellBC 218 (C.A.), at para. 58: "The better views, in my judgment, are . . . that a plea of guilty saves the community a great deal of expense. . .." Refer finally to *R. v. Johnston*, [1970] 4 C.C.C. 64, 1970 CarswellOnt 255, [1970] 2 O.R. 780 (Ont. C.A.), applying *R. v. de Haan* (1967), [1967] 3 All E.R. 618, 52 Cr. App. R. 25, [1968] 2 Q.B. 108 (C.A.).

f) The mitigation, if any, arising from a guilty plea in a case of overwhelming evidence of guilt:

i) Introducing the rule in *R. v. Spiller*, [1969] 4 C.C.C. 211, 1969 CarswellBC 42, 6 C.R.N.S. 360, 68 W.W.R. 187 (C.A.)

A further area of controversy surrounds the question whether a guilty plea is entitled to any credit if the prosecution faces little challenge in demonstrating guilt. In other words, counsel is faced with the prosecution's submission that a guilty plea by an accused who is obviously guilty is without much mitigating importance as the outcome of the trial is a foregone conclusion.

Indeed, in the leading authority, *R. v. Spiller*, [1969] 4 C.C.C. 211, 68 W.W.R. 187, 6 C.R.N.S. 360, 1969 CarswellBC 42 (C.A.), Robertson J.A. remarked as follows at page 215 C.C.C., para. 12 "I do not think that any significant weight should be given to the plea of guilty here: The respondent knew that she was inescapably caught." In other words, although defence counsel had submitted that it was mitigating that the offender entered a guilty plea thus saving the Crown the expense of a trial, on the authority of Edmund Davies, L.J. in *R. v. de Haan* (1967), [1967] 3 All E.R. 618, 52 Cr. App. R. 25, [1968] 2 Q.B. 108 (C.A.), at p. 619: "It is undoubtedly right that a confession of guilt should tell in favour of an accused person, for that is clearly in the public interest." In response, the Court of Appeal advanced the following remarks: "With the greatest respect, I do not think that that is a principle of universal application, though it may well be appropriate to apply it in some cases, and I do not think that any significant weight should be given to the plea of guilty here: The respondent knew that she was inescapably caught."

In this section, attention is drawn to the parameters of this doctrine as developed in the case law, to the legislatives changes since it was advanced, and to the emerging view that defence counsel should urge upon the Court that it should not matter whether the offender could hope to escape conviction in light of the other societal interests fostered by a guilty plea.

ii)   Discussing the application of the *Spiller* doctrine:

A)   The course of justice is not advanced by a guilty plea where no successful defence is possible

Many cases have applied the *Spiller* judgment and the rationale that it promotes to the effect that little mitigating weight should be assigned to a guilty plea that fails to advance the course of justice. For example, *R. v. Fitzgerald* (1991), [1991] B.C.J. No. 1030, 1991 CarswellBC 1723 (C.A.) stands for the proposition that where a guilty plea is entered in the face of overwhelming evidence of guilt, the plea should not attract a great discount in sentence. As we read at para. 6, "For my part, I recognize that there are cases in which a plea of guilty will play a considerable part in the sentencing process. As was pointed out, however, where the circumstances are such that the plea of guilty is offered in the face of overwhelming evidence of guilt it will not attract so great a discount."

See also *R. v. Macki*, [2001] B.C.J. No. 574, 2001 CarswellBC 758, 2001 BCSC 427 (S.C.), wherein Romilly J. remarked at para. 56: "An early guilty plea merits considerable weight in sentencing disposition . . . It does not merit such weight, however, where the accused knows he or she is inescapably caught: *R. v. Spiller*, [1969] 4 C.C.C. 211 (B.C.C.A.). . .". In an earlier judgment, Mr. Justice Romilly had observed that "An early guilty plea does not merit such [mitigating] weight where the accused knows he is inescapably caught: *R. v. Spiller*. . ." Refer to para. 18 of *R. v. Cabrera* (1998), [1998] B.C.J. No. 175, 1998 CarswellBC 175 (S.C.).

There are other examples of the influence of *R. v. Spiller, supra*. Among the many that might be cited from non-British Columbia courts, reference is made to para. 9 of *R. v. Ching* (2002), [2002] N.W.T.J. No. 57, 2002 CarswellNWT 61 (Terr. Ct.), we read: "I take into account the guilty plea, however, one has to recognize that the accused was essentially caught red-handed." Further, in *R. v. Rey* (2002), [2002] M.J. No. 321, 2002 CarswellMan 363 (Prov. Ct.), Mr. Rey was identified as the culprit of a robbery by reason of red dye found within the money he stole. Indeed, the trial judge thrice observed that the offender was caught red-handed, at paragraphs 2, 9 and 12 of the judgment, and concluded that the guilty plea ought not to receive the weight that it might in other, less compelling, circumstances of guilt. Of note, although the Court of Appeal intervened and held that a conditional term of two years less a day was fit, as opposed to the 30- month penitentiary term selected at trial, it did not criticize or even comment on the decision in the first instance to discount almost wholly the guilty plea. See *R. v. Rey*, [2002] M.J. No. 26, 163 Man. R. (2d) 76, 2002 CarswellMan 25, 2002 MBCA 16, 269 W.A.C. 76 (C.A.) and para. 24 of *R. v. D. (L.R.)* (1992), [1992] N.S.J. No. 37, 109 N.S.R. (2d) 133, 1992 CarswellNS 303, 297 A.P.R. 133 (Co. Ct.).

Note as well *R. v. United Keno Hill Mines Ltd.* (1980), [1980] Y.J. No. 10, 1 Y.R. 299, 10 C.E.L.R. 43, 1980 CarswellYukon 9 (Terr. Ct.), at para. 25:

> Voluntarily reporting the violation to authorities indicates a genuine desire to act responsibly. The bulk of environmental regulation depends upon the integrity of corporations to provide full disclosure of the impact of their operation on the environment. Voluntarily reporting breaches must be acknowledged as a mitigating circumstance by the courts in sentencing. Pleas of guilty are not of any significance if detection and conviction were inevitable (see: *R. v. Spiller*, [1969] 4 C.C.C. 211.)

I refer as well to the comments consigned in *R. v. Helpard* (1995), [1995] N.S.J. No. 426, 145 N.S.R. (2d) 204, 418 A.P.R. 204, 1995 CarswellNS 511 (C.A.), at para. 32: "While Mr. Helpard's guilty plea is a matter that should have some mitigating effect, it should be borne in mind that it was entered on the fifth court appearance when it was clear that the circumstantial evidence linking Mr. Helpard to the crime was compelling. The plea might be characterized as a "recognition of the inevitable", quoting *R. v. Faulds* (1994), 79 O.A.C. 313, 20 O.R. (3d) 13, [1994] O.J. No. 2145, 1994 CarswellOnt 147 (C.A.).

Returning briefly to British Columbia case law, a number of other judgments support the view that little, if any, weight need be assigned to a guilty plea in circumstances in which the offender is caught red-handed. By way of limited example, note para. 1 of *R. v. Swanson* (June 15, 1981), Doc. Vancouver 810336, [1981] B.C.J. No. 880 (C.A.), para. 7 of *R. v. Bassett* (1992), [1992] B.C.J. No. 1021, 13 B.C.A.C. 169, 24 W.A.C. 169, 1992 CarswellBC 989 (C.A.), page 35.

In addition, refer to page 35 [C.C.C.], para. 11(g) of *R. v. Scherer* (1984), [1984] O.J. No. 156, 5 O.A.C. 297, 16 C.C.C. (3d) 30, 42 C.R. (3d) 376, 1984 CarswellOnt 79 (C.A.), leave to appeal refused (1984), 58 N.R. 80n, 7 O.A.C. 80n, 16 C.C.C. (3d) 30 (note) (S.C.C.). Indeed, in the last noted case, Martin J.A. remarked: "The mitigating effect of the appellant's guilty plea was diminished by reason of his being caught 'red-handed' and having no possible defence."

Expressed in its simplest terms, the *Spiller* doctrine holds that no "significant" weight ought to be assigned to the sentencing equation in the case of an offender who would be found guilty at the conclusion of the trial: The cases appear to suggest that it is not necessarily an expression of remorse, as contrasted to the situation in which the offender pleads guilty without regard to the likelihood of conviction, on the one hand; to substantially discount the sentence might result in impairing the value of denunciation and deterrence, both general and specific, on the other. Thus, the course of justice is not advanced by the guilty plea under either rationale.

B) What if the guilty plea does advance the course of justice by saving court time?

Of interest, *R. v. Spiller, supra*, has been applied with an element of flexibility in cases in which the offender's actions resulted in saving valuable court time and resources, even though conviction was inevitable. For example, in *R. v. Gerhard* (1995), [1995] A.J. No. 392, 168 A.R. 370, 1995 CarswellAlta 628 (Prov. Ct.), para. 15 records the following instruction:

> I agree with the Crown that the guilty plea given by the accused is a mitigating factor. Obviously a trial was avoided and as well all the time and work that would have been involved therein. . . . This also was a case where it seems that inevitably the accused would have been caught because once the basic premises upon which he had obtained the contract with the Government of Canada were shown to be non-existent, his entire house of cards, as it were, was doomed to come crashing down.

In other words as the British Columbia Court of Appeal said some two decades ago in the now well-known case of *The Queen v. Spiller*, the accused, in the instant matter, was inextricably caught up by the evidence here and it would not have been a difficult case to prove even though it might have taken some time and expense. Nevertheless he has pleaded guilty and that in itself is in mitigation of his position to some degree.

In this respect, note para. 26 of *R. v. Canning* (1996), [1996] O.J. No. 4134, 1996 CarswellOnt 4517 (Prov. Ct.), para. 23 of *R. v. Lui* (April 12, 1994), Vaillancourt Prov. J., [1994] O.J. No. 736 (Prov. Ct.) and para. 4 of *R. v. Gillis* (1989), [1989] P.E.I.J. No. 114, 77 Nfld. & P.E.I.R. 136, 1989 CarswellPEI 86, 240 A.P.R. 136 (T.D.).

C)   *What if the guilty plea does advance the course of justice, by promoting a sense of responsibility?*

Having noted that there is a societal interest in promoting guilty pleas to permit savings in court time, it will be appropriate to point to the possible involvement of s. 718(f) in the selection of a fit sentence, a legislative enactment not yet foreseen in 1969. Recall that s. 718 reads in part that "The fundamental purpose of sentencing is to contribute, along with crime prevention initiatives, to respect for the law and the maintenance of a just, peaceful and safe society by imposing just sanctions that have one or more of the following objectives: . . . f) to promote a sense of responsibility, and acknowledgment of the harm done to victims and to the community."

In this respect, reference is made to *MacMillan Bloedel Ltd. v. Simpson*, [1994] B.C.J. No. 268, [1994] 7 W.W.R. 259, 92 B.C.L.R. (2d) 1, (*sub nom.* MacMillan Bloedel Ltd. v. Brown) 44 B.C.A.C. 241, 88 C.C.C. (3d) 148, (*sub nom.* MacMillan Bloedel Ltd. v. Brown) 71 W.A.C. 241, 1994 CarswellBC 218 (C.A.). Of note, the majority reviewed the fitness of "discounting" otherwise appropriate periods of custody to reflect the fact of a guilty plea. In particular, attention is drawn to para. 55, pages 155-156 [C.C.C.]:

[55] The trial judge declined to reduce their sentences on [account of guilty pleas] because they did not show remorse. I think, with respect, that remorse in a case such as this where the Appellants acted deliberately for unrecanted reasons of conscience, is not the only factor to be considered in relation to the effect of a plea of guilty on the severity of a sentence. In my judgment, a plea of

guilty in these circumstances represents an acknowledgment of responsibility for which some credit should be given.

Ought not some mitigating weight to be assigned to the fact that there was no attempt to escape responsibility, or to unfairly minimize the part played, notwithstanding the fact that the offence appears to be easily established by reason of the offender being caught red-handed. In this respect, note para. 26 of *R. v. Canning* (1996), [1996] O.J. No. 4134, 1996 CarswellOnt 4517 (Prov. Ct.), para. 23 of *R. v. Lui* (April 12, 1994), Vaillancourt Prov. J., [1994] O.J. No. 736 (Prov. Ct.) and para. 4 of *R. v. Gillis* (1989), [1989] P.E.I.J. No. 114, 77 Nfld. & P.E.I.R. 136, 1989 CarswellPEI 86, 240 A.P.R. 136 (T.D.).

At the end of the day, one cannot help but agree with the observations consigned in *R. v. Davis* (1980), 2 Cr. App. R. (S.) 168. The Court referred to the fact that some accused waste much public time and money and added that: "They should be encouraged to stop these sort of tactics. In this case they did not try to hoodwink the Court in any way. They did not try to cause as much trouble as they could." Quote at para. 56 of *MacMillan Bloedel Ltd. v. Brown, sub nom* MacMillan Bloedel Ltd. v. Simpson, [1994] B.C.J. No. 268, [1994] 7 W.W.R. 259, 92 B.C.L.R. (2d) 1, 44 B.C.A.C. 241, 88 C.C.C. (3d) 148, (*sub nom.* MacMillan Bloedel Ltd. v. Brown) 71 W.A.C. 241, 1994 CarswellBC 218 (C.A.).

D) What if the guilty plea does advance the course of justice, by evidencing remorse?

Guilty pleas, even by offenders with no hope of a defence, may be consonant with the promotion of the course of justice if they demonstrate an element of remorse, often seen as a precursor to self-rehabilitation. Thus, in *R. v. Schwan* (1994), [1994] A.J. No. 605, 154 A.R. 85, 1994 CarswellAlta 579 (Prov. Ct.), we read at para. 12 the following instruction that I have chosen to quote at length:

> [Both counsel] referred to the early guilty plea of the accused as being a mitigating factor. In the particular circumstances of this case I agree that it is a mitigating factor and that it is a mitigating factor of signal significance. . . . A guilty plea is not always an indication of true remorse but can be, depending upon all of the circumstances, as the B.C. Court of Appeal said in *The Queen v. Spiller* (1969) 6 C.R.N.S. 361, where the Court noted that often times persons will plead guilty because they are inextricably

caught up by the evidence and have very little chance, realistically, of escaping criminal liability. That circumstance of course does not mean then that there cannot be real remorse on the part of the accused but in such circumstances such remorse is much more difficult to divine although it may still be assumed if there are other indicators pointing towards its existence.

E)   What if the guilty plea does advance the course of justice, by sparing victims the trauma of testifying?

By parity of reasoning, it is important not to overlook the fact that a guilty plea by one without a defence nevertheless serves to spare the victim(s) from having to testify. Refer again to para. 12 of *R. v. Schwan* (1994), [1994] A.J. No. 605, 154 A.R. 85, 1994 CarswellAlta 579 (Prov. Ct.): "It is often said that a plea of guilty is mitigating because it can show remorse, because it can save individuals the stress and difficulty of appearing as witnesses before the Court. . .". Support for this view is found in *R. v. S. (S.)* (1990), [1990] P.E.I.J. No. 84, 84 Nfld. & P.E.I.R. 102, 1990 CarswellPEI 72, 262 A.P.R. 102 (T.D.), with direct reference to *R. v. Spiller, supra.*

F)   What if the guilty plea does advance the course of justice, by promoting the search for the truth?

In his judgment styled *R. v. Chung* (November 17, 1993), Doc. Burnaby 46000, [1993] B.C.J. No. 2646 (Prov. Ct.), Judge Romilly, as he then was, set forth certain pointed comments that are illuminating in terms of the present debate. In particular, I wish to highlight paras. 37-39:

> [37] I mean no disrespect when I say that while the position taken by the Court it, *Fitzgerald, supra,* may have been applicable when the case of *Spiller, supra,* was heard, one wonders whether the same position is applicable today in the era of the Charter of Rights.

> [38] Today one is entitled to ask: "What is the meaning of 'overwhelming evidence' of guilt?" Was there not "overwhelming evidence of guilt" in *R. v. Mack* (1988) 4 C.C.C. (3d) 513? Was there not "overwhelming evidence of guilt" in *R. v. Greffe* (1990) 5 C.C.C. (3d) 161 S.C.C.? Was there not "overwhelming evidence of guilt" in *R. v. Hebert* (1990) 77 C.R. (3d) 145? The simple answer is "yes" yet we know that these cases and many others

have been successfully argued before the courts and pleas of not guilty entered after trials.

[39] The plain truth is that since the promulgation of the Charter of Rights there are fewer and fewer guilty pleas to any charges in our courts. Search for the truth is no longer the main guiding principle in criminal law.

Refer as well to *R. v. Ali* (May 11, 1993), Doc. Coquitlam 40968RT, Burnaby 46000T, [1993] B.C.J. No. 1267 (Prov. Ct.), at paras. 21-23.

G)   The emerging challenge to the Spiller doctrine

There is an emerging school of thought that holds that it is not consonant with proper sentencing principles to discount the mitigating weight to be assigned to a guilty plea on the basis of the strong likelihood of conviction. Reduced to its most fundamental expression, proponents of this principle can identify no compelling rationale to refuse to credit a guilty plea, and thus refuse so to do. In other words, since the guilty plea serves to reduce trial time, spares the victim(s) from having to testify, and indicates a resolve to act in a pro-social fashion by acknowledging guilt, it is worth some credit, all other factors being equal.

The leading case in this respect is *R. v. Santos* (1993), [1993] O.J. No. 2539, 67 O.A.C. 270, 1993 CarswellOnt 1156 (C.A.). The Court held that a trial judge commits an error of law in discounting a guilty plea or in refusing to acknowledge it as a significant mitigating factor by reason of the overwhelming evidence against the offender. No less weight is to be assigned, though the offender "has been inescapably caught". Refer to para. 2, pages 270-271. The judgment of *R. v. Bruce* (1982), [1982] P.E.I.J. No. 12, 35 Nfld. & P.E.I.R. 530, 99 A.P.R. 530, 28 C.R. (3d) 247, 1982 CarswellPEI 11 (C.A.) was cited as authority. Refer in particular to pages 252-253 [C.R.], para. 14 which reads in part:

> . . . It has also been stated that a guilty plea should be given less weight where there is such a preponderance of evidence against the accused that the only reasonable choice or option left open is a plea of guilty. *R. v. Spiller*, [1969] 4 C.C.C. 211 (B.C.C.A.). In the present case the respondent had signed a statement in which she had admitted her guilt and it could be said that her only choice was to plead guilty. However, if the rationale for a policy of decreasing sentence where a guilty plea had been

entered, is based on the consideration of the time saved by not having a trial, I am unable to accept the proposition that there should be less weight given to a guilty plea from a person who has been inescapably caught. I would agree with the trial judge that the guilty plea by the respondent should be a mitigating circumstance.

Thus, the Court was of the view that it is necessary to examine the circumstances of each case and that, in effect, all offenders who are "guilty as sin" have to be shown to be so, with attendant loss of judicial economy and potential secondary harm to witnesses. Notice has also been taken of *R. v. Sarao* (1995), 80 O.A.C. 236 (C.A.), at para. 4: "It must also be taken into consideration that he pleaded guilty to the charges (albeit in the face of overwhelming evidence) and thereby saved the victims' family the trauma of a trial and he saved the state the time and expenses of a lengthy trial."

In this light, it is instructive to observe that in *R. v. K. (B.S.)* (September 20, 2002), Watt J., [2002] O.J. No. 4006 (S.C.J.), Watt J. situated the guilty plea within the particular dynamics of the actions of the offender. "B.S.K. has also pleaded guilty. He waived the preliminary inquiry and consented to his committal for trial. Neither is this a courthouse door plea of guilty. It was mentioned early, and there has been no change of heart. The overwhelming nature of the evidence against him does not diminish its significance. See *R. v. Santos* (1993), 67 O.A.C. 270, 270-271." To the same effect is *R. v. McDonald* (2000), [2000] O.J. No. 4398, 2000 CarswellOnt 4277 (C.J.), at para. 8.

Mr. Justice Hill identified an additional element in *R. v. Hoang*, [2002] O.J. No. 1355, [2002] O.T.C. 229, 2002 CarswellOnt 1340 (S.C.J.), at para. 110: the guilty plea brings finality to the proceedings in a public setting. Refer as well to His Honour's earlier judgment to the same effect in *R. v. Holder* (1998), [1998] O.J. No. 5102, 21 C.R. (5th) 277, 83 O.T.C. 161, 1998 CarswellOnt 4728 (Gen. Div.) at pages 281-2 [C.R.], para. 17.

In the final analysis, it is obvious that a guilty plea by a defendant who cannot secure an acquittal at trial is not on the same footing as a guilty plea advanced by a similarly situated offender who implicates others in the offence and who discloses the location of incriminating evidence, not otherwise known. In this respect, note the comments consigned at para. 19 of *R. v. Gagnon* (2000), [2000] O.J. No. 3410, 136 O.A.C. 116, 147 C.C.C. (3d) 193, 2000 CarswellOnt 3317 (C.A.).

It is suggested that in light of the general acceptance that mitigation arises in situations in which a guilty plea or pleas results in manifesting remorse, or saving court time, or sparing victims from having to testify or in demonstrating a sense of responsibility in the offender or even in bringing finality to proceedings that could otherwise result in acquittals by reason of potential Charter breaches, mitigation of some significant weight should be assigned even if it can be said that the offender was caught red-handed or could not escape responsibility. From one perspective, this is merely applying the *Spiller* doctrine as it has developed. From another, it may be seen as a repudiation of the *Spiller* doctrine. It remains for the Courts of Appeal to resolve this controversy.

g) The mitigation, if any, arising as a result of a not guilty plea:

i) Introduction

At the heart of this debate is the question of co-operation with the authorities, and the question of an offender's co-operation with the authorities is always a difficult issue. On the one hand, as will be seen in the forthcoming discussion, the rule in *R. v. Kozy* (1990), 74 O.R. (2d) 545, 41 O.A.C. 27, 58 C.C.C. (3d) 500, 80 C.R. (3d) 59, 1990 CarswellOnt 113 (C.A.) holds that no reduction in an otherwise fit sentence may arise out of the conduct of the defence. Nevertheless, an offender who pleads not guilty may not profit by the reduction in sentence often associated with sparing the witness from having to testify and the saving of valuable court time, to name but two factors discussed earlier.

What counsel may wish to stress, however, is that *R. v. Kozy, supra*, held at p. 550 [O.R.], p. 64 [C.R.], para. 13, that a not guilty plea is not necessarily inconsistent with remorse. This point is not often advanced, and rarely with any vigour.

In the circumstances, the heart of the discussion will focus on the rule in *Kozy* in order to make plain that, at the very least, no discredit arises from a not guilty plea and, at worst, no credit is available that might otherwise have been assigned had an early guilty plea been advanced.

ii) The ruling in *R. v. Kozy*:

On behalf of Griffiths and Osborne, JJ.A., Mr. Justice Carthy identified the issue as follows: "... whether it was proper for the trial judge to increase an otherwise appropriate sentence because the accused gave evidence at trial which was construed as a series of blatant lies, demonstrating an absence of remorse and a need for rehabilitation." Refer to p. 546 [O.R.], p. 60 [C.R.], para. 1. Of note, His Lordship observed in the following paragraph that "This is not the case of an accused shading the truth to protect himself from the charge. His evidence recklessly maligned the complainant [in a sexual assault trial] and was palpably false." A review of para. 3, p. 547 [O.R.], p. 61 [C.R.], makes plain that the offender's account was implausible and an incredible fabrication.

In sentencing Mr. Kozy, the trial judge remarked "But there is another factor that I am taking into consideration, and that is the character of the accused as demonstrated by his false statements in Court, under oath, which demonstrate a need for rehabilitation and a lack of remorse." Refer to p. 547 [O.R.], p. 61 [C.R.], para. 4. In advancing these comments, the trial judge acknowledged that the cases were divided as to the propriety of taking the conduct of the defence into account. Later on, he added that it was the lack of remorse and the need for rehabilitation that were of paramount concern, not the fact of perjury. Refer again to p. 547 [O.R.], p. 61 [C.R.], para. 5.

Thus, the Court of Appeal had no difficulty in concluding that the trial judge had "added some measure to the sentence he would have considered fit had it not been for the untruthful evidence given by the accused at trial." Refer to pp. 547-48, p. 62 C.R., para. 6.

Carthy J.A. remarked that there was appellate authority supporting the view that a higher sentence may be imposed, not to punish perjury, but to address reformation of a deficient character, with reference to *R. v. Tews*, 45 C.C.C. 116, 1926 CarswellAlta 13, 22 Alta. L.R. 161, [1926] 1 W.W.R. 321 (C.A.), at p. 118. It was followed by the Nova Scotia Court of Appeal in *R. v. Cornett* (1949), 96 C.C.C. 316 (N.S. T.D.), holding it appropriate to look to the conduct of the accused in giving evidence at trial as part of the assessment of character.

The Court of Appeal also noted that in a later holding, the Alberta Court of Appeal came to a very different conclusion, by means of a "fully reasoned judgment", that did not refer to *R. v. Tews, supra*. In *R. v. Sawchyn* (1981), 30 A.R. 314, 22 C.R. (3d) 34, 124 D.L.R. (3d) 600, [1981] 5 W.W.R. 207, 60 C.C.C. (2d) 200, 1981 CarswellAlta 274 (C.A.), leave to appeal conviction not granted 33 A.R. 198, 39 N.R. 616, [1981] 2 S.C.R. xi], the Court held that "... the only consideration which may be given to the conduct of the accused at trial is in answer to a plea for leniency", observing that it may be difficult to perceive remorse in cases in which there has been misconduct in the defence. In addition, it is not proper to treat misconduct as an aggravating factor attracting an additional sentence. Refer to p. 548 [O.R.], p. 62 [C.R.], para. 7 and to para. 28-35, pp. 208-211 of the C.C.C. report of *R. v. Sawchyn, supra*.

Of note, Carthy J.A. remarked that the Québec Court of Appeal has also advanced inconsistent instruction on this issue. In one decision, *R. v. Paradis* (1976), 38 C.C.C. (2d) 455, 1976 CarswellQue 82 (C.A.), leave to appeal conviction denied [1977] 1 S.C.R. xi, Kaufman J.A. expressed the view that while a plea of guilty may be considered as evidence of remorse in passing sentence, perjury should be ignored, even if barefaced and brazen, on the theory that such concerns should be dealt with in subsequent proceedings.

In a further decision, *R. v. Maruska* (1983), 8 C.C.C. (3d) 74, 1983 CarswellQue 353 (C.A.), the Court held that untruthful testimony given by the accused could be taken into consideration as indicating a need for incarceration for the purpose of rehabilitation. As remarked by Carthy, J.A., "The courts did not see this as in conflict with *Paradis* because the sentence was being imposed for rehabilitation, not for perjury." His Lordship added, at pp. 548-549 [O.R.], p. 63 [C.R.], para. 8.

> That is precisely the rationalization that has, in my opinion, induced the disparities among the authorities. If conduct at trial is looked to for any reason, it will invariably be discreditable conduct and will tend to increase the sentence. Clothing the rationale in the character of the convicted person or the need for rehabilitation cannot hide the fact that in the *Maruska* case, for instance, the accused was jailed for lying in Court.

Turning to the English authorities, the Ontario Court of Appeal observed that they are consistently against giving any consideration to matters arising from the conduct of the defence, citing *R. v. Dunbar* (1966), 51 Cr. App. R. 57 (Eng. C.A.), *R. v. Skone* (1966), 51 Cr. App. R. 165, [1967] Crim. L.R. 249, 116 New L.J. 1713 (Eng. C.A.) and *R. v. Harper* (1967), 52 Cr. App. R. 21 (Eng. C.A.).

The Court in *R. v. Kozy, supra*, then reviewed the few Ontario judgments that had considered this issue. The first case noted was *R. v. Cranwell* (1958), 120 C.C.C. 402 (Ont. C.A.). Laidlaw J.A. suggested that a trial judge could properly consider the conduct of the accused at trial in deciding upon punishment. There is no elaboration of this obiter statement in light of the fact that the sentence was upheld.

Next, the well-known judgment of *R. v. Willmott* (1966), 1 C.C.C. 171, 1966 CarswellOnt 18, [1966] 2 O.R. 654, 49 C.R. 22, 58 D.L.R. (2d) 33 (C.A.) was cited for the proposition that the offender's attitude during the trial is a factor which may be weighed in the selection of a fit and proper sentence. Refer to p. 179 [C.C.C.]. This reference was also unnecessary for the Court to have reached its decision. Carthy J.A. went on to note that in *R. v. Johnston*, noted at (1976-77), 19 Cr. L. Q. 284, the Ontario Court of Appeal reduced a sentence for contempt from ten years to two years because the trial judge had taken into account that the offender had perjured himself and was the "kingpin" in a conspiracy to defeat justice through giving false testimony in a murder trial. The Court had ruled that the only offence established was that of contempt in refusing to answer questions and that the sanction had to be restricted to that offence. See *R. v. Kozy, supra*, at p. 549 [O.R.], p. 63 [C.R.], para. 10.

Mr. Justice Dubin's brief observation in *R. v. Doren* (1982), 66 C.C.C. (2d) 448, 1982 CarswellOnt 1308, 36 O.R. (2d) 114, 135 D.L.R. (3d) 258 (C.A.), varied (1982), 66 C.C.C. (2d) 448 at 458, 135 D.L.R. (3d) 258 at 268 (Ont. C.A.), at p. 457 [C.C.C.], was not reproduced. On behalf of Zuber and Blair, JJ.A., His Lordship remarked that "Although a plea of guilty is a mitigating factor, a plea of not guilty is not an aggravating factor."

Mr. Justice Carthy went on to set his instruction on this question, at pp. 549-550 [O.R.], pp. 63-64 [C.R.], para. 12. By reason of the significance of the guidance provided, it is set out at length:

> The root of the inconsistency is found in the blurring of the edges between sentencing for the crime that is before the Court and finding a sentence which suits the individual. In sentencing the individual, a trial judge engages in what is, in part, a subjective assessment of the character of the convicted person. A broad range of sources of information feed that assessment and the personal contact between judge and accused, eye to eye, in the courtroom, is bound to leave its mark. Yet, in terms of the administration of justice both the right to full answer and defence and the right not to be punished for a crime of which an accused has not been convicted point in the direction of ignoring the conduct of the defence.

The Court of Appeal took pains to identify an important policy consideration for the rule against attaching aggravating weight to a not guilty plea: the fear that any other sentencing principle would impair the right to make full answer and defence. Indeed, "... any perceived impingement upon the manner in which a defence is to be conducted, such as fear that a particular tactic might induce a heavier penalty, would impair the right to full answer and defence. In the view of the Court, the manner of presenting the defence, whether it be "counsel's viciousness in attacking a complainant" or "lies told by an accused", are of no moment in the selection of a fit sentence. Refer to p. 550 [O.R.], p. 64 [C.R.], para. 14. Having selected a fit sentence, it is not thereafter reduced to reflect the presence of a mitigating feature such as the remorse inherent in a guilty plea.

Hence, an increased sentence is not justified by reason of the fact that an accused person put in motion a full trial. In few words, no penalty flows from a plea of not guilty. In the worst case scenario, the offender may not qualify for the mitigation of the otherwise fit sentence that should result from a guilty plea. The Court added further instruction: "This limited use [of evidence touching upon the actions of the accused] is not inconsistent with the right to full answer and defence. It is simply saying that in the sentencing process a convicted person's assertion of facts supporting a mitigated sentence will be measured against any sworn testimony at trial which indicates the contrary." Refer to p. 551 [O.R.], p. 65 [C.R.], para. 15.

A) The application of the rule in Ontario

R. v. Kozy, supra, was interpreted by the Court of Appeal as follows in *R. v. Bigelow* (1991), [1991] O.J. No. 1739, 1991 CarswellOnt 1780 (C.A.) at para. 7: "It is not clear that the trial judge increased the sentence, which he would otherwise have imposed, because of his findings that the appellant had lied at trial. If he had done so it would have been an error in principle."

In *R. v. N. (J.)* (1994), 95 C.C.C. (3d) 121, 77 O.A.C. 8, [1994] O.J. No. 2965, 1994 CarswellOnt 1830 (C.A.), Galligan and Weiler, JJ.A., remarked that "An appropriate sentence cannot be increased to demonstrate a Court's displeasure at the manner in which a defence was conducted. If that were permitted, the fear of an inappropriately high sentence might impinge upon an accused person's right to make full answer and defence". Refer to p. 126 [C.C.C.], para. 17.

Subsequently, in *R. v. Valentini* (1999), 132 C.C.C. (3d) 262, 43 O.R. (3d) 178, [1999] O.J. No. 251, 1999 CarswellOnt 271, 118 O.A.C. 1 (C.A.), it was noted that the trial judge had listed the offender's lack of remorse as an aggravating factor in sentencing. See pp. 295-296 [C.C.C.], para. 80. At p. 296 [C.C.C.], para. 82, we are instructed that "Lack of remorse is not, ordinarily, an aggravating circumstance. It should only be considered aggravating in very unusual circumstances such as where the accused's attitude towards the crime demonstrates a substantial likelihood of future dangerousness. Even then the trial judge must be careful not to increase the sentence beyond what is proportionate having regard to the circumstances of the particular offence." The Court added, at pp. 296-297 [C.C.C.], para. 83:

> The problem with treating lack of remorse as an aggravating factor is similar to treating the conduct of the defence as an aggravating circumstance. In this case, the lack of remorse appeared to rest on nothing more than the continued assertion of innocence in the face of a guilty verdict following a trial. To treat lack of remorse as an aggravating factor in those circumstances comes perilously close to increasing the sentence because the accused exercised his right to make full answer and defence

At p. 299 [C.C.C.], para. 91, the Court emphasized that it is an error in principle to consider lack of remorse as an aggravating circumstance.

Turning to a number of unreported judgments and endorsements, Catzman J.A. observed that "... the trial judge erred in attributing to the appellant a lack of remorse in insisting upon a trial", at para. 2 of *R. v. Hansen* (April 13, 1995), Doc. CA 17242, [1995] O.J. No. 1016 (C.A.). Note as well the brief passage at para. 5 of *R. v. Smith* (1997), [1997] O.J. No. 404, 1997 CarswellOnt 265 (C.A.): "... there is a serious error in principle having regard to the disparity between the sentence of 12 years imposed on the appellant and the sentence of three and one-half years imposed on the co-accused. While the appellant has a somewhat more serious criminal record, unlike the co-accused, he did not plead guilty. This did not justify an eight and one-half year difference." This appears to suggest, does it not, that it did justify some degree of disparity?

Consider also the endorsement of McMurtry, C.J.O., Robins and Charron, JJ.A., in *R. v. Jamieson* (1997), [1997] O.J. No. 1111, 1997 CarswellOnt 5825 (C.A.), at para. 2: "While the appellant is correct in his submission that lack of remorse and a plea of not guilty are not aggravating factors and should not have been identified as such by the sentencing judge ... the absence of these mitigating factors can properly be taken into account in determining the fitness of sentence."

See also para. 1(d) of *R. v. Fuentes* (1997), [1997] O.J. No. 1547, 1997 CarswellOnt 966 (C.A.) in which the Court of Appeal found inappropriate the trial judge's criticism of the appellant for pleading not guilty. To consider the conduct of the accused during trial as an aggravating circumstance was held to be an error in principle by the Court of Appeal in *R. v. Dragomir* (1998), [1998] O.J. No. 1907, 1998 CarswellOnt 1948 (C.A.), at para. 1.

Of interest, the rule has been applied to overturn a ruling of an administrative body imposing a harsher penalty by reason of a failure by the person charged with misconduct to acknowledge guilt. See *College of Physicians & Surgeons (Ontario) v. Gillen* (1990), 42 O.A.C. 173, 1 O.R. (3d) 710, [1990] O.J. No. 2280, 1990 CarswellOnt 851 (Div. Ct.), affirmed (1993), 1993 CarswellOnt 1836, 13 O.R. (3d) 385, 64 O.A.C. 83 (C.A.), at para. 4. Along the same lines, see *Brock-Berry v. Registered Nurses' Assn. (British Columbia)* (1995), [1995] B.C.J. No. 1876, 127 D.L.R. (4th) 674, 63 B.C.A.C. 198, 1995 CarswellBC 569, 12 B.C.L.R. (3d) 169, 104 W.A.C. 198, 34 Admin. L.R. (2d) 76 (C.A.), at para. 16.

A number of Ontario trial divisions are worthy of note, especially *R. v. Holder* (1998), 21 C.R. (5th) 277, [1998] O.J. No. 5102, 1998 CarswellOnt 4728 (Gen. Div.), at para. 21, that "In sentencing, an offender must not be punished because her testimony under oath was clearly disbelieved. This feature of the case, however, can serve to negate any other evidence of remorse", citing *R. v. Kozy, supra*.

The Court added, "An accused is not to be otherwise penalized for the manner of presenting the defence case". In the case at Bar, the Court found that the offender was undeserving of the leniency which is associated with a guilty plea. Hill J. repeated this instruction in *R. v. Hayes* (1999), [1999] O.J. No. 938, 1999 CarswellOnt 893, 95 O.T.C. 207 (Gen. Div.), at para. 29 and 31. See also para. 23-25 of *R. v. Raycraft* (1995), [1995] O.J. No. 3958, 1995 CarswellOnt 3620 (Gen. Div.) and para. 13 of *R. v. Walker* (1998), [1998] O.J. No. 3856, 1998 CarswellOnt 3723 (Gen. Div.).

My colleague, Mr. Justice Fraser, has interpreted the rule in these terms, having found that the accused fabricated a story in answer to the accusations: "... this finding is not to be given any weight at the sentencing stage except to negate any other evidence of remorse which might have been a mitigating factor in sentencing." Refer to para. 8 of *R. v. Deane* (1997), [1997] O.J. No. 3578, 1997 CarswellOnt 3431 (Prov. Div.), affirmed (2000), 2000 CarswellOnt 398, [2000] O.J. No. 403, 143 C.C.C. (3d) 84, 129 O.A.C. 335 (C.A.), affirmed 2001 CarswellOnt 119, 2001 CarswellOnt 120, 2001 SCC 5, 265 N.R. 1, 152 C.C.C. (3d) 96, 140 O.A.C. 269, [2001] 1 S.C.R. 279. Note as well *R. v. Frost* (January 4, 1991), Morrissey J. (Ont. Gen. Div.).

In addition, I wish to point out that Mr. Justice Kurisko, who had sentenced Mr. Kozy at trial, had occasion to apply the instruction of the Court of Appeal in a subsequent decision, *R. v. F. (M.)* (1993), [1993] O.J. No. 1568, 1993 CarswellOnt 3423 (Gen. Div.), affirmed (1994), 1994 CarswellOnt 3025 (C.A.), at para. 7. His Honour stated, "... no weight should have been given to the accused's conduct in his defence except to negate any other evidence of remorse which might have mitigated the fit sentence."

R. v. Nelson (2001), [2001] O.J. No. 2585, 2001 CarswellOnt 2297, 147 O.A.C. 358 (C.A.) is authority for the proposition that "Sentences cannot be increased to express disapproval of the conduct of the defence." Refer to para. 18.

Having noted the appellate level case law from outside of Ontario that was cited by Carthy J.A., it will be of assistance to review developments since the release of *R. v. Kozy, supra.*

B)   The application of the rule in Québec

In the Province of Québec, the Court of Appeal appears to have maintained the view that the conduct of the defence is not to be taken into account in the determination of a fit sentence. Nevertheless, a number of trial decisions suggest that it may be an appropriate foundation for denying a measure of leniency, particularly with respect to the granting of discharges.

Touching firstly the instruction of the Court of Appeal, in *R. v. Tait* (1992), [1992] Q.J. No. 874, 1992 CarswellQue 667 (C.A.), Fish J.A. remarked how the trial judge had not been impressed by the "shameless perjury" that the accused committed. Refer to para. 15. In His Lordship's opinion, this led to the selection of an extreme and unwarranted severe sentence. For the Court, Mr. Justice Fish agreed with the judgment in *R. v. Kozy, supra,* and held as well that the issue was resolved by the earlier decisions *R. v. Paradis, supra,* and *R. v. Maruska, supra.*

In a subsequent judgment, *R. c. Savard* (1998), [1998] Q.J. No. 4014, 1998 CarswellQue 3773 (C.A.), at para. 36-39, Mr. Justice Biron noted that the trial judge was of the view that the testimony of the accused, charged with multiple frauds, "flew in the face of an overwhelming testimonial and documentary case" and spoke volumes about his state of mind. This led the trial judge to conclude that the offender had not begun his rehabilitation. This conclusion was held to be contrary to the instruction found in the above-noted remarks from *R. v. Tait, supra*, and *R. v. Kozy, supra*. Of interest, the Court of Appeal observed that in considering the conduct of the accused, post-offence, it would be appropriate to evaluate not only the conduct at trial but the absence of further offences and other favourable steps towards rehabilitation such as employment, etc. Refer to para. 40.

Turning now to the judgments of the Superior Court, in *R. c. Abenaim*, [1996] A.Q. No. 1173, [1996] R.J.Q. 1911, 1996 CarswellQue 562 (S.C.), Mr. Justice Béliveau observed, "Il est évident qu'une sentence plus élévée ne peut être imposée du fait que le juge croit qu'un accusé a trompé la cour en témoignant", [[Translation] "It is trite to say that a sentence cannot be increased to reflect the trial judge's belief that the accused attempted to mislead the Court while testifying], citing *R. v. Johnston, supra*, and *R. v. Tait, supra*. Refer to para. 14.

At the next paragraph, the Court went on to ask itself whether the conduct of the accused may be a ground for refusing to grant a lenient disposition. Béliveau J. noted that the earlier judgment of *R. v. Paradis, supra*, the accused himself had not testified but had presented three alibi witnesses whose evidence was rejected and a fourth who attempted to accept responsibility for the accusations of attempted murder. His evidence was also disbelieved. Nevertheless, Mr. Justice Kaufman made plain that the accused cannot be sentenced for "an offence [perjury and conspiracy to commit perjury] for which he has not yet been convicted." Refer to p. 462 of *R. v. Paradis, supra*, and to para. 19 of *R. c. Abenaim, supra*.

Moreover, Béliveau J. remarked that although a more severe sentence may not be upheld on the basis of misconduct by the accused in his defence, it is nevertheless appropriate to weigh such misconduct in deciding whether a discharge ought to be granted. Refer to para. 20. Support for this view was found in the judgment of Mr. Justice Greenberg in *R. v. Sabloff*, [1979] C.S. 1077, 1979 CarswellQue 26, 13 C.R. (3d) 326 (S.C.), at p. 1079 [C.S.]: "Now, this Court obviously does not have the right or the function to punish [accused] for being untruthful in her evidence before the jury. However, it is certainly one factor to be considered as indicative of a need for incarceration for the purpose of rehabilitation." Of note, Greenberg J. had not concluded that the jury had found that she had perjured herself: "It was at worst perjury and at best a heavy shading of the truth, in an attempt to avoid conviction", as noted at para. 21 of *R. c. Abenaim, supra.*

Mr. Justice Béliveau also noted the further judgment of Greenberg J. in *R. c. Lévesque* (1980), 19 C.R. (3d) 43, 1980 CarswellQue 27 (S.C.) in which his colleague had observed that it was not within his province to punish the accused for perjury committed in the course of defending the accusations of sexual assault and kidnapping but that it was consonant with proper sentencing principles to remark how rehabilitation had not yet been achieved. Refer to p. 52 [C.R.], cited at para. 22 of *R. c. Abenaim, supra.*

Béliveau J. also found comfort for his conclusions in *R. v. Maraska, supra,* at p. 76. In that judgment, McCarthy J.A. did not criticize the trial judge's opinion that, on the one hand, the Court does not have the function or the right to punish the accused for being untruthful in his testimony and, on the other, "... it is certainly one factor to be considered as indicative of a need for incarceration for the purpose of rehabilitation."

At length, Mr. Justice Béliveau addressed the issue of the constitutional right to make full answer and defence and observed, "... la Charte ne confère pas non plus à l'accusé le droit de se parjurer." [Translation: "... the Charter does not grant to an accused the right to commit perjury.]

Returning to the narrow issue at hand, the merits of a discharge in the case of testimony that was rejected as being false and misleading, Mr. Justice Béliveau opined "La Cour ajoute que la possibilité de prendre en compte le parjure de l'accusé pour lui refuser la clémence peut se justifier encore davantage en matière d'absolution." [Translation: "The Court wishes to add that the possibility of taking into account perjury committed by the accused as a ground for denying leniency finds greater justification in cases of discharges.] Refer to para. 35.

His Honour remarked that the decision to grant or not a discharge requires an examination of the public interest. In that respect, the Court is bound to consider the credit that the criminal justice system enjoys in the eyes of a reasonable well-informed person, and how it might be diminished if leniency is awarded to a person who has attempted to mislead the Court. Mr. Justice Béliveau did add that it would be an error to interpret his judgment as the justification for refusing a discharge in such cases; in his view, misconduct must be considered as a factor in the selection of a fit sentence, together with all of the other relevant circumstances. Refer to para. 35.

Béliveau J. summarized his findings at para. 36. Firstly, perjury committed by the accused can never justify a sentence greater than what is appropriate in accordance with well-recognized principles. Secondly, perjury by an accused is a factor that a sentencing Court may consider in evaluating whether an offender is remorseful and, in the absence of remorse, it may be appropriate to refuse to mitigate the otherwise fit sentence. Thirdly, it is essential that a sentencing court exercise care in order to ensure that the application of the latter principle does not result in failing to honour the former. Fourthly, in the case of discharges, it is consonant with well-recognized sentencing principles to consider perjury by an accused in judging the public interest criterion but this factor need not be decisive. The Court added, as a fifth conclusion, that under no circumstances can the fact that the accused was found guilty after trial, and not by reason of a guilty plea, result in a decision to decline to grant a discharge. Lastly, the case-law in Québec supports the view that perjury by an accused is a factor that may be weighed in selecting the rehabilitative component of the sentence. His Honour repeated these factors in a subsequent judgment, *R. c. Rondeau* (1997), [1997] A.Q. No. 1841, 1997 CarswellQue 716 (S.C.), reversed (2000), 2000 CarswellQue 850 (C.A.), at para. 153.

In closing, note the insistence of the Court in *R. c. Abenaim, supra,* on the threshold finding that an accused committed palpable perjury, a factor repeated at para. 43 wherein the Court tracked the language of Carthy J.A. in *R. v. Kozy, supra,* "evidence ... palpably false" by contrast to "an accused shading the truth to protect himself from the charge". It remains to be seen whether palpable perjury committed by others called by the accused may lead to a refusal to exercise leniency or a decision to emphasize the need for rehabilitation.

C) The application of the rule in Alberta

What of the developments in Alberta? It will be instructive for counsel to note the many useful judgments discussed below. As noted previously, the Court of Appeal in *R. v. Sawchyn, supra,* held that it was not proper to treat misconduct as an aggravating factor attracting an additional sentence although it may be difficult to assign any mitigating value on the grounds of remorse in cases of misconduct. It will be of assistance to review the judgment at greater length.

Firstly, it is noteworthy that the misconduct of the accused was not an act of perjury—his misconduct was in attempting to intimidate or corrupt witnesses. He had not been prosecuted for these offences but merely failed to challenge these accusations in any way. Refer to p. 208 [C.C.C.], para. 28. The Court remarked that the Crown urged, as a result, a more severe sentence. This submission was rejected by Laycraft, J.A., on behalf of Chief Justice McGillivray and Holmes, J. (ad hoc). "Evidence of remorse, as for instance by a plea of guilty, will often justify reduction of a sentence below the level which would otherwise be appropriate for the offence committed. In my view, however, evidence of misconduct by an accused in the course of his defence cannot justify an increase in sentence beyond that which is appropriate for which he has been convicted." Refer to pp. 208-209, para. 29.

Support for this principle was found in the English Court of Appeal judgment of *R. v. Dunbar, supra*, and in the writings of Dr. D.A. Thomas, at p. 51 of *Principles of Sentencing* (Second Edition):

> Where a sentencer reacts to the manner in which the defence has been conducted by imposing a sentence in excess of what the facts of the offence warrant, the Court will normally reduce the sentence. ... Quashing the sentence the Court stated that if he was rightly convicted he lied to the police and the Court which convicted him ... this is a reason for not being especially lenient or merciful, and it might even be a reason for proceeding against him for perjury ... but it is a not a good reason for sending him to prison where the other circumstances of the case did not warrant such punishment. ... it is now a well established principle ... that behaviour of a defendant ... such as attacking a prosecution's witness's character or giving evidence which is or may amount to perjury is not a basis upon which what would otherwise be an appropriate sentence may be increased.

Refer to para. 32, p. 209 [C.C.C.].

In the next paragraph, Laycraft J.A. continued the analysis touching upon the possible loss of leniency. "Misconduct by an accused in the course of his defence may indirectly affect his sentence by negating the existence of remorse. A plea for leniency leading to a sentence lower than otherwise appropriate may fail because the misconduct will prove that the accused has no contrition for the offence committed and that the process of rehabilitation has not commenced." Refer to p. 209 [C.C.C.], para. 33.

His Lordship remarked that Mr. Clayton C. Ruby has criticized this rule in his book, but that Dr. Thomas agrees with a principle according to which an accused is not to be penalized in terms of his sentence for exercising his rights although he may lose some of the mitigation which would otherwise be attributable to remorse. Refer to *Principles of Sentencing, supra,* at p. 50 and to *Sentencing (Second Edition)* [Toronto: Butterworths, 1980), at p. 194.

As set out at pp. 209-210 [C.C.C.], para. 33, Mr. Ruby opined that "This is nevertheless a difficult principle to understand. If the sentence is to be longer because of lack of remorse (as indicated by the conduct of the defence), then there is very little difference between that indirect course of action and increasing sentence directly because of the conduct of the defence." Mr. Ruby submitted that the supposed distinction is illusory for either an accused is or is not penalized for that reason. He added, "... the above formulation looks suspiciously like an attempt to ride two horses at the same time."

Mr. Justice Laycraft responded to this criticism in these terms: "To adopt this submission is to say that an accused receives the same sentence whether or not he is remorseful. I respectfully disagree". Refer to p. 210 [C.C.C.], para. 34. Laycraft J.A. was of the view that "It is simply a fact that it will be much more difficult to perceive the existence of remorse where there has been misconduct in the defence." See p. 210 [C.C.C.], para. 34. His Lordship did add that Mr. Ruby's comments emphasize the care that must be taken by a Court to ensure that the absence of mitigating factors does not lead to a sentence higher than appropriate for the offence.

In sum, the Alberta Court of Appeal held that "It remains a valid principle that remorse, or indeed any other mitigating factor, justifies leniency; an accused who shows no remorse will, all other factors being equal, receive a higher sentence than an accused who does not. It is also a valid principle that an accused is not to receive a sentence higher than appropriate for the offence of which he has been convicted because of misconduct in his defence." I pause to emphasize that the Court went on to indicate that in such circumstances, an accused may lose the benefit of leniency arising from factors in mitigation. Again, see p. 210 C.C.C., para. 34. The Court disregarded the actions of the accused respecting the witnesses but did observe that he displayed no remorse for the offence he committed.

D) *The minority view: R. v. V. (J.T.) (1998), [1998] B.C.J. No. 549, 105 B.C.A.C. 42, 1998 CarswellBC 751, 171 W.A.C. 42 (C.A.)*

I have uncovered no further decision of the Alberta Court of Appeal, or of any other level from that province, in which these pronouncements had been challenged or distinguished. In fact, save for one notable exception, *R. v. Kozy*, *supra*, has been followed consistently by other courts, notably by the British Columbia Court of Appeal in *R. v. Dycko* (1997), 94 B.C.A.C. 177, [1997] B.C.J. No. 1502, 1997 CarswellBC 1327, 152 W.A.C. 177 (C.A.), at para. 3, wherein the Court criticized the trial judge for observing that the accused had "put the victim through the agony of a trial", holding that a plea of not guilty was his right and that no aggravating circumstance arose in the circumstances. See also *R. v. Dixon* (1991), 3 B.C.A.C. 228, [1991] B.C.J. No. 2786, 1991 CarswellBC 1107, 7 W.A.C. 228 (C.A.), *R. v. Martel* (July 30, 1986), Doc. GDC-6249, [1986] P.E.I.J. No. 70 (S.C.) and R. v. Reid (1997), [1997] O.J. No. 2167, 1997 CarswellOnt 1987 (Gen. Div.), varied (1999), 1999 CarswellOnt 2558 (C.A.).

The one significant exception is *R. v. V. (J.T.)* (1998), 105 B.C.A.C. 42, [1998] B.C.J. No. 549, 1998 CarswellBC 751, 171 W.A.C. 42 (C.A.), which is examined below.

In essence, it is held that *Kozy* is wrongly decided on the scope of defence tactics in cross-examination. On behalf of Finch and Donald, J.A., Mr. Justice Esson remarked that "... insofar as the judgment in *Kozy* depends on having resort to full answer and defence, it is wrong in law." Refer to para. 13. Mr. Vickers was accused of having taken part in a simulated robbery, that is to say a robbery that involved the willing participation of the victim. At trial, he testified that he had nothing to do with the matter, contradicting the testimony of the victim, who was co-operating with the prosecution.

Further, he called one B., who swore that he had committed the robbery. As noted at para. 4, "The neat defence came unraveled ... when the Crown [demonstrated that B. was in jail that day]. He justified that on the ground that he had forgotten he was in jail that day and, as far as he knew, his buddy [Vickers] didn't do it. 'He thought maybe by some miracle of the world you would believe me.'" Of course, Mr. Vickers was found guilty.

As recorded at para. 8, the trial judge was concerned that "Mr. Vickers sat in the witness box and, without batting an eye, lied to me under oath. ... And in addition to that, sat by and listened and watched Mr. B. commit perjury, and then clearly, through submissions made by counsel, I gather and I must infer, instructed you to submit that someone else must have committed this robbery." Of interest, the Court was prepared to find that the accused and Mr. B. had not collaborated on B.'s perjury.

The British Columbia Court of Appeal reviewed Mr. Justice Carthy's instruction in *R. v. Kozy, supra,* including the lengthy passages from *R. v. Sawchyn, supra.* Of especial interest, Esson J.A. set out the following observations from the judgment of Carthy, J.A., at para. 12 [p. 506 C.C.C.]:

> Just as an accused should never apprehend that a penalty will flow from a plea of not guilty, there should also be no perceived impingement upon the manner of presenting the defence. This is so whether it be counsel's viciousness in attacking a complainant or lies told by the accused. The latter may lead to its own penalty on a trial and conviction for perjury, but within the trial for the offence of sexual assault both rank as tactics of the defence, however ill-conceived and they are embraced within the right to full answer and defence. . .

Mr. Justice Esson responded, again at para. 12:

> That formulation has some rather startling implications and, in my respectful view, unnecessarily extends the scope of the right to make full answer and defence. Our law accords wide latitude to defence counsel but, except in the passage quoted above, I am not aware that it has been suggested that there are no limits on cross-examination. If counsel indulges in vicious and irrelevant attacks on a witness, the trial judge may interfere. If, as the passage implies, the accused has a constitutionally protected right to lie on the stand, it would follow that he could not be prosecuted for perjury. That cannot be the law.

At all events, having stated his concerns, Esson J.A. went on to make plain that the holding of the Ontario Court of Appeal was not necessary to reach the result it sought to achieve. "The whole of the ground covered by the argument based on full answer and defence is covered by the traditional formulation that the accused is not to be punished for a crime of which he has not been convicted..." Refer to para. 13 wherein Mr. Justice Laycraft's judgment in *R. v. Sawchyn, supra,* is reviewed. In the final analysis, Esson J.A. opined that "While I disagree with that aspect of the reasoning in *Kozy*, I accept in all other respects that it was correctly decided. If the references to full answer and defence were to be deleted, no other aspect of the decision would be affected." Refer to para. 15. His Lordship noted as well that "It is well settled that the rule against punishing an offender for a crime of which he was not convicted does not preclude all consideration of the conduct of the defence in determining sentence." Again, refer to para. 15.

h)   A summary for advocates

The present discussion has highlighted the difficulties in practice of avoiding that the right to make full answer and defence be undermined by the fear that the course of the defence may be held to have aggravated the sentence. Many thorny issues have been identified, notably the need for greater transparency in the allocation of aggravating weight in the decision to grant or not a discharge and the outstanding *Vickers* issue respecting the lengths to which defending counsel may go in conducting the defence.

2.   MITIGATION INHERENT IN SECONDARY PENALTIES:

a)   Introduction

An important step in advocating a fit sentence is to evaluate, if appropriate, the weight to be assigned to secondary penalties that might have resulted from the wrongdoing that serve to blunt (or to dismiss) the reach of denunciation or general deterrence. *R. v. Millar* (October 4, 1990), Charron J. (Ont. Gen. Div.) provides a compelling example of the loss suffered by an offender prior to the imposition of sentence. Shortly put, Mr. Millar killed his infant child by reason of shaking and pled guilty to criminal negligence causing death. He received a suspended sentence with probation for only one day in recognition of the pre-trial detention, the social opprobrium visited upon him, the lengthy separation from his family, and the crushing reality that he would face each new day of his life with the understanding that his actions led to the death of his beloved infant!

It is therefore incumbent upon counsel to identify the various elements that comprise this secondary penalty and to urge the sentencing court to assign appropriate mitigating weight to the "sanctions" that the offender has already been subjected to. These may include the as yet not felt consequences of a criminal record, without regard to the sentence.

b)   Sentencing requires a balancing of competing factors

At the outset, it will be useful to note the instruction provided by Mr. Justice LaForest in *R. v. L. (T.P.)*, [1987] S.C.J. No. 62, [1987] 2 S.C.R. 309, 44 D.L.R. (4th) 193, 80 N.R. 161, 82 N.S.R. (2d) 271, 37 C.C.C. (3d) 1, 61 C.R. (3d) 1, 32 C.R.R. 41, 207 A.P.R. 271, 1987 CarswellNS 41, 1987 CarswellNS 342, at p. 22 [C.C.C.], at para. 26, in addressing the various sentencing principles as they were known prior to the massive sentencing reform giving rise to the present Code provisions, in force as of September 3, 1996:

> In a rational system of sentencing, the respective importance of prevention, deterrence, retribution and rehabilitation will vary according to the nature of the crime and the circumstances of the offender. No one would suggest that any of these functional considerations should be excluded from the legitimate purview of legislative or judicial decisions regarding sentencing.

In other words, no single sentencing principle may trump one or all of the others save if the facts surrounding the offence and the offender permit the Court to conclude that it must be given priority. As made plain in *R. v. Luxton*, [1990] S.C.J. No. 87, [1990] 2 S.C.R. 711, 112 N.R. 193, [1990] 6 W.W.R. 137, 76 Alta. L.R. (2d) 43, 111 A.R. 161, 58 C.C.C. (3d) 449, 79 C.R. (3d) 193, 50 C.R.R. 175, 1990 CarswellAlta 144, 1990 CarswellAlta 658, it is of cardinal importance to structure a sentence to take into account the individual accused and the particular crime.

In this regard, it is suggested that the case law discussed in this section favours the view that a significant element of denunciation is present as a result of the speedy apprehension, public arrest, public trial and public imposition of a sentence, leaving aside entirely the penalties to be imposed. Stated otherwise, it is not necessary for the Court to select the same allocation of correctional resources in such cases, be they monetary penalties, periods of confinement, etc., in recognition of the fact that the offender has already been punished to a certain extent. As made plain in *R. v. Freedman* (1975), 25 C.C.C. (2d) 58 (Ont. C.A.), in order to protect the public, under our system of justice, "we do not rely only on a jail sentence but on the whole public process from investigation and arrest, including sentence, which process hopefully culminates in the rehabilitation of the offender and the deterrence to others".

c)   Punishment arising out of the mere fact of a public prosecution

Although it is not often characterized as such, and at times this factor is ignored in sentencing submissions, secondary penalties arise from the speedy apprehension, public arrest, public trial and public imposition of a sentence. In few words, the very fact of a trial amounts to punishment. Any punishment, it is suggested, must be assessed and weighed in conformity with the principle of proportionality found at s. 718.1.

In this vein, note the early case of *R. v. Code* (1908), 13 C.C.C. 372, 1 Sask. L.R. 295, 7 W.L.R. 814 (C.A.). The report records at page 373 [C.C.C.] that the offender was ordered to pay the Crown costs of $2.00 for the "rent of hall for holding court." The secondary punishments that are considered herein are of the same nature: costs or penalties that are incurred by an offender prior to, or independent of, the actual sentence but that serve to assess a sanction, albeit in indirect fashion. A further example is seen in *R. v. Schurman* (1914), 23 C.C.C. 365, 1914 CarswellSask 272, 7 Sask. L.R. 269, 7 W.W.R. 680, 19 D.L.R. 800 (C.A.). The offender was ordered to pay to the prosecution the costs of having himself transported to the jail. See page 302 [C.C.C.].

The first judgment that is of interest to us was penned by Dubin J.A., later the Chief Justice of Ontario, in the case of *R. v. Pearce* (1974), [1974] O.J. No. 1213, 16 C.C.C. (2d) 369 (C.A.). Although His Lordship's considered opinion did not rally the support of the two other members of the panel, it did serve to introduce an element of mitigation that had not been recognized in such direct terms previously. That denunciation arises in the eyes of the public merely by reason that the offender has been subjected to:

1)   speedy apprehension and arrest;

2)   a criminal record that resulted from the Court proceedings; and

3)   the fact that a custodial term will be imposed

By reason of the importance of the reasoning advanced, I have elected to quote from the judgment at length. Para. 14, p. 371 [C.C.C.] records that:

In giving effect to the principle of deterrence in sentencing, I do not think that the length of the term imposed is decisive. The knowledge of speedy apprehension and arrest, the imposition of a criminal record, and the fact that a custodial term will be imposed are also important considerations. It ought not to be overlooked that it is important that persons in prison who are to be released at some time will not return to a life of crime but will become self-supporting, capable of assuming new responsibilities and turn in the direction of becoming useful members of society. If a prison term is of such a length as to endanger the future rehabilitation of an accused, then the term of imprisonment imposed on him will not protect society in the future. Therefore, there has to be a balance between what is appropriate as a punishment and as a deterrent with the recognition that the accused will be released at some time. At the age of 23 this man is at a critical stage of his life when one considers his chances of learning a trade, settling into a family life and establishing his roots.

Dubin J.A., added, at para. 15, p. 271 [C.C.C.]:

In my view a sentence of four years imprisonment for a first offender is not a lenient sentence, but a heavy sentence. It is a long term for a young man. Any longer term is one which I fear may require him to be maintained in the penitentiary beyond the time when the discipline and training that he will receive and which he requires will continue to be effective. Any longer term, in my opinion, would likely result in his inability to reconstruct his life, and reduce his incentive to reform.

Although this opinion did not question the need for a prison term, the principle advanced has been applied and refined over the years, as will be seen. At present, denunciation is inherent in the eyes of the public by reason of the "knowledge of speedy apprehension and arrest, of trial, the imposition of a criminal record, and potentially of a jail sentence". See *R. v. C. (S.P.)* (October 26, 1998), Stroud J., [1998] N.S.J. No. 451 (Prov. Ct.) at para. 15. In fact, the judgment is so well-regarded by reason of subsequent application in further decisions that it is often overlooked that Mr. Justice Dubin was in the minority with respect to the result.

The next important judgment in this line of cases also dates back to 1974, *R. v. Meneses* (1974), [1974] O.J. No. 736, 25 C.C.C. (2d) 115 (C.A.). On behalf of Gale C.J.O. and Kelly J.A., Dubin J.A. remarked, at para. 10, p. 117:

The argument that a conviction and fine against this accused must stand to effect a more apparent deterrent to others must give way when other considerations are more paramount, and when the broad view of the public interest is considered. In our opinion, the knowledge of speedy apprehension, arrest and trial should be an effective deterrent to persons such as the accused who may be tempted to commit such an offence. A conviction and a fine would not be a deterrent to a professional shoplifter, but, of course, such a person would not receive either an absolute or conditional discharge.

Two things are noteworthy. Firstly, the remarks set out above represent the unanimous view of the Court of Appeal. Secondly, the refinement of "speedy apprehension, arrest and trial" was brought about by reason of the minor nature of the accusation. Nevertheless, the Court made plain that deterrence is served by the process of the Court even prior to the imposition of the sentence. Refer as well to *R. v. Totten* (July 9, 1992), Vaillancourt Prov. J., [1992] O.J. No. 2805 (Prov. Div.), R. v. Deschamps (April 4, 1989), Doc. Nipissing DC 712/89, [1989] O.J. No. 936 (Dist. Ct.), R. v. Dash (1990), [1990] O.J. No. 2398, 1990 CarswellOnt 1517 (Gen. Div.), *R. v. Khan* (November 10, 1975), Gale C.J.O., Dubin J.A., MacKinnon J.A., [1975] O.J. No. 1039 (C.A.) and to *R. v. Liu* (1996), [1996] O.J. No. 2908, 1996 CarswellOnt 2993 (Prov. Div.).

That the application of the "speedy apprehension, arrest and public trial" principle remained controversial was made plain the next year in *R. v. Prieduls* (May 27, 1975), Brooke J.A., Dubin J.A., Lacourciere J.A., [1975] O.J. No. 589 (C.A.). Dubin J.A. had occasion to consign these remarks in his dissenting judgment:

However, in my opinion, the knowledge of speedy apprehension, arrest and trial, and the fact that for an offence such as this even a first offender will carry with him a criminal record and a term of imprisonment, should be an effective deterrent to persons such as the accused who may be tempted to commit such an offence in the future. The sentence imposed by the provincial judge would not be a deterrent to professional criminals, who would, of course, receive a more severe sentence.

His Lordship added, at para. 8:

To uphold the sentence imposed by the provincial judge could result in the accused being unable to continue his education in an orderly fashion and could have severe consequences upon his future. In my opinion the public interest could best be served by imposing a shorter term of imprisonment plus a period of probation. It is never to be overlooked that a person on probation is not a free man during his term. He is under supervision and must earn his ultimate freedom. In my opinion society can best be protected in a case such as this by a shorter term of imprisonment with a lengthy term of probation. Nothing will be gained, in my opinion, by insisting that the accused serve a longer term in prison than the term I would have imposed, and the longer term could entail an unnecessary risk for his future.

The next case that is worthy of attention is *R. v. Demeter* (1976), 3 C.R. (3d) S-55, 32 C.C.C. (2d) 379, 1976 CarswellOnt 31 (C.A.), a striking example of conduct said to be "completely out of character". The youthful offenders robbed a pizzeria while brandishing an unloaded pellet gun. It appears that their object was not the $265.00 stolen, but to satisfy some sort of challenge. "A pre-sentence report gave a favourable prognosis as to his being able to respond under probation supervision." Refer to page S-56 [C.R.], p. 380 [C.C.C.].

Dubin J.A., as he then was, observed further: "In considering what is an appropriate sentence for the very young, the paramount consideration must be their immediate rehabilitation. Speedy apprehension, arrest, public trial and a criminal record, with its consequences, should be the best deterrent for those young persons who may be tempted to commit an offence such as this." Refer to page S-57 [C.R.], pp. 381-382 [C.C.C.]. Hence, the Court concluded that "...a short custodial term followed by a period of probation, in my opinion, affords the best prospect for their immediate rehabilitation, and if that is accomplished, the protection of the public and the interests of society are best served." Refer to p. 382 [C.C.C.]. See *R. v. M. (N.)* (1991), [1991] O.J. No. 2406, 1991 CarswellOnt 2035 (Gen. Div.), R. v. O. (J.) (1992), [1992] O.J. No. 680, 1992 CarswellOnt 3090 (Gen. Div.) and R. v. P. (C.) (December 9, 1991), Vaillancourt Prov. J., [1991] O.J. No. 2519 (Prov. Div.).

R. v. C. (V.K.) (November 5, 1976), Dubin J.A., Houlden J.A., Blair J.A., [1976] O.J. No. 1032 (C.A.) is also apposite. The judgment includes these remarks, at para. 4:

> This is a case of two young men alone in this country, in strange surroundings. Although they had access to a distant relative, they had no parental guidance. They made a serious mistake. The issue is whether a conviction and suspended sentence

must stand as a deterrent to others of like mind, notwithstanding the apparent serious consequences that a criminal record will have on the future of these two young men. We do not think that a suspended sentence is a greater deterrent to youths that may be tempted to steal than a discharge, certainly not a conditional discharge with probation. The fact of speedy apprehension, arrest and trial with the public disgrace and jeopardy which is thereby occasioned should be a sufficient deterrent, and the future of these two young men need not be jeopardized by insisting that they bear a criminal record. The purpose of the introduction by Parliament of the provision for absolute and conditional discharges is to permit the Court in appropriate cases to. . .

Yet another 1976 judgment on this point is *R. v. D. (M.)* (November 19, 1976), Dubin J.A., Houlden J.A., Blair J.A., [1976] O.J. No. 1129 (C.A.). As noted at para. 9: "In considering what an appropriate sentence is for the very young, the paramount consideration must be their immediate rehabilitation. Speedy apprehension, arrest, public trial and a criminal record, with its consequences, should be the best deterrent for those young persons who may be tempted to commit an offence such as this."

Consider also the guidance found in *R. v. Jover* (1977), 41 C.C.C. (2d) 24, 1977 CarswellOnt 1199 (Prov. Ct.). The accused was a 16-year-old boy who was being sentenced for pointing a firearm. In completely innocent circumstances, while "fooling around" with his close friend, a rifle which he had pointed at the friend went off and the friend was killed. Having reviewed in some detail the sad facts of the case and the applicable law, Nosanchuk P.C.J. remarked, at pp. 30-31:

It must be observed that the prosecution, in any case, took the view that it was not opposed to a conviction and a suspended sentence. In this respect, I refer to the case of *R. v. Cheung and Chow* (1976-77), 19 Crim. L.Q. 281, a decision of the Ontario Court of Appeal. [Cited earlier as *R. v. V.K.C.*, [1976] O.J. No. 1032 (C.A.)] In that case—that case did involve a theft of items from a store, totalling approximately $30. The Court of Appeal, in that case held that the Provincial Judge erred in failing to grant a discharge, merely because more than one item of goods were taken. The Court went on to say as follows, and this is pertinent to the submission of the Crown in this case:

A suspended sentence is not a greater deterrent to youths tempted to steal than a discharge, certainly not a conditional discharge. Speedy apprehension, arrest and trial with the public disgrace and jeopardy which is occasioned should be sufficient deterrent. The purpose of the provisions for discharges is to permit the Court in appropriate cases to relieve a person of a criminal record and the consequences which may far outweigh the gravity of the offence.

In my opinion, the public interest does not only necessarily restrict to a punitive interest, but in appropriate cases can involve dealing humanely with the unique circumstances of any case, and in this case, where there is no element of hostility between the accused and the deceased, where the offence is entirely, as I believe it to be, a technical pointing, where the consequences were not in [the] mind of the accused at all, and were entirely consistent, as the Crown pointed out, with the matter being a horrible accident, it is, in such circumstances, to the public interest that the accused be granted a discharge.

As well, note the comment of Robert J.A. in *R. c. Scraire* (1998), 132 C.C.C. (3d) 210, 1998 CarswellQue 4560, [1998] Q.J. No. 3659, [1999] R.J.Q. 89, 10 M.V.R. (4th) 48 (C.A.), wherein he stated at p. 217: "In the case at bar, it is difficult to see how imprisonment, which would necessarily force the appellant to suspend his studies and to leave his job, would be of any use to him or to society in general." Full text is also available in French, [1998] A.Q. No. 3659.

Reference may also be made to *R. c. Gaudreault* (21 mars 2000), no Québec 200-36-000729-996, [2000] J.Q. No. 1228 (C.S.) at para. 10: "Le tribunal adhère à la position de la Cour d'appel de l'Ontario qui, dans *R. c. Cheung and Chow*, (1977) 19 C.L.Q. 280 [cited earlier as *R. v. C. (V.K.)* (November 5, 1976), Dubin J.A., Houlden J.A., Blair J.A., [1976] O.J. No. 1032 (C.A.)] a dit: "A suspended sentence is not a greater deterrent to youths tempted to steal than a discharge, certainly not a conditional discharge. Speedy apprehension, arrest and trial with the public disgrace and jeopardy which is occasioned should be sufficient deterrent." Refer as well to *R. v. Bigg* (January 12, 1994), Doc. North Vancouver 24993, [1994] B.C.J. No. 174 (Prov. Ct.), at para. 14.

The judgment in *R. v. Robinson* (1993), [1993] M.J. No. 509, 88 Man. R. (2d) 191, 51 W.A.C. 191, 1993 CarswellMan 251 (C.A.). Para. 7 records:

In balancing the public interest against the offender's needs, a sentencing judge should bear in mind that the reformation of a criminal is the best guarantee against recidivism. Where there is a real prospect of rehabilitating an offender, a conscious effort should be made to avoid a sentence which might be counterproductive to that end. This is particularly true where the offender is very young. In *R. v. McCormick*, [1979] M.J. No. 21, 47 C.C.C. (2d) 224, [1979] 4 W.W.R. 453, 7 Man. R. (2d) 30, 9 C.R. (3d) 248 (C.A.), the majority quoted with approval the following passage from the judgment of Dubin, J.A. (as he then was) in *R. v. Demeter* (1976), 32 C.C.C. (2d) 379 (Ont. C.A.) at p. 381:

> In considering what an appropriate sentence is for the very young, the paramount consideration must be their immediate rehabilitation. Speedy apprehension, arrest, public trial and a criminal record, with its consequences, should be the best deterrent for those young persons who may be tempted to commit an offence such as this.

Please note that in *R. v. McCormick*, the Court added these comments at para. 21: "I agree with Dubin, J.A., that the criminal record itself, and the consequences which it carries, becomes part of the punishment, and should be so considered by the judge imposing sentence."

Subsequently, the Manitoba Court of Appeal provided further instruction. In *R. v. Leask* (1996), *[1996] M.J. No. 587,* 113 Man.R. (2d) 265, 131 W.A.C. 265, 112 C.C.C. (3d) 400, 1996 CarswellMan 577 (C.A.), additional reasons at (1996), 1996 CarswellMan 576, 112 C.C.C. (3d) 400 at 405, 113 Man. R. (2d) 265 at 269, 131 W.A.C. 265 at 269 (C.A.), Twaddle J.A. observed, at para. 1: "Three very young adult offenders without prior criminal involvement appeal from a sentence of one year's imprisonment imposed on each of them for a brutal assault causing bodily harm to a stranger. The issue is whether the sentencing judge sacrificed the rehabilitation of these young men to the need for deterrence." In the next paragraph, the Court observed, "The governing principle in a case like this, approved repeatedly by this Court, is that stated by Dubin J.A. (as he then was) in *R. v. Demeter* (1976), 32 C.C.C. (2d) 379, 1976 CarswellOnt 31, 3 C.R. (3d) S-55 (C.A.) at pp. 381- 382 [C.C.C.]:

> In considering what an appropriate sentence is for the very young, the paramount consideration must be their immediate rehabilitation. Speedy apprehension, arrest, public trial and a criminal record, with its consequences, should be the best deterrent for those young persons who may be tempted to commit an offence such as this.

Of interest, note the comments consigned at para. 3: "Obviously, the principle is not absolute. Some offences are so serious that even extreme youth is not a ground for leniency and some offenders will have demonstrated by their past conduct that they are not entitled to it. But the transition from statutorily-defined young person to adult should not be marked by an immediate abandonment of rehabilitation as the primary goal in cases where the prospect of successful rehabilitation is real."

Consider as well some of the submissions noted by the Court of Appeal in *R. v. Pierce* (1997), [1997] O.J. No. 715, 97 O.A.C. 253, 1997 CarswellOnt 682, 32 O.R. (3d) 321, 5 C.R. (5th) 171, 114 C.C.C. (3d) 23 (C.A.), leave to appeal refused (1997), 105 O.A.C. 319 (note), 224 N.R. 154 (note), 34 O.R. (3d) xv, 117 C.C.C. (3d) vi (S.C.C.), at para. 33: "In response, and as an alternative to the Crown's interpretation of 'safety of the community', counsel for the appellant submits that the imposition of a conditional sentence does result in the creation of general deterrence. He refers to the recognized deterrent effect resulting from arrest, public trial, conviction, impediments to future employment and a criminal record."

A further judgment that is worthy of attention is *R. v. S. (M.L.)*, [2000] M.J. No. 490, 153 Man. R. (2d) 61, 238 W.A.C. 61, [2001] 2 W.W.R. 262, 149 C.C.C. (3d) 410, 2000 CarswellMan 541, 2000 MBCA 112 (C.A.). Reference is made at para. 9 to *R. v. Robinson*, at para. 7, quoted earlier.

That the mere fact of the proceedings may import punishment, and at times significant if not sufficient punishment, has been discussed in other recent cases. For example, the Court of Appeal imposed a nominal penalty to mark the fact that the "secondary" penalties that an offender had incurred under this heading, leaving aside the cost and time involved in defending the accusation, in *R. v. Seaway Gas & Fuel Ltd.* (2000), [2000] O.J. No. 226, 47 O.R. (3d) 458 (Eng.), 128 O.A.C. 268, 2000 CarswellOnt 163, 142 C.C.C. (3d) 213, 183 D.L.R. (4th) 412, 47 O.R. (3d) 468 (Fr.) (C.A.). Refer to para. 45. In the circumstances, an absolute discharge was imposed in the case of sales of cigarettes to minors.

Note also para. 51 of *R. v. Beyo* (2000), [2000] O.J. No. 888, 47 O.R. (3d) 712, 131 O.A.C. 150, 144 C.C.C. (3d) 15, 2000 CarswellOnt 838 (C.A.), leave to appeal refused 2000 CarswellOnt 3927, 2000 CarswellOnt 3928, [2000] S.C.C.A. No. 239, 263 N.R. 392 (note), 145 O.A.C. 198 (note), [2000] 2 S.C.R. vi. "The appellant was given a conditional discharge on that count. It is now over eight years since these events and the appellant has been through a preliminary inquiry and two trials. Accordingly, I would allow the appeal from the finding of guilt ... set aside the verdict, order a new trial and enter a stay of proceedings...".

d)   "Dead time": Mitigation as a result of secondary penalties associated with pre-trial detention:

i)   Introduction

If it is well understood that secondary penalties blunt the need for the assignment of correctional resources by reason of the fact that the offender has already been made to "suffer" some punishment, it will be of advantage to examine the most common example of this form of alternative penalty: pre-trial detention or "dead time".

In this situation, the offender has been jailed already. Moreover, s/he has had to undergo more difficult imprisonment by reason of the absence of programs, the denial of leave or opportunities for employment or education outside of the institution, the uncertainty surrounding the date of release, the lack of early release and remission, added to the burdens inherent in incarceration notably overcrowding. In other words, not unlike the situation involving public trials discussed above, the offender who is made to undergo pre-trial detention necessarily suffers some element of punishment, prior to the formal imposition of sentence, and that it is the duty of counsel to advocate for the proper recognition of this secondary penalty.

ii)   The recent instruction of the Supreme Court of Canada

"Dead time", as it is often referred to, has been the subject of consideration by the Supreme Court of Canada of late, and it will be of assistance to review briefly the instruction received in *R. v. W. (L.W.)*, (*sub nom.* R. v. Wust) [2000] S.C.J. No. 19, [2000] 1 S.C.R. 455, 184 D.L.R. (4th) 385, 252 N.R. 332, 134 B.C.A.C. 236, 143 C.C.C. (3d) 129, 32 C.R. (5th) 58, 219 W.A.C. 236, 2000 CarswellBC 749, 2000 CarswellBC 750, 2000 SCC 18, *R. v. W. (L.W.)*, [2000] S.C.J. No. 21, (*sub nom.* R. v. Arrance) [2000] 1 S.C.R. 488, (*sub nom.* R. v. Arrance) 184 D.L.R. (4th) 410, (*sub nom.* R. v. Arrance) 252 N.R. 319, (*sub nom.* R. v. A. (C.R.)) 134 B.C.A.C. 268, (*sub nom.* R. v. Arrance) 143 C.C.C.

(3d) 154, (*sub nom.* R. v. A. (C.R.)) 219 W.A.C. 268, 2000 CarswellBC 747, 2000 CarswellBC 748, (*sub nom.* R. v. Arrance) 2000 SCC 20, and *R. v. W. (L.W.)*, [2000] S.C.J. No. 20, (*sub nom.* R. v. Arthurs) [2000] 1 S.C.R. 481, (*sub nom.* R. v. Arthurs) 184 D.L.R. (4th) 405, (*sub nom.* R. v. Arthurs) 252 N.R. 325, (*sub nom.* R. v. Arthurs) 134 B.C.A.C. 274, (*sub nom.* R. v. Arthurs) 143 C.C.C. (3d) 149, (*sub nom.* R. v. Arthurs) 219 W.A.C. 274, 2000 CarswellBC 745, 2000 CarswellBC 746, (*sub nom.* R. v. Arthurs) 2000 SCC 19.

At para. 45 of *R. v. W. (L.W.)*, *supra*, Arbour J. remarked that "[i]n the past, many judges have given more or less two months credit for each month spent in pre-sentencing detention. This is entirely appropriate even though a different ratio could also be applied...". Of note, in *R. v. W. (L.W.)*, *supra*, the sentence imposed at trial was reinstated. The trial judge had granted the appellant one year credit for his seven months of pre-sentencing custody. Refer to para. 46. In other words, the denial of two-for-one credit was upheld, as a matter of discretion.

iii)   The normal rule is for credit on a "two for one" basis

The instruction of the Supreme Court of Canada therefore is to the effect that it is entirely appropriate to grant enhanced credit on a two-for-one basis for trial detention, though a different ratio could also be applied. What is of interest, however, is that appellate courts appear to have selected "two for one" as the norm.

Indeed, as we read in a judgment that preceded *R. v. W. (L.W.)*, *supra*, "The normal rule is that credit is given on a two-for-one basis for pre-trial custody." This is the view advanced by McMurtry C.J.O., Doherty and Rosenberg JJ.A. at para. 2 of *R. v. Warren* (1999), [1999] O.J. No. 4591, 127 O.A.C. 193, 1999 CarswellOnt 3950 (C.A.). Of note, the question of the credit to be assigned was squarely before the Court for para. 1 sets out that the first issue was whether the trial judge erred in principle in the manner in which he dealt with pre-trial custody.

It will be of assistance to consider briefly at this stage a number of pre-*W. (L.W.)* judgments to then refer to post- *W. (L.W.)* judgments in order to demonstrate the strength of this view respecting secondary penalties.

Mr. Justice Laskin noted at para. 25 of *R. v. Rezaie* (1996), [1996] O.J. No. 4468, 96 O.A.C. 268, 31 O.R. (3d) 713, 112 C.C.C. (3d) 97, 3 C.R. (5th) 175, 1996 CarswellOnt 4753 (C.A.), that "...trial judges, in deciding on an appropriate sentence, frequently give credit for double the time an accused has served."

At para. 16 of *R. v. K. (M.)* (1996), [1996] O.J. No. 1587, 90 O.A.C. 394, 28 O.R. (3d) 593, 107 C.C.C. (3d) 149, 1996 CarswellOnt 1677 (C.A.), the Court of Appeal held "...if the appellant were to receive what is sometimes regarded as an appropriate credit, namely a multiplier of two for the "dead time" of pre-trial custody...".

At para. 11 of *R. v. McDonald* (1998), [1998] O.J. No. 2990, 111 O.A.C. 25, 40 O.R. (3d) 641, 127 C.C.C. (3d) 57, 17 C.R. (5th) 1, 54 C.R.R. (2d) 189, 1998 CarswellOnt 3025 (C.A.), Rosenberg J.A. remarked, "[b]earing in mind that trial judges will often give credit of two days for each day spent in pre-trial custody...". His Lordship added at para. 65:

> Under s. 719(3), it is left to the sentencing court to "take into account" any pre-sentence custody "in determining the sentence". The subsection does not provide any fixed rule as to how much credit should be taken into account. For the reasons expressed by Professor Friedland, Mr. Trotter and Laskin, J.A., in *R. v. Rezaie*, trial judges generally give double credit for pre-sentence custody. I see no reason to depart from this practice, where appropriate, in cases of minimum punishment, although the sentence imposed would be less than four years. I appreciate that this injects a certain imprecision in the sentencing. On the other hand, such a lack of precision already exists where the proposed sentence far exceeds four years and the trial judge intends to give credit for pre-sentence custody. The sentencing judge will, however, have to be satisfied that when the proposed sentence and the pre-sentence custody are combined, the effective "punishment" is at least four years. Moreover, the sentencing judge is not bound to give credit for the full period of pre-sentence custody. And, of course, the judge is entitled to impose more than the minimum four year sentence.

For example, in *R. v. Thompson* (2000), [2000] O.J. No. 2270, 133 O.A.C. 126, 146 C.C.C. (3d) 128, 2000 CarswellOnt 2097 (C.A.), it was noted that the offender "...should have received credit on a two-for-one basis ... for the time served in pre-trial custody." Refer to para. 81. It noted as well that no cogent reasons were disclosed to deny credit on a two-for-one basis. It seems that the Court was influenced greatly by the fact that the offender sought to serve his 14-month period of pre-trial detention in a federal institution and that the denial of this request resulted in depriving him of the opportunity of engaging in programs of education, retraining and rehabilitation. Refer again to para. 81.

Many other examples are known of such enhanced credit. In *R. v. S. (D.C.)* (2000), [2000] O.J. No. 885, 47 O.R. (3d) 612, 131 O.A.C. 396, 2000 CarswellOnt 840 (C.A.) the Court remarked at para. 1, "...if the usual two-for-one credit had been given...". In *R. v. Quance* (2000), [2000] O.J. No. 2243, 133 O.A.C. 276, 146 C.C.C. (3d) 153, 2000 CarswellOnt 2066 (C.A.) the Court of Appeal noted without adverse comment that 18 months of pre-trial detention was credited as the equivalent of three years. See para. 37. In *R. v. Zhang* (2000), [2000] O.J. No. 1617, 132 O.A.C. 159, 2000 CarswellOnt 1548 (C.A.), as set out at para. 28, credit is given on a two-for-one basis. In *R. v. Davy* (2000), [2000] O.J. No. 3519, 137 O.A.C. 53, 2000 CarswellOnt 3397 (C.A.), at para. 29, the two-for-one credit was not criticized. The same comment applies to para. 2 of *R. v. F. (J.S.)* (2000), [2000] O.J. No. 3316, 135 O.A.C. 396, 2000 CarswellOnt 3079 (C.A.), leave to appeal refused (2001), 2001 CarswellOnt 866, 2001 CarswellOnt 867, 268 N.R. 400 (note), 149 O.A.C. 392 (note) (S.C.C.). In *R. v. Bates* (2000), [2000] O.J. No. 2558, 134 O.A.C. 156, 146 C.C.C. (3d) 321, 35 C.R. (5th) 327, 2000 CarswellOnt 2360 (C.A.), para. 2 also records an instance of two-for-one credit being noted without adverse comment.

In *R. v. Allison-McLeish* (2000), [2001] O.J. No. 845, 2001 CarswellOnt 653, 142 O.A.C. 50 (C.A.), the offender was convicted of robbery and sentenced to three and one-half years' imprisonment. As set out at para. 12, "The trial judge was of the view that a sentence of five years' imprisonment was appropriate. He imposed a sentence of three and one-half years' imprisonment after giving the appellant credit for nine months of pre-trial custody." In other words, nine months of dead time was reckoned to be the equivalent of 18 months, a two-for-one credit.

Note as well *R. v. Nelson* (2001), [2001] O.J. No. 2585, 147 O.A.C. 358, 2001 CarswellOnt 2297 (C.A.), at para. 14: "Assuming the usual two-for-one credit given for pre-trial custody...". The Court went on to assign such credit, criticizing the trial judge's refusal to grant enhanced credit on the theory that the offender's defence disentitled him to such leniency. See para. 18. As made plain, "...there is no connection between the reason credit is given for pre-trial custody and the trial judge's conclusion that an accused has advanced a 'perjurious defence'."

In *R. v. Burke* (2001), [2001] O.J. No. 1119, 143 O.A.C. 286, 2001 CarswellOnt 929, 41 C.R. (5th) 134, 153 C.C.C. (3d) 97, 53 O.R. (3d) 600, 61 O.R. (3d) 256 (note) (C.A.), reversed 2002 CarswellOnt 1970, 2002 CarswellOnt 1971, 2002 SCC 55, 164 C.C.C. (3d) 385, 213 D.L.R. (4th) 234, 2 C.R. (6th) 1, 290 N.R. 71, 160 O.A.C. 271, [2002] 2 S.C.R.

857, the Court of Appeal indirectly commented that the offender received credit on a two-for-one basis. See para. 51. See also *R. v. Melanson* (2001), [2001] O.J. No. 869, 152 C.C.C. (3d) 375, 142 O.A.C. 184, 2001 CarswellOnt 657 (C.A.), additional reasons at (2001), [2001] O.J. No. 1500, 2001 CarswellOnt 1319 (C.A.), leave to appeal refused (2001), 2001 CarswellOnt 3797, 2001 CarswellOnt 3798, 284 N.R. 196 (note), 158 O.A.C. 200 (note) (S.C.C.), *R. v. Coelho* (2001), [2001] O.J. No. 2866, 148 O.A.C. 83, 2001 CarswellOnt 2501, 13 M.V.R. (4th) 171 (C.A.), *R. v. Hall* (2001), [2001] O.J. No. 3704, 2001 CarswellOnt 3241 (C.A.), and *R. v. Higginbottom* (2001), [2001] O.J. No. 2742, 156 C.C.C. (3d) 178, 2001 CarswellOnt 2343, 150 O.A.C. 79 (C.A.).

An interesting situation may arise in the case of a conviction arising on a re-trial if the accused had been incarcerated at the conclusion of the first. See *R. v. Sabourin* (2001), [2001] O.J. No. 4649, 2001 CarswellOnt 4254 (C.A.), at para. 4: "In considering whether to proceed with a new trial, the Crown will no doubt take into account that the appellant has already served the sentence imposed." Should the offender be re-tried and further convicted, the prior period of detention would no doubt receive enhanced credit, chiefly due to the reluctance to re-incarcerate offenders who have undertaken rehabilitative steps. In such a case, however, it would be necessary to take into account the fact that there was an opportunity to participate in programs, and that remission and parole might have been at play. In sum, in calculating "dead time", credit must be given for any period of time spent in custody following conviction, and prior to a new trial being ordered on appeal.

The Court of Appeal remarked at para. 9 of *R. v. DaSilva* (2002), [2002] O.J. No. 4695, 166 O.A.C. 295, 2002 CarswellOnt 4159 (C.A.). "We cannot be certain that [the trial judge] gave the appellants credit as he intended to do, and we see no reason credit should not be given to the appellants at the customary two-for-one rate."

Para. 5 of *R. v. Clarke* (2003), [2003] O.J. No. 1966, 2003 CarswellOnt 1922, 172 O.A.C. 133 (C.A.) underscores these additional penalties in this fashion: "The considerations respecting two-for-one credit for pre-trial detention all apply here. Pre-trial custody cannot be used to earn remission towards parole; there are few rehabilitative programs available in detention centres, and the conditions in detention facilities are more crowded than in correctional facilities such as penitentiaries." See also *R. v. White* (2003), [2003] O.J. No. 2544, 2003 CarswellOnt 4106, 176 C.C.C. (3d) 396 (C.A.) and *R. v. Camkiran* (2003), [2003] O.J. No. 703, 2003 CarswellOnt 670 (C.A.) which includes the brief observations at para. 1: "In all the circumstances, in our view the appeal from sentence should be allowed by varying the sentence in order to give two-for-one credit for pre-trial custody." Nothing else is known of the facts.

In addition, recent instruction from the Court of Appeal is of interest. *R. v. Fice* (2003), [2003] O.J. No. 2617, 2003 CarswellOnt 2494, 13 C.R. (6th) 174, 65 O.R. (3d) 751, 177 C.C.C. (3d) 566 (C.A.) settles the question whether it is open to a sentencing judge to take into account pre-sentence custody in determining whether the sentence to be imposed falls within the range of sentences that engages the conditional sentencing regime. The Court of Appeal held that it is open to a trial judge to do so. It is not without interest to set out Her Ladyship's remarks at para. 21 that "This methodology may of course result in situations in which an offence that would normally merit a penitentiary sentence instead garners a conditional sentence because of the effect of pre-sentence custody." Such a result, we are told, is not unacceptable.

> It is not in my view absurd to allow that the appropriate range of sentence may change depending on the presence of pre-sentence custody. There are many factors to be taken into account in sentencing, of which pre-sentence custody may be one pursuant to s. 719(3), and a variation in any of the factors may result in a different appropriate range of sentence. Where a particular offender has served a substantial amount of time in pre-sentence custody, it might not be appropriate, in the view of the sentencing judge, for that offender to receive a sentence in the penitentiary range.

Para. 21 goes on to remark that a sentencing judge might conclude, given that pre-sentence custody is often served in harsher circumstances than the punishment ultimately calls for . . . that a penitentiary term would no longer be proportionate to the offence.

Of further interest, the Court of Appeal went on to highlight that even after concluding that the appropriate range of sentence is a term of imprisonment of less than two years, a sentencing judge would still have to be satisfied that a conditional sentence would not endanger the safety of the community and would be consistent with the fundamental purpose and principles of sentencing. This result will be less likely where the offence is one that would merit a penitentiary term, absent the pre-sentence custody. Refer to para. 22 and to *R. v. Persaud* (2002), 26 M.V.R. (4th) 41, 2002 CarswellOnt 1596, [2002] O.J. No. 1883, 159 O.A.C. 134 (C.A.) and the observation at para. 1 that "it will be the rare and exceptional case that a trial judge, who is otherwise of the view that a penitentiary sentence is warranted, will ultimately impose a conditional sentence after factoring in time spent in pre-trial custody."

R. v. Keevil (2003), [2003] O.J. No. 112, 2003 CarswellOnt 113, 167 O.A.C. 329 (C.A.) is of interest in upholding a total sentence of seven years and nine months, after giving credit on a two-for-one basis for the 326 days he had served in pre-trial custody, for a slew of offences including six break and enters of residential properties, possession of a stolen vehicle, and aggravated assault endangering life, dangerous driving, possession of property obtained by the commission of a crime with a value under $5000 (x3), possession of a controlled substance (*Controlled Drugs and Substance Act*) and failure to stop (*Highway Traffic Act*). Refer to paras. 1-2. The offences involved three separate periods.

For ease of understanding, it should be noted that the key components of the sentence were: aggravated assault endangering life – six years (seven years less 183 days time served on a two-for-one basis); 1998 break and enter offences – nine months; 1999 break and enter offences – 12 months (15 months less 45 days time served on a two-for-one basis; and 1999 possession of a stolen vehicle – six months time served (90 days time served on a two-for-one basis).

iv)   "Two for one" is the normal rule, not the inflexible rule:

A)   *As an exercise of discretion*

There are countless examples of sentencing courts upholding credit for pre-trial and sentence detention on a scale inferior to that of "two-for-one". There is little benefit to be gained in referring to much of this jurisprudence and it will suffice to note but a few examples. The first, taken from the Supreme Court of Canada, is found in *R. v. Morrisey*, [2000] S.C.J. No. 39, 191 D.L.R. (4th) 86, 259 N.R. 95, 148 C.C.C. (3d) 1, 36 C.R. (5th) 85, 2000 CarswellNS 255, 2000 CarswellNS 256, 2000 SCC 39, 77 C.R.R. (2d) 259, [2000] 2 S.C.R. 90, 187 N.S.R. (2d) 1, 585 A.P.R. 1. As set out at para. 11, the trial judge was of the view that a three-year sentence would be appropriate and he reduced it by one year to credit the five months served in pre-trial detention. There was no adverse comment by our highest Court respecting the granting of enhanced credit superior to two-for-one; to the contrary, the Court noted at para. 57 that "[a] one-year credit for five months of pre-trial custody is not demonstrably unfit."

Secondly, as noted, in *R. v. W. (L.W.)*, *supra*, the Supreme Court of Canada unanimously held that Parliament intended to preserve the judicial discretion to consider pre-sentencing custody under s. 719(3) and ensure that justice is done in the individual case, notwithstanding the introduction of minimum jail terms. Refer to para. 9. Further, it was noted that two-for-one is the often-applied ratio and that "it is entirely appropriate even though a different ratio could also be applied." The Court added that a rigid rule must be avoided. See para. 45.

At para. 25 of *R. v. Rezaie*, *supra*, Mr. Justice Laskin instructs us that: "Although [section 721(3) of the Criminal Code] is discretionary, not mandatory, in my view a sentencing judge should not deny credit without good reason. To do so offends one's sense of fairness. Incarceration at any stage of the criminal process is a denial of an accused's liberty." His Lordship went on to point out the usual reasons to justify the granting of credit, and for granting credit on an enhanced basis.

Rosenberg J.A. pointed out in *R. v. McDonald*, *supra*, that prior to the introduction of legislation governing the effect of pre-sentence custody, sentencing courts might take into account such periods. The applicable sentencing principle was expressed in *R. v. Sloan* (1947), 87 C.C.C. 198, 1947 CarswellOnt 7, 3 C.R. 107 (C.A.), at pp. 198-199 [C.C.C.]:

> This Court has had occasion to recently point out in *R. v. Patterson*, 87 Can. C.C. 86, [1947] O.W.N. 146, that there is no authority for the "dating back of any sentence". The sentence can only bear the date on which it is imposed and any term of imprisonment contained therein cannot begin to run earlier than the date of the sentence itself. This is not to say that the Court can not take into consideration, in imposing sentence, any period of incarceration which the accused has already undergone between the date of his arrest and the date of the sentence, but such period cannot form part of the term imposed by the sentence. If the Court is of the opinion that the circumstance justifies such a course, it may reduce the term of imprisonment, which it would otherwise impose, by the whole or part of the period of imprisonment already served.

Note the submission, not adopted by the Court of Appeal, that the sentencing judge erred in not giving the offender a two-for-one credit for pre-trial custody in *R. v. Shott* (2002), [2002] O.J. No. 3215, 2002 CarswellOnt 2817 (C.A.), at para. 1. Further examples include *R. v. Miller* (2002), [2002] O.J. No. 3589, 2002 CarswellOnt 3057, 163 O.A.C. 63 (C.A.). The judgment records that the offender shot a police officer at very close range and was convicted of aggravated assault. The trial judge sentenced the appellant to a term of eight years, which included pre-trial custody of 27 months, for which she accorded four years' credit. Although the Court of Appeal intervened to increase the sentence to ten years, it maintained the same credit, that is to say four years' credit for a pre-trial custody period of 27 months. See para. 10.

In the final analysis, counsel must be mindful of *R. v. Larocque* (1999), [1999] O.J. No. 2547, 1999 CarswellOnt 2473 (C.A.) stands for the proposition that "... where a trial judge declines to give credit for pre-trial custody on a two-for-one basis that this is not an error in principle." Refer to para. 1.

B)   *To promote other sentencing principles*

R. v. Warren, supra, also makes plain that the normal rule of credit on a two-for-one basis is not an inflexible principle. The Court noted that the trial judge indicated that he would take the "dead time" into account, but he was not prepared to give it "straight arithmetic credit". In fact, as recorded at para. 2:

> The trial judge gave as his reason for not giving full credit for the pre-trial custody that the appellant was "in jail for one reason only and it is your fault". The trial judge then referred to the fact that the appellant was eventually held in custody because he repeatedly violated the conditions of the recognizance.

Note also that at para. 7, the Court observed: "The appellant had been given every opportunity to remain at large so that he would not suffer the prejudice from pre-trial custody. By his own actions, he jeopardized his bail status and ultimately he had to be detained pending his trial ... in the circumstances we cannot say that it was an error in principle for the trial judge to refuse to give a full two-for-one credit." Note in addition the remarks at para. 27, "I don't intend to give him any credit for the time he spent in custody at all. This man, when he was released, within the very next month jumped his bail, attempted to leave the country and flee the country."

Hence, the Court of Appeal upheld the sentencing judge's exercise of discretion as a means of upholding the principle that bail orders must be respected and general respect for the administration of justice.

One questions whether the same result would follow in the case of far fewer and far less grave breaches of bail orders. In the case of Mr.

Warren, he was found guilty of four separate serious breaches and sentenced to a total of 12 months in jail, in addition to a total of four years in prison for sexual assaults. As recorded at para. 7, "[i]t will be seen that the appellant was repeatedly released in the period from 1994 to 1997 and that he violated the terms of his release on many occasions. These were flagrant violations of important terms designed to protect society and ensure the good conduct of the appellant until these serious charges could be dealt with."

R. v. Rezaie, supra, points out the reluctance of the Court of Appeal to uphold the complete denial of all credit in the absence of an appropriate factual foundation and objective legal rationale. Although it requires a lengthy reference to para. 28 to illustrate the Court's concerns, it will be of assistance to do so:

> ...the sentencing judge suggested that the appellant should be denied credit because his pre-trial custody resulted from his illegal acts and abuse of the legal process [by dismissing his lawyer]. No evidence was led to suggest that the appellant dismissed his lawyer solely to delay the trial and to force the Crown to bring the victim back to Canada again. However, even if Crossland, J.'s, reasons justified refusal of credit, these reasons related only to the second period of detention, that is, the five-month period beginning after the appellant had served his sentence for failing to appear (July 1, 1994), and ending when he was convicted (November 24, 1994). These reasons had nothing to do with either the first period of detention (the four and one-half months before the appellant was released on bail) or the third period (the two months occasioned by the Crown's request that the sentencing hearing be adjourned). In effect, the trial judge took into account irrelevant considerations in denying credit for at least six and one-half months of pre-trial and pre-sentencing custody. Taking into account irrelevant considerations constitutes an error in principle.

Accordingly, the sentence imposed by the trial judge was not entitled to deference and was subject to review, but the Court of Appeal concluded that the five-year sentence was fit, even giving credit for pre-trial and pre-sentencing custody.

Hence, it is within the province of counsel to attempt to refute any suggestion that the general rule should be displaced as a matter of discretion to promote other sentencing principles. In this light, counsel must be aware of the following cases as well.

Firstly, *R. v. Thompson* (2000), [2000] O.J. No. 2270, 133 O.A.C. 126, 146 C.C.C. (3d) 128, 2000 CarswellOnt 2097 (C.A.), at para. 85. Of note, the judgment may be distinguished on the grounds that the offender was serving the remnant of an earlier sentence while awaiting trial. Refer to para. 74.

Secondly, counsel must advance cases such as *R. v. Stewart* (2002), [2002] O.J. No. 3391, 2002 CarswellOnt 2872, 163 O.A.C. 391 (C.A.), to support the view that the cases that support enhanced credit on a two-for-one credit on appeal are legion but far fewer in number are those in which denial of enhanced credit is upheld on appeal. For example, para. 10 of *R. v. Stewart, supra*, includes these remarks that I have underlined:

> With respect to sentence, the appellant's sentence is effectively equivalent to nine years and nine months. The appellant submits that the disparity between his sentence and that of the co-accused, Tim Lindsay, who received a sentence of three years in addition to 15 months' pre-trial custody is an error in principle. Mr. Lindsay pled guilty in separate proceedings to a lesser number of charges. We do not agree that the sentence is an error in principle. The appellant instigated the assault. Unlike Mr. Lindsay, he was on probation at the time of the offences and on bail. *Allowing double credit for pre-trial custody in these circumstances was not required.*

Counsel should be vigilant to press the Court to apply the general rule, in the absence of sufficient justification in the circumstances. In this vein, noteworthy is *R. v. V. (R.C.)* (2003), [2003] O.J. No. 1644, 2003 CarswellOnt 1621 (C.A.), at para. 6. The Court found the circumstances of the case to be sufficiently exceptional in light of the delays attaching to the ultimately abandoned dangerous offender application and the undue length of time it took to complete 30 days of evidence, particularly in light of the appellants' express wish to have the trial and sentencing dealt with more expeditiously, to justify an order that two-for-one credit for pre-trial custody be granted. In the result, he received credit for five years and four months.

It is suggested that this is not authority for the proposition that only exceptional circumstances justify enhanced credit, in light of the numerous cases in which such credit is assigned as a matter of course. If anything, it is authority for the view that exceptional circumstances readily justify enhanced credit. Counsel would be well advised in such situations to correspond with the prosecution and the correctional authorities to stress the prejudice being experienced by the detainee, as well as the Court at the remand stage, to then renew these petitions at the time of sentencing.

The case law therefore should be read as requiring enhanced credit as a matter of course and always in cases of exceptional circumstances. That being said, one general class of cases in which enhanced credit is denied (or credit on at least a two-for-one basis) is denied involves misconduct by the offender.

The paucity of examples of such an exceptional regime is illustrated in *R. v. Clarke* (2003), [2003] O.J. No. 1966, 2003 CarswellOnt 1922, 172 O.A.C. 133 (C.A.). As we read at para. 5, the trial judge sentenced the appellant to a term of 14 years' imprisonment, and awarded credit of two years for the pre-trial custody period of 18 months. In reaching the conclusion to deny credit on a two-for-one basis, reliance was placed on the factor that the defendant "had prolonged the length of his custody because he changed counsel and lost his first trial date." However, the Crown conceded that there was no evidence that Mr. Clarke had changed counsel for any improper purpose and, thus, the trial judge erred in principle because he took into consideration an irrelevant factor. In the opinion of the Court of Appeal, Mr. Clarke should have received a credit of at least three years for the time spent in custody.

Note that in *R. v. Veaudry* (2000), [2000] O.J. No. 1818, 132 O.A.C. 258, 2000 CarswellOnt 1776 (C.A.) the offender had served six weeks of his 15-month jail term. Nevertheless, the Court of Appeal did not reduce the 15-month term when it was converted into a conditional period of imprisonment.

v) May pre-trial detention be granted nil credit?

In *R. v. W. (L.W.)*, *supra*, Arbour J. remarked at para. 1 that a trial judge may give credit for pre-sentencing credit. Thus, the trial judge is not required to grant any credit.

It is of interest to note that in *R. v. Warren*, *supra*, the Court of Appeal commented, "Like the trial judge, we would not refuse to give the appellant any credit for pre-trial custody." Refer to para. 7. The Court underscored that the offender was repeatedly released in the period from 1994 to 1997 and that he violated the terms of his release on many occasions. "These were flagrant violations of important terms designed to protect society and ensure the good conduct of the appellant until these serious charges could be dealt with." Refer again to para. 7. Thus, some credit ought to be awarded, but not the usual "two-for-one".

The instruction of the Court of Appeal for Ontario in *R. v. Rezaie, supra,* at para. 25, is that a judge should not deny credit absent justification, which should be placed on the record. After all, it is a denial of liberty. At para. 26, the Court noted that "...absent justification, sentencing judges should give some credit for time spent in custody before trial (and before sentencing)." In other words, it may be possible to assign no credit.

In this respect, note the remarks of Laskin J.A. at para. 26 of *R. v. Rezaie, supra*:

> Nothing said in *R. v. C.A.M.* detracts from this proposition. In that case, the trial judge, in imposing a cumulative 25 year sentence, denied any credit for approximately eight months of pretrial custody. In restoring the trial judge's disposition, Lamer, C.J.C., observed at pp. 568-569 [S.C.R.]:
>
> > After taking into account all the circumstances of the offence, the trial judge sentenced the respondent to 25 years' imprisonment. In imposing that term of imprisonment, Filmer, Prov. Ct. J., was at liberty to incorporate credit for time served in custody pursuant to s. 721(3) of the Code, but chose not to. I see no reason to believe that the sentencing order of Filmer, Prov. Ct. J., was demonstrably unfit.

Laskin J.A. added, "[t]he trial judge and the Supreme Court may simply have been of the view that the eight-month period would have had no practical impact on this lengthy custodial sentence. Cf. *R. v. Squires* (1975), 8 Nfld. & P.E.I.R. 103, 8 A.P.R. 103, 25 C.C.C. (2d) 202, 1975 CarswellNfld 15 (Mag. Ct.), varied on other grounds (1977), [1977] N.J. No. 4, 11 Nfld. & P.E.I.R. 457, 22 A.P.R. 457, 35 C.C.C. (2d) 325, 1977 CarswellNfld 117 (Nfld. C.A.)." Refer again to para. 26.

Rosenberg J.A. points out that the sentencing judge is not bound to give credit for the full period of pre-sentence custody. See para. 65 of *R. v. McDonald, supra*.

vi)   Dead time and the maximum sentence

The credit (or denial of credit) to be given to "dead time" may also be controversial with respect to the selection of the maximum period of detention. In this respect, note the instruction of the Ontario Court of Appeal in *R. v. Legere* (1995), 77 O.A.C. 265, 1995 CarswellOnt 1711, [1995] O.J. No. 152, 22 O.R. (3d) 89, 95 C.C.C. (3d) 555 (C.A.). Shortly put, the accused was charged with trespassing and vagrancy and was released on bail with conditions that, inter alia, he not communicate with any person under the age of 16. Legere was followed upon his release and was seen kneeling down in front of two approaching children, who fled. There was no indication as to whether he spoke to them or made any gestures. He was arrested and charged with two counts of breaching his recognizance.

The Ontario Court, General Division, convicted the accused of breaching his recognizance and sentenced him to imprisonment for two years less a day plus three years' probation. Of note, Legere spent 11 months in custody pending trial.

Finlayson, Austin and Laskin, JJ.A., allowed the conviction appeal and substituted acquittals, holding that the prosecution had not established that the accused "communicated" with the children. Of particular assistance is the following passage from the trial judge's reasons: "Now, while it is normally recognized, I know, that pre-trial custody is taken into account, it is my view that under the exceptional circumstances found here about public safety, there remains a proper exercise of discretion by giving the accused no credit whatsoever for pre-trial custody." [Refer to para. 23 of the judgment of Laskin, J.A.]

It will be convenient to set out at length the reasons for judgment of Mr. Justice Laskin touching upon the sentence appeal, with reference to the original paragraphs:

[34] Since I would allow the conviction appeal, there is no need to address the appellant's appeal against sentence. Moreover, by the time this appeal was argued the appellant had already served his term of imprisonment. Nonetheless, I would like to make a few brief observations about the custodial portion of his sentence.

[35] That the trial judge found dealing with the appellant's sentence "an extremely difficult and troublesome task" is understandable. That he wanted to protect the public by imposing the maximum periods of imprisonment and probation permitted by law is also understandable in the light of the evidence before him. I think, however, that there are two difficulties with the sentence the appellant received. The first arises out of the trial judge's refusal to give any credit for the appellant's pre-trial custody. A sentencing

judge may deny any credit for time spent in custody. But to do so and then impose the maximum sentence for the offence is, I think, inappropriate.

vii) Any period of imprisonment is to be excluded from the credit to be assigned for "dead time"

Rosenberg J.A. points out at para. 65 of *R. v. McDonald*, supra, that "it must be clear that the pre-sentence custody was for the [offence in question]. Otherwise it cannot be said to be time spent in custody 'as a result of the offence', as required by s. 719(3)...". This is not necessarily a self-evident proposition in every case. See para. 23(I) of *R. v. Rezaie*, supra. An offender who is serving a term of incarceration may be denied access to programmes and facilities, and may not be considered for work release, temporary absence, and for parole, while awaiting trial after a loss of "bail" in another matter. In such circumstances, counsel should press for enhanced credit.

viii) Rationales for the rule of crediting "dead time":

A) The absence of a statutory "credit" scheme

As set out at para. 25 of *R. v. Rezaie, supra* "...other than for a sentence of life imprisonment, legislative provisions for parole eligibility and statutory release do not take into account time spent in custody before trial (or before sentencing)." This may justify the granting of credit for pre-trial detention as it is more onerous than post-sentence custody. This is one of the reasons for describing it as "dead time".

B) The absence of programmes of rehabilitation

It is often remarked by sentencing courts that "...local detention centres ordinarily do not provide educational, retraining or rehabilitation programs to an accused in custody waiting trial." See again para. 25 of *R. v. Rezaie, supra*. This is another reason for describing pre-trial detention as "dead time". See the comments at para. 28 of *R. v. W. (L.W.), supra*.

Of course, it would be ironic that an offender who enjoyed access to programmes of education and rehabilitation and who took full advantage of these would be denied a measure of leniency, i.e., two-for-one credit, on the grounds of access to these programmes; the focus ought to be on the enhanced prospects for rehabilitation, it would seem.

C) The conditions at the jails are trying

Closely related to the issue of lack of programmes is the often difficult conditions of detention when not under sentence. In his text, *The Law of Bail in Canada* (Toronto: Carswell, 1992), at p. 28, Prof. Gary Trotter summarizes the effects of pre-trial detention in the following terms, as quoted at para. 33 of *R. v. McDonald, supra*:

> A number of commentators have stressed the hardships which prisoners held without bail must endure. Remand prisoners, as they are sometimes called, often spend their time awaiting trial in detention centres or local jails that are ill-suited to lengthy stays. As the Ouimet Report stressed, such institutions may restrict liberty more than many institutions which house the convicted. Due to overcrowding, inmate turnover and the problems of effectively implementing programs and recreation activities, serving time in such institutions can be quite onerous. This is no doubt why pre-trial detention, which is punctuated by inactivity, has come to be known as "dead time" and is sometimes taken into account by sentencing judges.

At para. 38, the majority observed: "Similarly, in *Sanchez v. Metropolitan Toronto West Detention Centre* (1996), (*sub nom*. R. v. Sanchez) [1996] O.J. No. 7, 1996 CarswellOnt 45, 34 C.R.R. (2d) 368 (C.A.), at para. 23-26, Austin, J.A., recognized that the conditions under which remand prisoners are held arguably could in some circumstances constitute 'punishment', even if such prisoners are not being 'punished' so as to violate their rights under ss. 7 and 12 of the Charter...".

Arbour J. remarked at para. 28 of *R. v. W. (L.W.), supra*:

> In addition, and in contrast to statutory remission or parole, pre-sentence custody is time actually served in detention, and often in harsher circumstances than the punishment will ultimately call for. In *R. v. Rezaie* [[1996] O.J. No. 4468] (1996), 96 O.A.C. 268; 31 O.R. (3d) 713; 112 C.C.C. (3d) 97 (C.A.) ... Laskin, J.A., succinctly summarizes the particular features of pre-trial custody that result in its frequent characterization as "dead time" at p. 104 [C.C.C.]:

...in two respects, pre-trial custody is even more onerous than post-sentencing custody. First, other than for a sentence of life imprisonment, legislative provisions for parole eligibility and statutory release do not take into account time spent in custody before trial (or before sentencing). Second, local detention centres ordinarily do not provide educational, retraining or rehabilitation programs to an accused in custody waiting trial.

At para. 38 of *R. v. W. (L.W.)*, *supra*, Arbour J. again qualified "dead time", selecting in this instance the words, "the usually harsh nature of pre-sentencing custody".

Of course, the ease with which counsel can demonstrate trying conditions of detention will promote enhanced credit. In other words, greater "enhanced" credit may be awarded due to exceptional hardship. In this respect, refer to the discussion of *R. v. O. (E.)* (2003), [2003] O.J. No. 563, 2003 CarswellOnt 544, 169 O.A.C. 110 (C.A.) at para. 11:

> The appellant had been placed while in pre-trial custody in a "lock down" situation, which segregated him from the general inmate population and reduced his time out of his cell to approximately one or two hours a day. The trial judge recognized that consideration of that aggravating factor would further reduce the sentence. Finally, the trial judge considered the desirability of imposing a term of probation, which required imposition of a sentence of imprisonment of less than two years duration. In the result, the trial judge reduced the 27-month sentence to an 18-month sentence of imprisonment, followed by three years probation. The trial judge's stated approach to arriving at that sentence indicates that he clearly credited the appellant with 138 days of pre-trial custody, on a two-for-one basis.

Another example is seen in *R. v. DaSilva* (2002), [2002] O.J. No. 4695, 2002 CarswellOnt 4159, 166 O.A.C. 295 (C.A.). Para. 9 is of assistance in terms of the proper credit for pre-trial detention. As we read, "[t]he trial judge was aware of the period of the approximately one year of pre-trial custody that the appellants spent in prison. He rejected the Crown's submission that no weight should be attached to the pre-trial custody and stated that he did not intend to ignore it."

R. v. Barton (2002), [2002] O.J. No. 4105, 2002 CarswellOnt 3584, 165 O.A.C. 294 (C.A.) provides guidance on the issue of the mitigating weight to be assigned to a period of pre-trial custody served in segregation. In this respect, para. 16 sets out the following:

The trial judge declined to treat time spent in segregation as a discrete mitigating factor concerning sentence. In his view, a decision to place an accused in segregation is a decision made by the relevant correctional institution based on institutional considerations. However, the trial judge also stated that time spent in segregation could be considered "as part of time served awaiting trial." It thus appears that, in determining the credit to be given to the appellant for pre-trial custody, the trial judge did take the nature of the appellant's pre-trial custody into account, in addition to its duration. In our view, it was proper for the trial judge to do so. Segregation is a relevant factor to be considered in determining an appropriate credit for pre-trial custody. In this case, the appellant requested segregation, in the interests of his own safety. The trial judge afforded the appellant significant credit for pre-trial custody [to wit: credit of 40 months for about 23 months of "dead time"].

D)   Dead time is a form of punishment

At para. 8 of *R. v. W. (L.W.)*, *supra*, Arbour J. quoted these comments from the judgment of a five-judge panel of the British Columbia Court of Appeal in *R. v. Mills*, [1999] B.C.J. No. 566, 119 B.C.A.C. 284, 194 W.A.C. 284, 133 C.C.C. (3d) 451, 1999 CarswellBC 578, 1999 BCCA 159, 23 C.R. (5th) 384, 65 C.R.R. (2d) 1 (C.A.), at pp. 458-459 [C.C.C.]: "[i]ncarceration, whether before or after disposition, is a serious deprivation of liberty, and being forced to ignore it as a part of sentencing is inherently unjust." Subsequently, at para. 30, Her Ladyship commented on the "severe nature" of pre-sentencing custody.

At para. 32 of *R. v. McDonald*, *supra*, it was noted by the majority that in virtually all respects, persons in custody awaiting trial are indistinguishable from those in custody serving sentences. Indeed, it is a form of punishment and it is true today, as it was 40 years ago, that persons confined pending trial are subject to conditions which are more oppressive and restrictive than those applied to convicted and sentenced offenders.

E)   To not credit dead time may lead to disparity

Moreover, in *R. v. W. (L.W.)*, *supra*, at para. 8, Arbour J. set out the comments of a five-judge panel of the British Columbia Court of Appeal in *R. v. Mills*, [1999] B.C.J. No. 566, 119 B.C.A.C. 284, 194 W.A.C. 284, 133 C.C.C. (3d) 451, 1999 CarswellBC 578, 1999 BCCA 159, 23

C.R. (5th) 384, 65 C.R.R. (2d) 1 (C.A.), at pp. 458-459 [C.C.C.], to the effect that ignoring pre-sentence detention can lead to unjust discrepancies between similarly situated offenders. Refer as well to para. 42.

F)   The denial of credit might lead to unfairness

Note the strong language found in *R. v. W. (L.W.)*, *supra*, at para. 11. Arbour J. remarked on "...the absurdity and the unfairness that results from an interpretation of the Criminal Code that precludes granting credit for time served prior to sentencing." As noted, the offender was detained following his guilty plea, but while awaiting sentence. "Such delay is often necessary to permit the Court to make a better informed decision about the appropriate sentence by obtaining input from a pre-sentence report, or otherwise through materials collected by the parties. This is particularly important in the case of a first-time offender about whom little may be known." The Court concluded, "[i]t would be grossly unfair if this period of time, which after a guilty plea is undoubtedly part of the punishment, were to be added to the minimum required by law, rather than computed as part of it."

An interesting twist is discussed in *R. v. McCullough* (2000), [2000] O.J. No. 32, 142 C.C.C. (3d) 149, 2000 CarswellOnt 18 (C.A.). As set out at para. 44, the offender was given no credit for "dead time" by the trial judge in light of the fact that his pre-trial custody would be taken into account on the parole eligibility for murder pursuant to s. 746 of the Criminal Code. Once that conviction was set aside, it became appropriate to take the pre-trial custody into account.

ix)   What of a mathematical formula?

At the outset, note the instruction of the Supreme Court of Canada in *R. v. W. (L.W.)*, *supra*, at para. 44:

> I see no advantage in detracting from the well-entrenched judicial discretion provided in s. 719(3) by endorsing a mechanical formula for crediting pre-sentencing custody. As we have re-affirmed in this decision, the goal of sentencing is to impose a just and fit sentence, responsive to the facts of the individual offender and the particular circumstances of the commission of the offence. I adopt the reasoning of Laskin, J.A., in *Rezaie*, at p. 105 [C.C.C.], where he noted that: ...provincial appellate courts have rejected a mathematical formula for crediting pre-trial custody, instead insisting that the amount of time to be credited should be determined

on a case by case basis ... Although a fixed multiplier may be unwise, absent justification, sentencing judges should give some credit for time spent in custody before trial (and before sentencing). [Citations omitted]

In the next paragraph, the Court added that the "...often applied ratio of two-for-one reflects the harshness of detention in custodial centres lacking in educational, vocational and rehabilitation programs and the absence of any remission. "...[C]redit cannot and need not be determined by a rigid formula and is thus best left to the sentencing judge, who remains in the best position to carefully weigh all the factors which go toward the determination of the appropriate sentence, including the decision to credit the offender for any time spent in pre-sentencing custody."

In *R. v. Warren, supra,* the Court of Appeal did not criticize the trial judge's comment that "...he would take the 'dead time' into account, but he was not prepared to give it 'straight arithmetic credit'". See para. 2.

In *R. v. Rezaie, supra,* the Court held as follows, at para. 26:

> Still, this Court and other provincial appellate courts have rejected a mathematical formula for crediting pre-trial custody, instead insisting that the amount of time to be credited should be determined on a case by case basis: *R. v. M.N.T.* [[1991] O.J. No. 946] (1991), 51 O.A.C. 37 (C.A.); R. v. Tallman, Laboucan and Auger [[1989] A.J. No. 119] (1989), 94 A.R. 251; 68 C.R. (3d) 367 (C.A.), and the cases referred to in Nadin-Davis and Sproule, eds., *Canadian Sentencing Digest* (1982) at pp. 141-144.

Of interest, the Court of Appeal added, "...a fixed multiplier may be unwise...".

x)   The fixing of credit is to occur on a case-by-case basis

As noted, in *R. v. Rezaie, supra,* Laskin J.A. agreed that a mathematical formula for crediting pre-trial custody is not appropriate, adding that "...a fixed multiplier may be unwise". As set out at para. 26, the Court insisted that the amount of time to be credited should be determined on a case by case basis, with reference to *R. v. T. (M.N.)* (1991), [1991] O.J. No. 946, 51 O.A.C. 37, 1991 CarswellOnt 707 (C.A.), *R. v. Tallman* (1989),

[1989] A.J. No. 119, 94 A.R. 251, 68 C.R. (3d) 367, 1989 CarswellAlta 17, 65 Alta. L.R. (2d) 75, 48 C.C.C. (3d) 81 (C.A.), and the cases referred to in Nadin-Davis and Sproule, eds., *Canadian Sentencing Digest* (1982) at pp. 141-144.

Note as well *R. v. Nurse* (1993), [1993] O.J. No. 336, 61 O.A.C. 128, 83 C.C.C. (3d) 546, 1993 CarswellOnt 772 (C.A.), at para. 38. It tends to make plain how vague may be the calculation of credit. "Terrence Nurse received a ten-month sentence on count one and a one-year sentence on count two, the sentences to be served consecutively. He, too, has a lengthy criminal record but, as the trial judge noted, he served a lot of 'dead time'".

xi)   Pre-trial credit and minimum jail sentences:

At the outset, note that in *R. v. W. (L.W.), supra*, Arbour J. opined that "[t]his appeal raises a legal issue of deceptive simplicity, which has generated a number of contrary decisions in several courts of appeal. The issue is whether, when Parliament has imposed a mandatory minimum sentence, the courts may deduct from that sentence the time spent by the accused in custody while awaiting trial and sentence, if this has the effect of reducing the sentence pronounced by the Court to less than the minimum provided by law." Refer to para. 1.

At para. 9, the Court observed:

> The task before this Court is to settle the controversy regarding whether or not s. 719(3) may be applied to sentences imposed under s. 344(a), and, by implication, to mandatory minimum sentences in general. For the reasons that follow, I find Rosenberg J.A.'s, analysis in [*R. v. McDonald, supra*] compelling. [That] decision makes it clear that this Court can uphold both Parliament's intention that offenders under s. 344(a) receive a minimum punishment of four years imprisonment and Parliament's equally important intention to preserve the judicial discretion to consider pre-sentencing custody under s. 719(3) and ensure that justice is done in the individual case.

This issue was addressed by the Court of Appeal for Ontario in *R. v. McDonald, supra*. As set out at para. 2, "[t]he appellant spent over six months in pre-sentence custody. [Counsel argues] that even if s. 344(a) is constitutional, it was open to the trial judge to have sentenced the appellant to less than four years to take into account this pre-sentence custody in accordance with s. 719(3) of the Code." Rosenberg J.A. then noted, "[i]n my view, properly interpreted, s. 719(3) of the Criminal Code allows the sentencing judge to take pre-sentence custody into account in fixing the term of the sentence of imprisonment for an offence under s. 344(a). Absent that interpretation I would have found s. 344(a) to be unconstitutional." Refer to para. 3.

At para. 18, the Court observed, "[t]his appeal then raises the following issues for determination: I. Irrespective of the Charter does s. 719(3) of the Code permit a judge to deduct time spent in pre-sentence custody from the sentence to be imposed under s. 344(a)?" His Lordship concluded, at para. 19, that "[s]ection 719(3) allows a sentencing court to deduct time spent in pre-sentence custody from the four-year minimum punishment prescribed by s. 344(a). As a result, s. 344(a) does not infringe s. 12 either in this case or in other reasonable hypothetical circumstances. The section is therefore valid and there is no need to consider s. 1. If I am wrong and pre-sentence custody cannot be taken into account, I would have found that s. 344(a) violates s. 12."

A) Are sentencing courts empowered to give credit even if it serves to reduce a minimal period of incarceration?

The short answer is "yes".

One of the compelling rationales advanced by the Supreme Court of Canada for concluding that pre-sentence detention may be taken into account revolves around the application of the *Corrections and Conditional Release Act* and the *Firearms Act*. In the view of the Court, as penned by Arbour J., the fact that Parliament did not seek to introduce a special regime respecting parole for those sentenced to a minimum period for serious weapons offences involving fatalities makes plain that "...it did not see fit to alter the general administration of sentences in a way that would distinguish the new mandatory minimums from other sentences." Further, "[i]t therefore follows that a rigid interpretation of s. 719(3), which suggests that time served before sentence cannot be credited to reduce a minimum sentence because it would offend the requirement that nothing short of the minimum be served, does not accord with the general management of minimum sentences, which are in every other respect 'reduced' like all others, even to below the minimum." Refer to para. 27.

Shortly put, offenders sentenced to a minimum four-year term are entitled to parole on the same footing as others. Had Parliament wished offenders guilty of these serious offences involving firearms to be detained for longer periods, it would have altered the administration of the sentences. It did not. Note as well the remarks consigned at para. 32: "...when Parliament enacted s. 344(a) as part of the *Firearms Act* in 1995, Parliament did not also modify s. 719(3), to exempt this new minimum sentence from its application, any more than it modified the applicability of the provisions of the *Corrections and Conditional Release Act* to mandatory minimum sentences."

Note as well the remarks of Arbour J., found at para. 1 of *R. v. W. (L.W.)*, *supra*: "I determined in *Wust* that a sentencing judge may give credit for time served in pre-sentencing custody, even if that credit results in a sentence below the mandatory minimum, since this reflects the intention of Parliament that all sentences be administered consistently within the context of the criminal justice system's sentencing regime."

R. v. McDonald, *supra*, includes these comments, at para. 35-38, per Rosenberg J.A.:

> ...In my view, [subsection 719(3)] ... was also intended to give the judge an express power to take into account pre-sentence custody where the statute prescribed a minimum punishment. This is made clear both in the House of Commons Debates and in a text published at the time of the *Bail Reform Act* was enacted. During House of Commons Debates (5 February 1971) at second reading of Bill C-218, Amendment of Provisions of the Criminal Code relating to Arrest and Bail, the Minister of Justice, John Turner, stated clearly the government's intention in reference to the new provision at p. 3118:

> Generally speaking, the courts in deciding what sentence to impose on a person convicted of an offence take into account the time he has spent in custody awaiting trial. However, under the present Criminal Code, a sentence commences only when it is imposed, and the Court's hands are tied in those cases where a minimum term of imprisonment must be imposed. In such cases, therefore, the Court is bound to impose not less than the minimum sentence even though the convicted person may have been in custody awaiting trial for a period in excess of the minimum sentence. The new version of the bill would permit the Court, in a proper case, to take this time into account in imposing sentence.

. . .

This was also the understanding of John Scollin. I find his views of particular assistance since he was with the Department of Justice at the time the *Bail Reform Act* was introduced and testified before the Standing Committee on Justice and Legal Affairs. In his text, *The Bail Reform Act: An Analysis of Amendments to the Criminal Code Related to Bail and Arrest* (Toronto: Carswell, 1972), at p. 91, he summarizes the effect of the new provision:

> This subsection gives statutory sanction to the practice of the courts in taking into account in determining sentence the time that an accused has already spent in custody as a result of the offence. An important extension, however, is that the Court will now be able to take such time into account even in the case where there is a minimum sentence which would otherwise not commence until it is imposed.

xii)   A word for advocates

As a general proposition, two-for-one credit is granted by sentencing courts as a matter of discretion to promote fairness and proportionality, and to take into account the secondary penalty undergone by the offender.

As has been discussed, sentencing Courts emphasize that the granting of credit for pre-trial detention is a matter of discretion to be exercised by the trial judge, but that the usual situation involves awarding enhanced credit, typically on a two-for-one basis. Thus, sentencing courts now take a more liberal view of the credit to be assigned to pre-trial detention and that it no longer is loath to employ a mathematical formula, notwithstanding many earlier judgments disapproving of the practice. It must be understood that this general rule of assigning some enhanced credit for pre-trial detention rests upon a foundation of fairness, and to serve the proportionality rule. In addition, it is presumed to promote rehabilitation. If these goals were not advanced, then greater consideration may be given to denying enhanced credit, as has been seen.

It is urged upon advocates to identify all secondary penalties, not just dead time, that an offender "suffers" or experiences for they must be considered in sentencing as they form part of the coercive and rehabilitative process that serves to correct anti-social behaviour. To fail to credit any incidental punishment visited upon an offender is to fail to ensure that a proportionate sentence has been selected. In this respect, pre-trial detention or "dead time" is perhaps the best known of all of the secondary penalties. In many ways, it symbolizes the consequences that may arise from the mere belief that wrongdoing has occurred.

A final word on advocacy respecting dead time is apposite. In *R. v. Howlett* (2002), [2002] O.J. No. 3525, 2002 CarswellOnt 2977, 163 O.A.C. 48 (C.A.) para. 8(a) sets out the suggestion of the offender that the trial judge "...failed to give the appellant credit for the time he spent in pre-trial custody." Although this complaint was dismissed, it is suggested that the better practice is for counsel to specifically request the credit to be given, to shelter the record. In that fashion, if the sentencing court disagrees with the suggestion, it can be debated.

e)   Restrictive bail conditions as a secondary penalty

The same rationales identified previously with respect to public prosecutions and with respect to "dead time", namely the infliction of punishment prior to the selection of a sentence, the need for fairness and a proportionate penalty, are identified as justifying the selection of a lesser penalty than might otherwise be appropriate in the case of an offender who has been subject to restrictive bail conditions.

This factor has received greater emphasis and consideration in the last few years, principally as a result of the Supreme Court of Canada's decision in *R. v. Askov*, [1990] 2 S.C.R. 1199, 59 C.C.C. (3d) 449, 79 C.R. (3d) 273, 1990 CarswellOnt 111, 1990 CarswellOnt 1005, [1990] S.C.J. No. 106, 49 C.R.R. 1, 74 D.L.R. (4th) 355, 75 O.R. (2d) 673, 113 N.R. 241, 42 O.A.C. 81. Indeed, as expressed in *R. v. Morin*, [1992] 1 S.C.R. 771, 134 N.R. 321, 53 O.A.C. 241, 71 C.C.C. (3d) 1, 1992 CarswellOnt 75, [1992] S.C.J. No. 25, 1992 CarswellOnt 984, 12 C.R. (4th) 1, 8 C.R.R. (2d) 193, at p. 786 [S.C.R.], "The right to security of the person is protected in s. 11(b) by seeking to minimize the anxiety, concern and stigma of exposure to criminal proceedings. The right to liberty is protected by seeking to minimize exposure to the restrictions on liberty which result from pre-trial incarceration and restrictive bail conditions ...".

R. v. P. (L.) (2003), [2003] O.J. No. 251, 2003 CarswellOnt 193, 168 O.A.C. 170, 172 C.C.C. (3d) 195 (C.A.) provides an example of mitigating weight on the grounds of restrictive bail conditions, as a form of secondary penalty. In particular, refer to para. 26: "[he] has been under a form of house arrest since July 1999, that he has been on bail pending appeal on very strict terms including house arrest since March 2001...". Many other examples spring to mind easily, including curfews, non-association orders, restrictions on travel, consumption of alcohol, limitations on the operation of a motor vehicle, etc.

It is the duty of counsel to identify for the sentencing court all of the restrictions on the offender's liberty that have resulted in visiting upon that person some form of punishment, and to request a discounted sentence as a result.

f)   Secondary penalties and ostracism

To date, the discussion has focused on secondary penalties that are the direct result of state action: the fact of a public prosecution, and the decision to detain an offender prior to sentencing or to limit that person's liberty to a significant degree. At this stage, attention is drawn to a secondary penalty that is suffered without any direct role being assigned to the administration of justice: the ostracism or social opprobrium felt by the offender.

As illustrated briefly by the following cases, when an offender is shunned or ostracized by his peers and community, it may be open to defence counsel to argue successfully that some "punishment" has already been inflicted and it is not necessary that the same sentence that would otherwise be appropriate be selected. One significant example of this mitigating element is seen in *R. v. Power* (2003), [2003] O.J. No. 2414, 2003 CarswellOnt 2764, 176 C.C.C. (3d) 209, 174 O.A.C. 222 (C.A.). Refer in particular to para. 9: "He is truly remorseful for his actions and the negative repercussions those actions have had on his family and others. He has felt the wrath of the community in a very direct way, but continues to enjoy the strong support of his immediate family and those in charge of the school he attends."

Note the full catalogue of secondary harm visited upon the offender in *R. v. Cohen* (2001), [2001] O.J. No. 1606, 144 O.A.C. 340, 2001 CarswellOnt 1440 (C.A.), at para. 19. The Court remarked that the offender, guilty of several counts of distribution and possession of child pornography had also suffered the wrath of his community. As we read, ". . . these proceedings have already had a significant deterrent effect upon the appellant. The arrest, trial and conviction of the appellant on these charges have led to what the trial judge described as 'harassment' from the community. His two youngest children were, as found by the trial judge, 'subjected to abuse from their peers and adults'. The appellant and his family had to move to another community to escape." The Court of Appeal concluded that the sentence imposed by the trial judge failed to reflect the devastating effect these proceedings have already had upon the appellant and his family.

An earlier well-known example of the secondary penalties associated with a notorious case is found in *R. v. Bunn* (1997), [1997] M.J. No. 543, 118 Man. R. (2d) 300, 149 W.A.C. 300, 125 C.C.C. (3d) 570, 1997 CarswellMan 502 (C.A.), leave to appeal allowed (1998), 227 N.R. 297 (note), 129 Man. R. (2d) 157 (note), 180 W.A.C. 157 (note) (S.C.C.), affirmed 2000 CarswellMan 16, 2000 CarswellMan 17, [2000] S.C.J. No. 10, [2000] 4 W.W.R. 1, 2000 SCC 9, 140 C.C.C. (3d) 505, 30 C.R. (5th) 86, 182 D.L.R. (4th) 56, 249 N.R. 296, [2000] 1 S.C.R. 183, 142 Man. R. (2d) 256, 212 W.A.C. 256, at para. 19:

> The architect of his own nightmare, Mr. Bunn is very cognizant of what he has already lost in personal terms. With a 20-year career in ruins, the subject has had to face and accept the opprobrium associated with charges of professional misconduct. With the disapproval, if not scorn, of both the public and his peers, Mr. Bunn's reputation has been sullied irreparably. The humiliation and torment for the subject can only be amplified with the realization that his invalid wife and teenage daughter must share in the embarrassment and debasement of his personal debacle.

In *R. v. Foley* (1982), 2 C.C.C. (3d) 570, 1982 CarswellBC 800 (C.A.) we read, "In a case such as this I think it important that there be punishment, that punishment be seen by others who know of the circumstances and that it be seen by the respondent himself". See page 571. He was ordered to perform 1,000 hours of community service in the creation of a work of art that would be a visible expression of his wrongdoing.

In closing, it may be assumed that there is a secondary penalty even in the absence of direct evidence of ostracism at times, in light of the available evidence. For example, in *R. v. Johnston* (2000), [2000] O.J. No. 3539, 136 O.A.C. 190, 2000 CarswellOnt 3354 (C.A.), at para. 37, the Court recorded these comments:

> In particular, the trial judge paid importance to the evidence of the appellant's good character and reputation in the community. He considered the devastating consequences that the charges and the trial had had on the appellant: he lost his privacy, he lost his job as a Crown Attorney, his career as a lawyer was in jeopardy, he was experiencing financial difficulties and had disgraced his family. The trial judge also recognized that, during the course

of these offences, the appellant had been affected by severe depression and alcoholism.

In few words, public disgrace is a strong form of punishment.

g)   Secondary penalties and poor health

The imposition of secondary penalties and the offender's poor health is a somewhat controversial issue. It is suggested that an individual whose health results in making confinement particularly difficult triggers consideration of the secondary penalty principle. Obviously, a lesser period of confinement will produce a greater degree of "punishment" in the case of one who suffers from poor health, all other things being equal.

In an outstanding example of weight being assigned to the co-operation and compliance shown by an offender post-sentence, the Court of Appeal refrained from setting aside a conditional term in a case of prolonged and grave sexual violence in the context of abuse of trust. In *R. v. C. (D.W.)* (2000), [2000] O.J. No. 3759, 2000 CarswellOnt 3519 (C.A.), it noted that the offender's behaviour during the first year of the conditional period was exceptional, and that his health had deteriorated somewhat due to the stress of the proceedings. It was not in the interests of justice to order him to be incarcerated at this time. Refer to para. 15.

Here again, it is incumbent upon counsel to seek out all relevant information in order that the sentencing court may render a fully informed judgment. In the case of *R. v. Fuentes* (2003), [2003] O.J. No. 2545, 2003 CarswellOnt 2453 (C.A.), the Court of Appeal underscored how the trial judge had expected the offender to receive appropriate medical attention, including surgery for his very serious eyesight condition, while incarcerated. As this expectation had not been met, and the offender's condition continues to deteriorate, appellate intervention was required and the sentence was reduced to time served, not otherwise described.

As we read at para. 1, "This is a completely unacceptable situation and has resulted in [his] serving sentence on extremely harsh conditions."

The mitigating impact of poor health is illustrated in *R. v. Aquino* (2002), [2002] O.J. No. 3631, 2002 CarswellOnt 3078 (C.A.) wherein the Court of Appeal remarked, "[t]aking into consideration the serious stroke suffered by the respondent after the imposition of sentence, the Crown submits that the appropriate range is three to five years. We agree. Given the extremely serious circumstances underlying the offence, it is our view that a term of imprisonment of four years is the appropriate sentence." Refer to para. 1.

In this respect, para. 2 records that he is seriously disabled and will require special care and rehabilitative therapy for the duration of the time he will spend in custody. "The correctional authorities are obliged under the *Corrections and Conditional Release Act* to provide inmates with essential health care. For that purpose, the respondent should be assessed immediately and appropriate steps taken to provide the proper medical care, including the rehabilitative treatment which the evidence indicates that the respondent requires." Unfortunately, the offence is not described.

The impact on sentencing of an offender's poor health was also considered in *R. v. Cann* (2001), [2001] O.J. No. 1867, 2001 CarswellOnt 1655 (C.A.) and (May 22, 2001), Doc. CA C34374, [2001] O.J. No. 1881 (C.A.). The offender's poor health resulted in an order that he serve his sentence, not otherwise described, pursuant to s. 742.1. Of interest, the Court pointed out at para. 7 that the health had deteriorated to the point that it is now precarious. Further, "He is confined to his house with the exception of visits or trips for medical treatment." Accordingly, he was to serve the sentence on the same terms and conditions as the conditional sentence he is currently serving for another offence." Although not clear, it seems that he had received a penitentiary-length sentence at trial.

In closing, a complete consideration of this topic requires the reader to review the discussion surrounding the "Elderly offender".

h)   Secondary penalties and harm to the innocent members of the offender's family

In the section that follows, a further type of secondary harm is considered, namely the "harm" that an offender's family loved ones suffer as a result of the factors discussed earlier. As noted in *R. v. Cohen, supra*, at para. 19, ". . . these proceedings have already had a significant deterrent effect upon the appellant. The arrest, trial and conviction of the appellant on these charges have led to what the trial judge described as 'harassment' from the community. His two youngest children were, as found by the trial judge, 'subjected to abuse from their peers and adults'. The appellant and his family had to move to another community to escape."

It will be useful to begin the review of this principle by considering the mitigating perspective that is associated with this element in sentencing. In this respect, the Court of Appeal remarked at para. 1 of *R. v. Malik* (2002), [2002] O.J. No. 3877, 2002 CarswellOnt 3341 (C.A.) that by reason of the failure to obtain a discharge, the offender could no longer travel abroad in his work as a chartered accountant and had lost his livelihood. The Court then focused on the fact that his conviction had hindered his ability to find suitable employment, and this resulted in an inability to meet his obligations towards his children from a previous marriage and the members of his new family. As set out at para. 4: "Loss of employment results in direct financial hardship for those children as well as the appellant."

On occasion, defence counsel are able to "pull at the heart strings" of the Court when dealing with offenders who face extraordinary secondary penalties. A frequent example touches upon the plight of the pregnant offender who faces incarceration. Although the offence and the offender may be such that incarceration is warranted, it may be appropriate for the Court to exercise a degree of leniency by reason of mercy.

The endorsement by the Court of Appeal in *R. v. Cater* (2003), [2003] O.J. No. 1781, 2003 CarswellOnt 1696, 171 O.A.C. 178 (C.A.) is of interest in this respect. As we read at para. 2, the sentence of 16 months plus three years probation was fit when issued. "However, the passage of time and the appellant's current pregnancy with twins, expected in November, has caused us to look at the circumstances anew. We agree with the Crown that this offence calls for a period of custody. The Crown at the same time agrees that we should be concerned that under the Provincial system her babies will be taken from her if born in prison." In the result, the sentence was reduced to one of six months custody plus three years probation on the terms imposed by the trial judge except for the term as to seeking out employment.

It is suggested that counsel forge a submission on other than the anvil of mercy, however. Indeed, it is suggested that the secondary penalty associated with the fear and anxiety of losing her children and the concomitant hoped-for resolve to act responsibly in order to enjoy the freedom to raise the children may be sufficient to justify the conclusion that further wrongdoing is unlikely. If the community no longer need fear harm, there is a corresponding lessening of the imperatives justifying resort to imprisonment.

Perhaps the best example known of a secondary penalty in this respect is drawn from *R. v. Millar* (October 4, 1990), Charron J. (Ont. Gen. Div.), a judgment of Charron J., as she then was. The offender had killed his infant child by reason of shaking and had pled guilty to criminal negligence causing death. He received a suspended sentence with probation for only one day. Among the many mitigating elements that were weighed by the trial judge was the primary fact that the offender would have to live his life knowing he had killed his own child. In addition, for a seven-year period since the child died, Mr. Millar and his family had been subject to intense scrutiny by child welfare authorities who now had no concerns with respect to the accused's ability as a parent and was described as otherwise law-abiding and non-aggressive. Further, he had spent some 45 days in custody and for a period of several years was prevented from living with his family as a result of the outstanding charge.

On the other hand, one cannot always resort to one's family as a form of shield or protective measure to insulate against punishment. In other words, the sentencing court may not be able to assign much by way of mitigating weight to this element in sentencing when confronted with a serious offence. For example, in *R. v. Owens* (2002), [2002] O.J. No. 2599, 2002 CarswellOnt 2249, 161 O.A.C. 229 (C.A.), although the offender had a positive background, no criminal record, a supportive family and prospects of rehabilitation, and though the Court was not unmindful of the tragic consequences of the convictions on his family and the consequences of a penitentiary term for the offender, as set out at para. 11, it could not interfere by reason of the gravity of the planned wrongdoing. To abuse a position of trust as a police officer to intimidate potential victims of a bank robbery carries significant moral blame.

As stated immediately above, secondary harm to the family is not always of such a nature as to ensure that mitigating weight is found. Further example is drawn from *R. v. Bajada* (2003), [2003] O.J. No. 721, 2003 CarswellOnt 617, 169 O.A.C. 226, 173 C.C.C. (3d) 255 (C.A.). Though the Court referred to the offender's young family at para. 8, a six-year term for possession of cocaine for the purpose of trafficking was found to be a fit sentence.

Further guidance on the issue of the needs of dependent family as a mitigating feature is seen in *R. v. R. (D.)* (2003), [2003] O.J. No. 561,

2003 CarswellOnt 543, 169 O.A.C. 55 (C.A.). Para. 7 in particular sets out that ". . . in light of the respondent's pre-trial custody and his *alleged involvement in the on-going care of his other children*, the respondent submits that the terms of his sentence should reflect his counselling and family obligations. In our view, while there are cases where the needs of a dependent family will affect mitigation of sentence, that is not this case."

A comment on advocacy that arises in the circumstances: These examples highlight the imperative need for proof of such family involvement and counsel's duty to seek out such information.

i) Secondary penalties and immigration consequences

Defence counsel may be advantaged in stressing that an offender already has suffered some form of sentence or penalty, on the one hand, and that s/he now enjoys a better understanding (and respect) for the laws and rules of organized society, on the other, as a result of the infliction of some secondary penalty.

A simple illustration may be drawn from the case of *R. v. Lacroix* (2003), [2003] O.J. No. 2032, 2003 CarswellOnt 1970, 172 O.A.C. 147 (C.A.). Mr. Lacroix was sentenced on a joint submission to two years in a penitentiary followed by three years probation. On appeal he sought to vary the custodial part of his sentence to two years less a day, and the Crown did not oppose the variation. As we read at para. 2, "The appellant faces a deportation order. Under the *Immigration and Refugee Act* he can appeal that order only if his sentence is less than two years. At the time of sentencing the appellant was unaware of and, therefore, did not make known to the trial judge the immigration consequences of his sentencing. These consequences are a relevant consideration on sentence. No disservice to the fitness of the sentence would be caused by the variation the appellant seeks."

It must be stressed that it is the anxiety associated with the uncertainty of the result of the proposed inquiry that provides the additional penalty, not just the fact of an actual deportation should such an order be made. In most instances, defence counsel will be well placed to argue that the offender has learned the necessary lesson and no further (or greater) allocation of correctional resources is required to ensure that he assimilates the desired pro-social values.

A good example is found in the case of *R. v. White* (2003), [2003] O.J. No. 2544, 2003 CarswellOnt 4106, 176 C.C.C. (3d) 396 (C.A.). Para.

28 underscored how the offender's mild disposition made him vulnerable in jail, and how the pre-hearing custody had marked him significantly, to the extent that he was now capable of recognizing that his relationship with his wife was over and his need to seriously pursue treatment and counselling. In addition, the renewed or enhanced understanding of the potential penalties for any further transgression serves to foster specific deterrence.

In *Ontario (Attorney General) v. Brenton* (March 17, 1970), Aylesworth J.A., MacKay J.A., Kelly J.A., [1970] O.J. No. 209 (C.A.), passing reference is made at para. 2-3 to the possible deportation that might result from the conviction for mail fraud.

In general, note *R. v. Zhang* (2000), [2000] O.J. No. 1617, 132 O.A.C. 159, 2000 CarswellOnt 1548 (C.A.). The Court of Appeal remarked that deportation was the obvious outcome but did not attach much weight to this factor.

j)   Secondary penalties and "automatic" fines

R. v. Henry Heyink Construction Ltd. (1999), [1999] O.J. No. 238, 118 O.A.C. 261, 1999 CarswellOnt 254 (C.A.) is of interest in making plain that even automatic additional penalties must be considered as a form of secondary penalty.

The judgment is authority for the proposition that all penalties that an offender is subject to, including administrative ones imposed by outside agencies, are to be evaluated by a sentencing court. The offender pleaded guilty to offences under the *Occupational Health and Safety Act* and fines of $35,000 and $7,000, respectively, were imposed. "By automatic operation of s. 60.1 of the *Provincial Offences Act* ... surcharges of 20 percent were added to each fine." See para. 1.

On appeal, the reviewing Court took into account the surcharges and the other circumstances of the case and reduced the fines to $30,000 and $5,000 respectively. The Court of Appeal upheld this result, holding that it was entirely appropriate for the Court to consider the surcharges in determining the fitness of the sentence imposed at trial. Refer to para. 11. As set out at para. 13, "In imposing sentence a trial judge can properly have regard to the surcharge and its economic impact on the accused. Having in mind the surcharge does not mean simply a proportionate reduction in the fine so that with the surcharge added, a predetermined amount is reached. Rather, in passing sentence it means taking account of the surcharge as a real life consideration that affects the economic circumstances of the accused and his or her capacity to pay."

k) Confiscation as a secondary penalty

The criminal courts are faced with an increasing number of situations in which secondary penalties in the nature of confiscations and forfeitures arise, from the loss of a motor vehicle associated with smuggling to loss of rifles involved in the commission of crimes. See *R. v. Mc-Gregor* (1956), [1956] M.J. No. 7, 19 W.W.R. 199, 64 Man. R. 206, 116 C.C.C. 55, 24 C.R. 216, 1956 CarswellMan 40 (C.A.), in which the common "secondary penalty" of forfeiture of a vehicle involved in drug trafficking is discussed at length. Note in particular the language found at page 59 C.C.C. indicating clearly that forfeiture is part of the sentence or punishment. It was also described as an added punishment. *R. v. Bertoia* (1961), [1961] O.J. No. 177, 130 C.C.C. 416 (C.A.) also makes plain that any secondary penalties, such as the confiscation of a vehicle, may be taken into account.

This is not a new development, as evidenced in *R. v. Hagen* (1920), [1920] O.J. No. 151, 33 C.C.C. 208, 53 D.L.R. 479, 47 O.L.R. 384 (H.C.) and we can draw some instruction from prior judgments. As we read at page 210 [C.C.C.], para. 9: "Section 70 [of the *Ontario Temperance Act*] does not create an offence at all. It merely provides how, under certain circumstances, liquor which is seized while unlawfully in transit shall be dealt with. The destruction of the liquor is not a penalty for any offence, but is one of the consequences of the impounding of the liquor, which, by reason of its unlawful possession or its unlawful destination, has become a prohibited article." *Hardy v. Alain* (1920), 35 C.C.C. 128 (Que. Sess. Peace) records a sentence for possession of a still as follows, at page 130 C.C.C.: a fine of $200 and costs and, in default of payment, to an imprisonment of six months, and declares the still and other apparatus and effects seized in the present case to be confiscated in favour of the Crown.

Gambling offences are often the subject of such confiscations but one exception is seen in *R. v. Johnson.* (1915), 25 C.C.C. 124, 35 O.L.R. 215, 27 D.L.R. 607 (S.C.). The moneys seized from the person of an offender convicted of keeping a gaming house was not ordered forfeited. See page 128.

On occasion, it may be appropriate to note that certain secondary penalties have been assessed and that they may attenuate, in whole or in part, the penalty to be imposed. For example, in *Smith, Re*, 74 C.C.C. 374, 1940 CarswellSask 80, [1940] 3 W.W.R. 371 (K.B.), it was noted that the trial judge found that "the records of the above named accused were inaccurate and incomplete" in contravention of the *Fur Act* and thus 101 muskrat skins together with the records seized were ordered to be forfeited to His Majesty represented by the Minister. No fine was imposed, although $5.50 in costs was levied. Refer to page 374 [C.C.C.].

Counsel must be alert to identify these "secondary losses" even though not arising out of a prosecution in direct terms, in order that the sentencing court understand fully the extent of the penalty visited upon the offender.

l)   Compensation, not restitution, to the victim

It is suggested that a secondary penalty scenario arises in a case in which the offender must pay compensation for harm caused or loss occasioned, as opposed to restitution. In other words, the welfare fraud resulting in a "gain" of $3,000 that must be repaid does not result in any loss—nothing is lawfully taken from the offender as a result of a restitution order. By contrast, to pay compensation does result in a secondary loss. An early example is found in a case of assault, *Goodwin v. Hoffman* (1909), 15 C.C.C. 270, 10 W.L.R. 613, 1909 CarswellAlta 84 (Dist. Ct.). See page 614 [W.L.R.], page 271 [C.C.C.]. In the civil action, the victim recovered $150.00 for loss of wages and medical bills. Refer to page 615 W.L.R., page 273 [C.C.C.].

In this respect, note the discussion of *R. v. Michigan Central Railway* (1907), 17 C.C.C. 483, 1907 CarswellOnt 234, 10 O.W.R. 660 (H.C.). Riddell J. advances the principle that the fact of paying civil damages mitigates the reach of deterrence and denunciation.

m)   Civil driving penalties

No authority is required to justify the inclusion, as a secondary penalty, of the automatic driving licenses and prohibitions from operating motor vehicles that arise from certain criminal convictions. Indeed, a number arise from the very fact of being prosecuted. In such cases, the sentencing court cannot ignore the hardship that this will bring about, such as loss of employment.

Of interest, note the unusual secondary penalty selected at trial, and upheld on summary conviction appeal, in *Bogdane v. R.* (1962), [1963] 1 C.C.C. 283, 1962 CarswellSask 40, 39 W.W.R. 641 (Dist. Ct.). Upon being convicted of dangerous driving, the trial judge made an order directing that 12 points be entered against the driving record of the accused pursuant to the *Vehicles Act.* He was also prohibited from driving for three months, and fined $100.00. Refer to page 284 [C.C.C.]. The District Court refused to entertain an appeal from the points order, but it did reduce the prohibition to the equivalent of "time served", in light of the concerns respecting employment. See page 285 [C.C.C.].

n)   Professional disqualifications

Again, little reference to authority is required to substantiate the submission that the loss of professional standing and qualification as a result of an offence is a mitigating factor as a secondary penalty. In *R. v. D. (C.),* [2000] O.J. No. 1668, 132 O.A.C. 133, 2000 CarswellOnt 1569 (C.A.), support is found for the suggestion that a criminal record for sexual violence will disqualify someone from employment in many fields that involve the public.

o)   The adverse consequences of being convicted

In the course of Mr. Justice Tritschler's dissenting opinion in the case of *R. v. Iwaniw* (1959), 30 W.W.R. 590, 127 C.C.C. 40, 32 C.R. 389, 1959 CarswellMan 72 (C.A.), His Lordship advanced the following remarks, at pages 68-69 [C.C.C.]: "Now no one suggests that Overton or Iwaniw require a longer sentence as a deterrent to themselves. The disaster which has overtaken them is tragic. No one has suggested that imprisonment of these men is needed for its reformative effects. But it is said that a longer sentence for Iwaniw is necessary as a deterrent to others." In this respect, His Lordship added:

> Does this sentence meet the criteria of deterrence—not deterrence to anyone but to those in a situation similar to that of these young men? The distinction is important and is basic to an appreciation of the view of the learned trial Judge. Will young men of hitherto blameless lives yield to the temptation to commit a wrong of this sort because if caught they will suffer only 18 months in prison, *separation from wife and child, loss of employment and career and the black future which awaits the "ex-convict" so well known to those who concern themselves in the sad field of ex-prisoner rehabilitation?* We must not fall into the error of consid-

ering whether the sentence now under review would be a deterrent to other potential wrongdoers whose situation was not similar to that of these prisoners, for example, men with different backgrounds or with a bad or even any prior record. Such persons would not receive a sentence of 18 months nor would they expect it. With respect I feel that much of the argument addressed to us on the question of deterrence ignored this. If the sentence given Iwaniw, accompanied as it is by other punishing factors, will not be a deterrent, will it become a deterrent by adding some months to it—and how many? In the difficult field of punishment there is great diversity of opinion. Members of this Court sometimes differ about sentences. Uniformity in sentencing is often spoken of but seldom with sufficient recognition of the fact that cases can seldom be matched. Despite similar elements, important facts will distinguish cases and always behind the facts is the unique personality of the prisoner—an important, if not the most important, consideration.

I have italicized a passage for emphasis.

p)   The impact of improper or flawed proceedings

Further, it must be stressed that secondary penalties may arise in a number of ways. For example, the offender may have been subject to a prosecution that was void from the outset and thus, was never sentenced in any fashion that the law acknowledges. Such a situation arose in *R. v. Lowery* (1907), 15 O.L.R. 182, [1907] O.J. No. 40, 13 C.C.C. 105 (C.A.). Boyd C. noted at para. 6, page 183 that "Everything was of the most informal character, and no conviction was drawn up. . . he was not charged with any criminal offence, but only with taking a horse, and he was put in prison because he had 'committed a breach of the law.'" Hence, should a further prosecution have been initiated, it would have been proper for the sentencing court to credit all of the secondary harm suffered by the offender.

q)   Injuries suffered by offender in course of offence

In *R. v. Nagy* (1989), [1989] O.J. No. 2374, 1989 CarswellOnt 2012 (C.A.) the Court noted a number of mitigating features. As set out at para. 1, "The trial judge carefully considered all relevant factors in imposing sentence. We are of the view, however, that in light of the circumstances of the accused including his very serious injuries, the disparity in criminal records between him and his co-accused and the trial judge's very proper desire to emphasize general deterrence, a more appropriate sentence would have been 18 months imprisonment together with probation." The Court selected a one-year period of probation, with a term requiring his attendance for treatment of the drug addiction as required by his probation officer. See also *R. v. Abbott* (1985), 36 Man. R. (2d) 187 (C.A.).

Note the dissent in *R. v. Abbott* (1985), [1985] M.J. No. 420, 36 Man. R. (2d) 187, 1985 CarswellMan 355 (C.A.), leave to appeal refused (1985), 64 N.R. 157n (S.C.C.), Monnin C.J.M. observed at para 1: "The accused appeals a sentence of ten years imposed on him by James, P.J., on a count under s. 79 of the Criminal Code, causing the explosion of an explosive substance, namely a home-made bomb placed under a car." The dissenting judgment added these observations:

> [3]   The accused managed to blow himself up in a vain attempt to place a homemade bomb in or under the car of one Mr. Weir. The motive is not entirely clear, but it seems to have been jealousy. A sentence of ten years was imposed upon the accused after he entered a plea of guilty to a charge under s. 79 of the Criminal Code.

> [4]   It would be difficult to assert that the sentence was unfit under normal circumstances. But there are three factors which lead me to the view that the sentence was too severe in this particular case. Firstly, the accused, now 23, had a clear record. Secondly, the accused sustained massive injury in the explosion, losing the lower part of his left arm, and three fingers off of his right hand. Injuries of such severity are a reasonable consideration in determining the appropriate sentence. Thirdly, the accused has pre-existing health problems, which make institutional confinement even more of a punishment than it usually is. Under these circumstances, I would reduce the sentence from ten years to five years.

r)   Summary for advocates: Any element of punishment inherent in the proceedings must be considered to be mitigating

Little authority is required to justify the proposition that any element of punishment that has been visited upon an offender by the very fact of the proceedings should serve to mitigate the sentence that the Court may impose. Indeed, since sentencing serves to deter the offender and to impress upon others who might be tempted to emulate the misconduct in question that they will also suffer a sanction, in conformity with s. 718, together with other objectives, the duty of the sentencing court to impose a proportionate penalty pursuant to s. 718.1 would be violated by failing to take into account these "secondary penalties".

In the final analysis, however, care must be taken not to overlook that many sentencing scenarios will disclose that an offender is the author of his/her own misfortune and that although the imposition of secondary penalties must be taken into account, all other things being equal, the Court may not assign any significant weight to the hardship endured by the offender prior to trial. In this respect, Riddell J. remarked at para. 114, page 667 of *R. v. Leach* (1908), 17 O.L.R. 643, [1908] O.J. No. 89, 14 C.C.C. 375 (Div. Ct.), affirmed (1908), 1908 CarswellOnt 774, 21 O.W.R. 919, 18 C.C.C. 487 (C.A.): "I feel no regret at coming to the conclusions just set out: Anyone who wilfully disregards and disobeys a law of the land should be punished, and has only himself to blame if he finds himself in the unhappy condition of this defendant." The duty of counsel is to attempt to lessen the reach of this "perspective" by insisting on a principled approach to the selection of a fit and proper sentence.

3. EXPERT EVIDENCE: CAPACITY FOR REHABILITATION

Counsel must consider the wisdom of seeking and introducing expert evidence as to the offender's capacity for rehabilitation. This might address the ability to overcome addiction, or to achieve anger management, or to accept the end of a relationship, etc. For example, in *R. v. Wang* (2001), [2001] O.J. No. 1491, 144 O.A.C. 115, 153 C.C.C. (3d) 321, 2001 CarswellOnt 1321 (C.A.), additional reasons at (2001), [2001] O.J. No. 1961, 2001 CarswellOnt 1773 (C.A.), at para. 67, expert testimony suggested a capacity for empathy and thus, of rehabilitation, that was not in evidence if the sentencing court had focused solely on the facts of the offence. A more favourable result was obtained as some mitigating weight could be attached to the conduct or, in the alternative, by reducing the aggravating weight otherwise available. In few words, the offender wasn't beyond hope of reform.

4. MORAL BLAME: THE DEGREE OF VIOLENCE

R. v. Price (2000), [2000] O.J. No. 886, 144 C.C.C. (3d) 343, 33 C.R. (5th) 278, 72 C.R.R. (2d) 228, 140 O.A.C. 67, 2000 CarswellOnt 837 (C.A.) provides guidance on the pains that counsel must take to identify the correct degree of moral blame attaching to the offender's conduct in circumstances of non-sexual violence. The Court of Appeal remarked that as the driver of the "get away car", the actual degree of violence that could fairly be attributed to the offender was quite inferior to that which the co-offenders faced. Indeed, para. 55 reads in part: "Although [he] may have played a significant role in the planning of the robbery, he was not directly involved in the assaultive behaviour and threats of bodily harm . . . Nor is there any evidence that he either countenanced or envisaged the violence that occurred."

It is an appropriate generalization to suggest that the greater the harm suffered by the victim, or threatened, the greater must be the allocation of aggravating weight on the scale of offending, all other things being equal, by reason of the moral blame assigned to the infliction of violence. By way of simple illustration, a modest push with an open hand does not result in the same harm as a vicious blow with a closed fist. By way of limited reference, note *R. v. Hanifan* (2001), [2001] O.J. No. 1576, 2001 CarswellOnt 1442, 144 O.A.C. 110 (C.A.). The offender received a six-year term for manslaughter arising out of a pool hall fight. The Court of Appeal made plain at page 28 that "...given the severe blow struck by the appellant, its tragic consequences and the appellant's criminal record, this sentence was within the appropriate range for this offence." The fact remains that had the victim been able to duck, or the blow land even an inch away, the matter might not have been reported to the authorities.

The context, however, may result in the allocation of greater moral blame in the one case than in the other. For example, to push ever so gently a bereaved individual so that s/he will fall into an open gravesite during a burial ceremony is far more reprehensible, as measured on a moral scale, than a punch delivered by someone who willingly agreed to a fight involving equally matched protagonists. In the same vein, to stain a friend's shirt in a deliberate fashion to embarrass them during an end-of-year hockey banquet featuring copious imbibing of intoxicants pales next to inflicting the same stain on a rival's wedding dress on the steps of the church.

Consider as well the useful enumeration of aggravating features in *R. v. Drisdelle* (2002), [2002] O.J. No. 3901, 165 O.A.C. 107, 2002 CarswellOnt 3384 (C.A.) with a view to ensuring that no greater moral blame attaches to the offender than what is attributable to the actions disclosed in the evidence. The majority judgment remarked at para. 13 that "...the appellant's conduct in the robberies is to be contrasted with that of his accomplices. While the appellant's role was serious, and not insignificant, it did not involve the use of violence or weapons, an attempt at disguise, threats to the victims of the robberies or verbal abuse of them."

Again, counsel is urged to place the degree of offending on the scale of wrongdoing and it is a proper exercise in advocacy in the circumstances, to argue that the offender, as in the case of Mr. Drisdelle, did not use a weapon. If the offender did, it is to be argued that it was not fired. If it was, the submission would be that it was not fired in such a way as to harm anyone directly, etc.

5.   VIOLENCE: PLACING THE HARM ON A SCALE

Sentencing courts are concerned to a significant extent with the harm done to the victims of violent crime and generally select a sentence that is commensurate with the harm done. As a generalization, the greater the actual or foreseeable harm, the greater will be the reach of general deterrence and denunciation.

Emphasis must be placed on the harm, as it may be inflicted without actual infliction of direct violence. For example, in *R. v. Llorenz* (2000), [2000] O.J. No. 1855, 132 O.A.C. 201, 145 C.C.C. (3d) 535, 35 C.R. (5th) 70, 2000 CarswellOnt 1884 (C.A.), Sharpe J.A., dissenting as to the convictions appeals, observed that "... [the] trial judge pointed out that this was a case of protracted abuse in which the appellant had effectively terrorised the complainant and her mother through exploitative distortion of their religious and spiritual beliefs. The appellant preyed on the vulnerability of the complainant and subjected her to a form of mental torture. The complainant had suffered significant trauma as had her mother." Refer to para. 71.

In the result, counsel may be advantaged in a given case by advocating how the offender in question limited the reach of the violence or attenuated it to a certain extent. This is not to suggest that any credit is given to the offender for only snatching the purse from the elderly victim after pushing her to the ground. To the contrary, the sentencing court's attention is drawn to the absence of wanton, or gratuitous violence. The crime remains one of violence but one that is not as elevated on the scale of wrongdoing as in other cases.

Two further examples may be useful to illustrate this proposition. In the first case, consider the great weight being attached to the serious consequences to the victim of the sexual violence perpetrated against her in *R. v. C. (D.W.)* (2000), [2000] O.J. No. 3759, 2000 CarswellOnt 3519 (C.A.). In that appeal, the Court would have set aside a conditional term on the grounds that it failed to accord sufficient weight to denunciation in the case of an extremely serious offence of prolonged sexual violence involving a breach of trust, but did not due so to exceptional grounds of hardship. In fact, the child was abused in the presence of the baby she was caring for, making it impossible for her to resist. See para. 10-12. The consequences to her included having to move away and the loss of family and friends.

No less grave is the second example. Indeed, in *R. v. L. (J.)* (2000), [2000] O.J. No. 3806, 2000 CarswellOnt 3704, 137 O.A.C. 1 (C.A.) para. 24 sets out that: "The impact on the victims has been profound and is ongoing." The offender is an older brother of the young victims and he employed a significant degree of physical force and threats of harm over the years to further his abuse over the years, starting when the victims were quite young.

As is readily apparent, the moral blame attached to such exploitative conduct is quite high. The Court's response must be in keeping with the lack of restraint demonstrated, the extent of the infliction of harm and the adverse, serious consequences, to name but three factors. Nevertheless, on the scale of wrongdoing, many situations may be identified as embracing far more serious lack of restraint, greater infliction of harm, and even worse consequences.

The goal is not, of course, to point to the existence of potentially worse offences, but to ensure that the offence is evaluated on the basis of what took place, in an objective manner. The resulting placement on the scale of wrongdoing, for violent offences in this first example, involves certain philosophical concerns, as it tends to disparage the harm suffered by those at the lesser end of the scale. Nonetheless, the offence must be situated on such a scale if the range principle, for example, is to be applied fairly. Thus, in *R. v. Krushel* (2000), [2000] O.J. No. 302, 130 O.A.C. 160, 31 C.R. (5th) 295, 142 C.C.C. (3d) 1, 2000 CarswellOnt 325 (C.A.), leave to appeal refused (2002), 2002 CarswellOnt 4384, 2002 CarswellOnt 4385, (*sub nom.* R. v. Grey) [2002] S.C.C.A. No. 293, 307 N.R. 200 (note) (S.C.C.) it is important to assess that the offence ". . . had a dramatic effect on the lives of the victim and his children", as made plain at para. 31. It would be of equal import to note the absence of any such harm, if such were the case.

Counsel must seek an individualized sentence, not a typical or "range" sentence, in most cases, as this will be advantageous. The case of *R.*

v. Turcotte (2000), [2000] O.J. No. 1316, 48 O.R. (3d) 97, 131 O.A.C. 311, 144 C.C.C. (3d) 139, 32 C.R. (5th) 296, 2000 CarswellOnt 1251 (C.A.), a case of manslaughter involving the strangulation death of a 71-year-old woman at the hands of her 47-year-old son, will serve to highlight how difficult is the placement of a case on the appropriate scale of wrongdoing. This judgment illustrates the success that counsel may enjoy in advocating for an individualized disposition if a compelling sentence submission is crafted, and in countering the need for a "range" sentence.

By a two-to-one majority, the trial judge's sentence of a two-year less one-day conditional term of imprisonment was upheld. Catzman J.A., Abella J.A. concurring, and Justice MacPherson, in dissent, all found that a term of imprisonment in the penitentiary was not required. The majority and minority judgments were of the view that the offence of manslaughter embraces a wide range of conduct and provincial reformatory periods are well within the range. At para. 19, we see that *Proulx* is cited as support for the view that conditional sentences are not inappropriate for serious offences including manslaughter, with reference to paras. 80-81 of Chief Justice Lamer's judgment.

In the view of the majority, however, no grounds existed to interfere with the sentence imposed by the trial judge. It did emphasize that appropriate conditions were selected to ensure appropriate residence, abstention from alcohol, counselling and treatment, and community service. See para. 24.

The forceful dissent concluded that the selection of a sentence to be served within the community was demonstrably unfit by reason of the particularly violent nature of the offence in question. It underscored the agony of the victim, her helplessness in light of her age and drunken state, the viciousness of the strangulation, and set about to place this offence within the context of domestic violence, a far too prevalent feature within our society, it found. See para. 37 and 42-43.

In sum, to fail to jail the offender was to fail to assign sufficient weight to the principle of denunciation and general deterrence, leaving aside the insufficient attention the conditional term drew to the moral blameworthiness or responsibility of the offender. See para. 39.

In other words, the majority and the minority differed strongly on the emphasis to be placed on the offender's degree of moral blameworthiness.

6. INDIVIDUALIZED SENTENCES AND DRINKING AND DRIVING OFFENCES

In *R. v. L. (J.)* (2000), [2000] O.J. No. 2789, 135 O.A.C. 193, 147 C.C.C. (3d) 299, 5 M.V.R. (4th) 76, 2000 CarswellOnt 2649 (C.A.), the Court of Appeal provides signal instruction on the sentencing of drivers guilty of serious harm while impaired, at para. 3, together with direct guidance on counsel's ability to influence to a great extent the selection of the sentence based on individualized submissions:

> The only principle that can be stated with assurance concerning this offence is that, where the offence involves not only reckless driving conduct but the consumption of alcohol, the sentences have tended to increased severity over the past 20 years. Otherwise, the particular offence is very much driven by individual factors, especially the blameworthiness of the conduct. The more that the conduct tends toward demonstrating a deliberate endangerment of other users of the road and pedestrians, the more serious the offence and the more likely that a lengthy prison term will be required.

Stated otherwise, counsel must demonstrate so far as possible that the conduct was not such as to demonstrate deliberate endangerment. In so doing, it must be understood that the evaluation of these factors by sentencing courts is by no means a uniform task and disparity of views is not uncommon, as will be illustrated below. Hence, it is an area of sentencing in which great effort by the advocate may be well rewarded.

What is being advanced is that the selection of a fit sentence is a complex task at the best of times and it may become quite controversial in drinking and driving cases featuring the heretofore-good citizen guilty of an egregious crime. This complexity made plain in *R. v. Godfree* (2000), [2000] O.J. No. 3409, 2000 CarswellOnt 3316, 136 O.A.C. 49, 7 M.V.R. (4th) 60 (C.A.), a case of impaired driving causing death. For the majority, Feldman J.A. remarked that no error in principle had been shown in the selection by the trial judge of a 20-month conditional term of detention. There is no doubt that the offender was grossly intoxicated, combined medication to alcohol, and should have known that her driving would result in a disaster. This element is strongly suggestive of elevated moral blame.

However, it was balanced with evidence that the offender had been seeking treatment for many years, with some success, and that she was opposed to this type of conduct and that she was extremely remorseful. The evidence suggested that she did not pose a great risk of re-offending. See paras. 22-24. The pre-sentence report was positive, and their was strong family support.

After a thorough review of the case law, including the recent judgments of the Supreme Court of Canada, Feldman J.A. opined that no grounds existed to interfere with the trial court's sentence. The terms and conditions were onerous yet capable to addressing her needs and, in the final analysis, as made plain at para. 35, "...there appear to be sufficient controls in place to ensure that [she] will comply with the conditions of her sentence and will not be a threat to the community." Of interest, the Court was not informed of any breach since the imposition of the sentence. Refer again to para. 35.

The dissenting judgment focused particular attention on the fact that "[t]here is, in reality, nothing to prevent [her] from leaving her home, consuming alcohol and then driving again." See para. 10. The Court noted that the Crown submitted that:

> ...these conditions are inadequate. Many persons who have committed the offence of impaired operation of a motor vehicle causing death are sincerely remorseful for the harm they have caused and promise they will not drink and drive in the future. The respondent is not under the care or supervision of anyone on a continuous basis. She does not work outside the home or attend education classes during the day. She has no ongoing responsibilities such as the care of children to act as a form of moral dissuasion. She is not subject to unannounced random alcohol testing. There is, in reality, nothing to prevent the respondent from leaving her home, consuming alcohol and then driving again. This province does not have a system for monitoring whether a person serving a sentence in the community is actually abiding by the requirement to remain in his or her residence. The conditional sentence of the trial judge contained no external controls on the respondent to ensure she did not drink and drive.

At bottom, para. 15 records that the dissent found justification to intervene as a result of the trial judge's decision to consider her mental condition as relevant to the event. Denunciation could not be met without actual deprivation of liberty, in the circumstances. See para. 18.

7.   RANGE OF SENTENCES AND EXCEPTIONAL CASES

Not unlike counsel's duty to assert that the case calls for an individualized sentence, in appropriate cases, there is an obligation to seek an exceptional sentence in certain situations. In this respect, note *R. v. Habib* (2000), [2000] O.J. No. 3036, 147 C.C.C. (3d) 555, 135 O.A.C. 329, 2000 CarswellOnt 2863 (C.A.). The Crown submitted that the appropriate sentence for an aggravated assault conviction involving Shaken Baby Syndrome is three to five years. In response, the Court noted, "While the typical case may receive such a sentence, the range must extend to accommodate the rare or exceptional case, such as this." See para. 10. A reformatory term was not unknown and not so low as to be outside the range.

With respect to the contention that a conditional term provides inadequate weight to the factors of denunciation and general deterrence given that this was a Shaken Baby Syndrome case, the Court of Appeal responded, "Just as we cannot exclude the conditional sentencing possibility from categories of offence, we cannot do so for subcategories such as all Shaken Baby Syndrome cases." See para. 12. It added, "While there is no doubt that the assault of an infant will always be a very serious matter, the appropriate sentence must depend on the particular facts in each case." A conditional term was upheld.

8. HARDSHIP: AVOIDING UNDUE HARDSHIP AS A JUSTIFICATION FOR LENIENCY

On occasion, the typical or range sentence is not selected by reason of an exceptional feature such as undue hardship. An example is drawn from the report of *R. v. C. (D.W.)* (2000), [2000] O.J. No. 3759, 2000 CarswellOnt 3519 (C.A.). The Court of Appeal would have set aside a conditional term on the grounds that it failed to accord sufficient weight to denunciation in the case of an extremely serious offence of prolonged sexual violence that included intercourse of a minor in a clear violation of a breach of trust, but did not due to exceptional grounds of hardship. See para. 10.

A common situation involves the reluctance to re-incarcerate offenders, or to impose as lengthy a sentence as might otherwise be appropriate, in the case of those who have served a term of imprisonment and who appear to be on the path leading to a successful rehabilitation. In *R. v. Young* (January 15, 1971), MacKay J.A., McGillvray J.A., Arnup J.A., [1971] O.J. No. 81 (C.A.), MacKay J.A. observed that the offender was detained for over 11 months prior to being released on bail, having been sentenced to nine months' definite and 18 months' indeterminate. When the matter came on for hearing some eight months later, it was not thought necessary to re-incarcerate him.

R. v. T. (S.L.) (1989), [1989] O.J. No. 2399, 1989 CarswellOnt 1555 (C.A.) is apposite as well. The Court observed that Mr. Thompson has served the custodial portion of his sentence and, although, as indicated, the sentence was low, it was held that it would not be in the interests of justice that he now be re-incarcerated. Refer to para. 1.

It must be stressed that certain fact situations justify the return of an offender to a custodial facility. For example, in *R. v. Miles* (1989), [1989] O.J. No. 2351, 1989 CarswellOnt 2039 (C.A.), the Court of Appeal characterized the assault under s. 245.1(1)(a) as being "very serious", ". . . involving the use of a knife and a threat of death. . .". The Court in directing a nine-month period of detention, remarked, at para. 1, ". . . the sentence imposed failed to adequately reflect the principles of general and specific deterrence. Were it not for the fact that the respondent has served the sentence imposed by the trial judge and the particular hardship which further incarceration will impose on his family, the sentence which we propose to impose would be longer."

At the end of the day, if the goal of sentencing is to protect the community, then it is often appropriate to temper the reach of severity, selected to further the reach of denunciation and general deterrence, with the objective of safeguarding the offender's rehabilitation. In addition, the same principle of restraint in the selection of a jail sentence must apply to restraint in the selection of a further period of detention.

9.   AGGRAVATING FEATURE: THE LENGTH OF TIME THE OFFENCE OCCURRED

As a general rule, the greater the period of time during which an offence (or offences) of sexual violence has occurred, the greater is the moral blame assigned to the offender. In simple terms, s/he demonstrated an inability to cease an activity that is plainly harmful to the victim(s). *R. v. Krushel* (2000), [2000] O.J. No. 302, 130 O.A.C. 160, 31 C.R. (5th) 295, 142 C.C.C. (3d) 1, 2000 CarswellOnt 325 (C.A.), leave to appeal refused (2002), 2002 CarswellOnt 4384, 2002 CarswellOnt 4385, (*sub nom.* R. v. Grey) [2002] S.C.C.A. No. 293, 307 N.R. 200 (note) (S.C.C.) illustrates the principle that specific and general deterrence may have to be emphasized in cases in which "...the conduct spanned a number of years...". Refer to para. 31.

That the duration of the sexual wrongdoing may be decisive as demonstrating an elevated degree of moral blame was seen in *R. v. L. (J.)* (2000), [2000] O.J. No. 3806, 2000 CarswellOnt 3704, 137 O.A.C. 1

(C.A.) at para. 24. The offender is an older brother of the young victims and he employed a significant degree of physical force and threats of harm to further his abuse over the years, starting when the victims were quite young. Refer as well to the dissent in *R. v. W. (A.G.)* (2000), [2000] O.J. No. 398, 130 O.A.C. 78, 2000 CarswellOnt 358 (C.A.), paras. 8-9.

The rejection of a conditional sentence in a case of sexual interference was upheld in *R. v. Knight* (2002), [2002] O.J. No. 3392, 2002 CarswellOnt 2873 (C.A.), at para. 14. The offender's "deuce less" was held to be fit in light of the fact that "[he] was in a position of trust to T.E.; the abuse continued over a period of six years with numerous incidents; she suffered serious psychological harm that is ongoing. The appellant is not a first offender and has a criminal record for property offences and crimes of dishonesty."

The aggravating impact of repeated offences of sexual violence against same victim over a lengthy period of time was underscored in *R. v. Singh* (2002), [2002] O.J. No. 3604, 163 O.A.C. 199, 2002 CarswellOnt 3060 (C.A.). Para. 5 includes this information: "The sentence, three years, was appropriate given that several acts of sexual intercourse with a 12- to 18-year-old girl were proved against the appellant."

Note also *R. v. P. (D.)* (2001), [2001] O.J. No. 2865, 148 O.A.C. 56, 2001 CarswellOnt 2502 (C.A.). The offender was found guilty of sexual assault and of two counts of touching a young person for a sexual purpose. He received a five-year term for the assault offence, and two two-year sentences, concurrent, for the sexual touching charges. In sum, the misconduct involved his stepchild when she was aged 12 to 14, and involved full intercourse on a regular basis. Para. 3 records that the victim was threatened should she disclose the wrongdoing.

Para. 46 sets out that the sentence was at the high end of the range. Nevertheless, it was upheld, as the crimes were extremely serious, involving as it did a young stepchild in acts of sexual intercourse and other forms of sexual violence on a repeated basis over a substantial period of time, committing thus a gross breach of trust. "In the circumstances, we are satisfied that a lengthy penitentiary term was warranted and that the global sentence of five years imposed at trial was appropriate."

By way of contrast, as a general rule it is mitigating that anti-social behaviour was brief and has been corrected by means of self-rehabilitation. *R. v. Vandervoort* (2002), [2002] O.J. No. 3471, 2002

CarswellOnt 2912 (C.A.), provides an example of a conditional sentence being substituted for a jail sentence in circumstances in which the Court of Appeal concluded that although "[t]he offence was serious and clearly called for a custodial disposition", the progress shown by the youthful adult offender would be compromised by a period of imprisonment. Refer to paras. 1 and 4. Although not involving sexual violence, this judgment illustrates the importance of the duration of the wrongdoing.

It will be useful to add that of primary importance to the Court's determination that leniency was appropriate was the threshold finding that "[t]his young person fell off the rails for a short period of time but had fully rehabilitated herself by the time of sentencing. She had returned to live with her family, resumed her schooling, was employed part-time, become involved in community work including counselling troubled youth." See para. 2. Paragraph 4 makes plain how that "[t]o send this young person to jail would undermine the outstanding effort she had made to straighten out her life." Accordingly, the appellate tribunal disagreed with the emphasis placed by the trial judge on denunciation.

It may be helpful as well to refer briefly to *R. v. Nelles* (2000), [2000] O.J. No. 3034, 135 O.A.C. 265, 2000 CarswellOnt 2861 (C.A.). The trial judge was clear in his findings that he had a reasonable doubt as to whether the complainant consented to the first sexual act but that, with respect to the second one, he found confirmation in the admissions of the appellant that the complainant did not consent. The offender had testified that the complainant ". . . wasn't the same . . . I kind of figured she didn't want to the second time . . . I agree I ignored my own observations and I wanted to have sex . . . From my observations she lost all interest . . . I asked if she wanted to try again. She gave no answer."

What is significant is that at the sentence stage, the Court of Appeal found the term of nine months excessive in the circumstances. As we read at para. 4, "The sexual acts were of a short duration and, with respect to the second one that he was convicted of, he desisted when the complainant protested."

10. SECONDARY HARM: OBLIGATION TO MOVE TO BE FREE OF POTENTIAL HARM AND TO LESSEN FEARS

An example of great weight being attached to the serious direct and secondary harm suffered by the victim of sexual violence is found in

R. v. C. (D.W.) (2000), [2000] O.J. No. 3759, 2000 CarswellOnt 3519 (C.A.). A child was abused in the presence of the baby she was caring for, making it impossible for her to resist. See para. 10-12. The consequences to her included having to move away and the loss of family and friends.

11. VICTIM'S VULNERABILITY

The aggravating impact of repeated offences of sexual violence against same quite vulnerable victim over a lengthy period of time was also underscored in *R. v. C. (D.W.)* (2000), [2000] O.J. No. 3759, 2000 CarswellOnt 3519 (C.A.). In that appeal, the Court would have set aside a conditional term on the grounds that it failed to accord sufficient weight to denunciation in the case of an extremely serious offence of prolonged sexual violence involving a breach of trust, but did not due to exceptional grounds of hardship. In fact, the child was abused in the presence of the baby she was caring for, making it impossible for her to resist. See para. 10-12.

12. NEUTRAL FEATURE: THE ABSENCE OF A RECORD IN THE CASE OF DRINKING AND DRIVING: THE TYPICAL OFFENDER IS LAW-ABIDING

A cursory review of the cases under the rubric of "First offenders" will suggest that the absence of a criminal record typically is a mitigating feature in sentence. Nevertheless, this factor is accorded little weight in the case of very serious offences of drinking and driving for two reasons. The first is that the offender is very often a law abiding individual and to award any significant mitigating weight might serve to counter the reach of denunciation and general deterrence. Secondly, an offender who commits an offence involving a tremendously high degree of moral blameworthiness cannot expect much by way of leniency notwithstanding the absence of a record.

In *R. v. McVeigh* (1985), [1985] O.J. No. 207, 11 O.A.C. 345, 22 C.C.C. (3d) 145, 1985 CarswellOnt 1389 (C.A.), a 31-year-old professionally employed married man without a criminal record was convicted of criminal negligence causing death arising out of a motor vehicle accident. Mr. McVeigh was very drunk when the motor vehicle he was driving struck and killed a 14-year-old boy at 7:30 p.m. while the child was sitting on his bicycle less than a foot from the curb under a street lamp on a well-lit and dry multi-lane residential parkway. In other words, an offender guilty of an offence manifesting such an elevated degree of moral blameworthiness cannot point to the absence of a record in mitigation. S/he certainly cannot point to that blameless criminal history as proof that s/he knows right from wrong. . ..

Secondly, the prosecution may lead evidence suggesting that despite the lack of a record, the offender has engaged in such conduct in the past, and is therefore not entitled to claim the full (or any) credit for the absence of a criminal record. In the case of Mr. McVeigh, page 148 [C.C.C.] underscores his drinking "problem" for years. He stated to the probation and parole officer who prepared the pre-sentence report that alcohol became a real problem for him around the age of 21 and he described himself as a "binge drinker" who would be sober all week and become "totally smashed" on weekends. "Although his excessive drinking was causing problems in his marriage, he took no steps to resolve his alcohol problem until after the tragic events. . .". In such circumstances, the refusal to take any steps to avoid the type of harm that resulted carries with it an elevated degree of moral blame, even in the absence of a prior conviction.

Recall that in *R. v. McVeigh, supra,* evidence was considered by the Court of Appeal suggesting heavy and sustained alcohol abuse in the past. It was not made plain, however, that the offender had operated a motor vehicle while impaired in the past, although the inference was not far removed. . . The case report of *R. v. Levesque* (2001), [2001] O.J. No. 210, 30 M.V.R. (4th) 246, 2001 CarswellOnt 176 (C.A.), provides a direct example of such a finding of prior criminal misconduct, and not just of an inference. It provides a typical example of the controversy that surrounds the prosecution's attempt to advance evidence of prior, unprosecuted misconduct, as an aggravating element in sentencing.

Finlayson, Labrosse and Laskin, JJ.A. observed in the course of their brief oral endorsement that:

> [3] The pre-sentence report indicated that the appellant began drinking at the age of 16 and that there was ample evidence of a more longstanding substance abuse problem than the appellant would suggest. He admitted to a previous conviction for Over 80 mgs. and Care and Control in 1971-72. Contrary to the appellant's perception, the information provided by his ex-wife and his common-law wife is indicative of alcohol-related problems right up to the time of the current offence.

Although he had a prior record involving one conviction under s. 253(b), what is of relevance for present purposes is the consideration by the Court of the evidence that he committed this type of offence on other occasions, though he was not prosecuted or convicted.

Of note, the offender pleaded guilty to impaired operation causing bodily harm. He was involved in a serious motor vehicle accident when he made a left turn without warning and collided with an approaching vehicle. His passenger, his common-law wife, sustained significant bodily injuries as a result of the accident. The breathalyzer readings were 294 and 288, more than three times the legal limit. Paragraph 1 of the judgment records the view of the Court that the readings are ". . . indicative of a conscious decision to drive despite severe intoxication." In other words, of an elevated degree of moral blame.

In the course of their decision to uphold a jail term of nine months, and to reject a plea for a conditional endorsement, their Lordships assigned significant weight to the trial judge's conclusion that, on the whole, the offender failed to recognize the seriousness of his alcohol abuse. Refer to para. 5. This conclusion was predicated upon the negative opinion advanced by the author of the pre-sentence report. In effect, the report tipped the scales against the granting of a measure of leniency.

As a result of the review of these two cases, counsel must be careful to not limit the submissions to the mere absence of a record, or the limited nature of the prior history, but must prepare full submissions addressing all prior misconduct that has been disclosed. Indeed, in certain situation to be discussed herein, it may be advantageous to press submissions in which greater wrongdoing is communicated to the sentencing court than was disclosed.

In *R. v. Dharamdeo* (2000), [2000] O.J. No. 4546, 139 O.A.C. 137, 149 C.C.C. (3d) 489, 6 M.V.R. (4th) 175, 2000 CarswellOnt 4575 (C.A.), the Court of Appeal indicated that conditional sentences for drinking and driving offenders, in which repeated injuries are caused, will be upheld only in exceptional circumstances. Shortly put, on two occasions the offender was grossly impaired in the early hours of the morning and caused accidents resulting in serious and multiple injuries. In fact, on the first, he was operating a motor vehicle alone, in contravention of his learner's permit; in the second instance, the offence occurred while he was awaiting trial.

The offender was described as a heavy "weekend drinker" in the pre-sentence report and it was noted further that he failed to complete a residential alcohol treatment program. His parents were unable to control his actions. The Court of Appeal reviewed the sentencing principles enunciated in various cases touching upon drinking and driving offences and remarked that "[i]mprisonment has been recognized by the courts as properly promoting general deterrence and denunciation in the context of drinking and driving related offences." Refer to para. 22. Further, that "[g]eneral deterrence in these cases should be the predominate concern, and such deterrence is not realized by over emphasizing that individual deterrence is seldom needed once tragedy has resulted from the driving."

Further yet, quoting *R. v. Biancofiore* (1997), [1997] O.J. No. 3865, 119 C.C.C. (3d) 344, 1997 CarswellOnt 3218, 29 M.V.R. (3d) 90, 35 O.R. (3d) 782, 103 O.A.C. 292, 10 C.R. (5th) 200 (C.A.), at paras 22-24 (para. 25 of *Dharamdeo*):

> There is nothing to indicate that the need for harsh measures in the interests of general deterrence has abated. Only two years ago, Cory J. again drew attention to the problem of drinking and driving in *R. v. Bernshaw*, [1994] S.C.J. No. 87, 95 C.C.C. (3d) 193 (S.C.C.) at 204:
>
>> Every year drunk driving leaves a terrible trail of death, agony, heartbreak and destruction. From the point of view of numbers alone, it has a far greater impact on Canadian society than any other crime. In terms of the deaths and serious injuries resulting in hospitalizations, drunk driving is clearly the crime which causes the most significant social loss to the country.

The Court of Appeal then cited *Proulx*, at para 129: "Moreover, dangerous driving and impaired driving may be offences for which harsh sentences plausibly provide general deterrence. These crimes are often committed by otherwise law-abiding persons with good employment records and families. Arguably such persons are the ones most likely to be deterred by the threat of severe penalties." Having concluded that the sentencing judge erred in law in failing to give proper consideration to the principle of general deterrence and the need for a denunciatory sentence, the Court substituted a five-month jail term, effective that date, which would have been longer but for the prior completion of the six-month conditional sentence.

In *R. v. Mould* (2000), [2000] O.J. No. 3040, 135 O.A.C. 294, 6 M.V.R. (4th) 150, 2000 CarswellOnt 2890 (C.A.), the offender was found guilty after trial of impaired driving causing death and impaired driving causing bodily harm. The circumstances, as in all such cases, were tragic. He and two of his friends were drinking together and his driving caused the death of one friend and injury to the other friend. The trial judge imposed a conditional sentence of 15 months with a five-year suspension from driving. The Crown's appeal was dismissed, no grounds for interference having been shown. One suspects that the judgment can be distinguished from *Biancofiore* and the subsequent judgment in *Dharamdeo* on the grounds that they involved repeated instances of dangerous conduct.

13. ROAD RAGE

A brief word touching upon road rage will be of assistance. In *R. v. McCalla* (2000), [2000] O.J. No. 399, 2000 CarswellOnt 415 (C.A.) involving a dangerous driving related offence unrelated to alcohol, the offender received a sentence of 15 months to be followed by three years probation. He was guilty of an attack on the driver of another car that he thought was guilty of reckless driving. In effect, he followed the complainant intent upon exacting revenge and introduced a dangerous weapon into the confrontation and used it to inflict a very serious injury on the complainant. See para. 7. Notwithstanding the favourable aspects, notably that he was a first time offender and by all accounts a hardworking decent person enjoying a positive background, the Court of Appeal did not consider it a fit case for a s. 742.1 sentence. As the trial judge said, "the facts called out for a deterrent sentence". Refer again to para. 7.

14. THE TRAGIC CONSEQUENCES OF THE OFFENDER'S ACTIONS

As a matter of common sense, sentencing courts will weigh the tragic consequences of criminal wrongdoing but in this respect, as in all other matters susceptible of being influenced by advocacy, care must be taken not to let the unfortunate results obscure the objective evaluation of the conduct and the moral blame attributable to the offender. Indeed, as a matter of common experience, tragic consequences may result from comparitively innocuous events while nothing remarkable may flow from incredibly dangerous incidents.

An example of the general rule is seen in *R. v. LeBeau* (2001), [2001] O.J. No. 3241, 148 O.A.C. 256, 14 M.V.R. (4th) 166, 2001 CarswellOnt 2782 (C.A.). The Court dismissed a sentence appeal brought by the offender. At para. 14, it noted that the trial judge "concluded that because of the enormity of the tragic consequences of the appellant's actions, his duty was to impose a sentence that would send a 'clear and unequivocal message' emphasizing the principles of general deterrence." Thus, a conditional sentence of imprisonment would "in no way act as a general deterrent or properly reflect society's denunciation of the appellant's actions." Refer again to para. 14.

No error in principle was disclosed by the sentence or the reasons behind it. The offender was found guilty of four counts of criminal negligence causing death, one count of criminal negligence causing bodily harm, four counts of impaired causing death and one count of impaired driving causing bodily harm. She was sentenced to fours years in jail, and to a driving prohibition of 15 years. As set out at para. 2, the offender was involved in a tragic high-speed car crash that left four young passengers dead, and seriously injured two others, including herself, although that factor was not noted further.

In this respect, note the four-year sentence meted out in *R. v. Colbourne* (2001), [2001] O.J. No. 3620, 157 C.C.C. (3d) 273, 149 O.A.C. 132, 19 M.V.R. (4th) 29, 2001 CarswellOnt 3337 (C.A.), at para. 1. The offender was convicted of impaired causing death and thus, charges of dangerous driving and "over .08" were stayed, following the entry of findings of guilt. See Note 1. The Court did not discuss the merits of the sentence.

R. v. Mascarenhas (2002), [2002] O.J. No. 2989, 2002 CarswellOnt 2517, 60 O.R. (3d) 465, 162 O.A.C. 331, 29 M.V.R. (4th) 1 (C.A.) illustrates rather dramatically the philosophy of the courts that as the moral blame attaching to the conduct increases, so should the severity of the sentence, all other things being equal. Indeed, the Court of Appeal took pains to demonstrate that it was concerned with a sentence appeal as against a total term of 12 years [reduced to 10.5 by reason of pre-trial credit] in circumstances that included blood-alcohol readings above 338 milligrams, the inability to control a vehicle such that it struck down two people walking on a roadside path, the further inability to control the vehicle after the fatal collision, not to mention a horrendous drinking and driving record and bail conditions prohibiting both drinking and driving. Very little could be said in mitigation, save for guilty pleas at various stages of the proceedings, and some efforts to overcome alcoholism.

The issue came down to this: whether the global sentence was open to appellate intervention as being outside the appropriate range. Dealing first with the nine-year term, prior to credit, for the counts of criminal negligence causing death, it upheld this disposition chiefly on two grounds: Firstly, as set out at paras. 15-21, the case-law supported a continuing need to increase the severity of sentences in such cases of "deliberate endangerment" in order to highlight the principle of general deterrence; secondly, Parliament's repeated intervention in increasing the sentencing regime marks its wish to protect the community by means of more exacting penalties. Support for this proposition is seen at paras. 22-25.

In the same vein, the Court of Appeal did not find any reason to intervene in the trial judge's decision to impose two consecutive terms of six months for the breaches of the recognizance prohibiting drinking and the operation of a motor vehicle. Recognizing that the principle is to direct concurrent dispositions in cases of offences arising out of the same transactions, it nevertheless held that in accordance with *R. v. Gummer* (1983), 1 O.A.C. 141, 1983 CarswellOnt 119, [1983] O.J. No. 181, 38 C.R. (3d) 46, 25 M.V.R. 282 (C.A.), sentences for offences arising in such cases may be made consecutive if the offences "constitute invasions of different legally protected interests, although the principle of totality must be kept in mind." See para. 31. Accordingly, as the prohibitions found in the recognizance were attempting to protect other interests than merely the prevention of impaired operation, they could be the subject of consecutive penalties.

15. BREACH OF COURT ORDERS DESIGNED TO PROTECT THE PUBLIC

Prosecuting counsel achieve great success by emphasizing the type of moral blame described in the case of *R. v. Biancofiore* (1997), [1997] O.J. No. 3865, 119 C.C.C. (3d) 344, 35 O.R. (3d) 782, 103 O.A.C. 292, 10 C.R. (5th) 200, 29 M.V.R. (3d) 90, 1997 CarswellOnt 3218 (C.A.). Shortly put, the offender was convicted of dangerous driving causing bodily harm, "over 80" and take automobile without consent. The Court of Appeal emphasized the following remarks at para. 28 and 31:

> [28] The pressing need to ensure that the drinking and driving offences not be destigmatized might not be met by a conditional sentence in this case. More importantly, there is no reason why the denunciatory burden should not be borne by this offender. This was a particularly serious case, not merely because of the consequences. The course of conduct included breach of probation, the unlawful taking of the vehicle and a pattern of driving dangerously while his blood-alcohol level exceeded the maximum

permitted by law, which led to the maiming of another human being.

[31] The moral culpability of the respondent in this case was high, particularly having regard to the intentional risk-taking manifested in the manner of driving and the consequential harm caused. For the same reasons, I am also satisfied that a period of incarceration would be consistent with the other principle of restraint expressed in s. 718.2(d), which requires that the Court not deprive the offender of his liberty "if less restrictive sanctions may be appropriate in the circumstances"

Of further interest, para. 32 begins by emphasizing that no single factor may be decisive. In other words, counsel might succeed in blunting the reach of the moral blame associated with the conduct, but it is presumed that breaching a court order placed to protect the community is an indication of the need for the allocation of greater, not lesser, correctional resources.

16.   THE MORAL BLAME ASSOCIATED WITH DRUG OFFENCES:

As in the case of violence in general, and in the case of driving offences in particular, the more significant is the harm, the more likely it will be that the Court will respond with a significant sentence. This is true as well in the case of drug offences for the moral blame assigned to a pursuit that yields great profit, on the one hand, and great harm to the community in terms of both ruined lives by addiction and the commission of crimes to obtain funds, on the other, is quite elevated. Again, care must be exercised by counsel to ensure that no aggravating weight is assigned that is not justified, particularly with respect to the many stereotypical elements that are associated with drug trafficking.

a)   The scale of offending and moral blame

The case of *R. v. Wu* (2002), [2002] O.J. No. 4758, 2002 CarswellOnt 4233, 170 C.C.C. (3d) 225, 167 O.A.C. 141 (C.A.) underscores that the more dangerous the drug, and the more extensive the degree of criminal involvement, the greater the sentence, all other things being equal. Thus, para. 72 reads as follows: "First, heroin is clearly one of the most deadly and devastating of all the proscribed drugs. That is the drug—in a 92 per cent pure form—the appellants carried." In addition, para. 73 reads: ". . . importation is the most serious of all the drug offences. That is the offence the appellants committed."

b)   The scale of the offence in terms of value

R. v. Wu (2002), [2002] O.J. No. 4758, 2002 CarswellOnt 4233, 170 C.C.C. (3d) 225, 167 O.A.C. 141 (C.A.) also records that the appellants imported 60 bricks of heroin with an estimated street value of $50,400,000. This quantity of heroin would have provided about 1,680,000 individual hits on the street. This was seen as particularly aggravating. See para. 74.

c)   The potential for profit and moral blameworthiness

This issue was discussed briefly in *R. v. Pham* (2002), [2002] O.J. No. 2545, 2002 CarswellOnt 2121, 161 O.A.C. 80, 167 C.C.C. (3d) 570, 94 C.R.R. (2d) 371, 6 C.R. (6th) 373 (C.A.), a case involving the smuggling of cigarettes but whose instruction is valuable to drug cases in general.

The Court stressed the direct link between the size of the fine and the quantity of the illegal substance. "Those who possess larger quantities are clearly players in larger criminal enterprises with larger illegal profits for whom larger minimum fines are rationally founded. The use of this factor, which is both objective and reasonable, to regulate the size of the minimum fine ensures that the punishment will not be grossly disproportionate." Refer to para. 19. As a result, if it is suggested that such fines are disproportionate to "mules", as opposed to the "brains", the Court would respond that the "brains" should receive far greater fines... See para. 20.

d)   Drug offences lead to destruction of individuals and communities

An excellent and somewhat rare example of expert evidence being led to substantiate aggravating factors in sentencing is found in the case of *R. v. A. (F.)* (1989), [1989] O.J. No. 2453, 1989 CarswellOnt 1501 (C.A.). The Court was informed of the serious adverse effects resulting from ingesting crack cocaine, on the one hand, and of disruption to the community by crack consumption, on the other. As we read at para. 1:

> The appellant was convicted of trafficking in cocaine, more precisely, crack, and being in possession of cocaine (crack) for

the purpose of trafficking. The dispositions under appeal were 12 months secure and 6 months open custody respectively. The expert evidence of a doctor described the serious medical consequences, especially mental and emotional disturbances, resulting from the use of crack. The expert evidence of a community relations counsellor employed by the Metro Toronto Housing Authority described the terrible disruptive effects in the community caused by crack dealers. These facts, taken together with the extremely negative pre-disposition report, which showed that the appellant had not responded to three previous dispositions where terms of probation were imposed, were properly relied on by the trial judge. In our view, the disposition is not inconsistent with the purposes of the *Young Offenders Act.*

17. THE WORST-CASE ANALYSIS: THE REFORMED RULE

Consideration in greater depth of the extreme end of the scale touching upon the severity of harm reveals that extreme violence is typically visited with extremely severe sentences. In this respect, more severe sentences are typically upheld in the case of sexual offenders described as sexual predators. For example, in *R. v. H. (T.)* (2000), [2000] O.J. No. 4644, 2000 CarswellOnt 4711 (C.A.), the Court of Appeal did not interfere with a nine-year sentence imposed in the case of sexual offences occurring between 1966 and 1969 and involving two step-daughters who were between four and nine years of age. He was guilty of numerous incidents of various kinds of sexual assault including rape and physical abuse, which took place in the homes in which the appellant resided with his step-daughters and their mother. At para. 11, the Court noted, "...the trial judge characterized this case as unusual and as probably one of the worst case scenarios. As pointed out by the Crown, the appellant was a sexual predator in his own home. He abused the position of trust and authority vested in him and frequently and seriously abused two children in his care. Under the circumstances, we think that the sentence was fit."

R. v. DaSilva (2002), [2002] O.J. No. 4695, 2002 CarswellOnt 4159, 166 O.A.C. 295 (C.A.) provides a valuable illustration of the reformed rule respecting the "worst group of offences and a worst group of offenders" type of situation as described in *R. v. Olsen* (1999), [1999] O.J. No. 218, 131 C.C.C. (3d) 355, 1999 CarswellOnt 186, 22 C.R. (5th) 80, 116 O.A.C. 357 (C.A.). The offenders were convicted of numerous offences as a result of the car jacking, kidnapping, assault, extortion and robbery of two innocent victims. As made plain at para. 1, "[t]he horrendous night of terror that followed the car jacking lasted 11½ hours. The victims were abducted, unlawfully confined both in their car and in the trunk of the car, and then in an apartment, severely assaulted repeatedly, robbed, threatened with a firearm, and forced to supply their home access code so that the appellants could enter and burglarize their home. Their confinement would have continued to unknown results but for their fortuitous escape from a co-accused..."

With respect to the consequences for the victims, para. 2 informs us that "[t]he offences have had, and continue to have, a lasting and profound psychological effect on the two victims and a physical effect on one victim who sustained serious injuries during the vicious assaults."

The trial judge sentenced L.D., who was 22 years old at the time of sentencing, to 18 years' imprisonment and a parole ineligibility order was made requiring that he serve one-half of his sentence. As for T.M., who was 23 years old at sentencing, he was sentenced to 16 years imprisonment and a similar parole ineligibility order was made. These sentences were upheld, the only success the offenders enjoyed on appeal being a precise endorsement touching upon credit on a two-for-one basis for the substantial pre-trial detention they underwent.

Para. 6 is instructive in setting out the following remarks:

> The trial judge categorized these offences as one of those few examples of a crime that goes beyond pure horror. The nature of the offences, coupled with the offenders' motive, fall within that category of criminal conduct requiring the strongest form of denunciation. It is wrong to compare cases in search of some comparable level of horror as the appellants appear to do. In the words of Laskin J.A., speaking for this court in *R. v. Olsen and Podniewicz*, [*supra*], this case fits the description of a "worst group of offences and a worst group of offenders".

In other words, we are no longer to focus on the traditional "worst case, worst offender" test, in which the focus is on an absolute standard, but rather on a standard of superlatives in the sense it is within the class or group of "worst" offences and offenders. To the extent that the two situations are among the class deserving of the most extreme condemnation, then the most severe sentencing response is merited. In other words, to be concerned solely with pointing to a worse case or offender serves to insulate grave offender and offences from the proper degree of sanction. In this respect, note that the Court then set out these observations, at para. 7:

> The trial judge considered all the relevant factors in arriving at a global sentence. He was justified in imposing a sentence that reflected the gravity of the offences, reinforced the principles of denunciation and general deterrence, and maintained public respect for the administration of justice. The appellants have failed to show that the sentences are demonstrably unfit or that they represent a substantial and marked departure from sentences in similar circumstances so as to justify the intervention of this Court.

A further issue touched upon the background of the offenders. As set out at para. 5, "[t]he trial judge found that the appellants were career criminals who had intentionally embarked upon a violent criminal path of life and had treated jail and the criminal justice system as mere occupational hazards." In addition, "[b]oth appellants had amassed significant criminal records which began as young offenders and carried into adulthood. Their records include serious crimes of violence."

R. v. Thongdara (2000), [2000] O.J. No. 1832, 132 O.A.C. 256, 2000 CarswellOnt 1872 (C.A.) includes this observation, at para. 4: "It is difficult to imagine a worse case than this [of robbery and extortion] and the offender, despite his youth, approaches the worst offender status." Hence, the Court refused to interfere with a total sentence of 18 years, notwithstanding two years of pre-trial detention.

I pause to once again urge counsel to be vigilant in their duty in that advocacy remains a quite valuable instrument at this stage of sentencing. It is not because the situation seems quite bleak that efforts ought not to be made to canvass closely the elements of the case law that are favourable. Indeed, it is quite precisely because the situation appears so bleak that the offender and the Court require signal assistance. In this respect again, it must be repeated that no single orthodox position governs and courts may reach quite divergent views.

For example, *R. v. Y. (T.)* (2002), [2002] O.J. No. 3473, 2002 CarswellOnt 2915 (C.A.), illustrates this richness of perspectives. The majority opinion emphasized that "[t]he facts supporting the offence of criminal negligence causing death are not often seen to be much worse than this case. Moreover, the appellant meets the general description of the worst offender. The victim impact was serious." Refer to para. 1. In addition, although it found the sentence of eight years to be a lengthy one, it was found to be fit in the circumstances. See para. 3. By contrast, the dissenting judgment is reduced to a cryptic "Charron J.A. would have reduced the global sentence of eight years to one of six years." Refer to para. 4. For present purposes, what is significant is the example of how reasonable individuals can draw quite different judgments of the same facts.

18. CASES OF "STARK HORROR"

At the extreme end of the scale are offences that are described as being of "stark horror". As a general rule, sentencing courts will select a life sentence in cases of "stark horror" to reflect the greatly elevated moral blame arising in such cases. In *R. v. Cheddesingh* (2002), [2002] O.J. No. 3176, 2002 CarswellOnt 2660, 162 O.A.C. 151, 60 O.R. (3d) 721, 168 C.C.C. (3d) 310 (C.A.), leave to appeal allowed (2003), [2003] S.C.C.A. No. 112, 2003 CarswellOnt 3302, 2003 CarswellOnt 3303 (S.C.C.), Justice Abella, Carthy and Macpherson JJ.A., concurring, up-held a life sentence imposed in the case of a rape and manslaughter of a 76-year-old woman by a 20-year-old offender, without a single reference to the case law. Indeed, the brutal and abhorrent facts were so vile that the Court of Appeal had no difficulty in concluding that the offence was one of "stark horror", and thus deserving of the imposition of the maximum sentence of life imprisonment. In sum, the offender broke into two separate dwellings earlier on the evening in question, throwing a bottle of gasoline at the feet of one occupant, to then ransack the apartment of an 82-year-old male who did not awake. Thereafter, he entered the apartment of his next victim, and engaged in conduct that is movingly described by the trial judge at para. 14. The degra-dation, both physical and psychological, led to her death within a month...

Hence, para. 15 records the Court's conclusion in this respect in re-jecting the submission that life imprisonment was an excessive dis-position: "This compelling depiction manifestly justifies the decision to characterize this offence as one of 'stark horror'. I would not, therefore, interfere with the imposition of a sentence of life imprisonment."

By way of contrast, however, the Court of Appeal was reluctant to endorse this "loaded expression" in *R. v. Zhang* (2000), [2000] O.J. No. 1617, 132 O.A.C. 159, 2000 CarswellOnt 1548 (C.A.). Although it saw it as a borderline case, it held that a review of the relevant authorities did not lead to the conclusion that the offence and the circumstances surrounding warranted that label. It did add, however, "...no doubt ... that this was one of the worst cases of aggravated assault imaginable and as such, it called for a severe sentence."

By way of summary only, note that the victims were his wife and an elderly man he suspected was involved with her. Both victims suffered extreme injuries, including cuts to the head, hands and legs of his wife, severe bruising and a fractured jawbone. The scarring on her leg is permanent and the event has left her emotionally and psychologically traumatised. The other victim was set on fire, was in surgery for five hours and received 13 to 15 units of blood. He was hospitalized for nine days and then spent three months undergoing rehabilitative treatment. He suffered extensive lacerations to his head, face and neck. His hands were badly injured and two of his fingers had to be amputated. He lost eight teeth and now has to wear a denture. A fracture to the tibia bone in his left leg has left him unable to kneel and he suffers from drop foot, which causes him to walk with a limp.

19.   HARM TO MEMBERS OF PROTECTED CLASSES:

Here again counsel's duty is to select a placement of the offence(s) on the scale of wrongdoing based on the nature and severity of the harm, by and large, with the additional concern touching on the status of the victim as a member of a protected class. Indeed, the same harm visited on a differently situated individual may result in a greater allocation of moral blame, all other things being equal.

It seems that the rationale is that persons employed in certain livelihoods or in certain relationships have no choice but to expose themselves to greater risk than is otherwise the situation for the community at large. Stated otherwise, some individuals expose themselves to would-be robbers to a greater extent than the community at large. For example, taxi drivers accept fares at all hours of the day and at the most secluded of places. In the same vein, police officers must risk their lives to protect members of the community.

Hence, those who would seek to take advantage of this comparative vulnerability are considered more reprehensible than those who do not. Although this type of reasoning may be subject to the attack that it rests upon a chivalrous notion of "a fair fight", that it is less worthy of extra condemnation to attack an individual of the same size in broad daylight, it does appear to have widespread support. It should not be thought, however, that the reverse proposition is attractive—it is not mitigating to attack or rob members of non-protected classes, but in such cases no added moral blame is assigned.

a)   Peace officers

The aggravating impact of violence against a peace officer, as a member of a protected class, was made plain in *R. v. Miller* (2002), [2002] O.J. No. 3589, 2002 CarswellOnt 3057, 163 O.A.C. 63 (C.A.). Para. 4 records that the offender shot a police officer at very close range. It must be noted that the offender had been charged with attempted murder and unlawfully trafficking in cocaine, but the jury returned a verdict of not guilty of attempted murder, but guilty of the lesser included offence of aggravated assault, and guilty of trafficking in a controlled substances. See para. 5. On the conviction for aggravated assault, the trial judge sentenced the appellant to a term of eight years, which included pre-trial custody of 27 months, for which she accorded four years' credit. She also sentenced him to six months on the trafficking charge, to be served concurrently.

It will be useful to note the contents of para. 6. "The Crown submitted that the trial judge erred in principle in failing to give effect to the principle of parity now codified in sec. 718.2(b) of the Criminal Code and that, in light of this Court's decision in *R. v. Osbourne*, [1984] O.J. No. 2633, 94 C.C.C. (3d) 435, a sentence of 12 years, less credit for pre-trial custody, was required." The Court then observed, at para. 7: "The trial judge did not ignore Osbourne nor was she unmindful that the victim was a police officer, of whose profession this Court has said:

> Police officers, in the performance of their duties, are the representatives of the whole community, and an attack upon them is an attack upon the structure of a civilized society. Further, police officers, in the performance of their duties, are often in a position of special vulnerability and are entitled to such protection as the law can give. *R. v. Forrest* [1986] O.J. No. 330, 15 O.A.C. 104, at 107, per Zuber J.A.

In the Court's view, although the trial judge adverted to the requisite considerations, she gave inadequate considerations to them and, in consequence, imposed a sentence that did not reflect the gravity of the offence and was below the appropriate range. See para. 8. This error justified appellate interference. Of interest, the Court of Appeal rejected the Crown's contention that, because this case is so similar to Osbourne, parity demands a 12-year sentence. "Parity is only one of a number of principles that must be taken into consideration in imposing an appropriate sentence, and it cannot in and of itself dictate the result in all cases involving similar offenders committing similar crimes." See para. 9.

In the result, it held that taking into account all of the circumstances, an appropriate sentence that should have been imposed in the present case was ten years, less the credit the trial judge gave for pre-trial custody. In other words, a six-year term was imposed.

b) Internationally protected individuals

An outstanding example of violence against an internationally protected individual is found in the report of the assault of former Soviet Premier Kosygin. See *R. v. Matral*, [1972] 2 O.R. 25, 6 C.C.C. (2d) 62, 17 C.R.N.S. 30, 1972 CarswellOnt 1 (Prov. Ct.), affirmed [1972] 2 O.R. 752, 6 C.C.C. (2d) 574, 1972 CarswellOnt 889 (C.A.). Of interest, it was held that too great a degree of severity had been shown.

c) Employees of businesses targeted for robbery

In *R. v. Crowe* (1989), 76 Sask. R. 246, 1989 CarswellSask 368 (C.A.), we read:

> Public confidence in the administration of justice will be undermined if this serious offence of robbery with a weapon is not visited with a substantial term of imprisonment. This Court has frequently stated that robbery is the type of crime from which the public is entitled to be protected and that the sentence imposed must leave no doubt that such conduct will not be tolerated. Small shops, confectioneries and taxi operators are particularly vulnerable to this type of attack. Robbery is particularly serious because of its inherent danger to human life. Escalation of violence or a threat of violence toward a victim can easily result in death or serious bodily harm, particularly if the victim decides to resist the offender.

Refer to *R. v. Allison-McLeish* (2001), [2001] O.J. No. 845, 2001 CarswellOnt 653, 142 O.A.C. 50 (C.A.) for an example of gratuitous violence that results in an elevated degree of moral blame. In particular, para. 2 and 12-13 indicate that the offence was the robbery of a Mac's Milk at night, with a firearm, in which the victim was pistol-whipped. As noted at para. 13, "[a]lthough he had no adult record, the appellant had three prior convictions as a young offender. The trial judge was entitled to consider that general deterrence was the paramount consideration."

d) Persons enjoying the protection of court orders as members of a protected class

By way of general introduction to the question of moral blame associated with breaching court orders, refer to discussion surrounding *R. v. Biancofiore, supra*. In addition, in order to evaluate the potential aggravating impact of offences showing disrespect for court orders, reference is made to *R. v. Howlett* (2002), [2002] O.J. No. 3525, 2002 CarswellOnt 2977, 163 O.A.C. 48 (C.A.). The judgment makes plain at para. 3 that the offender's criminal record spanned a period of 15 years from 1985 to 2000 and included more than 50 convictions, ten of which were for driving while disqualified and numerous others for disrespecting court orders. The Court thus underlined not only a lengthy period of wrongdoing, but a lengthy period during which the offence in question, driving while disqualified, was committed on ten occasions. The Court also highlighted the fact that the offender was often guilty of other offences showing disrespect for court orders. At bottom, this shows a lack of insight into criminal behaviour, a failure to reform despite numerous court warnings, and unwillingness to act in a pro-social manner.

It is of interest to note that the Court of Appeal did not criticize in any way the two-year less a day conditional sentence imposed in *R. v. Casey* (2000), [2000] O.J. No. 71, 128 O.A.C. 185, 30 C.R. (5th) 126, 2000 CarswellOnt 79, 141 C.C.C. (3d) 506, 70 C.R.R. (2d) 225 (C.A.), leave to appeal refused (2000), 2000 CarswellOnt 4632, 2000 CarswellOnt 4633, [2000] S.C.C.A. No. 382, 266 N.R. 198 (note), 142 O.A.C. 398 (note) (S.C.C.) for the theft of 18 swim suits and a failure to appear. It does not lead support for the view that a conditional sentence is not available for those who breach court orders. Also, note the language recorded at para. 56: "In my opinion, the variation of the conditional sentence order was fit ... The partial revocation of the appellant's community sentence represented an appropriate remedy in light of his almost immediate disregard of the conditions of his original conditional sentence."

Turning directly to the moral blame attaching to violence directed against a person enjoying the protection of the Courts, note *R. v. Ward* (2000), [2000] O.J. No. 301, 2000 CarswellOnt 323 (C.A.). This judgment provides an example of a harsh response by the Court to sanction repeated instances of domestic violence in a case of an offender subject to a probation order protecting the victim. Note as well that in *R. v. Pupovic* (2000), [2000] O.J. No. 4427, 138 O.A.C. 193, 2000 CarswellOnt 4112 (C.A.), leave to appeal refused (2001), 2001 CarswellOnt 872, 2001 CarswellOnt 873, 271 N.R. 192 (note), 149 O.A.C. 199 (note) (S.C.C.), the offender breached the condition requiring him to stay away from the home of the victim. See para. 12.

In *R. v. Krushel* (2000), [2000] O.J. No. 302, 130 O.A.C. 160, 31 C.R. (5th) 295 (C.A.), the Court was influenced against the granting of a conditional sentence in part by the offender's failure to honour a peace bond. Refer to para. 31. A breach of recognizance may be decisive in the decision to refuse a conditional endorsement. See para. 1 of *R. v. S. (D.)* (2000), [2000] O.J. No. 2611, 2000 CarswellOnt 2486 (C.A.).

20.   TAKING INTO ACCOUNT OTHER WRONGDOING

In the evaluation of the objective harm caused to victims of crime, it is permissible in certain instances with the consent of the offender for the aggravating impact of having other misconduct taken into account as illustrated in *R. v. Howlett* (2002), [2002] O.J. No. 3525, 2002 CarswellOnt 2977, 163 O.A.C. 48 (C.A.). It provides an example of a sentencing court taking into account, and acting upon in the selection of a fit and proper sentence, information suggesting other misconduct, even though it will not result in a separate finding of guilt. This case serves as a good example of the operation of the "*R. v. Garcia and Silva*" rule, and of its contemporary manifestation as s. 725 of the Code.

Firstly, note the comments found at para. 4:

> At the time of sentencing, certain facts relating to a charge of threatening were read in on consent of both Crown and defence counsel. On February 7, 2002, the police attended the appellant's residence in reference to another investigation involving the appellant's spouse, Brenda Howlett. In relating her version of events, she advised the police officers that, on a prior date, the appellant had threatened to punch her glasses from her face. The appellant was charged accordingly. Those facts were admitted to by the appellant through his counsel. Both the Crown and defence counsel took the position that these facts could be taken into account pursuant to the principle of sentencing in *Garcia v. Silva*. The charge of threatening was then withdrawn.

Paragraph 5 records the following information in this respect.

Counsel also acknowledged in his submissions that Crown counsel would be seeking a probation order in relation to the threatening incident, on conditions that the appellant take an anger management course and that he not communicate with Ms. Howlett without her consent and the consent of the probation officer. Counsel indicated that the appellant wanted to take an anger management course and specifically asked that this condition be made part of the probation order. Counsel further indicated that his client realized that the non-communication condition would be imposed and that he had a place to stay upon his release.

Secondly, note that the prosecution sought a probation order in relation to "the charge not pled to" on the same conditions that had been described by defence counsel. Refer to para. 6.

In the result, the trial judge concluded that the situation was aggravated in part "by the other facts that were read in 'pursuant to the principle in *Garcia v. Silva*'." Refer to para. 8. Of interest, para. 8(b) sets out the offender's ground of appeal according to which the trial judge erred in sentencing him to a period of probation in relation to a threatening charge that was withdrawn.

By reason of the importance of the guidance advanced by Justice Charron, it will be useful to set out at length the holding as set out at paras. 10-14.

[10] I see no reason to interfere with the imposition of the probation period in relation to the threatening charge. The facts related to the threatening charge were read in on consent of both Crown and defence counsel and agreed to by the appellant through his counsel. Both counsel acknowledged that the Court could take these facts into account in sentencing. It is apparent from the record that they also agreed that these facts would form the basis for the imposition of a probation order on conditions as set out by counsel. The charge was then withdrawn by Crown counsel.

[11] Express reference was made to the principle in *R. v. Garcia and Silva*, [1970] 1 O.R. 821, [1970] 3 C.C.C. 124 (C.A.), as the basis for following this procedure. This Court in *Garcia and Silva* recognized that where an accused is sentenced for one offence, a judge may take into consideration other convictions and, on some occasions and under proper safeguards, other outstanding charges. This procedure has been codified by parts of s. 725 of

the Criminal Code: see *R. v. Edwards* (2001), 54 O.R. (3d) 737
(C.A.), for an analysis of the principles governing the use of untried
offences in sentencing.

[12] As this Court recognized in *Edwards,* s. 725 is consistent
with the presumption of innocence as it allows for the punishment
or sentencing of an offender for untried offences only when appropriate safeguards are taken. Of particular relevance to this case
are the provisions contained in s. 725(1)(b.1) . . .

21.   HARM TO ADMINISTRATION OF JUSTICE

In *R. v. D. (C.)* (2000), [2000] O.J. No. 1668, 132 O.A.C. 133, 2000
CarswellOnt 1569 (C.A.), the Court noted that the proper range for
perjury depends on the purpose served by the falsehood. Refer to p.
134, para. 7. "Perjury is a serious offence ... it strikes at the heart of
the administration of justice. In the present case, it was committed for
the intended personal benefit of the appellant [to secure] his release
from custody pending his appeal ... We recognize that the offence can
be committed in a graver setting, for example, in giving evidence in a
trial of a serious offence in which case the sentence would, generally,
be heavier." The Court upheld a one-year sentence, while noting that
the sentence might have been shorter and still have been within the
acceptable range.

22.   FIRST OFFENDERS TO INCORRIGIBLE OFFENDERS: AN EXAMINATION:

a)   Introduction

Broadly formulated, offenders who have no criminal history are entitled
to claim a large measure of leniency from the sentencing courts, all
other things being equal. The animating rationale may be expressed
in two parts:

> i) it is presumed that the previous good conduct supports
> the view that the offender has well assimilated the community's
> socialization and understands right from wrong, and

> ii) it is presumed that s/he has developed a sufficient "moral
> compass" that the process of reformation begins upon arrest.

In the result, fewer correctional resources need be assigned by the sentencing court to correct what is considered to be an aberrant display of morally blameworthy conduct.

By way of further introductory comment, recall the guidance in this century-old case. In *R. v. Hayward* (1902), [1902] O.J. No. 12, 5 O.L.R. 65, 6 C.C.C. 399 (H.C.), Boyd C. observed that the offender pleaded guilty to stealing 88 cents out of the church box. He was sentenced to a "term of two years to the provincial reformatory." The trial judge appears to have been informed that he was "over 17". Boyd C. remarked at para. 12, page 67, "The defendant has been imprisoned since the 2nd of October . . . As a first offender, he has perhaps been sufficiently convinced that it is not advisable to depart from the paths of honesty, and in hope that he may not again offend I now order his discharge." It was then December 12.

b) First offenders: The absence of a prior record demonstrates a capacity for pro-social conduct:

i) In the case of no prior blameworthy conduct

As a general rule, a measure of leniency is often extended to first offenders on the grounds that they have a functioning "moral compass", as evidenced by a history of pro-social conduct, and that whatever wrongdoing occurred is a manifestation of aberrant conduct, often associated with a temporary or episodic "triggering" event.

Hence, if the nature of the offence or the circumstances of its commission are such that the Court can have but little confidence in the ability of the offender's "conscience" to guide further pro-social conduct, it will intervene to a greater extent than would otherwise be appropriate or necessary. Sexual violence involving an adult offender in a situation of trust and a vulnerable child (or children) extending over a period of time including escalating abuse provides one of many possible examples of a heightened need for intervention. In the case of *R. v. L. (J.)* (2000), [2000] O.J. No. 3806, 2000 CarswellOnt 3704, 137 O.A.C. 1 (C.A.), para. 24 sets out that "The impact on the victims has been profound and is ongoing." The offender is an older brother of the young victims and he employed a significant degree of physical force and threats of harm over the years to further his abuse starting when the victims were quite young.

If we reverse the proposition, this view may be expressed as follows: A first offence resulting from a minimal degree of morally blameworthy conduct not indicative of an offender committed to an anti-social lifestyle may not require much by way of correctional or punitive resources. An example is found in *R. v. Flores* (2000), [2000] O.J. No. 1991, 2000 CarswellOnt 1886 (C.A.). The Court of Appeal for Ontario underscored that an individualized disposition was possible even in cases of extreme violence if it can be shown that it was an isolated instance of wrongdoing "borne of adolescent jealousy." Refer to para. 2.

Doubtless, in this situation as in most other sentencing scenarios, counsel must be skilful in attempting to address the underlying tension between the wish of the sentencing court to be lenient in the case of first offenders and the imperatives of denunciation and general deterrence.

For example, no success was enjoyed in *R. v. Cameron* (1991), [1991] M.J. No. 502, 75 Man. R. (2d) 290, 6 W.A.C. 290, 1991 CarswellMan 366 (C.A.), the Court noted at page 7 (Q.L.): "The factors cited in mitigation, such as the accused's alleged drunkenness on the night in question, the favourable pre-sentence report, the absence of a previous criminal record and the accused's relatively settled family life and work history, neither individually nor collectively justify a reduction of the sentence from the three-year starting point." In other words, the "punitive" elements in sentencing were awarded pride of place by reason of the morally elevated nature of the misconduct.

By way of contrast, in the somewhat unusual case of *R. v. MacDougall* (1995), [1995] M.J. No. 531, 107 Man. R. (2d) 236, 109 W.A.C. 236, 1995 CarswellMan 459 (C.A.) the offender was led by her son to attempt to smuggle narcotics into the jail in which he was detained. At para. 3, the Court noted: "The accused co-operated with police authorities and entered a plea of guilty. A pre-sentence report indicates that the accused realizes the gravity of her wrongdoing, and is remorseful." She had no record and was trying to protect her son from harm he said would befall him unless she delivered the narcotics. The Court of Appeal agreed with the trial judge that such exceptional circumstances including ". . . her desire to help her son out of difficulties, the fact that no money was involved, her clear record, and her personal circumstances" militated in favour of leniency. Refer to para. 5.

It is suggested that the reason for leniency being held out in the latter case, and not in the former, resides in the Court's characterization of the moral blame attached to the conduct. Hence, it is counsel's duty to frame submissions in which not only is the moral blame addressed, it is neutralized whenever possible. In light of the fact that the absence of a prior record demonstrates a capacity for pro-social conduct, and presumably permits leniency to be at the forefront of the Court's sentencing options at the outset, counsel has an advantage at the outset.

ii) In the case of prior blameworthy conduct not resulting in a record: If the offender can cease harmful conduct?

We now turn our attention to a situation in which there is some element of prior blameworthy conduct, but no prior record. Recall the facts of *R. v. L. (J.)* (2000), [2000] O.J. No. 3806, 2000 CarswellOnt 3704, 137 O.A.C. 1 (C.A.). The offender was involved in sexual violence over a period of time and in breach of a situation of trust. This simple example demonstrates that although no prior record was in evidence prior to sentencing, the offender could not point to the same degree of morally blameless conduct, as would one who only offended on one occasion, or on fewer occasions.

Simply put, the moral blame increases with the number of prior "offences", even if not prosecuted. The rationale is that with each instance of wrongdoing, the offender is given an opportunity to draw back from the wrongful conduct, and to correct the behaviour as a result of the operation of one's conscience or "moral compass" as I choose to describe it. The failure to do so is aggravating and the repeated failure to do so is greatly aggravating.

In such situations, counsel should strive to identify elements of mitigation. A first area of advocacy would be in reference to the period between any and each such misconduct not unlike the application of the "gap" principle, discussed elsewhere. Counsel might also seek to present evidence of the offender's efforts at overcoming addiction, even if not successful, as this demonstrates a responsible attitude and an attempt at "fixing the blame on the bottle", etc., which may be of some benefit. This form of submission would be apt in a case of longstanding drug involvement, for example.

In this respect, note is made of *R. v. Morrison* (1999), [1999] O.J. No. 2655, 123 O.A.C. 203, 1999 CarswellOnt 2191 (C.A.) and of *R. v. H. (J.)* (1999), 118 O.A.C. 354, [1999] O.J. No. 1308, 135 C.C.C. (3d) 338, 1999 CarswellOnt 1048 (C.A.) in which we are instructed that it is improper to reject the objective of rehabilitation simply because an offender has previously tried treatment programmes and failed, even when treatment was a term of interim release! Counsel might also wish to advance submissions to indicate that an unusual element was at play that no longer need concern the Court. An example might involve the influence of the lead offender whose influence has been neutralized.

c) Prior blameworthy conduct not resulting in a record: Domestic violence

A further area of general concern for counsel in sentencing in this respect involves evidence of prior wrongdoing suggesting the commission of domestic violence although not resulting in a conviction. Again, counsel must be industrious in attempting to answer the question, what is to be done with information suggesting prior misconduct that was not prosecuted? There is no advantage to repeating the earlier discussion. As a result, only one example from the case law need be reviewed briefly.

The case of *R. v. Zhang* (2000), [2000] O.J. No. 1617, 132 O.A.C. 159, 2000 CarswellOnt 1548 (C.A.) is noteworthy in this respect. The offender's wife, the victim of severe beating, testified as to prior assaults she suffered as part of the narrative and to explain certain actions she took. These were taken into account by the trial judge in assessing penalty and the Court of Appeal did not raise any concerns about this procedure. See para. 25. Indeed, it was seen as a significant aggravating feature.

Counsel might wish to distinguish the case on the grounds that the evidence was not challenged, and raise the concern that any misconduct outside of the scope of the charging instrument is denied. Obviously, care must be taken not to permit the prosecution to lead too wide ranging testimony in this respect, but to challenge all evidence of prior misconduct might lead to undesirable consequences including the need to recall the victim. The submission of a victim impact statement must also be considered and dealt with as fully as possible.

d) Prior blameworthy conduct not resulting in a record: Sexual and other violence advanced as similar fact

One further area touches upon the aggravating weight to be advanced in cases of successful prosecutions in which evidence is led of sexual or other violence which is advanced as similar fact evidence. This question admits of no simple answer but it seems that general principles of sentencing and s. 724 of the Code are not offended by the prosecution submitting that evidence of such misconduct may be considered.

Two examples are known. In one report, *R. v. Batte* (2000), (*sub nom.* R. v. W.B.) [2000] O.J. No. 2186, (*sub nom.* R. v. W.B.) 133 O.A.C. 3, 145 C.C.C. (3d) 498, 34 C.R. (5th) 263, 76 C.R.R. (2d) 189, 2000 CarswellOnt 2114 (C.A.), the prosecution was stayed due to unreasonable delay. Nevertheless, the misconduct that was the subject matter of the "stay" by reason of delay was advanced and considered in the companion prosecution, *R. v. Batte* (2000), [2000] O.J. No. 2184, 49 O.R. (3d) 321, 134 O.A.C. 1, 145 C.C.C. (3d) 449, 34 C.R. (5th) 197, 2000 CarswellOnt 2113 (C.A.).

R. c. Ménard (2002), [2002] J.Q. No. 5271, 2002 CarswellQue 2626 (C.A.), is also apposite. Para. 18 reports that the trial judge was correct to emphasize the offender's prior record including similar facts respecting conduct in 1994. Although the case did not involve a first offender, it does support the view that such prior "unproven" misconduct may be considered at the sentencing stage.

e) Sprees: Prior misconduct not resulting in a record but that is aggravating at sentencing

A further area of concern in the case of first offenders surrounds the question of the commission of sprees. The guiding principle is that the offender remains a primary or first wrongdoer: S/he did not betray the Court's leniency by committing a further offence after receiving a first sentence that serves as an explanation of society's expectations and as a warning of future difficulties if there is any repetition of the wrongdoing. It is obvious that the offender did not have a sufficiently operative moral compass to provide a "brake" to arrest the misconduct at any point and the lack of fortitude and insight as to the harm being caused must be taken into account, but this is not as grave as in the case of one who has been sentenced.

Of course, it is always a question of degree. Thus, to commit two separate offences of impaired driving prior to being arrested for either is a serious matter, but less morally blameworthy than to have committed three. It is also less blameworthy than to have committed the second (and third, as the case might be), after being arrested and released without conditions of bail for the first, and so on. In this respect, refer in general to *R. v. Skolnick*, [1982] 2 S.C.R. 47, 138 D.L.R. (3d)

193, 42 N.R. 460, 68 C.C.C. (2d) 385, 29 C.R. (3d) 143, 16 M.V.R. 35, 1982 CarswellOnt 76, 1982 CarswellOnt 737.

In the case of an offender involved in a number of offences, be they car thefts, break and enters, et cetera, the duty of defence counsel is to point out that whatever failings may have been present respecting the offender's ability to recognize the misconduct for what it is, and to desist voluntarily, s/he did not enjoy the benefit of the assistance of the Court, nor the warning as to future punishment.

In this respect, refer to para. 32 of *R. v. De La Cruz* (2003), [2003] O.J. No. 1971, 2003 CarswellOnt 1921, 178 C.C.C. (3d) 128, 174 C.C.C. (3d) 554, 172 O.A.C. 177 (C.A.), additional reasons at (2003), 2003 CarswellOnt 3128 (C.A.). The misconduct in question was dealt with by the sentencing court in disorder, a common situation, in that some offences came to light prior to others that were committed earlier, but all arose prior to the first sentence. The sentencing court must be assisted to ensure that no "double punishment" arises and that no imputation of further offending after sentencing arises.

Leaving aside this unusual situation, reference is now made to the more traditional sentencing scenario. A simple example is seen in the case of *R. v. Sturge* (2001), [2001] O.J. No. 3923, 17 M.V.R. (4th) 272, 2001 CarswellOnt 3691 (C.A.). The Court granted a "discount" of sorts as the offences had taken place over a brief period of time, and without the intervention of court proceedings.

Note as well *R. v. Tame* (1965), [1966] 1 O.R. 497, [1966] 2 C.C.C. 183, 1965 CarswellOnt 234 (C.A.), leave to appeal allowed [1966] 1 O.R. 552n, [1966] 2 C.C.C. 185n (C.A.). Laskin J.A., later the Chief Justice of Canada, did not criticize or comment adversely in any fashion the trial judge's decision to suspend sentence and to place a 16-year-old offender guilty of six charges of break and enter on probation for two years.

It will now be advantageous to consider the very recent guidance in the case of *R. v. White* (2003), [2003] O.J. No. 2544, 2003 CarswellOnt 4106, 176 C.C.C. (3d) 396 (C.A.). Counsel will wish to stress that the offender in question, as in the case of Mr. White, had never offended until the onset of a serious period of wrongdoing and that there are now in place sufficient measures to address the temporary stressors that led to atypical behaviour. See paras. 20-21 and in particular the observation respecting "the appellant's lack of a criminal record prior to the break up of his family. . .".

A further useful example of the complexity of understanding the history of wrongdoing as opposed to the history of court sentences, understood as warnings that if unheeded demonstrate elevated moral blameworthiness is seen in the case of *R. v. Drozdz* (2003), [2003] O.J. No. 2146, 2003 CarswellOnt 2016, 172 O.A.C. 228 (C.A.). In this instance, the defendant was convicted of three counts of sexual assault and three counts of indecent assault involving four different young boys. The facts relating to a fifth boy were also considered for the purpose of sentencing.

As we read at para. 2, "The sexual assaults involved a serious breach of trust and were committed over a period of 12 years between 1980 and 1992." Further, para. 3 makes plain that Mr. Drozd had previously been convicted of indecent assault on five different child victims, committed prior to 1979 for which he received conditional sentences in September 2001. The Court of Appeal found the seven-year sentence to be within the appropriate range for similar cases.

In other words, although the offences were all grave ones, the resulting penalties were well inferior to the type of sanction that would have been appropriate had the offender been sentenced in respect to a further spree of sexually violent crimes, to then commit further offences of a like nature after his release. This case also makes plain that imprisonment, even a lengthy period of imprisonment, remains an available option in the case of a first offender.

In the final analysis, emphasis must be placed on the fact the offender has not had the benefit of the Court's guidance by means of an earlier sentence prior the next misconduct taking place results in greater moral blame being assigned to the offender than is warranted. A lack of insight and resolve to act responsibly on behalf of an offender is only fully engaged as a sentencing principle in the case of those who are given an opportunity to reform and who fail to take advantage of this opportunity.

f) Unprosecuted prior offences and pre-sentence reports: An examination:

i) Introduction

As has been seen, one of the most common sources of information respecting prior, unprosecuted wrongdoing is the probation officer's report. Thus, it will be useful to know when pre-sentence reports must be ordered. The instruction set out in *R. v. Priest* (1996), 93 O.A.C. 163, 1 C.R. (5th) 275, 110 C.C.C. (3d) 289, [1996] O.J. No. 3369, 30 O.R. (3d) 538, 1996 CarswellOnt 3588 (C.A.), at para. 15 is apposite: "This Court has stressed that before imposing a sentence of imprisonment upon a first offender, the trial judge should have either a pre-sentence report or some very clear statement with respect to the accused's background and circumstances." In the next paragraph, the Court remarked "This requirement of a pre-sentence report or statement about the offender is not a mere formality. As discussed below, the trial judge has a duty to consider whether any disposition other than imprisonment would be appropriate. Without some understanding of the accused's background, the trial judge cannot possibly make that determination".

Reference is also made to the instruction found at para. 15. "This Court has stressed that before imposing a sentence of imprisonment upon a first offender, the trial judge should have either a pre-sentence report or some very clear statement with respect to the accused's background and circumstances. See, for example *R. v. Bates* (1977), 32 C.C.C. (2d) 493, 1977 CarswellOnt 1097 (C.A.), at page 494 per Brooke, J.A. *"That principle has particular application in the case of a youthful offender like this appellant"* (Emphasis supplied). See also para. 16 of *R. v. G. (G.L.)* (January 11, 1982), Jessup J.A., Dubin J.A., Blair J.A., [1982] O.J. No. 193 (C.A.).

The difficulty is that to understand an offender's background, it may be necessary to ascertain previous events that amount to misconduct not formally found to be offences after trial.

ii)   May the probation officer report that an offender has engaged in a pattern of misconduct?

A)   *The traditional view: The Rule in R. v. Bartkow*

Many judgments follow the traditional or orthodox view espoused by Chief Justice MacKeigan in *R. v. Bartkow* (1978), 24 N.S.R. (2d) 518, 35 A.P.R. 518, 1 C.R. (3d) S-36, 1978 CarswellNS 11 (C.A.), on the issue of what information may properly be sought of an offender and consigned in a pre-sentence report. Generally speaking, it is thought that probation officers are not to concern themselves with allegations of wrongdoing that are not the subject of the proceedings. As noted at p. S-40 [C.R.], the report contained references such as "The grapevine has had it for the past couple of years that the accused would sell dope to anyone who had the money regardless of age. This was corroborated by his statement in interview that he was selling to 'everyone and his dog'". In response, the Court of Appeal remarked, "I wish that those who prepare such reports would realize that it is no part of their job to give any information, whether inculpatory or exculpatory, respecting offences which the accused committed, especially ones for which he has not been convicted." Refer again to p. S-40 [C.R.].

B)   The emerging view: Prior misconduct is germane

Are these guidelines respected at present? It is submitted that a careful review of the case law, the report of which is too lengthy for present purposes, serves to make plain that the answer is no. The following cases are offered as an illustration of present trends.

The case report of *R. v. Levesque* (2001), [2001] O.J. No. 210, 30 M.V.R. (4th) 246, 2001 CarswellOnt 176 (C.A.), provides a direct example of such a finding of prior criminal misconduct, and not just of an inference. It provides a typical example of the controversy that surrounds the prosecution's attempt to advance evidence of prior, unprosecuted misconduct, as an aggravating element in sentencing.

Finlayson, Labrosse and Laskin, JJ.A. observed in the course of their brief oral endorsement that:

> [3] The pre-sentence report indicated that the appellant began drinking at the age of 16 and that there was ample evidence of a more longstanding substance abuse problem than the appellant would suggest. He admitted to a previous conviction for Over 80 mgs. and Care and Control in 1971-72. Contrary to the appellant's perception, the information provided by his ex-wife and his common-law wife is indicative of alcohol-related problems right up to the time of the current offence.

Although he had a prior record involving one conviction under s. 253(b), what is of relevance for present purposes is the consideration by the Court of the evidence that he committed this type of offence on other occasions, though he was not prosecuted or convicted.

Of note, the offender pleaded guilty to impaired operation causing bodily harm. He was involved in a serious motor vehicle accident when he made a left turn without warning and collided with an approaching vehicle. His passenger, his common-law wife, sustained significant bodily injuries as a result of the accident. The breathalyzer readings were 294 and 288, more than three times the legal limit. Paragraph 1 of the judgment records the view of the Court that the readings are ". . . indicative of a conscious decision to drive despite severe intoxication." In other words, of an elevated degree of moral blame.

In the course of their decision to uphold a jail term of nine months, and to reject a plea for a conditional endorsement, their Lordships assigned significant weight to the trial judge's conclusion that, on the whole, the offender failed to recognize the seriousness of his alcohol abuse. Refer to para. 5. This conclusion was predicated upon the negative opinion advanced by the author of the pre-sentence report. In effect, the report tipped the scales against the granting of a conditional term.

It is obvious that the information in *R. v. Levesque*, *supra*, tends to depart from the guidelines set out by MacKeigan C.J.N.S., in particular, the suggestion of on-going alcohol-related problems. In my view, this is a euphemism for "he was driving drunk at times". Be that as it may, it appears that the information found in the *Levesque* pre-sentence report is not atypical of what is provided to judges. Attention is now drawn to some of these cases.

In *R. v. R. (M.)* (1998), [1998] O.J. No. 737, 107 O.A.C. 233, 1998 CarswellOnt 892 (C.A.), McMurtry, C.J.O., Charron and Borins, JJ.A., considered the fitness of a 15-month period of imprisonment to sanction an offence of sexual assault causing bodily harm. The victim was the offender's spouse, as was the case in *R. v. Levesque*. Of note, in evaluating whether a conditional sentence ought to be imposed in this case, the sentencing judge found as a fact that the safety of the complainant would not be endangered by the appellant serving his sentence in the community. Refer to para. 6. The Court of Appeal reviewed the reasons for judgment and concluded that it should not interfere with the sentencing judge's exercise of discretion in refusing to impose a conditional sentence in this case. See para. 9. It did reduce the term of imprisonment to six months, for these reasons, found at para. 10 of the judgment:

> However, we are of the view that the term of imprisonment was harsh. It would appear that the sentencing judge misapprehended the evidence when he concluded, on the basis of a statement found in the pre-sentence report, that there was "a pattern of abuse" between the appellant and his spouse. He noted that the sentence was not being imposed to punish the appellant "for

this conduct" but nonetheless found "the previous assaultive behaviour" a relevant factor in considering the background of the
appellant. While the evidence showed that there had been heated
arguments in the past between the appellant and his spouse,
which arguments were often followed by consensual sexual activity, there was no evidence to support a finding of any pattern
of abusive behaviour. It would appear that this offence was an
isolated act. This misapprehension of the evidence may have unduly influenced the sentencing judge in his determination of the
appropriate quantum of the sentence.

In other words, the information found in the pre-sentence report was
not reliable. Nevertheless, it does appear that the Court held that had
the information been reliable, it could be advanced by a probation officer
called upon to provide a sentence report under s. 721(3)(a) of the
Criminal Code.

R. v. Glassford (1988), [1988] O.J. No. 359, 27 O.A.C. 194, 42 C.C.C.
(3d) 259, 63 C.R. (3d) 209, 1988 CarswellOnt 59 (C.A.), is also of
assistance. At page 12, one reads: "There is some evidence that the
subject may experience a problem with alcohol and drugs, although the
subject believes his use of both alcohol and drugs is nonproblematic.
Sources also indicate the subject has a volatile temper which he has
difficulty controlling." These words echo the remarks found in *R. v.
Levesque*. In the same vein, the inclusion of these remarks appears to
go against the authority of *R. v. Bartkow*.

A further example is found in *R. v. Condo* (March 27, 1981), Howland
C.J.O., Jessup J.A., Martin J.A., [1981] O.J. No. 35 (C.A.), at para. 3.
Howland, C.J.O., Jessup and Martin, JJ.A., remarked that a 16-year-
old guilty of participating in a serious robbery had known a deprived
childhood and the pre-sentence report respecting him was generally
unfavourable. "It indicated he was physically aggressive to perceived
threats and defiant towards those in authority. He had also had a heavy
involvement with drugs." There was no criticism of the inclusion of such
information that had little to do with the robbery.

These references suggest that a sentencing court may consider collateral information found in pre-sentence reports, even to the point of
permitting an offender's self-evaluation to be impeached. This may have
adverse consequences with respect to both the type and term of sentence selected and counsel must be vigilant to ensure that no greater
use is made than what is consonant with appellate authority.

C)   *Whether pre-sentence reports may describe the abuse of alcohol by an offender not leading to offences "so found"?*

A review of the case law supports the opinion that probation officers are encouraged to point out any history of alcohol abuse that may have been at the heart of any criminal behaviour, whether prosecuted or not. For example, in *R. v. Gibson* (1984), [1984] O.J. No. 121, 4 O.A.C. 313, 1984 CarswellOnt 1294 (C.A.), the ". . . offender has a good work record. It was indicated in the pre-sentence report that the respondent's various contacts with the law have largely been the result of his drinking". See page 6 (Q.L.).

See also *R. v. Hackney* (January 17, 1983), Doc. 768/81, [1983] O.J. No. 10 (C.A.), at para. 3: "... the pre-sentence report ... is not altogether unfavourable to the appellant, but it stresses that his abuse of alcohol has been and continues to be the source of many of his problems. Indeed his criminal record, which consists mostly of relatively minor offences, suggests that many of them were alcohol-related."

In *R. v. McVeigh* (1985), [1985] O.J. No. 207, 22 C.C.C. (3d) 145, 11 O.A.C. 345, 1985 CarswellOnt 1389 (C.A.), we read at p. 348, para. 6:

> It is clear that the respondent has had a drinking "problem" for years. He stated to the probation and parole officer who prepared the pre-sentence report that he began drinking alcohol at the age of 15. He felt that alcohol became a real problem for him around the age of 21 and he described himself as a "binge drinker" who would be sober all week and become "totally smashed" on weekends. Although his excessive drinking was causing problems in his marriage, he took no steps to resolve his alcohol problem until after the tragic events of April 1, 1983.

g)   First offenders guilty of serious offences: The elevated moral blame may require severe sentences

As is well known, many judgments make plain that youth and the absence of a record, or the absence of a record in the case of mature offenders, will not suffice to avoid a jail sentence if the offence is quite serious. In the case of *R. v. Corpus* (2000), [2000] O.J. No. 549, 2000 CarswellOnt 497, 130 O.A.C. 84 (C.A.) at paras. 10-11, the Court upheld an effective sentence of 11 years although Mr. Corpus was a first offender and of previous good character, notably in light of the danger he continued to pose to his former wife, the victim of an attempted murder. A penitentiary term was judged fit in *R. v. Syed* (2000), [2000] O.J. No. 3535, 22 C.C.L.I. (3d) 163, 2000 CarswellOnt 3291 (C.A.) involving an arson of a residence. Refer to para. 15. Note also *R. v. Schwarz* (2000), [2000] O.J. No. 3851, 137 O.A.C. 5, 2000 CarswellOnt 3697 (C.A.) involving a home invasion. The Court of Appeal urged substantial penitentiary terms for such offences, as recorded at para. 2.

In *R. v. Syblis* (2001), [2001] O.J. No. 115, 140 O.A.C. 64, 2001 CarswellOnt 142 (C.A.), reference is made to *R. v. Cunningham* (1996), [1996] O.J. No. 448, 104 C.C.C. (3d) 542, 1996 CarswellOnt 482, 88 O.A.C. 143, 27 O.R. (3d) 786 (C.A.), "...suggesting that the range of sentence for first offender couriers who smuggle large amounts of co-caine into Canada for personal gain should be six to eight years in the penitentiary." Of course, first offenders guilty of significant sexual vio-lence will often be jailed for lengthy periods, as illustrated in *R. v. E. (P.)* (2000), [2000] O.J. No. 574, 129 O.A.C. 369, 2000 CarswellOnt 499 (C.A.) at para. 25.

Note also *R. v. Flores* (2000), [2000] O.J. No. 1991, 2000 CarswellOnt 1886 (C.A.). At para. 1, the Court of Appeal recorded that "This was a very serious offence. Despite the respondent's youth (18), his first of-fender status..." a severe sentence was called for. See also para. 25 of *R. v. Zhang* (2000), [2000] O.J. No. 1617, 132 O.A.C. 159, 2000 CarswellOnt 1548 (C.A.), para. 41 of *R. v. Shahnawaz* (2000), [2000] O.J. No. 4151, 51 O.R. (3d) 29, 137 O.A.C. 363, 149 C.C.C. (3d) 97, 40 C.R. (5th) 195, 2000 CarswellOnt 4094 (C.A.), leave to appeal re-fused (2001), 2001 CarswellOnt 1378, 2001 CarswellOnt 1379, 270 N.R. 195 (note), 149 O.A.C. 395 (note) (S.C.C.) and para. 15 of *R. v. Syed* (2000), [2000] O.J. No. 3535, 22 C.C.L.I. (3d) 163, 2000 CarswellOnt 3291 (C.A.).

One further example of an exemplary first sentence will suffice to make plain that although defence counsel will normally be able to demonstrate that the absence of a criminal record in the case of a mature individual in terms of age and professional achievement bodes well for future rehabilitation, the Crown may point to exceptional situations in which severe penalties were selected in the case of quite serious wrongdoing. Thus, in *R. v. Patterson* (2003), [2003] O.J. No. 1353, 2003 CarswellOnt 1414, 170 O.A.C. 376, 64 O.R. (3d) 275 (C.A.), additional reasons at (2003), 2003 CarswellOnt 1660, 174 C.C.C. (3d) 193 (C.A.) a lawyer engaged in violent and other misconduct with an elevated degree of moral obloquy was dealt with in an exemplary fashion. See para. 69 in particular. In sum, Mr. Patterson's first offender status did not shield him from a seven-year term.

It must be recalled, however, that a severe sentence "may" be required in cases of elevated moral blameworthiness. Nevertheless, many examples of leniency are known. In a score of other judgments, the Court of Appeal for Ontario has emphasized the traditional view that first offenders ought not to be taken into custody if this was not absolutely required, all other things being equal. No purpose is served in setting out all of the references so attention will be focused on only a limited number, the most important one being *R. v. Habib* (2000), [2000] O.J. No. 3036, 147 C.C.C. (3d) 555, 135 O.A.C. 329, 2000 CarswellOnt 2863 (C.A.), at para. 12. The offender was guilty of aggravated assault on a baby.

In *R. v. Fudge* (2000), [2000] O.J. No. 2780, 2000 CarswellOnt 2628 (C.A.), the Court of Appeal emphasized in the first paragraph that the offender committed a crime of violence, having accumulated a record for crimes of violence, making her a significant danger to the community and to herself, not just by her prior conduct but also by reason of her addictions and her mental state. In sum, she was a real risk to the safety of the community.

Nonetheless, great leniency was shown to her by reason of the fact in the two years between the commission of the offence and the imposition of sentence, she turned her life around. "She is in a positive relationship with her husband, has developed a strong support network in the community and has remained drug and alcohol free. She has continued her progress since this sentence was imposed some six months ago." Refer to para. 2.

The Court of Appeal accepted that the trial judge had selected appropriate terms of a conditional sentence to guard against a return to her prior lifestyle. "She crafted a conditional sentence which was directed very much to the specific situation and concerns raised by this particular offender. The terms imposed by the trial judge also contain a significant punitive component." Refer to para. 4. It did not interfere with the sentence.

h)   Repeat offenders: Assessing the blameworthiness of the misconduct:

i)   Introduction

In the case of repeat offenders, the duty of counsel is to attempt to demonstrate that the repeated nature of the misconduct ought not to result in assigning any greater degree of moral blame than what is absolutely necessary in the circumstances. To be plain, the first sub-mission has to be that no severity ought to be shown on the second offence, save when Parliament has required it as in the case of a second offence of impaired operation, and that no concept of "three strikes, you are out" exists in Canada, save for the recently introduced legis-lation touching upon violent young persons and three-time offenders in the context of impaired driving, and so on. . .

All in all, it is the severity of the past and future wrongdoing, the period of time between each event, the attitude of the offender after each offence, and a host of other factors that will decide the issue. Thus, in the case of *R. v. Edwards* (2003), [2003] O.J. No. 701, 2003 CarswellOnt 668 (C.A.), the Court remarked at para. 1: "The serious-ness of the offence, the appellant's extensive record, and the fact that he was on probation when the offence was committed, justify the term imposed."

ii)   The impact of a youth record

In *R. v. Rockey* (2001), [2001] O.J. No. 1672, 2001 CarswellOnt 1447 (C.A.), the Court's oral endorsement noted that "[t]he trial judge gave no reasons for so significantly departing from [the Crown's submission of 12 months imprisonment]". See para. 1. Recognizing that the of-fences were very serious, and that the offender had a lengthy youth record, it emphasized his early guilty plea, that he is still quite young, and that he suffered terrible abuse as a child. Hence, 18 months was a fit sentence, given the pre-trial custody, not otherwise described. See also *R. v. Allison-McLeish* (2001), [2001] O.J. No. 845, 2001 CarswellOnt 653, 142 O.A.C. 50 (C.A.), at para. 2 and 12-13.

The general instruction to be drawn is that each element of the record must be assessed, including the significance of the prior wrongdoing and the progress, if any, since that earlier event. The particular instruc-tion is that less weight may be attached, all other things being equal, to youthful transgressions, as recognized by Parliament's refinements in the *Youth Criminal Justice Act* mandating the "elimination from consideration" of prior records.

iii)   The impact of a minor record

Broadly stated, a record that is not significant may be ignored. Indeed, often prosecutors will not advance such entries. In the case of *R. v. Syblis* (2001), [2001] O.J. No. 115, 140 O.A.C. 64, 2001 CarswellOnt 142 (C.A.), the offender had 2.13 kilograms of cocaine in his bag when arrested after entering the country. The Court noted that he had no prior criminal record of any significance.

iv)   The impact of a recent but minor prior record

Little authority is required for the view that a recent related record disentitles an offender to leniency, all other things being equal. In *R. v. M. (C.)* (2000), [2000] O.J. No. 2790, 2000 CarswellOnt 2650 (C.A.) for example, the offender had spent nine and one-half months in pre-trial custody. "Given his record and that he was on probation at the time, we agree that it was open to the trial judge to impose a further period of imprisonment. However, the trial judge erred in principle in placing undue emphasis on the record. While [he] was certainly not entitled to any leniency, the sentence imposed had to be proportionate to what actually occurred. Refer to para. 8. Further, in *R. v. Pupovic* (2000), [2000] O.J. No. 4427, 138 O.A.C. 193, 2000 CarswellOnt 4112 (C.A.), leave to appeal refused (2001), 2001 CarswellOnt 872, 2001 CarswellOnt 873, 271 N.R. 192 (note), 149 O.A.C. 199 (note) (S.C.C.), the Court noted a prior record for related violent offences. See also para. 11 of *R. v. Bell* (2000), [2000] O.J. No. 4565, 2000 CarswellOnt 5464 (C.A.), additional reasons at (2002), 2002 CarswellOnt 925 (C.A.).

v)   The impact of a recent substantial record

On occasion, the impact of a recent and related record is not difficult to assess. In *R. v. Thomas* (2001), [2001] O.J. No. 2220, 146 O.A.C. 298, 2001 CarswellOnt 1986 (C.A.), the Court's oral endorsement included the remarks that the prosecution had sought a sentence of two years less a day but the trial judge imposed three years, on top of the three months pre-trial custody. The Court of Appeal upheld the sentence as not unfit, though at the upper end of the range for criminal harassment. In doing so, it noted the *Bates* decision, and the many aggravating circumstances included the lengthy criminal record, the two prior as-saults on the same victim, his lack of regard for Court orders in the past including the existence of three probation orders at the time of committing this offence. Further, para. 2 records the "victim's fear of the appellant has led her to change both her job and her residence."

The Court of Appeal noted by way of oral endorsement in *R. v. Innes* (2001), [2001] O.J. No. 1018, 2001 CarswellOnt 825 (C.A.) that "[t]he sentence would be high for a first offence of domestic violence but the appellant, now aged only 30, has an horrific criminal record for violence against women. This, coupled with a similarly poor record for non-compliance with court orders relating to compliance with recognizances, terms of probation and one of failure to comply with a disposition, merit the sentence of 18 months imprisonment." Refer to para. 1. The Court noted at para. 2 that he would benefit from all programs available to him during his period of incarceration.

vi)   The impact of an unrelated record

The impact on sentencing of an unrelated record is not an easy question to address. The Court will often take pains to note that though an offender has an "extensive criminal record", he or she had "little by way of violence", as in the case of *R. v. Sturge* (2001), [2001] O.J. No. 3923, 2001 CarswellOnt 3691, 17 M.V.R. (4th) 272 (C.A.) at paragraphs 2 and involving an offender who pleaded guilty to seven counts of robbery and to other serious violent offences.

In many instances, a more favourable sentence may be secured if counsel is successful in distinguishing the present offence(s) from the prior record in order to support the submission that the wrongdoing is out-of-character, or resulted from an exceptional situation that is unlikely to be encountered again, or sprang from provocation, etc. Shortly put, that the record may be disregarded and the defendant treated as a first offender.

What must be attempted, within the bounds of the offence(s) and the offender and the duties owed to the Court as one of its officers, is to make plain that the lessons that were attempted to be taught in the past by the imposition of various measures and penalties were well understood, but were "overlooked" by reason of an extraordinary set of circumstances. In sum, the Court need not resort to the full panoply of "correctional" resources as the offender well understands the im-portance of pro-social actions and outlook.

A simple illustration follows. Assume the Court is called upon to sentence an offender who committed a minor assault in circumstances that might amount to significant provocation. Assume further that the offender's chronic alcoholism has led him to commit many small thefts over the years, but that he has no record of violence. In such circumstances, the number of thefts has resulted in a prior jail term of some importance for the last conviction as the offender has had the benefit of discharges, suspended sentences, modest fines, short, sharp jail terms, and so forth. Nevertheless, it might be appropriate to submit that the selection of an individualized term is still an available option for a crime of violence.

Stated otherwise, the offender's failure to profit fully from the probation officer's assistance and to be deterred by reason of imprisonment with respect to theft offences should not be taken to mean that a brief jail term, followed by a period of probation, or a period of conditional confinement, might not be a suitable sentence.

It may be of assistance to illustrate the opposite scenario as well. In the case of *R. v. Morey* (2003), [2003] O.J. No. 1562, 2003 CarswellOnt 1560, 171 O.A.C. 36 (C.A.), the trial judge imposed a cumulative sentence of seven years with a recommendation for early parole. The offender argued on appeal that this resulted in a harsh and excessive penalty in all the circumstances, and that it was beyond the range of a sentence appropriate for the offences committed. In particular, para. 38 records the following mitigating factors: a) he had no relevant criminal record and should be treated as a first offender. In response, the Crown submitted that the appellant was the directing mind and will of a significant, long-term trafficking organization, a characterization that found favour with the trial judge for reasons set out in particular at para. 40.

Of note, the Court of Appeal could find no grounds to intervene, making plain that an unrelated record may result in an offender being treated as a first offender, but if s/he has been convicted of a very grave offence, no leniency (or very little) will result from this successful characterization as a first offender.

vii)   The impact of a lengthy but unrelated record

Refer to *R. v. Sturge* (2001), [2001] O.J. No. 3923, 2001 CarswellOnt 3691, 17 M.V.R. (4th) 272 (C.A.). The offender's record was described as "extensive", but the Court did observe that he had little history of violent offences. See para. 4.

viii) Repeat offenders and their motivation: The profit motive

R. v. Nguyen (2002), [2002] O.J. No. 4667, 2002 CarswellOnt 4362 (C.A.) provides a brief illustration of the sentencing objective in the case of an offender who has gone on to repeat an offence, notwithstanding the prior sentence, with a view to obtaining funds. As set out at para. 1, "[i]n light of the nature of the offender who had criminal convictions in 1993 for drugs-related offences and the nature of this offence which was described as a sophisticated marketing operation, we think that the sentence was fit." In other words, since the earlier wrongdoing involved a scheme to make large profits, and the sentence imposed was not sufficient to discourage further attempts at making profits illegally, greater severity had to be shown to deter the offender.

If this person attempts further criminal activity for profit, after this second warning, it stands to reason that the Court will be justified in placing the offender much higher on the aggravating end of the scale of offenders on the footing that the person is demonstrating a resolve to be a career criminal, a highly elevated element of moral blame. In such instances, society is at greater risk of harm and may thus justify the greater allocation of punitive resources. If it is shown that the further offending is of a lesser (or different) degree, than the assignment of greater aggravating weight may not be justified. The degree of moral blame would not be as great in such a case.

This issue was discussed briefly in *R. v. Pham* (2002), [2002] O.J. No. 2545, 2002 CarswellOnt 2121, 161 O.A.C. 80, 167 C.C.C. (3d) 570, 94 C.R.R. (2d) 371, 6 C.R. (6th) 373 (C.A.), a case involving the smuggling of cigarettes. The Court stressed the direct link between the size of the fine and the quantity of the illegal substance. "Those who possess larger quantities are clearly players in larger criminal enterprises with larger illegal profits for whom larger minimum fines are rationally founded. The use of this factor, which is both objective and reasonable, to regulate the size of the minimum fine ensures that the punishment will not be grossly disproportionate." Refer to para. 19. As a result, if it were suggested that such fines are disproportionate to "mules", as opposed to the "brains", the Court would respond that the "brains" should receive far greater fines... See para. 20.

By way of contrast, in the somewhat unusual case of *R. v. MacDougall* (1995), [1995] M.J. No. 531, 107 Man. R. (2d) 236, 109 W.A.C. 236, 1995 CarswellMan 459 (C.A.) the offender was led by her son to attempt to smuggle narcotics into the jail in which he was detained. At para. 3, the Court noted: "The accused co-operated with police authorities and entered a plea of guilty. A pre-sentence report indicates that the accused realizes the gravity of her wrongdoing, and is remorseful." She had no record and was trying to protect her son from harm he said would befall him unless she delivered the narcotics. The Court of Appeal agreed with the trial judge that such exceptional circumstances including ". . . her desire to help her son out of difficulties, the fact that no money was involved, her clear record, and her personal circumstances" militated in favour of leniency. Refer to para. 5.

ix)   Repeat offenders who continue to offend by reason of addiction

R. v. Lelieveld (2002), [2002] O.J. No. 4661, 2002 CarswellOnt 4121 (C.A.) provides an interesting example of emphasis being placed on the offender's admission to his probation officer that he "got loaded once a week." Refer to para. 2. He had a 1997 conviction for impaired driving. This admission justified the aggravating element that the offender was a long-term abuser of alcohol.

This case illustrates a halfway point in terms of aggravation and mitigation. On the one hand, there was only one prior entry on the record and thus, only one prior "warning" by the Court (and the community) as to the danger of drinking and driving and on the need for sobriety. On the other, there had been numerous failures to heed this warning and numerous failures to draw back from the improper (and illegal) conduct and to consider the need for treatment. His failure to do so is consistent with higher moral blame than in the case of a repeat offender who has only committed the offence on one further occasion after being sentenced, all other things being equal.

In *R. v. H. (C.N.)* (2002), [2002] O.J. No. 4918, 2002 CarswellOnt 4327, 170 C.C.C. (3d) 253, 62 O.R. (3d) 564, 167 O.A.C. 292, 9 C.R. (6th) 103 (C.A.), para. 21 refers to the relative moral blameworthiness of addicts ". . . who import not only to meet but also to finance their needs. . ." as compared to "cold-blooded" non-users.

x)   Repeat offenders who continue to offend by reason of some animus

An offender who has had the opportunity to reflect on a course of violent conduct after a conviction and who then engages again in the dangerous activity demonstrates an elevated degree of moral blame. In effect, an inability to demonstrate a functioning "moral compass and an inability to seek the necessary assistance to overcome this deficit. Note *R. v. Dobbs* (2002), [2002] O.J. No. 4828, 2002 CarswellOnt 4297 (C.A.). The Court highlighted the offender's clear animus against the M.N.R. and his possession of firearms and explosives notwithstanding the existence of a prohibition order. See para. 2.

In *R. v. Barton* (2002), [2002] O.J. No. 4105, 2002 CarswellOnt 3584, 165 O.A.C. 294 (C.A.), a sentence of 32 months, after 23 months of "dead time" for offences of sexual assault, confinement and breach of recognizance, was upheld. The offender's recent and related record for violence was emphasized.

It is an aggravating factor that offender has a related record, as made plain in *R. v. Baxter* (2002), [2002] O.J. No. 3565, 2002 CarswellOnt 3120 (C.A.). A 12-month sentence was within the appropriate range for a second offence of making a threat to the same victim. Of note, the threat was detailed and serious.

On occasion, the impact of a recent and related record is not difficult to assess. In *R. v. Thomas* (2001), [2001] O.J. No. 2220, 146 O.A.C. 298, 2001 CarswellOnt 1986 (C.A.), the Court's oral endorsement included the remarks that the prosecution had sought a sentence of two years less a day but the trial judge imposed three years, on top of the three months pre-trial custody. The Court of Appeal upheld the sentence as not unfit, though at the upper end of the range for criminal harassment. In doing so, it noted the *Bates* decision, and the many aggravating circumstances included the lengthy criminal record, the two prior assaults on the same victim, his lack of regard for court orders in the past including the existence of three probation orders at the time of committing this offence. Further, para. 2 records the "victim's fear of the appellant has led her to change both her job and her residence."

Note that in *R. v. Thomas* (2001), [2001] O.J. No. 2220, 146 O.A.C. 298, 2001 CarswellOnt 1986 (C.A.), the Court's oral endorsement included remarks at para. 2 pointing out many aggravating circumstances including the two prior assaults on the same victim and his lack of regard for court orders in the past including the existence of three probation orders at the time of committing this offence.

In the final analysis, the offender who has learned nothing (or next to nothing) from prior sentences poses quite a challenge for counsel. It has been argued herein that if it can be shown that an offender has learned much, if not all, that a correctional measure may provide by way of instruction respecting pro-social attitudes and actions, *and* that the further wrongdoing was exceptional in nature or circumstances, then an individualized disposition may be fit. The corollary to this proposition is that an offender who appears to have learned little, if anything, from prior punitive measures may well require a greater allocation of punitive measures to bring home the earlier message that was ignored or poorly understood.

For example, *R. v. Fazekas* (2003), [2003] O.J. No. 1615, 2003 CarswellOnt 1603, 171 O.A.C. 115 (C.A.) includes these observations, at para 10: "In imposing sentence, the trial judge was particularly concerned that the appellant did not appear to understand the impact of his actions on the complainant and on other persons. The trial judge was concerned about the repetitive nature of the appellant's offences in the face of court orders [not to contact the complainant]." Indeed, the offender continued to make harassing calls from prison! In such circumstances, it is unlikely that a plea for leniency would be well received.

xi)   Repeat offenders who continue to offend in cases of driving prohibitions

R. v. Howlett (2002), [2002] O.J. No. 3525, 2002 CarswellOnt 2977, 163 O.A.C. 48 (C.A.), makes plain the distinction between a lengthy record and a lengthy related record. As noted at para. 3, the offender's criminal record spanned a period of 15 years from 1985 to 2000 and included more than 50 convictions, 10 of which were for driving while disqualified and numerous others for disrespecting court orders. The Court thus underlined not only a lengthy period of wrongdoing, but also a lengthy period during which the offence in question, driving while disqualified, was committed on ten occasions. The Court also highlighted the fact that the offender was often guilty of other offences showing disrespect for court orders.

At bottom, this shows a lack of insight into criminal behaviour, a failure to reform despite numerous court-warnings, and unwillingness to act in a pro-social manner.

xii)   Repeat offenders who continue to offend in general

R. v. Hebert (2002), [2002] O.J. No. 3307, 2002 CarswellOnt 2786, 162 O.A.C. 291 (C.A.) includes a notation at para. 9 that the extensive criminal record of the offender and the facts disentitled resort to a conditional sentence.

It may be apt to pause to describe an offender who is arrested every two months for causing a disturbance while intoxicated as "incorrigible", but the degree of moral blameworthiness is far from being as elevated as in the case of career criminals who commit otherwise serious offences, be they violent in nature or purely for gain. For example, the hopeless alcoholic who cannot avoid plying the bagpipes at all hours of the night and who then threatens to kill his neighbours when they challenge his conduct does commit a series of violent offences, but this misconduct pales in comparison to those who are committed to a life of crime that is more serious in nature.

xiii) Career criminals with extensive records:

The foregoing discussion on the motivation for further offending leads into a discussion of career criminals, and the response of the Court to a demonstrated unwillingness to conform to the dictates of organized society.

A) The general rule

To the degree and extent that offenders have demonstrated a long-standing refusal to abide by the rules of organized society, and a concomitant refusal to respond to any sentences whether individualized or severe, the sentencing courts will generally elect to assign ever increasing aggravating weight to further serious misconduct of the same general nature. For example, one who has been found guilty of repeated home invasions and who has been sentenced to increasingly significant terms of imprisonment may well be sentenced to a further and more significant jail term upon the commission of yet another home invasion.

The rationale appears to be the following in the case of offenders who seek profit from criminality. They are committed to crime in order to obtain money and appear to believe that the penalties meted out by the courts are mere licenses or irritants and are to be ignored or undergone and then forgotten. In such cases, the moral blame is high as they challenge one of the fundamentals of organized society: "Crime does not pay". The selection of ever-increasing penalties appears fully justified in order to vindicate one of our prime values and to deter them from further misconduct, in order to protect the community. As in all other situations, greater weight is assigned to greater degrees of wrongdoing and in accordance with the presence of other aggravating features such as violence or planning.

On the other hand, sentencing courts might well choose to assign little aggravating weight to an unrelated offence, let us say a first impaired driving infraction or an isolated "bar assault". In such a case, the offender has neither demonstrated a proclivity for engaging in such conduct nor a refusal to respect the community's values in this respect and to heed the warnings of the court as to this precise conduct.

B)   The exceptional disposition

The general rule is subject to an exceptional disposition if it can be shown that some new element is now present having a potential for mitigation that cannot be overlooked. For example, the offender is committed to seeking therapy for a substance abuse problem that has led to the accumulation of so many entries on the record, or s/he has found a supporting individual or network that offers a substantial degree of optimism that a fundamental change is in the offing.

C)   The emerging rule

When an offender's record of convictions for similar offences reaches a certain level that it cannot be placed at any point on the scale of offending short of the extreme end of aggravation, that person may fairly be described as a "career criminal", as did the Court of Appeal in *R. v. DaSilva* (2002), [2002] O.J. No. 4695, 2002 CarswellOnt 4159, 166 O.A.C. 295 (C.A.), at para. 5: "The trial judge found that the appellants were career criminals who had intentionally embarked upon a violent criminal path of life and had treated jail and the criminal justice system as mere occupational hazards." In addition, "[b]oth appellants had amassed significant criminal records which began as young offenders and carried into adulthood. Their records include serious crimes of violence." As a result, leniency was not an available sentencing option; to the contrary, lengthy jail terms and delayed parole orders were required to protect the public from seemingly incorrigible offenders.

Further, with respect to the values of the community, para. 7 of *R. v. DaSilva* (2002), [2002] O.J. No. 4695, 2002 CarswellOnt 4159, 166 O.A.C. 295 (C.A.) serves to highlight that "...a sentence that reflected the gravity of the offences, reinforced the principles of denunciation and general deterrence, and maintained public respect for the administration of justice."

It may be apt to describe an offender who is arrested every two months for causing a disturbance while intoxicated as "incorrigible", but the degree of moral blameworthiness is far from being as elevated as in the case of career criminals who commit otherwise serious offences, be they violent in nature or purely for gain. For example, the hopeless alcoholic who cannot avoid plying the bagpipes at all hours of the night and who then threatens to kill his neighbours when they challenge his conduct does commit a series of violent offences, but this misconduct pales in comparison to those who are committed to a life of crime that is more serious in nature.

23. VIGILANTISM:

a) Introduction

The case of *R. v. Dhillon* (1995), [1995] A.J. No. 272, 165 A.R. 239, 89 W.A.C. 239, 1995 CarswellAlta 550 (C.A.) provides an example of intervention leading to violent conduct involving a friend of a young female relative that was characterized in error by the trial judge as being "vigilantism." As we read at para. 2, "It is clear that he became involved, as the uncle of a young woman, in an effort to terminate the relationship between her and the victim. We are concerned about the trial judge's characterization of the incident, and of the accused, by terms such as 'enforcer' and 'vigilante'."

The Court added that the facts disclose a concerned uncle who had initially interceded to calm a dispute after the young woman became involved in an accident in the early morning hours. She had been at the home of the victim without the knowledge of her parents.

b) Taking the law into one's hands: The fear of general lawlessness

This leads to an indepth discussion of vigilantism. In *R. v. Hall*, [2002] S.C.J. No. 65, 167 C.C.C. (3d) 449, 4 C.R. (6th) 197, 165 O.A.C. 319, 2002 CarswellOnt 3259, 2002 CarswellOnt 3260, [2002] 3 S.C.R. 309, 2002 SCC 64, 217 D.L.R. (4th) 536, 293 N.R. 239, 97 C.R.R. (2d) 189, para. 26 makes plain the fear of vigilante justice being meted out should public confidence in the administration of justice be undermined for one reason or another. Indeed, "Where justice is not seen to be done by the public, confidence in the bail system and, more generally, the entire justice system may falter. When the public's confidence has reasonably been called into question, dangers such as public unrest and vigilantism may emerge."

The question to be discussed in this section is, how does the sentencing court address the issue of vigilantism? Is severity appropriate in light of the concerns that "self-help" methods that are typically violent attack both individuals who are entitled to the protection of the law and the legal system itself? May any mitigation arise out of a sense of injustice that is felt by those so moved to act? On the contrary, is the emphasis to be placed on denouncing violence and lawlessness?

The Manitoba Court of Appeal upheld a trial judge's decision to ignore a joint submission calling for a nine-month jail term and to impose a two-year less a day term of imprisonment for offences of break and enter and commit and of assault in *R. v. Weenusk*, [2003] M.J. No. 194, 2003 CarswellMan 240, 2003 MBCA 79, 173 Man. R. (2d) 318, 293 W.A.C. 318 (C.A.). As set out at para. 5, "There was animosity between the accused and members of the G. . . family. It would seem that the accused's brother had been assaulted a day or so previously, and the accused was of the belief that certain members of the Grieves family were responsible. It would also appear that the accused was unhappy with the police investigation into that assault. The accused and three of his friends decided to take the law into their own hands and seek retribution."

The offenders and his companions went to the G. . . home. After shouting threats outside the house, they broke down the door to the house and searched for those they believed were responsible. Essentially, the only member of the household that they encountered was a 12-year-old boy, who was punched and given a bloody nose and pushed head-first into a snow bank. Three members of the household successfully avoided confrontation by hiding in a crawl space, and others were successful in fleeing the scene. A destructive rampage followed in which all of the windows were smashed, the fridge was knocked over and the door ripped off. In addition, the television set was thrown out of a window and tables and chairs were shattered. Para. 7 reports that ". . .the accused and his friends trashed the place."

In the opinion of the Court of Appeal, the trial judge was correct to emphasize the harm done to the community and the need to denounce "a planned, calculated act of vigilantism" in which Mr. Weenusk played a leading role. See para. 10.

Having illustrated the nature of vigilante violence, at this stage of the discussion it will be of signal assistance to set out at length certain passages from the (always) scholarly judgment of Justice Fradsham in *R. v. B. (T.E.)*, [2000] A.J. No. 111, 373 A.R. 373, 2000 CarswellAlta 111, 2000 ABPC 17 (Prov. Ct.) touching upon the law's development away from such "self-help" methods. By way of factual background, suffice it to observe that the offender punched an accused person who was seated in the prisoner's box during the course of the latter's preliminary inquiry on an accusation of having sexually assaulted Mr. B.'s spouse. Evidently, Mr. B. believed that the accused had sexually assaulted his spouse. The relevant historical passages are found at paras. 26-30:

> [27] At the time of the Norman Conquest "an injury done was primarily the affair of the party injured and of his kindred—for in proportion as the bond of the community at large was weak the bond of the family was strong. It was for him and them to avenge the wrong on the wrongdoer and his kin, and to prosecute a 'blood feud' against them until the wrong originally done was wiped out by retaliation": *The English Legal System*, by Sir Geoffrey Cross and G.D.G. Hall (4th Ed. 1964), London, Butterworths, at p. 6.

> [28] Sir Frederick Pollock and Frederic Maitland described the development of the law in their classic work *The History of English Law* (2nd Ed. 1899, Cambridge, The University Press). At p. 46 of Volume 1, the learned authors stated:

>> "In Anglo-Saxon as well as in other Germanic laws we find that the idea of wrong to a person or his kindred is still primary, and that of offence against the common weal secondary, even in the gravest cases. Only by degrees did the modern principles prevail, that the members of the community must be content with the remedies afforded them by law, and must not seek private vengeance, and that, on the other hand, public offences cannot be remitted or compounded by private bargain."

> [29] It was the work of Henry II which resulted in the first great strides being made toward the adoption of the modern principles to which Pollock and Maitland referred. At p. 35 of *The English Legal System*, supra, the learned authors stated:

>> "In any event, by the end of the twelfth century we find a great advance in the administration of the criminal law. All

serious offences involving a breach of the peace are now Pleas of the Crown, and most Pleas of the Crown are now heard, in the royal court. The more serious crimes—homicide, for instance, and the graver cases of theft—wherever committed, place life and limb in the king's hands and are the subject of prosecution at the suit of the king and not merely at the suit of the injured party. Further, while the lesser criminal offences are still tried in the local or franchise courts, a system of discretionary money fines payable to the Crown or the holder of the franchise takes the place of the old system of compensation."

[30] The benefits of those centuries of judicial thought and social progress were brought to British North America by British settlers, and provided the firm foundation upon which our Canadian justice system is built. Crucial to that foundation is the concept that criminal acts are wrongs against society, and that the function of the criminal law is to address those wrongs on behalf of society. Generally speaking, it is to the civil law that individual subjects must turn in order to seek compensation for losses suffered by them as a result of criminal acts.

In addition, para. 31 makes plain that "We still steadfastly cling to the principle that it for society to determine culpability, and, if necessary, exact the appropriate punishment."

Having set out the legal principles decrying the type of violent "self-help" resorted to by the offender, the sentencing court remarked that the offender was guilty of having "visited upon the justice system the ugly spectacle of vigilantism." Refer to para. 34. In the circumstances, a 30-day jail term was selected.

Further historical insights are offered at pages 233-234 of *R. v. Strachan* (1986), [1986] B.C.J. No. 55, 25 D.L.R. (4th) 567, 24 C.C.C. (3d) 205, 49 C.R. (3d) 289, 21 C.R.R. 193, 1986 CarswellBC 446 (C.A.), affirmed (1988), 1988 CarswellBC 699, 1988 CarswellBC 768, [1988] S.C.J. No. 94, [1989] 1 W.W.R. 385, 56 D.L.R. (4th) 673, 37 C.R.R. 335, [1988] 2 S.C.R. 980, 90 N.R. 273, 46 C.C.C. (3d) 479, 67 C.R. (3d) 87. Again, in light of the richness of the ideas expressed, it will be of assistance to quote at length from these passages:

Although certain aspects of the history of police development in the United States have followed or paralleled that in the United Kingdom and Canada, there seems always to have been a difference in public attitudes to law enforcement which has reflected itself in the role of the police and in the degree of trust and respect accorded to them.

Those differences in attitude came into conflict during the early period of settlement in what are now the western provinces. Some of the feats of the Royal North West Mounted Police in imposing the rule of law in the territories in difficult circumstances, many of which were created by immigrants from the United States, are well known. The history of British Columbia, where the RCMP did not undertake general policing duties until 1950, provides illustrations of the same point. . . . British Columbia when it was a colony [experienced. . .] problems created at that time by the influx of Americans seeking their fortunes

> [. . .resulting in the creation of] the Vigilance Committees of that city, only recently disbanded and still much talked of, about the less-formally-organized vigilantes of the California mining camps, and about "Judge Lynch".

> All the colonial officials . . . dreaded similar consequences in British Columbia. Their fears proved groundless; California miners here never became, as has so often been thought, a lawless horde. What must be realized, though, is that colonial officials believed and worried that they might become lawless; they might turn to vigilantism; they might hold lynching parties; they might flout British law; and the officials reacted accordingly. Begbie, Brew, the few constables and the magistrates determined from the start that justice should be speedy and fair, regardless of race or colour. The latter statement may sound trite but the even-handed application of law to all segments of the heterogeneous mining community was, as much as anything else, responsible for the respect given to it. Within a short time, a few years only, the work was done; frontier justice in British Columbia never played the role it did in California and lynchings did not disgrace the colonial period; the only authentic one occurred long after, in 1884.

The case of *R. v. Young* (1989), [1989] P.E.I.J. No. 17, 74 Nfld. & P.E.I.R. 16, 231 A.P.R. 16, 1989 CarswellPEI 111 (T.D.) serves to underscore the menace to our cherished liberties as a result of the decision of an individual to take the law in his or her own hands. The offender was convicted of forcible confinement and of two counts of assault causing bodily harm involving two youths, having entered a guilty plea at mid-trial.

The incident was prompted when the complainants cut some hair from the head of Mr. Young's 12-year-old son. In particular, Mr. Young was frustrated with the justice system and he considered that some sort of legal jurisdictional challenge to the *Young Offenders Act* would delay getting his son's assailants off the streets. Indeed, the offender ignored the advice of two police officers that he bring his son into Police Head-quarters and advance a proper complaint.

Thus, Mr. Young set off with a friend and seized the boys on the street, dragged them off by the hair to his truck, bound their hands behind their backs and transported them to the site of a gravel pit ten kilometres away. Eventually, the two boys had their shoulder length hair removed to the scalp and were horsewhipped and left to find their own way home.

Para. 5 made plain that "The incident was a terrifying one for the complainants. They were left without their hair, and with minor cuts, bruises and the welts from more than half a dozen lashes. The memory of the ordeal haunted them for weeks."

The Court then remarked, "For the accused, the mission achieved its intended results. His justice was swift, his vengeance was sure, his message conveyed. By taking the law into his own hands, the accused first conducted his own investigation. He then presided at the trial of his victims, and finally he administered his own measure of punishment." Refer to para. 6. Campbell J. then observed, at para. 8: "And as a consequence, David Allen Young, in taking the law into his own hands, challenged the very foundation of the civilized society. He challenged the rule of law—a legal precept which promises all citizens—the judge and the judged—the same system and measure of justice as equally and fairly as human experience can guarantee."

I pause to emphasize that the trial judge reminded us of the following at para. 9:

> There are, no doubt, many who sympathize with the accused and agree with the course of action he has taken. The lessons learned on the streets of Northern Ireland, Lebanon and Miami must surely demonstrate the ultimate futility in the use of force as a means of obtaining voluntary civil obedience. The *Young Offenders Act* may not be the perfect means of dealing with deviant behaviour on the part of some youthful citizens—but it is the means preferred by

our lawmakers and enacted by them in Parliament. The laws of Parliament must prevail, and those who usurp those laws by taking the law into their own hands are guilty of conduct deserving of condemnation and punishment.

Of interest, the Court emphasized at para. 10 that the sentence must "reflect a strong rejection of the kangaroo court and physical abuse set up and administered by the accused."

c) Violence begets violence "Rambo-style"

As discussed briefly in *R. v. B. (T.E.)*, [2000] A.J. No. 111, 373 A.R. 373, 2000 CarswellAlta 111, 2000 ABPC 17 (Prov. Ct.) and *R. v. Young* (1989), [1989] P.E.I.J. No. 17, 74 Nfld. & P.E.I.R. 16, 231 A.P.R. 16, 1989 CarswellPEI 111 (T.D.), the overarching fear of vigilantism is that it serves to promote violence. By eroding the rule of law by means of their unilateral decision to visit violence upon those who are "judged" guilty of some form of violent transgression, vigilantes invite further violence by the friends and loved ones of those upon whom they have meted out "jungle justice".

A vivid example is seen in the case of *R. v. Anderson*, [2001] N.S.J. No. 28, (*sub nom.* R. v. A. (S.F.)) 190 N.S.R. (2d) 240, (*sub nom.* R. v. A. (S.F.)) 594 A.P.R. 240, 2001 CarswellNS 28, 2001 NSSC 13 (S.C.), reversed 2002 CarswellNS 291, [2002] N.S.J. No. 151, 2002 NSCA 42, 203 N.S.R. (2d) 71, 635 A.P.R. 71 (C.A.). Cacchione J. remarked that the offender's girlfriend complained to him of having been raped by one L. As a result, Mr. A. lost his composure "and sought retribution for what he believed [L.] had done...". By way of aggravating element, he engaged the assistance of another man, R. by threatening him with grievous harm. See para. 5-6.

Thereafter, the report is replete with references to the various elements of violence inflicted on both L. and R. over nearly three hours including attempted insertion of a firearm into the anal cavity, threats of emasculation, pistol-whipping, death threats, assault with a weapon, etc.

Para. 20 records the suggestion that the offender acted out of a concern to protect others but the Court points out that the actions involved not protecting the victim from further harm, but in inflicting gratuitous violence. Indeed, para. 26 makes plain the fear that violence begets violence "Rambo-style":

One of the difficulties I see is Mr. A.'s lack of faith in the justice system as reinforcing his moral code. Mr. A., you cannot be Rambo. You cannot go around deciding who is going to get punished for what you believe they did as being wrong. I think it is quite clear that we all have to live within the rules of society. As a parent, and I put this to Mr. Craig this morning, certainly I can see how you could want to do harm to someone for having injured somebody that you care about. But you just cannot do it. Society does not allow that. If we did, well then basically everybody would just be allowed to walk around with a gun and shoot anybody they did not like or anybody they thought had hurt someone else. And if that is the kind of society you want to live in, well, it certainly is not the one I want to live in. I think if you looked at movies such as Blade Runner, you can appreciate what I am talking about, because that is what it leads to, just anarchy. We cannot have that sir. I do believe that you have the potential to change your thinking, and it is unfortunate that you have been cast throughout your life as an enforcer, as a protector and perhaps you may have had good hockey coaches in terms of hockey skills, but certainly what they instilled in you or what they demanded of you is unfortunate. It should not be.

In closing, it must be noted that this offender was himself convicted of sexual assault in the past and thus, one cannot avoid considering the irony of the situation: What if the friends and family of his victim had sought him out and brutalized as he himself did? How does the community profit from such acts of "vigilante terrorism", to track the language of the trial judge at para. 62? In the end, violence begets violence and this is the main reason for severity by the Courts in sentencing vigilantism.

d)   Concerns over mob violence

An additional concern seen in *R. v. Young* (1989), [1989] P.E.I.J. No. 17, 74 Nfld. & P.E.I.R. 16, 231 A.P.R. 16, 1989 CarswellPEI 111 (T.D.) and *R. v. Anderson*, [2001] N.S.J. No. 28, (*sub nom.* R. v. A. (S.F.)) 190 N.S.R. (2d) 240, (*sub nom.* R. v. A. (S.F.)) 594 A.P.R. 240, 2001 CarswellNS 28, 2001 NSSC 13 (S.C.), reversed 2002 CarswellNS 291, [2002] N.S.J. No. 151, 2002 NSCA 42, 203 N.S.R. (2d) 71, 635 A.P.R. 71 (C.A.) is the threat of gang or mob violence. In each case, someone aided the offender, thus depriving the victim of any mean of escape. One can easily envisage the type of lynch mob giving rise to public lynching. . .

e) Vigilante justice: A form of extortion

The discussion thus far has been predicated it seems on some form of "colourable" grievance of one kind or another, chiefly that the offenders sought to punish an offender for some form of violence inflicted upon others, violence that the police and the prosecutors would have been properly charged with investigating and denouncing. In the present case, attention is drawn to vigilante violence in the form of "debt collection". In other words, the victim of the vigilante violence could not be said to be a criminal in any sense. In this respect, note *R. v. Guest* (1998), [1998] S.J. No. 446, 168 Sask. R. 172, 173 W.A.C. 172, 1998 CarswellSask 380 (C.A.). Cameron J.A. underscored twice in a six-paragraph judgment the "violent vigilante form of justice" involved in seeking to collect a debt, or to punish the refusal to honour it to be more exact. See paras. 3 and 4. In essence, the offender who was employed as a bouncer was convicted of assault causing bodily harm after marching a man from his home with the help of another, driving him into the countryside, beating and stripping him, and them leaving him there to find his way back to the city. "The man owed him $800, and this was Mr. Guest's way of collecting the debt." See para. 1.

The Court held at para. 4 as follows: "Having regard for the gravity of the offence, the circumstances in which it was committed, and the character of the accused's conduct, which was fairly said to constitute a form of violent vigilante justice, we are satisfied that trial judge ought not to have ordered that the term be served in the community. The need to give effect to the fundamental principle of sentencing suggested otherwise, as did the objectives of denunciation and deterrence, the paramount objectives in this instance. So too did the need to uphold public confidence in the administration of justice."

f) Vigilantism and deliberation

One of the aggravating elements that emerge from the cases is the usual presence of deliberation in the seeking out of the victims. This was seen in *R. v. Young* (1989), [1989] P.E.I.J. No. 17, 74 Nfld. & P.E.I.R. 16, 231 A.P.R. 16, 1989 CarswellPEI 111 (T.D.) and in particular in *R. v. Anderson*, [2001] N.S.J. No. 28, (*sub nom.* R. v. A. (S.F.)) 190 N.S.R. (2d) 240, (*sub nom.* R. v. A. (S.F.)) 594 A.P.R. 240, 2001 CarswellNS 28, 2001 NSSC 13 (S.C.), reversed 2002 CarswellNS 291, [2002] N.S.J. No. 151, 2002 NSCA 42, 203 N.S.R. (2d) 71, 635 A.P.R. 71 (C.A.). In this respect para. 49 records as an aggravating feature the fact that the "long time" it took to find the victim ought to have permitted the offender to reflect and possibly to regain the mastery of his emotions. See also para. 3 of *R. v. Huynh* (1996), [1996] A.J. No. 448, 184 A.R. 156, 1996 CarswellAlta 417, 122 W.A.C. 156 (C.A.).

By way of contrast, leniency was shown in *R. v. Dhillon* (1995), [1995] A.J. No. 272, 165 A.R. 239, 89 W.A.C. 239, 1995 CarswellAlta 550 (C.A.), a case in which little time for deliberation was in evidence.

g) Vigilante justice: The multi-national perspective

In these troubled post-September 11 times, it is not easy to overlook the fear of vigilante justice, from twin perspectives. On the one hand, we may fear reprisals against any identifiable group and such violence would make hollow our cherished ideals of freedom and respect for others. On the other, we must fear any renewed acts of terrorism, a particular form of vigilante justice, by those who would wish to punish our society for any perceived wrongs. From either perspective, severity in sentencing is not only appropriate and wise; it is consonant with the amendments to the Criminal Code following the horrific acts of violence we have all had to endure.

In this respect, guidance is found in the well-known judgment of Mayrand, C.J.S.P. in *R. v. Cossette-Trudel* (1979), 52 C.C.C. (2d) 352, 11 C.R. (3d) 1, 1979 CarswellQue 8 (C.S.P.). In addition, refer to *R. v. Critton*, [2002] O.J. No. 2594, [2002] O.T.C. 451, 2002 CarswellOnt 2199 (S.C.J.), at para. 68-76.

h) Gang warfare

Little authority is required to remind us of the harm generated as a result of gang warfare. One need only consider all of the victims of the bombings in Québec including the young boy who was walking on the street when a bomb exploded.

i) Vigilantism and the wrong person

I pause to point out the concern held by all officials in the administration of justice that has been alluded to in a number of the cases selected in this article: What if the "victim" had done no wrong? Implicit in the justification advanced by the offenders is the belief that the person who was interfered with (to select a euphemism) is guilty of some wrongdoing. But that might not be the case. . .

j)   Summary for advocates

Vigilante injustice, for it is not justice as we have seen, typically results in a severe sentence as it contains the aggravating elements of severe violence, premeditation, "ganging up" on victims, the potential for escalation, and the overall degradation of public respect for the administration of justice. As pointed out by McKinlay J.A. in *R. v. Strachan* (July 19, 1991), Doc. 346/91, [1991] O.J. No. 3179 (C.A.) at para. 1: "The appellant unlawfully obtained possession of a restricted weapon with which he armed himself, fully loaded, in order to carry out vigilante justice. It is a reasonable inference that he armed himself in this manner with the knowledge that the person he sought out might be armed and that he could use the weapon in his possession with the consequent danger to the public peace and to the safety of any persons in the vicinity."

In the final analysis, the community cannot be subjected to the risk of harm as a result of such gun battles leaving aside the more common situation of one-sided armed violence. Thus, severity is the dominant element, all other things being equal.

24.   THE TOTALITY PRINCIPLE

Among the many examples of concurrent penalties being selected for offences occurring on separate days is *R. v. Bullock* (1903), [1903] O.J. No. 33, 6 O.L.R. 663, 8 C.C.C. 8 (C.A.). It was noted without comment that the offenders were convicted of separate offences, occurring on consecutive days, and that they received 23 months on each, concurrent. See para. 12, pages 664-665 [O.L.R.].

Note the example of an offender, convicted of robbery, who was sentenced to 18 months definite and 12 months indefinite to be served concurrently to a sentence then already being served in *R. v. Blackmore* (1970), 2 C.C.C. (2d) 397, [1971] 2 O.R. 21, 14 C.R.N.S. 62, 1970 CarswellOnt 44 (C.A.), affirmed (1971), 2 C.C.C. (2d) 514n, 15 C.R.N.S. 126, 1971 CarswellOnt 12 (S.C.C.). Refer to para. 1, page 398 [C.C.C.].

R. v. S. (D.W.) (1989), [1989] O.J. No. 2350, 1989 CarswellOnt 2041 (C.A.) includes the observation that "The learned trial judge was justified in imposing a disposition of secure custody but, on all the facts, we think the period of 24 months on the breaking and entering conviction was too long. Further, it is agreed that the total disposition exceeded that allowed by s. 20(4) of the *Young Offenders Act*." Refer to para. 1.

In the result, the disposition on the breaking and entering conviction was reduced to 18 months secure custody, and a concurrent term of one month secure custody was selected for the conviction for breach, instead of a consecutive period.

The endorsement in *R. v. Lumley* (1989), [1989] O.J. No. 2377, 1989 CarswellOnt 2135 (C.A.) reads in part as follows, at para. 1: "In our view, the sentences, individually or totally, and even in totality with respect to the assault sentence, which is not under appeal here, were fit. . .".

The case of *R. v. MacKinlay* (1989), [1989] O.J. No. 2352, 1989 CarswellOnt 2121 (C.A.) provides some assistance as to the appropriate mix of concurrent sentences and, as well, as to the corrections, if any, to be brought to the total sentence in cases of a successful appeal of one but not all convictions. As we read at para. 1, ". . . the conviction for uttering a death threat cannot stand . . . Although the sentence on that count was a concurrent one for six months, in our view, the totality of sentences must be reconsidered. A fit total sentence would be 30 months and to accomplish that result the sentences on the two break and enter convictions are each reduced to 30 months concurrent with each other."

In practical terms, what the Court did was to elect to treat each of the most serious offences (it appears that there were more) as being equal to each other. The practical result is that the next sentence hearing will proceed on the footing that the normal progression for a similar offence will be to consider starting at 30 months, all other things being equal. The Court might have imposed a lesser sentence for the first of the two, with a concurrent period for the second such that the total remained 30 months. For example, 15 and 30 months, concurrent. The "starting point" would remain 30 months in such a scenario. On the other hand, it might have chosen to impose 15 and 15, respectively, and to direct a consecutive endorsement, with the result that the "starting point" might be seen as being 15 months.

25. OFFENDER A GOOD PROVIDER

In *R. v. E. (P.)* (2000), [2000] O.J. No. 574, 129 O.A.C. 369, 2000 CarswellOnt 499 (C.A.), the 61-year-old first offender was described as having been a "good provider for his family." Refer to para. 25. It was noted in his favour but the irony remains patent—while he was providing well with respect to the material needs of his family, he was also guilty of prolonged serious sexual violence that took place at the same time. As noted at para. 26, "The offences were of considerable gravity and involved a high degree of moral blameworthiness. The appellant was in a position of trust. He abused that trust repeatedly over many years."

26. LITTLE PROFIT WAS OBTAINED FROM THE OFFENCE(S)

The question of the significance of the profit an offender may obtain from participation in a criminal venture was discussed briefly in *R. v. John* (1999), [1999] O.J. No. 175, 117 O.A.C. 100, 1999 CarswellOnt 132 (C.A.), at para. 2. "The trial judge found that the appellant's role in the conspiracy was a relatively minor one for which he gained little profit." This was a factor in his favour, as set out at para. 9: "His role in the conspiracy was a relatively minor one and he gained little profit from it." It is difficult to appreciate how to address such matters. If the enterprise is well thought out and foiled notwithstanding careful preparation, why should it matter? Counsel may wish to submit that the absence of profit when considered against the sentence and all of the negative elements associated with the arrest and trial may be sufficient to persuade the offender to abandon this type of activity.

In the case of *R. v. Cuzner*, [1970] 3 O.R. 222, [1970] 5 C.C.C. 187 (C.A.), the Court noted at page 188 [C.C.C.]: ". . . it was conceded by counsel for the Crown that the respondent did not make exorbitant profits from the sales. . .". This seems relevant from this perspective: If an offender makes great profit from the unlawful activity, it may be that he or she will be prepared to suffer the sentence to then return to the activity. Stated otherwise, the sentence must make the possibility of profit unappealing. This may be easier in cases in which the profit was not significant and thus, a lesser penalty may be appropriate as the need for particular deterrence is lessened. The same analysis is available for would-be offenders from the perspective of general deterrence.

In *R. v. Kovacs* (November 29, 1971), McGillivray J.A., Kelly, J.A., Brooke J.A., [1971] O.J. No. 894 (C.A.), Kelly J.A. remarked at para. 15 that it was somewhat mitigating that he "made no significant gains for himself from the [illegal] operation. . .".

27. LIMITED OR MINOR ROLE IN THE OFFENCE

In *R. v. Lascelle* (December 13, 1971) Gale C.J.O., MacKay J.A., Evans J.A., [1971] O.J. No. 928 (C.A.), Gale C.J.O. noted orally that the six-month sentence imposed for wilful damage be reduced to ten days with probation. The Court noted that they were young and had no records. See para. 3. It is thought that the decision to exercise a measure of leniency was influenced by their limited degree of participation in the offence. Para. 1 notes that "[They] were present when bottles were thrown through some of the plate glass windows in a public school. . .".

In *R. v. John* (1999), [1999] O.J. No. 175, 117 O.A.C. 100, 1999 CarswellOnt 132 (C.A.), para. 2 and 9 set out that the appellant's role in the conspiracy was a relatively minor one for which he gained little profit.

28. UNBLEMISHED BACKGROUND

Counsel may wish to emphasize in appropriate cases that not only does the offender have no record, but that s/he has an unblemished background. For example, in *R. v. John* (1999), [1999] O.J. No. 175, 117 O.A.C. 100, 1999 CarswellOnt 132 (C.A.), para. 9 sets out that "The appellant was a first offender with an unblemished background and history. His role in the conspiracy was a relatively minor one and he gained little profit from it." Further, "He chose to become involved at a time when he was out of work and unable to support his family." To be balanced, it must be noted: ". . . despite the appellant's exemplary background and degree of complicity, a custodial sentence was called for." See para. 4. The judgment makes plain that the absence of a criminal history is not identical to enjoying an unblemished background and history."

29. ECONOMIC HARDSHIP LED TO OFFENCE

R. v. John (1999), [1999] O.J. No. 175, 117 O.A.C. 100, 1999 CarswellOnt 132 (C.A.), sets out at para. 9 that the first offender with an unblemished background and history ". . . chose to become involved [in a serious offence] at a time when he was out of work and unable to support his family." To be balanced, it must be noted: ". . . despite the appellant's exemplary background and degree of complicity, a custodial sentence was called for." See para. 4. It should also be noted that following his apprehension, he obtained gainful employment and he is described as a valued, trustworthy and conscientious employee.

In *R. v. Kovacs* (November 29, 1971), McGillivray J.A., Kelly, J.A., Brooke J.A., [1971] O.J. No. 894 (C.A.), Kelly J.A. appeared to find that it was a mitigating feature that the offender did not set out to defraud

the public, but that he began to do so only when his business began
to fail. See para. 14-15.

30. FAVOURABLE EMPLOYMENT HISTORY:

a) In general

R. v. John (1999), [1999] O.J. No. 175, 117 O.A.C. 100, 1999
CarswellOnt 132 (C.A.), sets out at para. 9 that the first offender with
an unblemished background and history ". . . chose to become involved
[in a serious offence] at a time when he was out of work and unable
to support his family." To be balanced, it must be noted: ". . . despite
the appellant's exemplary background and degree of complicity, a custodial sentence was called for." See para. 4. It should also be noted
that following his apprehension, he obtained gainful employment and
he is described as a valued, trustworthy and conscientious employee.

In the case of *R. v. Bevacqua*, [1970] 5 C.C.C. 139, [1970] 2 O.R. 786,
11 C.R.N.S. 76, 1970 CarswellOnt 15 (C.A.), the Court was unanimous
that the 18- and 19-year-old first offenders should serve only three
months in jail, not the nine and six month definite, and six month indeterminate, terms imposed at trial for possession of offensive weapons. Para. 4 recorded that "Both have highly commendable reputations
. . . in the community and with their employers. Both have records of
steady, gainful employment." Note the further comment: "Obviously . . .
there really is no room in a consideration of sentence with respect to
these two for imposition of any sentence to answer to the element of
their rehabilitation because they need none. The remaining elements
for consideration are deterrence to them and deterrence to others." In
the result, the Court emphasized their clear records, their youth, favourable employment histories, and highly commendable community
reputations.

Consider *R. v. Jolin* (May 7, 1970), Doc. 471/69, [1970] O.J. No. 338
(C.A.) as an example of a case in which favourable work history was
noted, but without great weight being assigned to that factor, in light of
the elevated moral blame associated with the grave domestic violence.
In sum, the manslaughter victim was his estranged wife who had left
him to live with another man, together with the couple's two children.
"He discovered their whereabouts and sought with a sawed-off shotgun
to persuade his wife to return home. Argument followed in the course
of which he shot and killed his wife and injured her paramour." See
para. 3. He was of good character and had an excellent work record.

Refer to para. 4. Notwithstanding the claimed drunkenness and the provocation, the Court found the ten-year sentence unimpeachable.

R. v. McKimm (1969), [1970] 1 C.C.C. 340, [1970] 1 O.R. 819, 1969 CarswellOnt 925 (C.A.) points to the negative results flowing from the decision to jail for a lengthy period a mature offender guilty of a silly (albeit serious) offence who has a very good record, was married, and was regularly and appreciatively employed. To pay sufficient heed to reformation and rehabilitation, and if a jail term was required, "it ought to have had an indeterminate term as one of its ingredients." See pages 341-342 [C.C.C.].

R. v. Stockfish (November 15, 1971), McGillivray J.A., Kelly J.A., Brooke J.A., [1971] O.J. No. 857 (C.A.) provides an interesting example of an appellate court exercising leniency, and thus reducing a "deuce less" to a suspended sentence, based on the age of the offenders who were neither young nor elderly. Although we do not know their ages, the Court emphasized at para. 2 that they were business people, married with children, and that they had "very good previous records" in the community. This was repeated at para. 3. In other words, it appears that the Court of Appeal was satisfied that they had learned the necessary lesson by reason of their arrest, public trial, convictions and sentence. Although not stated, they had served some post-sentence period in custody.

The brief endorsement in *R. v. D. (B.K.)* (1989), [1989] O.J. No. 2344, 1989 CarswellOnt 2010 (C.A.) makes plain at para. 1 that the offender was guilty of ". . . a serious offence involving sexual abuse of a child by a person in a position of trust. There were no exceptional circumstances and a custodial sentence was required." Para. 2 highlights that but for the ". . . passage of time since the commission of the offence, the extreme remorse of the respondent, the good progress he has made under psychological treatment, the absence of any criminal record, and his exemplary work record, the sentence we imposed would be longer." Unfortunately, the sentence was not recorded.

R. v. Haggarty (1989), [1989] O.J. No. 2774, 1989 CarswellOnt 2103 (C.A.) provides instruction on the guiding principles in cases of extortion. As we read at para. 2, ". . . we think extortion is a serious offence." The Court of Appeal went on to remark, however: "This offence was not of a heinous nature." By that I understand Houlden J.A. to have meant that the offence of extortion was at the lower end of the scale of offending. The appellant had no prior criminal record and had an excellent work record. In the circumstances the panel held that a sentence of time served would be an adequate penalty. The probation order was allowed to stand." No other facts are known. Of course, this factor becomes aggravating if the moral blameworthiness is elevated.

b) Exceptional situations: Even a fair work record suffices

On occasion, the desire of the sentencing courts to offer an offender some measure of leniency will be predicated on a barely adequate work record. For example, in *R. v. M. (J.N.)* (May 20, 1970), Aylesworth J.A., McGillivray J.A., Jessup J.A., [1970] O.J. No. 370 (C.A.), a 17-year-old was successful in appealing the four, three-month definite and twelve-month indefinite concurrent terms, for three counts of auto theft and one of attempted auto theft. The Court held at para. 2 that had the trial judge been in possession of the further evidence he would have committed an error in principle had he not suspended sentence "on all of the facts of the case." The fresh information disclosed that the offender, although a good student, had decided to quit school quite against the wishes of his parents, people of good repute, and they invited him to leave their house. While living on his own, he became involved in these offences. After being released on bail, he returned to his parents' home and to his former employer, where he had a good or, at least, a noteworthy work record and prospects of continued employment. Refer again to para. 2.

He was sentenced to time served, and placed on probation for 15 months on conditions including no alcohol, residence with parents unless consent of probation officer obtained, no association with co-accused cousin "save as reasonably may be necessary in the employment of the two by the same employer".

It is therefore counsel duty to emphasize that even the prospects of employment suffice to justify leniency in the circumstances.

Another example arises in the case of *R. v. B. (N.W.)* (1989), [1989] O.J. No. 2538, 1989 CarswellOnt 1915 (C.A.). The Court of Appeal looked to the mere fact that arrangements for employment and residence with his brothers upon release were in place, together with other favourable information.

31.   FAVOURABLE FAMILY BACKGROUND:

a)   Provision of love from offender to family

R. v. John (1999), [1999] O.J. No. 175, 117 O.A.C. 100, 1999 CarswellOnt 132 (C.A.), at para. 10, underscores the importance of supporting one's family in non-economic terms: "The appellant is a devoted husband and caring father."

R. v. McKimm (1969), [1970] 1 C.C.C. 340, [1970] 1 O.R. 819, 1969 CarswellOnt 925 (C.A.) points to the negative results flowing from the decision to jail for a lengthy period a mature offender guilty of a silly (albeit serious) offence who has a very good record, was married, and was regularly and appreciatively employed. To pay sufficient heed to reformation and rehabilitation, and if a jail term was required, "it ought to have had an indeterminate term as one of its ingredients." See pages 341-342 [C.C.C.].

b)   Provision of support and encouragement from family to offender

On occasion, the desire of the sentencing courts to offer an offender some measure of leniency will be predicated on the support of a strong family having pro-social values and attitudes. For example, in *R. v. M. (J.N.)* (May 20, 1970), Aylesworth J.A., McGillivray J.A., Jessup J.A., [1970] O.J. No. 370 (C.A.), a 17-year-old was successful in appealing the four, three-month definite and twelve-month indefinite concurrent terms, for three counts of auto theft and one of attempted auto theft. The Court held at para. 2 that had the trial judge been in possession of the further evidence he would have committed an error in principle had he not suspended sentence "on all of the facts of the case." The fresh information disclosed that the offender, although a good student, had decided to quit school quite against the wishes of his parents, people of good repute, and they invited him to leave their house. While living on his own, he became involved in these offences. After being released on bail, he returned to his parents' home and to his former employer, where he had a good or, at least, a noteworthy work record and prospects of continued employment. Refer again to para. 2.

He was sentenced to time served, and placed on probation for 15 months on conditions including no alcohol, residence with parents unless consent of probation officer obtained, no association with co-accused cousin "save as reasonably may be necessary in the employment of the two by the same employer".

Note as well *C., Re* (1969), [1970] 2 O.R. 626, [1970] 2 C.C.C. 168, 1969 CarswellOnt 411 (H.C.). It provides an example of the Court seeking to avoid any form of custody if a suitable placement in a home could be found, in the case of a young person.

A further instance is seen in *R. v. B. (N.W.)* (1989), [1989] O.J. No. 2538, 1989 CarswellOnt 1915 (C.A.). The Court of Appeal interfered on the grounds that although the disposition imposed on the young person was fit when it was made, it no longer was fit. As we read at para. 1, ". . . the excellent post-disposition report filed at the hearing, which reported on the appellant's performance in high school, the prospects of him attending university, arrangements for employment and residence with his brothers upon release have persuaded us that the public interest would best be served by his immediate release."

c) Provision of financial support from offender to family

R. v. Stockfish (November 15, 1971), McGillivray J.A., Kelly J.A., Brooke J.A., [1971] O.J. No. 857 (C.A.) provides an interesting example of an appellate court exercising leniency towards offenders who were married with children. See para. 2-3. Many reasons may be advanced and they include sympathy for the innocent family members, concern for the well being of the children, loss of livelihood, etc.

d) Avoiding hardship on family

In *R. v. Miles* (1989), [1989] O.J. No. 2351, 1989 CarswellOnt 2039 (C.A.), the Court of Appeal characterized the assault under s. 245.1(1)(a) as being "very serious", ". . . involving the use of a knife and a threat of death. . .". The Court in directing a nine-month period of detention, remarked, at para. 1, ". . . the sentence imposed failed to adequately reflect the principles of general and specific deterrence. Were it not for the fact that the respondent has served the sentence imposed by the trial judge and the particular hardship which further incarceration will impose on his family, the sentence which we propose to impose would be longer."

32. GOOD CITIZENSHIP

R. v. John (1999), [1999] O.J. No. 175, 117 O.A.C. 100, 1999 CarswellOnt 132 (C.A.), at para. 10, underscores the importance of good citizenship: "The appellant is a devoted husband and caring father. As well, he has, for many years, actively engaged in charitable and volunteer work on behalf of his native community."

R. v. Stockfish (November 15, 1971), McGillivray J.A., Kelly J.A., Brooke J.A., [1971] O.J. No. 857 (C.A.) provides an interesting example of an appellate court exercising leniency, and thus reducing a "deuce less" to a suspended sentence, based on the age of the offenders who were neither young nor elderly. Although we do not know their ages, the Court emphasized at para. 2 that they were business people, married with children, and that they had "very good previous records" in the community. This was repeated at para. 3. In other words, it appears that the Court of Appeal was satisfied that they had learned the necessary lesson by reason of their arrest, public trial, convictions and sentence. Although not stated, they had served some post-sentence period in custody.

33.   ACADEMIC PURSUITS

It is instructive that in *R. v. Cuzner*, [1970] 3 O.R. 222, [1970] 5 C.C.C. 187 (C.A.), the Court observed at page 188 [C.C.C.]:

> It was strongly urged that because of his good character before the commission of the offences and his fine performance since and because he is in school, this respondent should receive some special treatment. In this respect, we adopt what was said by Tysoe, J.A., for the British Columbia Court of Appeal in the case of *R. v. Adelman*, [1968] 3 C.C.C. 311, at p. 322, 63 W.W.R. 294.

> The instances where a suspended sentence can properly be given for trafficking in drugs must be very rare indeed and arise only where there are exceptional circumstances. This is not such an instance. . .

34.   FAVOURABLE REPUTATIONS

In the case of *R. v. Bevacqua*, [1970] 5 C.C.C. 139, [1970] 2 O.R. 786, 11 C.R.N.S. 76, 1970 CarswellOnt 15 (C.A.), the Court was unanimous that the 18- and 19-year-old first offenders should serve only three months in jail, not the nine- and six-month definite, and six-month indeterminate, terms imposed at trial for possession of offensive weapons. Para. 4 recorded that "Both have highly commendable reputations . . . in the community and with their employers. Both have records of steady, gainful employment." Note the further comment: "Obviously . . . there really is no room in a consideration of sentence with respect to these two for imposition of any sentence to answer to the element of their rehabilitation because they need none. The remaining elements for consideration are deterrence to them and deterrence to others." In the result, the Court emphasized their clear records, their youth, favourable employment histories, and highly commendable community reputations.

35. THE RELATIVE ABSENCE OF SERIOUS INJURY

R. v. Lount (May 19, 1970), Aylesworth J.A., McGillivray J.A., Jessup J.A., [1970] O.J. No. 365 (C.A.) provides a good example of the relative leniency that may be shown in a case in which the violence, though serious, did not result in as grave an injury (or injuries) as might have been anticipated. The Court dismissed the Crown's appeal from a 33-month term for armed robbery, though it described the sentence as "so light" and "very lenient" and added, "one of such leniency as to constitute a rarity in connection with the offence of armed robbery." See para. 3. Although it did not interfere, it added comments to the effect that the offender was fortunate that the violence he inflicted did not result in more serious injuries and he should not expect similar leniency in the future "should he find himself in similar trouble in the future." Refer to para. 4.

That the sentencing court must consider the extent of the injuries to the victim is illustrated in *R. v. Moore* (December 13, 1971), Doc. 371/71, [1971] O.J. No. 892 (C.A.). MacKay J.A. noted that the appellant complained that the trial judge had failed to take into account that the assault involved only a mere shove causing no physical harm. See para. 2. At para. 3, His Lordship noted that no injuries were inflicted. Of course, in some cases, dramatic injuries result from a mere shove while nothing of consequence may result from a serious blow.

36. THE "JUMP" OR "STEP" PRINCIPLE

As has been discussed at various rubrics, in conformity with the general animating principle of restraint in the recourse to imprisonment, sentencing judges are to select the least lengthy period of incarceration when incarceration is warranted. By parity of reasoning, when selecting a sentence for a repeat offender in a situation in which incarceration is mandated, the increase from the last or most important jail term should not be excessive. In other words, the courts should, all other things being equal, step up from the last sentence as if climbing stairs, and not jump past a few steps unless such an increase is necessary. As expressed ably by Rosenberg J. in *R. v. Borde* (2003), 172 C.C.C. (3d) 225, 2003 CarswellOnt 345, (*sub nom.* R. v. B. (Q.)) [2003] O.J. No. 354, 8 C.R. (6th) 203, 168 O.A.C. 317, 63 O.R. (3d) 417 (C.A.) at para. 39: "[The jump principle] cautions a court against imposing a dramatically more severe sentence than the sentences imposed upon the offender for similar offences in the recent past. It has little application where the severity of the offender's crimes shows a dramatic increase in violence and severity."

A further example is found in *R. v. White* (2003), [2003] O.J. No. 2544, 173 O.A.C. 201, 176 C.C.C. (3d) 396, 2003 CarswellOnt 4106 (C.A.), para. 173 records: "...while a term of imprisonment was warranted, given his prior convictions for criminal harassment and breach of probation, the increase was excessive. His prior sentences were for short periods of incarceration (58 days and 30 days), both of which were to be served intermittently, and a conditional sentence."

To repeat, sentences should, as a general rule, be increased incrementally and not substantially, as if one were progressing step by step, not by leaps and bounds. Thus, in *R. v. Hall* (2001), [2001] O.J. No. 3704, 2001 CarswellOnt 3241 (C.A.), as endorsed at para. 1, the offender was convicted of aggravated assault and sentenced to four and one-half years' imprisonment in addition to time served treated as two years for a total of six and one-half years. Para. 4 sets out that the offender's "...record is a long one, but the longest term he has served is two years. In our view, it was an error in principle to jump to six and one-half years. Even given the ferocity of this attack, we think the sentence should have been five years with two years' credit for time served for an effective sentence of three years."

It must be underscored, of course, that significant increases are justified in appropriate cases. For example, in *R. v. Munro* (2003), [2003] O.J. No. 512, 2003 CarswellOnt 496, 168 O.A.C. 380, 173 C.C.C. (3d) 281 (C.A.), para. 69 records that the sentence was upheld notwithstanding that it represented quite an increase from his prior worst sentence, in keeping with the degree of violence and the significant injuries, leaving aside the breach of trust and the breach of parole.

Further, I wish to underscore the following guidance, found at para. 3 of *R. v. Yip* (2000), [2000] O.J. No. 2781, 2000 CarswellOnt 2625 (C.A.): "We also reject the appellant's contention that the trial judge failed to give adequate weight to the fact that [he] had not received a prior sentence of incarceration. Prior sentences are always a consideration in determining the appropriate sentence, but in this case the prior sentence was a very minor consideration given the other more relevant circumstances." Although the facts are sparse, it seems that the offender had a major mental disorder and a record for violence and thus, long-term incarceration was required to protect the community. He was sentenced to 12 years, after a year of pre-trial detention. Consider *R. v. Pisani* (March 19, 1970), Aylesworth J.A., MacKay J.A., Kelly J.A., [1970] O.J. No. 230 (C.A.) in this vein.

The Court of Appeal refused to interfere with the six-year sentence for passing spurious currency. It noted that the 30-year-old offender has been in almost continuous trouble with the authorities and that "Time and again he has been dealt with most leniency. Three times I think he has been given suspended sentence and on another occasion in a conviction for theft, a recurring type of offence [for him], he was given a sentence of six months definite and twelve months indefinite. He does not seem to have learned from this leniency." See para. 2. It noted that the offence was grave, causing losses to the victims, and remarked twice that it must be visited with a severe punishment, although not of the highest or most serious type.

With respect, it is quite a jump and a significant penalty no matter the background for a non-violent offence.

37.   SPONTANEOUS OR "UNPLANNED" WRONGDOING

Although it is obvious that spontaneous wrongdoing is deserving of less condemnation than is planned offending, the fact remains that it is a relative factor, as are so many others. At best, it may not serve to reduce a sentence, but merely to arrest the Court's hand in selecting a more severe sanction. Thus, *R. v. Sampson* (December 30, 1970), Doc. 533/70, [1970] O.J. No. 1012 (C.A.) provides an example of this scenario. Convicted of aiding an escapee, the offender received one year definite. He had a record dating back to 1962, including an offence of escaping custody and many liquor offences. He was helping someone to saw off handcuffs when arrested. It was a spontaneous act. The trial judge reported that he took into account the gravity of the offence, the young man's record and that he "has been appearing in my Courts far too often". See para. 3. Also, ". . . if his past record is taken into account with the seriousness of this charge that this young man should be incarcerated for as much of the term as possible." The Court refused leave to appeal.

324   MITIGATING AND AGGRAVATING PRINCIPLES

38. PERCEIVED UNFAIRNESS IN THE PROSECUTION TO SOME DEGREE

Consider the comments consigned in *R. v. Swan, Piper & Co.* (March 19, 1970), Aylesworth J.A., MacKay J.A., Kelly J.A., [1970] O.J. No. 213 (C.A.), at para. 3: "This litigation has had a troubled course and really comes about not only through the vigorous defence to the charges laid but by reason of the draftsmanship [of the offence. . .]". The Court found that the trial judge was right to convict of permitting machines to be operated without a device being present to automatically prevent a person operating from coming into contact with a dangerous part. The Court then imposed a fine of $500 in each case.

39. AVOIDING THE COLLATERAL HARM RESULTING FROM INCARCERATION

In light of the many earlier useful references to this theme, it will suffice at this stage to repeat the guidance advanced by Mr. Justice Rosenberg on the negative collateral consequences resulting from incarceration that His Lordship set out at pp. 36-38 C.C.C. of *R. v. W. (J.)* (1997), [1997] O.J. No. 1380, 33 O.R. (3d) 225, 99 O.A.C. 161, 115 C.C.C. (3d) 18, 5 C.R. (5th) 248, 1997 CarswellOnt 969 (C.A.):

> This is not to doubt the theory of general deterrence, or its application to the manner of service of the sentence of imprisonment. Requiring some offenders to serve the sentence in a correctional facility as opposed to the community can reasonably be expected to deter some persons from offending: see *R. v. Shropshire, supra,* at p. 202. However, these conclusions suggest that general deterrence is not a sufficient justification for refusing to impose a conditional sentence. In view of its extremely negative collateral effects, incarceration should be used with great restraint where the justification is general deterrence. These effects have been repeatedly noted with depressing regularity. Some of the comments have been collected by the Sentencing Commission at pp. 42-44 and bear repeating.
>
> 1969: Ouimet Committee, Report of the Canadian Committee on Corrections (p. 314):
>
> One of the serious anomalies in the use of traditional prisons to re-educate people to live in the normal community arises from the development and nature of the prison inmate subculture. This

grouping of inmates around their own system of loyalties and values places them in direct conflict with the loyalties and values of the outside community. As a result instead of reformed citizens society has been receiving from its prisons the human product of a form of anti-social organization which supports criminal behaviour.

1973: LeDain Commission, Final Report of the Commission of Inquiry into the Non-Medical Use of Drugs (pp. 58-59):

Perhaps the chief objection to imprisonment is that it tends to achieve the opposite of the result which it purports to seek. Instead of curing offenders of criminal inclinations it tends to reinforce them. This results from confining offenders together in a closed society in which a criminal subculture develops.

. . .

These adverse effects of imprisonment are particularly reflected in the treatment of drug offenders. Our investigations suggest that there is considerable circulation of drugs within penal institutions, that offenders are reinforced in their attachment to the drug culture, and that in many cases they are introduced to certain kinds of drug use by prison contacts. Thus imprisonment does not cut off all contact with drugs or the drug subculture, nor does it cut off contact with individual drug users. Actually, it increases exposure to the influence of chronic, harmful drug users [p. 59].

1977: Solicitor General of Canada. A Summary and Analysis of Some Major Inquiries on Corrections — 1938 to 1977 (p. iv):

Growing evidence exists that, as educational centres, our prisons have been most effective in educating less experienced, less hardened offenders to be more difficult and professional criminals.

The Sentencing Commission also points out that the other recurring themes in these earlier reports are the overuse of custodial sanctions; [. . .] the excessive length of sentences of imprisonment; the high cost of incarceration; and the stigmatizing effect of a jail term. These reports emphasize the need to resort to the least drastic alternative in sentencing. The Sentencing Commission concluded that it was only logical to recommend that imprisonment be used with extreme moderation (p. 44). Parliament has accepted this conclusion in principle through s. 718.2(d) and (e) and the courts are required to give it real effect in practice through liberal resort to the conditional sentence regime.

An early judgment of note touching upon the harm associated with imprisonment, particularly in the case of youthful or first offenders, is that of *R. v. Tardif* (May 20, 1970), Aylesworth J.A., McGillivray J.A., Jessup J.A., [1970] O.J. No. 369 (C.A.). The now 19-year-old had received a suspended sentence for break, enter and theft, and upon being shown to have breached his probation he was ordered to serve six months determinate and six months indeterminate. He was to attend school in one location and did so, obtaining the permission of the probation officer to live with his mother two hours away during the summer holiday. He found work during that period, and tried to obtain an amendment to his condition respecting schooling, but did not follow the appropriate steps with the result that when he failed to return to school, he was the subject of a revocation hearing.

The Court of Appeal was quite sympathetic, noting the misunderstanding about the duty to inform the probation officer and his sincere desire to be employed. He was sentenced to time served, plus probation for about 11 months. Noteworthy is the comment found at para. 3: "The trouble with that sentence [not a severe one in any event] is that . . . it errs in principle in that probation is for the rehabilitation of the offender and in that the offender does not exist for the sake of probation. [He] should be given an opportunity to prove himself under adjusted terms of probation." The conditions were that he report twice a month, reside with mother save with consent of probation officer, not associate or hold any communication with co-accused, make every effort to continue to be gainfully employed and make full restitution respecting stolen goods by $8.00 monthly payments through the probation officer or as the probation officer may arrange. Lastly, the Court noted: "With this extended leniency . . . we express every hope that his rehabilitation will become complete."

In essence, the Court saw leniency as being appropriate if it leads to rehabilitation. To reverse the proposition leads to this question: Why not simply have him serve the sentence? Because in some fashion it is counter-productive to rehabilitation, either because it continues to keep him away from employment, continues to expose him to criminals, furthers his potential stigmatization as an offender, interferes with potential restitution, promotes a sense of injustice, etc.

40.   A TECHNICAL BREACH OF THE LAW

An early judgment of note illustrating the comparatively diminished degree of moral blame associated with a technical breach of the law is that of *R. v. Tardif* (May 20, 1970), Aylesworth J.A., McGillivray J.A., Jessup J.A., [1970] O.J. No. 369 (C.A.). The now 19-year-old had received a suspended sentence for break, enter and theft, and upon being shown to have breached his probation he was ordered to serve six months determinate and six months indeterminate. He was to attend school in one location and did so, obtaining the permission of the probation officer to live with his mother two hours away during the summer holiday. He found work during that period, and tried to obtain an amendment to his condition respecting schooling, but did not follow the appropriate steps with the result that when he failed to return to school, he was the subject of a revocation hearing.

The Court of Appeal was quite sympathetic, noting the misunderstanding about the duty to inform the probation officer and his sincere desire to be employed. He was sentenced to time served, plus probation for about 11 months.

41.   THE PRESUMPTION OF GOOD BEHAVIOUR DURING A PERIOD OF NON-OFFENDING

Counsel should recall the instruction in *R. v. White* (March 17, 1970), Aylesworth J.A., MacKay J.A., Kelly J.A., [1970] O.J. No. 212 (C.A.) at para. 1 that the offender had not committed an offence for seven years "and one must assume was a proper citizen". In other words, the assumption that good citizenship was shown during any period in which no offence is committed is presumed, absent evidence to the contrary.

One example would arise in the case of on-going sexual violence, as in the case of *R. v. White* (June 8, 1971), Osler J., [1971] O.J. No. 545 (H.C. [In Chambers]). Osler J. remarked that the offender was convicted under s. 37 of the *Juvenile Delinquents Act*. He had sexual intercourse with his daughter and contributed to her becoming a juvenile delinquent. Para. 4 sets out that "The offence was a particularly serious one and the evidence made it quite plain that there had been a continuous course of conduct involving this child for something over three years before the charge was laid."

42. THE PRIOR RECORD MAY SHOW THE "ABILITY TO GO STRAIGHT"

Counsel will recall the ealrier lengthy discussion respecting the "gap" principle at Chapter 3(3)(f). In addition, in a minor case in the circumstances, *R. v. White* (March 17, 1970), Aylesworth J.A., MacKay J.A., Kelly J.A., [1970] O.J. No. 212 (C.A.), the offender, 40 years of age, "shamefully defrauded an elderly lady" out of $83.00. The Court took pains to point out the particularly serious nature of the wrongdoing, having to do with preying upon the old, the infirm and the like, making reference to *R. v. Major* (1966), 48 C.R. 296, 1966 CarswellOnt 17 (C.A.). Refer to para. 2. It added that unlike the *Major* case, this was an isolated instance. Nevertheless, it highlighted in para. 1 that he had not committed an offence for seven years "and one must assume was a proper citizen". It then made plain at para. 2 that he "has demonstrated his ability to go straight, as it were, for a great length of time considering his previous record and his previous inclinations as indicated by that record."

43. THE NEED FOR TRAINING TO ENHANCE EMPLOYMENT SKILLS:

a) Introduction

One of the most common optional probation conditions is the requirement that an offender "actively seek and maintain suitable employment". By way of limited example, in *R. v. Priest* (1996), 93 O.A.C. 163, 30 O.R. (3d) 538, 110 C.C.C. (3d) 289, 1 C.R. (5th) 275, [1996] O.J. No. 3369, 1996 CarswellOnt 3588 (C.A.), the Court directed that the young, unemployed first offender apply himself to finding a job under the supervision of a probation officer and with the assistance of his stepfather. See paras. 8-9 and 30. Mr. Justice Rosenberg was no doubt of the opinion that a regular pay envelope would obviate for the need to commit burglaries and would promote a sense of responsibility and self-esteem that would foster the offender's self-rehabilitation.

In this respect, counsel must draw to the attention of the Court the significance of employment (and under-employment) in sentencing. For example, as seen in *R. v. John* (1999), [1999] O.J. No. 175, 117 O.A.C. 100, 1999 CarswellOnt 132 (C.A.), para. 9 makes plain that the first offender who had an unblemished background and history ". . . chose to become involved [in a serious offence] at a time when he was out of work and unable to support his family."

b)   The general policy: Employment is an important mitigating factor in sentencing

The cases are legion in which sentencing courts look upon an offender's work history with favour. In fact, they tend to assign significant mitigating weight to a lengthy and satisfactory employment history and to accord far less importance to recently obtained work, such as the ubiquitous roofing job found within a few days of the sentence hearing. The best example known of the former category is found in *R. v. Q. (M.T.)* (1988), 25 O.A.C. 375, [1988] O.J. No. 105, 1988 CarswellOnt 883 (C.A.), leave to appeal refused (1988), 30 O.A.C. 375n (S.C.C.), at p. 378 [O.A.C.], para. 15: "He had an exemplary history of conscientious work to provide for his wife and family." See also the strong work ethic demonstrated in *R. v. Gregorczyk* (1999), [1999] O.J. No. 3758, 1999 CarswellOnt 3023 (S.C.), at para. 4.

The rationale for this policy may be stated in few words: A favourable work record tends to demonstrate industry and thus, an element of good character and, in addition, it tends to obviate for the fear that the offender is wedded to a life of crime.

However, certain concerns do arise that counsel must be prepared to address. Firstly, employment must not be seen as an economic lever with which to "purchase" leniency. For example, in *R. v. A.* (1974), 26 C.C.C. (2d) 474, 17 Crim. L.Q. 115 (Ont. H.C.), the male offender was guilty of sexually assaulting a female employee in the work place. Haines J. commented that "Imprisonment would be of no assistance to the accused. It is likely it would ruin his one-man business." Refer to p. 475. In the result, a non-custodial disposition was selected. Refer as well to the recent case of *R. v. Stuckless* (1998), 41 O.R. (3d) 103, 111 O.A.C. 357, 127 C.C.C. (3d) 225, 17 C.R. (5th) 330, [1998] O.J. No. 3177, 1998 CarswellOnt 3175 (C.A.), involving a former member of the staff at Maple Leaf Gardens. The Court of Appeal noted at para. 18 that the trial judge had considered correctly the offender's gainful employment during his adult life, notwithstanding that the grave sexual crimes he committed involved, in part, a breach of the trust reposed in him by his employers.

c)   The issue of lack of employment

Although rarely the subject of direct comment, it appears that the lack of industry shown by an offender may be taken into account in the selection of a fit sentence. Thus, the New Brunswick Court of Appeal in *R. v. Sargefield* (1981), 34 N.B.R. (2d) 506, 85 A.P.R. 506, 1981 CarswellNB 157 (C.A.) underscored the poor employment prospects of a 16-year-old in selecting a 15-month term to sanction a break and enter.

Shortly put, it is difficult to discern a rationale for this view. It is suggested that not unlike the controversy surrounding the weight to be assigned to a not guilty plea, the better view is that credit may be assigned to a positive work history but that no unfavourable conclusion should flow from its absence. That someone was unemployed at the time of the commission of an offence does not portend any greater future anti-social conduct than does the fact of employment. Indeed, if it may be said that the prospects for rehabilitation are poorer in the case of an offender who does not fear losing a job if jailed, what may be said in the case of someone who did not check anti-social behaviour notwith-standing that his or her employment was jeopardized?

At all events, it must be observed that on occasion, allowance is made for the fact that the offender has been incarcerated often in order to explain a poor work record. For example, in *R. v. S. (C.W.)* (1987), 20 O.A.C. 323, 37 C.C.C. (3d) 143, [1987] O.J. No. 2162, 1987 CarswellOnt 1079 (C.A.), it was remarked by expert witnesses that "... considering the amount of time he had been in jail, his work history was not too bad...". Refer to p. 330 [O.A.C.], para. 22.

d)   Overcoming challenges in achieving employment

It must be observed that many individuals have overcome significant limitations and have been successful in gaining employment. For ex-ample, in *R. v. G. (K.)* (1993), 63 O.A.C. 360, [1993] O.J. No. 1742, 1993 CarswellOnt 1502, 83 C.C.C. (3d) 140 (C.A.), the report of the case records these comments, at para. 3: "The appellant is now 61 years of age. ... He is virtually illiterate and of borderline intelligence, but during virtually all of his years in this country has been gainfully employed." Note as well that in *R. v. Merryweather* (January 28, 1985), Doc. 552/83, 565/83, [1985] O.J. No. 21 (C.A.) Martin, J.A., noted: "The appellant Merryweather is below average intelligence. He comes from a deprived background, but notwithstanding his disadvantages he has, generally speaking, a favourable pre-sentence report." See footnote 5.

To the same effect is *R. v. Koe* (1994), 47 B.C.A.C. 315, 76 W.A.C. 315, 1994 CarswellYukon 8 (C.A.). As set out at para. 5, the offender had a fairly impressive work history which went a long way in convincing the Court to grant him a measure of leniency not otherwise available in light of his horrendous antecedents. As set out at para. 12, "I cannot say that the trial judge imposed a sentence which was unfit, given his assessment of the clear chance Mr. Koe had of rehabilitating himself. This Court has recognized in many cases that it is not an error in principle, where the circumstances call for it, to take steps in imposing a sentence with a view to breaking the cycle of crime. The goal of sentencing is to protect society. The rehabilitation of Mr. Koe, if successful, would achieve that end."

On the other hand, some individuals are unable to overcome the challenges that they face. Thorson J.A. observed in *R. v. Audette* (July 27, 1983), Doc. 354/83, [1983] O.J. No. 724 (C.A.), at para. 5: "An earlier report describes him as dull and of impaired intelligence...". On the other hand, as was the case in *R. v. Standring* (March 4, 1993), Doc. Welland 872/92, [1993] O.J. No. 4233 (Gen. Div.), an offender may be criticized for a "... chaotic work history, with numerous short lived jobs, despite considerable intelligence." Refer to para. 45. See also p. 5 of *R. v. Browne* (December 19, 1991), Bovard Prov. J., [1991] O.J. No. 2560 (Prov. Div.).

e)   The sliding scale of descriptions of a work history

As a general rule, it is suggested that the likelihood that imprisonment may be avoided (or the term reduced if it can't be avoided) is enhanced by the work history that is presented. Hence, at one extreme, someone who is at risk of losing all pension credits if jailed will receive more favourable consideration than the offender who has no history of long-term employment, at the other.

In fact, it must be understood that not only will a positive work history merit leniency, as shown in *R. v. Johnston* (February 26, 1990), Doc. Brockville 306/88 & 322/88, [1990] O.J. No. 317 (Dist. Ct.), at p. 8, but so will a "reasonable" one, as in the case of *R. v. B. (J.)* (June 9, 1988), Merredew Prov. Ct. J., [1988] O.J. No. 2535 (Prov. Div.), at p. 27. See also *R. v. Gibson* (1984), 4 O.A.C. 313, [1984] O.J. No. 121, 1984 CarswellOnt 1294 (C.A.), at p. 314, para. 11.

Further, the Courts tend to attach neutral weight to a spotty work history, as shown in *R. v. D. (T.)* (1999), [1999] O.J. No. 3543, 1999 CarswellOnt 2977 (C.J.), at para. 7. Note the language selected in *R. v. Rivet* (January 13, 1997), Doc. CRIMF(F) 5984/95 & 5985/95, [1997] O.J. No. 5501 (Gen. Div.), at para. 6: "He has had a somewhat varying work history but obtained what is apparently, a good job as a production welder in July, 1996." However, if the Court characterizes the employment history as "sporadic", as in *R. v. S. (A.)* (March 25, 1994), Salhany J., [1994] O.J. No. 950 (Gen. Div.) or "checkered", found in *R. v. Marin* (February 9, 1994), Belleghem J., [1994] O.J. No. 1281 (Gen. Div.), at para. 2, the offender faces some difficulty; it goes without saying that nothing positive may be expected from the finding that the history is "pickled". See para. 30 of *R. v. Andrew* (July 11, 1990), Smith D.C.J., [1990] O.J. No. 2781 (Dist. Ct.).

In closing this section, it will be of assistance to note that it is not unheard of for courts to take judicial notice of the challenging economic conditions that are at play in certain areas and to observe that it is quite difficult for people to find work. Consider *R. v. Greene* (1993), 28 B.C.A.C. 35, 47 W.A.C. 35, 1993 CarswellBC 1030 (C.A.), at p. 35, para. 3 wherein Taggart J.A. considers the effects of the recession. See also *R. v. Carrier* (1992), 12 B.C.A.C. 287, 23 W.A.C. 287, 1992 CarswellBC 429, 36 M.V.R. (2d) 315 (C.A.), at p. 289, para. 8 and *R. v. Skinner* (1992), 17 B.C.A.C. 93, 29 W.A.C. 93, 1992 CarswellBC 1060 (C.A.), at p. 94, para. 7.

f)   Employment and the issue of welfare benefits

It is suggested that a sentencing court may take into account an offender's positive contributions to family and the community resulting from employment. Further, that it is far from evident that a negative conclusion may be drawn from an unfavourable work history. Attention is now drawn to the question whether a Court may consider the acceptance of social or other general welfare assistance.

In this regard, note the following comments drawn from para. 33 of *R. v. Crockford* (1995), [1995] O.J. No. 3264, 1995 CarswellOnt 3747 (Gen. Div.): "At the time of the unlawful killing of the deceased, he was gainfully employed at a local publishing company. He was a contributing member of the community, not a burden upon its social benefits programs." Note as well *R. v. Kelly* (1998), 74 O.T.C. 296, [1998] O.J. No. 3780, 1998 CarswellOnt 3654 (Gen. Div.), at para. 6: "The accused has a Grade 11 education. His probation officer states that he has not been able to get back on his feet since he left Australia, although he appears motivated to work, that the accused speaks with pride about his work history, and with shame and embarrassment about now receiving social assistance of $322 per month. He has taken job training courses since 1992, but feels that given his age, his prospects of employment are limited, as employers are reluctant to hire someone of his age."

Although other examples might be cited, these two will suffice to make plain that there appears to be an inclination to view in negative terms the fact of obtaining social assistance. With deference to contrary opinion, no articulated rationale seems to support this policy and counsel should be vigilant in opposing such views, lest the fact of qualifying for a basic entitlement lead to a harsher sentence than otherwise thought appropriate.

g) Unemployment and no apparent (lawful) means of support

It must be noted that the controversy surrounding the receipt of social assistance stands on a different footing from the negative view that a sentencing court may entertain of an offender who is unemployed and who does not have any obvious means of support. In this regard, note the comments consigned at para. 7 of *R. v. Pellerin* (1995), [1995] O.J. No. 4166, 1995 CarswellOnt 726 (Gen. Div.), affirmed (1996), 1996 CarswellOnt 478 (C.A.): "A pre-sentence report was obtained which indicates that his work history is sporadic and unsteady. Early in life, he made ends meet by odd jobs and day to day work. At the present time, the time of the preparation of the pre-sentence report, it is confusing as to his source of income. Having no steady employment and not being on social assistance, it is questionable as to his means of support." In other words, was the offender committing crimes in order to obtain money?

h) Employment and temporary absence

An important factor in the granting of a temporary absence permit recommendation may be the presence of employment. In *R. v. Smith* (1999), 123 O.A.C. 228, [1999] O.J. No. 2694, 1999 CarswellOnt 2214 (C.A.), the offender received such an endorsement notwithstanding the primary decision that his offences required an actual deprivation of liberty within a correctional facility to denounce spousal violence, and thus the setting aside of a conditional jail sentence. Refer to para. 7. See also *R. v. Lee* (February 16, 1990), Doc. Halton DCOM 3756/89, [1990] O.J. No. 524 (Dist. Ct.). Judge Clarke stated: "You'll be sentenced to ten months in the reformatory. In light of your commendable work history and your present job, I will strongly recommend the temporary absence program." Refer to the last paragraph, at p. 6.

i)   Unemployment as a neutral factor if the offender is challenged

Notwithstanding the foregoing, in many instances sentencing courts appear to discount wholly, or to a large extent, the absence of a favourable work history if it appears that the offender is unable to obtain or to maintain employment by reason of intellectual or physical challenges, however caused.

j)   Jail to enhance employment skills

This is a controversial question. Older authorities certainly favoured incarceration (or increased incarceration) to promote the acquisition of a trade. For example, in *R. v. Fox* (February 5, 1971), Doc. Toronto 516/70, [1971] O.J. No. 112 (C.A.), Schroeder J.A. commented that "The accused is 21 years of age and while he has had difficulties at home, being unable to adjust to the home environment, the case is certainly not one which calls for probation", in light of the prior record, it seems. Refer to para. 7. The Court agreed with the trial judge's remarks at para. 6 that the lack of training was a concern, and that a sentence of 12 months would not teach him anything that the previous short sentences had not, and that what was required was a term which would enable him "to learn a trade, a result which, if achieved, would be conducive to his eventual rehabilitation."

However, in light of the recognized negative collateral consequences associated with imprisonment, and the abundance of job training centres and facilities outside of prison, concerns as to employment skills enhancement ought not to weigh heavily in the final analysis.

44.   A CASUAL, VERSUS A PROFESSIONAL, OFFENCE

In many respects, sentencing courts refer to the concern that an offender is committed to a criminal enterprise and, at times, to a criminal lifestyle, by resorting to expressions that describe the Danny Ocean of "Ocean's Eleven" fame such as a "professional" criminal, or a sophisticated offender, or the offence as being "well-conceived" or well-planned. In essence, the moral blameworthiness is elevated as the offender has not heeded any pangs of conscience over whatever time the commission of the offence required, or was easily swayed by the potential profit. In such cases, the assignment of enhanced correctional resources appears perfectly justified.

For example, in *R. v. Bjellebo* (2003), [2003] O.J. No. 3946, 2003 D.T.C. 5659, 2003 CarswellOnt 3955, 177 O.A.C. 378 (C.A.), the appellants were convicted of two counts of fraud and two counts of uttering forged documents. Para. 1 reads in part: "The fraud entailed a complex scheme involving Overseas Credit and Guaranty Corporation (OCGC) and the sale of limited partnerships to approximately 600 investors. The Crown alleged that the investors were defrauded of approximately $22,000,000 and that approximately $118,000,000 in fraudulent tax losses were claimed. Bellfield was sentenced to ten years imprisonment and a fine of $1,000,000 and Minchella was sentenced to seven years imprisonment. The appellants appeal both conviction and sentence."

Para. 13 reinforces these comments by stating: "This was a highly sophisticated and massive fraud involving $118,000,000 against the public purse and $22,000,000 against more than 600 individuals. It was perpetrated over a lengthy period of time, and involved thousands of documents, off-shore companies and accounts." In addition, para. 15 reads as follows: "There was evidence from which the trial judge could infer that Bellfield had the capacity to pay a substantial fine and, in any event, s. 734.7(b)(ii) of the Criminal Code requires that before any warrant of committal be issued for failure to pay the fine, the Court must be satisfied 'that the offender has, without reasonable excuse, refused to pay the fine...'".

45. PROPORTIONALITY

In *R. v. Legere* (1995), [1995] O.J. No. 152, 22 O.R. (3d) 89, 77 O.A.C. 265, 95 C.C.C. (3d) 555, 1995 CarswellOnt 1711 (C.A.), the Court of Appeal provides the following guidance on the selection of a proportionate sentence, at pp. 566-567 [C.C.C.]:

That the trial judge found dealing with the appellant's sentence "an extremely difficult and troublesome task" is understandable. That he wanted to protect the public by imposing the maximum periods of imprisonment and probation permitted by law is also understandable in the light of the evidence before him. I think, however, that there are two difficulties with the sentence the appellant received. The first arises out of the trial judge's refusal to give any credit for the appellant's pre-trial custody. A sentencing judge may deny any credit for time spent in custody. But to do so and then impose the maximum sentence for the offence is, I think, inappropriate.

The second difficulty with the appellant's sentence arises out of the principle that a sentence should be proportionate to the seriousness of the offence. Otherwise, it is not fit: *R. v. Wilmott*, [1967] 1 C.C.C. 171 at pp. 178-9, 58 D.L.R. (2d) 33, 49 C.R. 22 (Ont. C.A.); "Report of the Canadian Sentencing Commission: Sentencing Reform: A Canadian Approach" (Ottawa: Ministry of Supply & Services Canada, 1987), at pp. 153-5. Obviously, the protection of the public is of paramount importance in determining a fit sentence. In *R. v. Lyons* (1987), 37 C.C.C. (3d) 1, 44 D.L.R. (4th) 193, [1987] 2 S.C.R. 309, wrote at p. 22:

> The imposition of a sentence which "is partly punitive but is mainly imposed for the protection of the public" ... seems to me to accord with the fundamental purpose of the criminal law generally, and of sentencing in particular, namely, the protection of society.

But I do not think that a judge can use his or her sentencing powers in the Criminal Code to impose a sentence disproportionate to the gravity of the offence on the ground that such a sentence is required to protect the public. I agree with the following passages from the majority judgment of the High Court of Australia in *R. v. Veen* (No. 2) (1988), 33 A. Crim. R. 230 at p. 235: *[page567]*

> The principle of proportionality is now firmly established in this country. It was the unanimous view of the Court in *Veen* (No. 1) that a sentence should not be increased beyond what is proportionate to the crime in order merely to extend the period of protection of society from the risk of recidivism on the part of the offender...

> It is one thing to say that the principle of proportionality precludes the imposition of a sentence extended beyond what is appropriate to the crime merely to protect society; it is another thing to say that the protection of society is not a material factor in fixing an appropriate sentence. The distinction in principle is clear between an extension merely by way of preventive detention, which is impermissible, and an exercise of the sentencing discretion having regard to the protection of society among other factors, which is permissible.

and at p. 236:

> It must be acknowledged, however, that the practical observance of a distinction between extending a sentence merely

to protect society and properly looking to society's protection in determining the sentence calls for a judgment of experience and discernment.

The reasons of Brooke J.A. in *R. v. B. (M.)* (1987), 36 C.C.C. (3d) 573, 1987 CarswellOnt 1080, 22 O.A.C. 100 (C.A.) at p. 575, are also apt:

> The principles which are applicable in imposing a disposition here include that stated by MacKinnon A.C.J.O. in *R. v. Keefe* (1978), 44 C.C.C. (2d) 193 at p. 199, 6 C.R. (3d) 35, where he said: "We are not entitled to impose a sentence not warranted by the facts merely because of the accused's mental deficiencies or retardation."

And at p. 200 where he said:

> "As I have said, a sentence disproportionate to the offence is not warranted merely because of the mental retardation or illness of the appellant. If the treatment the appellant receives in this connection is not successful and at the time of his release he presents a continuing danger to himself or the public, the authorities have available to them the provisions of the *Penitentiary Act*, R.S.C. 1970, c. P-6, s. 19(1), and provincial mental health legislation."

> For the same reason, a probation order ought not to be resorted to except in a proper case. It is, in fact, a restriction on the liberty of the subject and, of course, carries with it penal consequences if it is breached.

See also *R. v. Luther* (1971), 5 C.C.C. (2d) 354, 16 C.R.N.S. 14, [1972] 1 O.R. 634, 1971 CarswellOnt 25 (C.A.).

46. SENTENCING AN OFFENDER GUILTY OF COMMITTING A DIFFERENT OFFENCE THAN THE ONE THOUGHT TO BE COMMITTED

This kind of situation often involves possession of narcotics and smuggling. For example, a person is told that the sealed cube van s/he is hired to drive contains cigarettes when in fact it contains heroin. How is the Court to sanction such an offence? It is suggested that the answer resides in the evaluation of the moral blame attached to the conduct.

Some guidance is found in the case of *R. v. Burgess* (1969), [1970] 3 C.C.C. 268, 1969 CarswellOnt 936, [1970] 2 O.R. 216 (C.A.). As noted by Mr. Justice Brooke at page 270 [C.C.C.], ". . . the evidence was very strong that everyone involved believed that the substance was hashish rather than opium, including the R.C.M.P." As noted at the same page, the offender was then 18, in high school, and he has since enrolled at university where he is attending classes. Further, ". . . there is no evidence to suggest that this young man was an addict, there is no evidence to suggest that he needed to be prevented from repeating his crime. The evidence is consistent with the fact that it was an experiment which he and some of his friends were involved in." In the view of the Court, even if the trial Judge was right, that the offender believed the substance was opium, the young man ought to have received a suspended sentence, applying *R. v. Wilmott*, [1966] 2 O.R. 654, 1 C.C.C. 171, 58 D.L.R. (2d) 33, 49 C.R. 22, 1966 CarswellOnt 18 (C.A.). Hence, the nine months definite and 12 months indeterminate was set aside, and a suspended sentence for two years less one day was selected. In reaching this conclusion, the Court was influenced by a post-sentence report.

47.   EXPERIMENTATION

R. v. Burgess (1969), [1970] 3 C.C.C. 268, 1969 CarswellOnt 936, [1970] 2 O.R. 216 (C.A.) provides an example of the leniency often shown to offenders whose wrongdoing is rooted in experimenting. As noted by Mr. Justice Brooke at page 270 [C.C.C.], ". . . there is no evidence to suggest that this young man was an addict, there is no evidence to suggest that he needed to be prevented from repeating his crime. The evidence is consistent with the fact that it was an experiment which he and some of his friends were involved in."

48.   NO HOPE OF SUCCESS IN OFFENCE: ANY SIGNIFICANCE?

On occasion, courts are asked to consider that the offender had no hope of success, or that the offence indicates lack of planning, lack of sophistication, etc., such that the sentence need not be severe as the offender is likely to desist from further such nonsense. The theory is that a professional offender is well set in a criminal lifestyle and requires a severe term to be deterred. For example, in *R. v. Moore* (December 13, 1971), Doc. 371/71, [1971] O.J. No. 892 (C.A.), MacKay observed that the trial judge had commented that the robbery of a patron occurred in a restaurant in the presence of 35 or 40 people. See para. 3. Nothing else is said on the point.

49.   VOLUNTARY RETURN TO JURISDICTION AFTER FLEEING

In *R. v. Kovacs* (November 29, 1971), McGillivray J.A., Kelly, J.A., Brooke J.A., [1971] O.J. No. 894 (C.A.), it was noted at para. 15 that ". . . after taking flight he returned of his own accord to face the charges...". Note as well *R. v. Hudson* (1981), 65 C.C.C. (2d) 171, [1981] O.J. No. 384, 1981 CarswellOnt 1175 (C.A.), at p. 172:

> When his real estate development scheme was on the verge of financial collapse the appellant diverted a large amount of mortgage moneys to his own account in the United Kingdom and he fled this country. After two years his conscience drove him to returning to answer for his crime. He came back with $20,000 which is held in a trust account.

50.   THE CROWN'S ELECTION

In all cases in which the prosecution elects to proceed by way of summary conviction, or fails so to do and the matter is deemed to be by way of summary election, this must be brought to the attention of the sentencing court.

In sum, the choice of a summary prosecution substantially reduces the maximum penalty that may be imposed and reduces the range of sentences.

51.   THE CROWN'S POSITION ON SENTENCING

R. v. Stockfish (November 15, 1971), McGillivray J.A., Kelly J.A., Brooke J.A., [1971] O.J. No. 857 (C.A.) affords an example of an appellate tribunal reducing a deuce less to a suspended sentence, being "particularly influenced by the fact that the Crown does not oppose the request. . .". Refer to para. 2. *R. v. R. (J.J.)* (1989), [1989] O.J. No. 2512, 1989 CarswellOnt 1609 (C.A.) includes these comments at para. 1: "In the light of new evidence in the way of a post-disposition report received upon consent and having regard to the position taken by the Crown on appeal, leave to appeal is allowed to the extent that the sentence below is varied by reducing the sentence of nine months' secure custody to time already served."

R. v. Mikic (1989), [1989] O.J. No. 2507, 1989 CarswellOnt 1610 (C.A.) sets out these comments at para. 1:

> In accordance with the joint submission of Counsel for the appellant and for the respondent, with whom we agree: Leave to appeal granted, appeal allowed, the three-year sentence is reduced to two years consecutive to time served, to be followed by a term of probation of two years on the statutory terms and the following conditions: 1) that the appellant report forthwith to be under the supervision of a probation officer; 2) that the appellant take such treatment for his mental illness as may be directed by the probation officer.

In other words, before you win over the Court, win over the prosecution!

52.   DYSFUNCTIONAL BACKGROUND

The sympathy that an offender may garner by reason of not having enjoyed the advantages of a supportive and enriching family life in childhood is hinted at in *R. v. Williams* (November 22, 1971), Kelly J.A., Jessup J.A., Brooke J.A., [1971] O.J. No. 873 (C.A.), at para. 2. The offender had had a "disturbed family life". In addition, refer to the discussion surrounding the "sad life" of an offender, at Chap. 2(1).

53.   DISPARITY

Noteworthy on the question of the principle according to which disparate sentences are to be avoided is the quite useful instruction provided by the Court of Appeal in *R. v. H. (D.A.)* (2003), (*sub nom.* R. v. D.A.H.) [2003] O.J. No. 143, 168 O.A.C. 176, 171 C.C.C. (3d) 309, 10 C.R. (6th) 109, 2003 CarswellOnt 148 (C.A.). In particular, it provides guidance on the application of the "usual range" in a given case and the trial judge's duty to do justice in the individual case. Para. 33 sets out these remarks:

> In *R. v. B.* [[1990] O.J. No. 36], 36 O.A.C. 307, this Court held that the "usual range" of sentence in all cases of sexual abuse of children to whom the offender stands in loco parentis if the abuse involves sexual intercourse is three to five years. That decision has been repeatedly followed in this Court and nothing in these

reasons should be taken as a departure from that holding. However, the Court is required to consider the particular circumstances of the case in determining whether the usual range of sentence should be applied. Trial judges are required to do justice in the individual case and, in appropriate circumstances, this may require departure from the usual range of sentence. Bastarache J. made this clear in *R. v. Stone* [[1999] S.C.J. No. 27], 134 C.C.C. (3d) 353 (S.C.C.) at 450:

> One function of appellate courts is to minimize disparity of sentences in cases involving similar offences and similar offenders; see *M. (C.A.), supra*, at para. 92, and *McDonnell, supra*, at para. 16, per Sopinka J. In carrying out this function, appellate courts may fix ranges for particular categories of offences as guidelines for lower courts. However, in attempting to achieve uniformity, appellate courts must not interfere with sentencing judges' duty to consider all relevant circumstances in sentencing; see *McDonnell, supra*, at para. 43, per Sopinka J.; and at para. 66, per McLachlin J. In Archibald, McEachern C. J. clearly stated, at p. 304, that it would be wrong to assume that there is any "precise range that will apply to every case". In my opinion, this qualification reveals that the Court of Appeal in *Archibald* correctly intended for trial judges to balance uniformity in sentencing with their duty to consider the circumstances of the particular case.

In the final analysis, the Court found justification for a decision to derogate from the usual range, chiefly by reason of the horrible childhood suffered by the offender and the circumstances of his admission of guilt giving rise to a likelihood of reformation. Refer as well to para. 3 of *R. v. Parent* (2003), [2003] O.J. No. 217, 2003 CarswellOnt 191 (C.A.).

R. v. Rizek (2003), [2003] O.J. No. 3351, 2003 CarswellOnt 3279 (C.A.), illustrates "justified" disparity in sentencing based on the fact that one offender used a weapon while prohibited from having one in his possession (par. 1). See also *R. v. Liikane* (2003), [2003] O.J. No. 3495, 2003 CarswellOnt 3379 (C.A.). Para. 5 of *R. v. K. (S.)* (2003), [2003] O.J. No. 2690, 2003 CarswellOnt 2580 (C.A.), includes these observations by the Court of Appeal, at para. 5:

> Both appellants also appeal their dispositions, which were six months closed custody, followed by three months open custody and 15 months probation. We see no basis for interfering with

these dispositions. The appellants participated in an unprovoked and violent assault with machetes. They were both on bail for other offences at the time of the commission of the assault. They are very fortunate that the injuries to the complainant were not more serious, which in turn might have led to much more serious criminal charges. The fact that the adult co-accused, Khan received a lesser sentence—a suspended sentence—is not a disparity which entitles us to interfere with the appellants' dispositions. Khan pleaded guilty to simple assault, testified as a Crown witness at the appellants' trial, had no criminal record, and was not on bail at the time of the offences.

Finally, in the case of *R. v. Gillan* (2003), [2003] O.J. No. 2513, 2003 CarswellOnt 2364 (C.A.), disparity in sentencing was justified by reason of the fact the offender pleaded guilty to more charges than the related offender, that his record for break and enter is much worse than the co-accused's and the co-accused had an eight-year gap in his record while the offender was released three weeks before he committed these offences. See para. 2.

54.   OFFENDER ACTED IMPULSIVELY

In *R. v. Crawford* (1989), [1989] O.J. No. 740, 34 O.A.C. 308, 1989 CarswellOnt 989 (C.A.), the appellant was convicted on a plea of guilty to second degree murder and was sentenced to life imprisonment and it was ordered that he must serve 13 years in prison before he becomes eligible for parole. At para. 2, the Court of Appeal opined that "We agree with the trial judge that this was a very serious offence. There can be no doubt that it shocked the community in which the victim lived and caused great anguish to her family. The death of a young person by violence must always have this effect. The question that confronted the trial judge was whether the period of ineligibility for parole should be extended beyond the minimum period of ten years." At the next paragraph, we read,

In our view, the case is distinguishable from cases such as *R. v. Larcenaire* (1987), 20 O.A.C. 380 and *R. v. McGill* (1986), 18 O.A.C. 81. The conduct of the accused in those cases was more grave than in the case at bar. Here, the accused man's acts and actions were inexplicable and irrational. The repeated acts of violence which caused this young woman's death speak of frenzy rather than deliberation. In our view, the trial judge should have given greater weight to the opinion of Dr. Orchard when he said:

"It is my further opinion that he was unlikely in any state to deliberate or consider his actions. It is most likely that this action was quite impulsive and a suicidal equivalent."

In the circumstances, Brooke J.A. held that the appeal should succeed and the sentence was varied to life imprisonment without eligibility for parole until the appellant has served ten years.

55. PERSONALITY DEFECTS

The question of the personality defects the offender may be suffering from falls within the general rubric of diminished moral blameworthiness. In other words, by reason of the offender's lack of impulse control, or judgment, or ability to check his or her temper, etc., lesser aggravating weight is justified. Consider the discussion of the following case as a valuable illustration:

In *R. v. White* (2003), [2003] O.J. No. 2544, 2003 CarswellOnt 4106, 176 C.C.C. (3d) 396 (C.A.), the majority judgment found that the sentence selected at trial was excessive, and was reduced to a period of "time served", an effective term of 12 months. The dissenting opinion would have upheld the 18-month jail period, after 80 days of "dead time", credited on a two-for-one basis, followed by a period of probation of three years. As we read at para. 1, Mr. White pled guilty to, and was convicted of, criminal harassment, five counts of breach of probation and breach of recognizance. All of the offences occurred as a result of Mr. White's attempts to reconcile with his family after his marriage ended.

Noteworthy are the facts that the then 48-year-old offender had never had any interaction with the criminal justice system. He had been married for 15 years to J. White and they had two sons, P. and A., who were aged 12 and 9 respectively. He was a good employee with a good work history. Stress resulted from a decision to move from their home community, with Mr. White having to commute. As set out at para. 7, he started to experience severe anxiety that developed into palpitations, nervousness and tremors. He suffered from loss of sleep and lack of appetite and developed a pessimistic outlook on life. His behaviour took a toll on his marriage and, after his admission into hospital for the first of many psychological assessments, he and his wife separated.

Mr. White at one time was subject to three separate probation orders; a term of all three orders was that he not have contact with J. White, but he did so nevertheless.

His first conviction was for criminal harassment against J. White and breach of recognizance. He received a 58-day intermittent sentence followed by two years probation. By a term of probation, he was to have no contact with J., P. or A., except through a family court order. Subsequently, he was convicted of breach of probation on October 2, 2001 and given a three-month conditional sentence. On October 22, 2001, Mr. White was arrested again for contacting his wife and children. He was held in custody until November 2, 2001, at which time his conditional sentence was terminated. He served the remainder of the sentence in custody. He was released from custody on December 11, 2001. The following day, December 12, 2001, Mr. White approached his children at their school and was arrested for breach of probation. He received a sentence of 30 days intermittent followed by two years probation. A term of probation was that he have no contact with J., P., or A., except through a family court order. On April 23, 2002, he was convicted of criminal harassment and sentenced to two years probation. He had served 78 days of pre-sentence custody. A term of the probation order was that he have no contact with J., P. or A.

Not surprisingly, the trial judge who dealt with the most recent set of convictions concluded that general and specific deterrence were the dominant considerations, as prior sentences that focussed on rehabilitation had proven ineffective. See para. 18. In the view of the Court of Appeal, no objection could be taken to the trial judge's imposition of a period of imprisonment. As we read at para. 20, "In accordance with this Court's jurisprudence (see, for example, *R. v. Bates* (2000), 146 C.C.C. (3d) 321, 2000 CarswellOnt 2360, [2000] O.J. No. 2558, 35 C.R. (5th) 327, 134 O.A.C. 156 (C.A.)) and in light of the appellant's continued refusal to abide by court orders, a period of incarceration was required in order to denounce his conduct, provide specific and general deterrence and meet the complainant's safety needs."

The majority opinion, however, concluded that having regard to the circumstances of these offences and of this appellant, the period of incarceration was excessive. The following factors lead to this conclusion, as enunciated at para. 21:

a)   the absence of violence in the offences;

b)   the appellant's lack of a criminal record prior to the break up of his family;

c)   the significant increase in sentence;

d)   the appellant's emotional and psychological problems; and

e)   the fact that the appellant had taken steps to receive counselling.

In the final analysis, as observed by the majority of the Court of Appeal at para. 26, "The gravity of the appellant's offences is materially different from those in *Bates* and *Thomas*. There were no assaults, profanity, threats or home invasions. There was no violence and no threatened violence against the complainant. Indeed, there was no history of violence nor were there allegations that Mr. White was abusive or violent during the marriage. He had no record prior to the break up of his family." And, he did not harass the complainant's friends and family, took responsibility for the offences, turned himself in to the police and pled guilty to all of the offences.

More to the point, with respect to his personality disorder noted earlier at para. 21(d), it is important to note that several medical and psychiatric opinion letters were filed as exhibits at sentencing. All of the physicians agreed that the appellant was having difficulty coping with his personal situation. "While there was a divergence of medical opinion as to the root of the appellant's behaviour ...the consensus was that further treatment, either through continued medication, counselling, or both, should be implemented." See para. 28. The paragraph concluded that "The opportunity for rehabilitation through such treatment is hampered by incarceration."

Finally, the majority underscored how the appellant's "mild disposition" made him vulnerable in jail, how the pre-hearing custody had marked him significantly, and how he was now capable of recognizing that his relationship with his wife was over and his need to seriously pursue treatment and counselling. Hence, the time he had spent in custody both pre and post-trial had impressed upon him the need for rehabilitation.

As for the question of Mr. White's emotional and psychological problems, the dissent qualified them as being "sad and deserving of sympathy". However, at this juncture the sentencing judge was entitled to conclude that specific deterrence of the appellant and the safety of his family must take priority. See para. 47. Finally, the minority was not convinced of the appellant's commitment to counselling, describing it as doubtful at para. 48.

In *R. v. Harcourt* (1989), [1989] O.J. No. 2768, 1989 CarswellOnt 1570 (C.A.), Brooke and Krever JJ.A. concluded that the ". . . sentence is too long having regard to the frailties of the appellant's personality." In their opinion, a term of time served (six months) was appropriate." See para. 2. On the other hand, Galligan J.A. dissented and concluded that the sentence was a fit one.

56.   CHANGE IN RESIDENCE

R. v. B. (N.W.) (1989), [1989] O.J. No. 2538, 1989 CarswellOnt 1915 (C.A.) provides an example of the Court of Appeal interfering on the grounds that although the disposition imposed on the young person was fit when it was made, it no longer was fit. As we read at para. 1, ". . . the excellent post-disposition report filed at the hearing, which reported on the appellant's performance in high school, the prospects of him attending university, arrangements for employment and residence with his brothers upon release have persuaded us that the public interest would best be served by his immediate release." He was to be the subject of a probation order for one year.

57.   THE STRICT APPLICATION OF THE LAW HINDERS REHABILITATION

In this respect, note *R. v. L. (C.)* (1989), [1989] O.J. No. 2397, 1989 CarswellOnt 2079 (C.A.). As was reported at para. 1, "Although a disposition of three months open custody for this offence was not too severe, we are all of the opinion that in the circumstances of this young offender, noting in particular, the reports of her previous good character and her present attempts to rehabilitate, including attending a special school program in Hamilton, and the impossibility of her being able to complete the current school term in Hamilton while she is in open custody in Brampton, all lead us to conclude that the disposition should be changed as to custody." The custodial disposition was reduced to time served, and she was to comply with a probation order providing for community service.

Note as well *R. v. M. (R.)* (1989), [1989] O.J. No. 2346, 1989 CarswellOnt 2006 (C.A.). Para. 1 reads in part: "This disposition, which the trial judge imposed, was, at the time of its imposition, entirely appropriate. However, the information which we have received respecting the appellant's progress in open custody shows that at this point he has obtained all the benefit that could be accomplished by the disposition and that there is no useful purpose to be served by its continuation after the commencement of the next school year." As a result, the disposition was varied to substitute four and one-half months open custody for the eight months open custody imposed with respect to the first count with the result that the total disposition was to be eight and one-half months open custody.

58. GOOD CHARACTER AS A CONDUIT TO FRAUD OFFENCES

As noted by Finlayson J.A. in *R. v. Pierce* (1997), [1997] O.J. No. 715, 32 O.R. (3d) 321, 97 O.A.C. 253, 114 C.C.C. (3d) 23, 5 C.R. (5th) 171, 1997 CarswellOnt 682 (C.A.), leave to appeal refused (1997), [1997] S.C.C.A. No. 225, 105 O.A.C. 319 (note), 224 N.R. 154 (note), 34 O.R. (3d) xv, 117 C.C.C. (3d) vi (S.C.C.), the Court of Appeal for Ontario considers that it is an error to place too much weight on the prior good character of a mature offender guilty of fraud.

This is not a new view of the question. As made plain in *R. v. Foran* (1969), [1970] 1 C.C.C. 336, [1970] 2 O.R. 52, 1969 CarswellOnt 371 (C.A.), at page 337 [C.C.C.], ". . . the learned trial Judge seems to have placed undue emphasis upon the position of the accused in the community and seems to have relied on that as a mitigating circumstance. Any mitigation from that source would seem to us to be more than offset by the fact that the very nature of this type of crime requires that it be committed by persons who have an established place in the community and are allegedly honourable gentlemen. This was a fraud and one who did not have the respondent's position could not have succeeded in committing it as he did."

59. KICKING

In *R. v. Wilson* (March 1, 1971), Doc. Toronto 37/71, [1971] O.J. No. 256 (C.A.), a 12-month definite term, followed by a deuce less indeterminate period, was upheld, mainly on the basis of a record containing two assaults, an assault against a peace officer and a cause a disturbance. As noted at para. 7, at a rock festival, the offender hit and kicked the victim who "ended up with four stitches over his right eye."

60. BRAZEN OFFENCE: ANY SIGNIFICANCE?

In *R. v. Wardrop* (December 2, 1971), Doc. Toronto 107/71, [1971] O.J. No. 904 (C.A.), MacKay J.A. observed at para. 2 that the offender attempted to steal a car (or the contents, being sales samples) in a brazen fashion at 4:00 in the afternoon. He had smashed a window and when asked what he was doing, replied that he was trying to get into the car. When told to get away, he replied, "Come on, I'll slice you". He then left. It seems that a severe term was appropriate to deter a determined offender who learned little from prior lenient penalties involving short terms and probation. Leaving the record aside, any offender who acts in such a brazen fashion faces a more severe response as s/he indicates a determination not seen in a casual offender. See para. 250. A case of theft under $50.00 resulted in a term of 18 months definite and six months indeterminate in *R. v. Olsen*, [1965] O.J. No. 561 (C.A.). He broke into a car at a golf course in broad daylight. The offender had a record, his attitude did not impress the Court, and there was no restitution or recovery. Further, as found at para. 3, there was a concern as to the prevalence of this type of offence. In sum, "[w]hile the sentence imposed is severe, it cannot be demonstrated that there was any error in principle."

61. PLANNING: WHAT IF THE PLAN IS TO AVOID INJURY?

It seems logical to credit an offender who seeks to minimise the possibility of injury to the victims. Although the offence may be viewed seriously by reason the planning, the removal of a shot from a shotgun cartridge might be held in the offender's favour. In *R. v. Larocque* (December 1, 1971), Doc. Toronto 406/71, [1971] O.J. No. 901 (C.A.), MacKay J.A. remarked at para. 2 that "The appellant when arrested stated that a .410 shotgun had been used but that the shot from the cartridge had been removed." No comment is noted suggesting leniency. During the commission of a robbery, a staff member misunderstood a command and moved, and the co-accused fired at him.

62. RACIALLY MOTIVATED OFFENCES

R. v. Johnson (October 6, 1989), Doc. CA 711/89, [1989] O.J. No. 2529 (C.A.) includes these comments at para. 1: "The trial judge heard all of the evidence and was in a better position to assess the racial overtones. The agreed statement of facts was not complete enough to enable this Court to conclude that the trial judge was wrong. He was concerned that the Respondent with his borderline intelligence should not be made the scapegoat for what transpired. In all of the circumstances we are not persuaded that the sentence was unfit having regard to the findings of the trial judge. We are not to be taken as concluding that assaults with racial overtones should not be dealt with severely."

Consider as well *R. v. Wright*, [2002] A.J. No. 892, 303 A.R. 371, 273 W.A.C. 371, 2002 CarswellAlta 874, 2002 ABCA 170 (C.A.), at para. 4. Although a ten-year gap in the offender's record was underlined, it could not assist greatly in light of the quite serious offence involving planning, racial overtones, and the extreme degree of violence justifying a 12-year term.

63. CONSUMING NARCOTICS WHILE IN A MOTOR VEHICLE

Although the endorsement is flawed by the omission of a few words, it seems, *R. v. Woodcock* (1989), [1989] O.J. No. 2343, 1989 CarswellOnt 2023 (C.A.) appears to suggest that it is not incorrect to hold as an aggravating factor militating against the granting of a conditional discharge that the offender consumed narcotics while in a vehicle that was being operated, albeit by someone else. See para. 1. The natural concern would be that this might lead the operator to consume.

64. USE OF A RUSE

R. v. Williams (1989), [1989] O.J. No. 2341, 1989 CarswellOnt 2007 (C.A.) includes these observations at para. 1: "The circumstances were abhorrent. The victim, old and legally blind, was attacked and robbed in his house by his two grandsons who gained entry by the ruse of inquiring for his health. Nevertheless, in our opinion, the sentence was too heavy. Although this accused had a serious related record, we think a maximum appropriate sentence would be 18 months."

65. UNFORESEEN CONSEQUENCES

In the case of *R. v. Slusar* (1935), 65 C.C.C. 91, 1935 CarswellSask 49, [1935] 3 W.W.R. 284, [1936] 1 D.L.R. 96 (C.A.), pages 93-94 [C.C.C.] record that the offender, guilty of willful damage to property by night, was sentenced to nine months' imprisonment in the Prince Albert gaol, with hard labour. "The latter also appeals on the ground that this sentence is excessive. Having regard to the serious nature of the offence, however, and to the circumstances disclosed regarding its commission, we are not prepared to say that it is too severe." As set out at page 92, in essence, Mr. Slusar passed along the street in front of the office of the Monarch Lumber Co. at Alvena and, as he did so, he threw a rock at one of the office windows, in which there were some cans of paint. The rock went through the window, breaking the glass and two cans of red paint, with the result that their contents splashed the floor, walls and ceiling of the office, and went over the desk and papers therein. The damage to the window sash was valued at $1.78, the cost of putting in a new glass at 50 cents, and the value of the two cans of paint at $2.40; making in all $4.68. These items, together with the cost of cleaning up the paint from the office premises, were estimated to amount to well over $20.

In *R. v. Phillips* (1999), [1999] O.J. No. 2848, 123 O.A.C. 304, 138 C.C.C. (3d) 297, 26 C.R. (5th) 390, 1999 CarswellOnt 2351 (C.A.), we receive the following guidance on this issue: "... the unforeseen consequences of an offence can properly be seen as an aggravating factor on sentencing...". Para. 27 sets out that: "Unforeseen consequences are not logically connected to the objectives of specific and general deterrence, however, they unquestionably play a role in the denunciation purpose of imposing sentence."

66.   AN OFFENDER MUST NOT BE SENTENCED TWICE: "SO MUCH FOR THE OFFENCE AND SO MUCH FOR THE RECORD!"

Proceeding on the assumption that the prior difficulties are disclosed to the sentencing judge, it will be useful to note the remarks on the impact and limits of a record in sentencing in *R. v. Stewart* (2003), [2003] O.J. No. 1958, 2003 CarswellOnt 1856, 172 O.A.C. 76 (C.A.). The appellant pled guilty to a charge of uttering a threat to cause bodily harm to his common-law partner. Of note, he acknowledged the particulars of his criminal record, described at para. 9 as "substantial", and that the trial judge concluded on the basis of the record that Mr. Stewart was a dangerous person and, without further reasons, sentenced him to jail for 18 months, plus two years' probation.

Noteworthy is the observation at para. 9 of the reasons of the Court of Appeal that the trial judge "appears to have sentenced the appellant on his record, without consideration for the particulars of the offence." The Court added, and this must be underscored: "*It must be remembered that the appellant had already paid the price for his earlier convictions.*" The next paragraph highlights the conclusion that the sentence of 18 months' imprisonment is out of proportion with the gravity of the offence. It is unreasonable."

Refer to *R. v. O. (E.)* (2003), [2003] O.J. No. 563, 2003 CarswellOnt 544, 169 O.A.C. 110 (C.A.), at paras. 12-15 with respect to the grievance raised by the offender to the effect that "the trial judge erred by imposing a sentence designed to punish the appellant for past lenient sentences concerning other crimes..." In this regard, the Court held:

> [15] The appellant submits that those statements by the trial judge indicate that he sought to punish the appellant for what he perceived to be lenient sentences imposed in connection with past offences. We do not accept that submission. The full context of the trial judge's comments make clear that his references to sentences previously received by the appellant were directed to consideration of the "jump principle", whereby sentences for a repeat offender should increase gradually, rather than by large leaps. The reasons for sentence of the trial judge, in our view, do not demonstrate that he erred in analysis of that principle, or that he attached any improper significance to the sentences received by the appellant for past offences.

As has been demonstrated, the offender is not to be punished twice on the grounds of a record, but the record is relevant in assessing what response is required to avoid further harm to the community. In the case of *R. v. Goyette* (2003), [2003] O.J. No. 1929, 2003 CarswellOnt 1824 (C.A.), the Court endorsed the following, at para. 1: "The offences were extremely serious and given the appellant's background and history, the trial judge was on solid ground in concluding that a very substantial penitentiary sentence was called for."

Hence, even though a record of prior offending is relevant to the selection of a fit sentence, its influence must not be permitted to be disproportionate. In effect, it cannot trump the application of all mitigating principles, all other things being equal. Counsel must strive to direct the Court's focus to the moral blame attached to misconduct, in order to blunt any potential overreaching.

67. REPETITIVE MISCONDUCT

An offender who has engaged in repetitive misconduct stands in a slightly different footing from s/he who has breached court orders. In the latter case, s/he has shown an unwillingness to reform and to learn the lessons that were to be taught by the various penalties. Examples include *R. v. De La Cruz* (2003), [2003] O.J. No. 1971, 2003

CarswellOnt 1921, 178 C.C.C. (3d) 128, 174 C.C.C. (3d) 554, 172 O.A.C. 177 (C.A.), additional reasons at (2003), 2003 CarswellOnt 3128 (C.A.) at para. 35 and *R. v. Fazekas* (2003), [2003] O.J. No. 1615, 2003 CarswellOnt 1603, 171 O.A.C. 115 (C.A.) at para. 10. The former type of offender, by contrast, has demonstrated a defective moral compass in that until apprehension, the offender was intent on further anti-social behaviour. It is not as serious as a refusal to conform to the correction inherent in state-sponsored sanctions.

68.   OFFENDING SHORTLY AFTER RELEASE

In the case of *R. v. Gillan* (2003), [2003] O.J. No. 2315, 2003 CarswellOnt 2364 (C.A.), some emphasis was placed on the fact that the offender was released three weeks before he committed the subject offences. Refer to para. 2(c). Not surprisingly, a plea for mitigation fell on deaf ears as the offender had not shown that s/he had learned anything from the previous trial and sentence.

Note that in *R. v. Playford* (2003), [2003] O.J. No. 954, 2003 CarswellOnt 874, 169 O.A.C. 300 (C.A.), para. 2 records that "the previous conviction for extortion and the short period following the serving of the sentence on that conviction before this offence was committed were aggravating factors and we take them into account."

69.   RECORD FOR QUASI-CRIMINAL MISCONDUCT

Many cases disclose examples of pre-sentence reports making reference to "provincial" driving records. In *R. v. Hannibal* (1994), [1994] M.J. No. 265, 95 Man. R. (2d) 42, 70 W.A.C. 42, 1994 CarswellMan 317 (C.A.), para. 7 reads as follows: "The pre-sentence report indicates the accused has only one previous driving offence of speeding for which he paid a $45 fine. Otherwise, the report indicates that his conduct, work habits and behaviour as a citizen are blameless. He has always been fully employed and is so at the present time as a field supervisor with a fertilizer service as well as a heavy equipment operator, mechanic and truck driver. That report concluded by recommending the accused as a suitable candidate for a community probation disposition." See as well *R. v. Emes* (1990), [1990] M.J. No. 111, 63 Man. R. (2d) 282, 1990 CarswellMan 129 (C.A.), at pages 2-3, and *R. v. Gutoski* (1990), [1990] M.J. No. 7, 63 Man. R. (2d) 246, 1990 CarswellMan 1, 19 M.V.R. (2d) 12 (C.A.), at page 4.

70. IF THE OFFENDER CAN'T ABIDE BY THE RULES, MAY THE COURT CHANGE THE RULES?

Counsel should consider the lessons found in the case of *R. v. Skoro* (1993), 28 B.C.A.C. 77, 47 W.A.C. 77, 1993 CarswellBC 1033 (C.A.). The Court dealt with an appeal from a curfew. The offender, who had been convicted of some 25 theft and break and enter offences, mainly as a young offender, was prohibited from being away form his place of residence between the hours of 11:00 p.m. and 6:00 a.m., "on any date except whilst in possession of written permission from that date for that date from your probation officer." See para. 3. The Court reviewed the circumstances of this 19-year-old individual, to then conclude that "... the imposition of a curfew on this 19-year-old young man is not one that is workable."

The following comments are also found in the judgment: "I am sure that if proper representations had been made in the Court below that the Provincial Court judge may well not have made such a condition. I feel that such a condition would be unworkable under the circumstances." See para. 8. In the result, the requirement of the curfew was deleted. It is submitted that no compelling rationale was articulated to justify the deletion of such a condition. If it was thought that the need to obtain written permission was potentially too onerous with respect to the demands upon the time of the probation officers, the possibility of obtaining such permission ought to have been deleted. The public interest would have been better served by requiring the offender to be bound by an absolute curfew than by removing this salutary restraint on his activities.

Note that in *R. v. Butler* (1988), 69 Nfld. & P.E.I.R. 126, 211 A.P.R. 126, [1988] P.E.I.J. No. 6, 5 M.V.R. (2d) 8, 1988 CarswellPEI 3 (T.D.) Campbell, J., remarked at p. 6 that "I must also consider the age, the mode of life, the character and personality of the offender". All of these factors may be usefully summarized under the rubric "Personal Circumstances of the Offender" as did Jenkins, J., in *R. v. Gauthier* (1996), 137 Nfld. & P.E.I.R. 246, 428 A.P.R. 246, [1996] P.E.I.J. No. 3, 1996 CarswellPEI 14 (T.D.) at para. 16, with reference to "Age, mode of life, character and personality". Hence, Parliament appears to have codified many of the factors that have been considered by the courts for many years in sentencing.

71. PROOF OF AGGRAVATING ELEMENTS: KNOWLEDGE OF HARM

In cases involving two or more offenders, counsel must contest any attempt to have aggravating features assigned to an offender unless shown beyond a reasonable doubt, notably the offender's knowledge as to the degree of harm that might result from the offence. In this respect, *R. v. Price* (2000), [2000] O.J. No. 886, 144 C.C.C. (3d) 343, 33 C.R. (5th) 278, 72 C.R.R. (2d) 228, 140 O.A.C. 67, 2000 CarswellOnt 837 (C.A.) provides the following guidance:

> [para. 54] The appellant was not in the store during the robbery. He was the driver of the car that transported all three accused to and from the robbery. There was no evidence that the appellant fired any of the shots.

> [para. 55] It would appear that the trial judge was of the view that both the appellant and the co-accused Montgomery should be treated identically in so far as sentence was concerned. In my view, in so doing the trial judge erred in principle, given the disparity between the criminal records of the two and the different roles that the appellant and Montgomery performed with respect to the robbery. Although the appellant may have played a significant role in the planning of the robbery, he was not directly involved in the assaultive behaviour and threats of bodily harm which, according to the victim impact statements, so traumatized those present in the store at the time of the robbery. Nor is there any evidence that he either countenanced or envisaged the violence that occurred.

The instruction to be drawn from this lengthy passage is that the facts of the offence must be scrutinized with care in order that no aggravating weight be assessed that is not fairly attributable to the offender and that no available mitigating weight be overlooked.

Index

ABORIGINAL OFFENDERS
background factors, 35, 37, 39, 41, 42-43
balancing of sentencing factors, 35
conditional sentence
   granted, 36-37, 38
Criminal Code, s. 718.2(d), 34
Criminal Code, s. 718.2(e), 34-35, 36, 39, 40, 77, 98
denunciation, and 37, 40, 41
deterrence, and, 37, 40, 41
discrimination against, 37
generally, 34-35, 42-43
imprisonment, 35-38, 40-41
moral blameworthiness, and, 39-42
overincarceration of, 40
R. v. Borde, 39-42
R. v. Fireman, 34-35, 42
R. v. Gladue, 35, 36, 37, 39, 40, 42, 43
R v. Wells, 35, 36, 37, 39, 40
racism and, 39, 41
rehabilitation and, 37
restorative justice, 38, 40
restraint principle and, 42
seriousness of offence as factor in sentencing, 35, 40, 41
separation, and, 40, 41
systemic factors, 35, 37, 39, 41

ADDICTION
drug offences and, 264, 266
expert evidence re, 246
generally, 57, 60, 104, 138, 145, 265-266
overcoming, 90, 91-92, 103, 106, 114, 141
probation condition re, 245
relapse, 103, 106, 114
repeat offenders and, 296
therapeutic remand and, 90-91

AFRICAN CANADIAN OFFENDERS
Criminal Code, s. 718.2, 44
discrimination against, 45

moral blameworthiness, and, 43-46
overincarceration of, 44, 45
racism, systemic, and, 43-46
R. v. Borde, 39, 43-46
R. v. Gladue, 43, 44, 46
R v. Wells, 44
seriousness of offence as factor in sentencing, 45, 46

AGGRAVATING FACTORS
administration of justice, harm to, 276
absence of, 4
brazen offence, 347-348
breach of bail conditions, 120, 216
breach of court orders, 120,138-139, 216, 263-264, 273-274
breach of trust, 135, 238, 255, 266, 279, 313, 316, 322
drug offences
   addiction, 264, 266
   dangerousness of drug, 264-265
   harm
      individual, 265-266
      social, 265-266
   profit
      actual, 265, 295-296
      potential, 265
   scale of offending, 264-265
duration of wrongdoing, 254-256, 257
factors wrongly identified as
   lack of co-operation, 132, 183
   lack of remorse, 188-189
   not guilty plea, 186-189
gap in commission or record of offences as, 105-106, 115
harm *see also* victim; violence
   administration of justice, to, 276
   individual, 265-266
   secondary, 256-257, 276
   social, 265-266
hate motivation, 348-349
fraud
   magnitude of, 74, 125

AGGRAVATING FACTORS —
  continued
narcotics consumption in motor
  vehicle, 349
offending shortly after release, 352
planning, 124-127
profit, 265, 295-296
proof of
  expert evidence, 265-266
  knowledge of harm, 5-6, 354
  multiple accused, 5-6, 354
  onus on prosecution, 5
record of offences, 291-301
road rage, 261
sexual predation, 266
social harm, 265-266, 276
sprees, 281-283, 351-352
"stark horror", 269-270
unforeseen consequences, 349-350
unprosecuted misconduct, 258-259,
  274-276, 279-288
victim related factors
  impact
    general, 268, 277
    psychological, 267
  protected status
    convenience store employees,
      272-273
    generally, 270-271
    internationally protected
      persons, 272
    peace officers, 271-272
    persons protected by court
      orders, 273-274
    taxi drivers, 272
    vulnerable employees,
      272-273
  secondary harm to, 256-257
  unprosecuted misconduct
    involving, 274-276
  vulnerability, 257, 270-272
vigilantism, 301-311
violence
  degree of, 246-248, 266-270
  denunciation and, 248, 268
  deterrence and, 248, 268
  escalation of, 119-120, 277
  moral blame and, 246-248, 272

peace officers, against, 271-272
persons protected by court
  orders, against, 273-274
propensity for, 73, 268
scale of harm, 248-250, 269-270
"stark horror", 269-270
vulnerable employees, against,
  272-273

ALCOHOLISM, 57, 60, 91, 103,
  111, 124, 140, 143, 146, 148,
  235, 258, 259, 285-286, 288, 294,
  296

ATTITUDE OF OFFENDER
breach of court orders and, 138-139,
  216, 263-264, 273-274
generally, 127-128, 186
positive
  examples of
    apology, 128-129, 140
    co-operation with authorities,
      129-132
    desire to reform, 132-133
    pre-sentence report,
      favourable, 133-134
rehabilitation and, 127, 131, 132,
  136, 140, 141
religious scruples and, 139
remorse
  generally, 134-137
  impact on sentencing, 134-137
  lack of
    potential for reform and,
      137-138
    recidivism and, 137
test cases and, 139
willingness to make amends
  court-ordered amends, and,
    148-149
  generally, 140-141
  lack of
    as neutral factor, 146-147
    threat of re-offending and, 147
  restitution, early, 146
  support network and
    generally, 141-144
    support from family, 145-146

ATTITUDE OF OFFENDER —
continued
  support from victim, 144-145
  vow to reform and, 147-148

BAIL
breach of order
  effect on sentencing, 120,
    216-218
  reducing credit for "dead time",
    216-218
conditions, restrictive
  mitigation and, 232-233

BALANCING
sentencing factors, of, 1, 36, 63,
  161, 186, 199-200

BEHAVIOUR OF OFFENDER
addiction
  overcoming, 90, 91-92, 103, 106,
    141
  relapse, 103, 106, 114
awaiting sentence, while, 90,
  118-119
brazen offence, 347-348
callous behaviour, 124
counselling
  effect of successful, 81
delay in sentencing and, 118-119
driving behaviour, 124, 251-252
employment and, 81-82
"gap" in record of offence and, *see*
  "GAP" PRINCIPLE
generally, 80
intimidating witnesses, 194
parole, during, 113, 120-121
passage of time and, *see*
  PASSAGE OF TIME
planning and, 124-127
probation, during, 121
provocation and, 122-124
therapy or treatment
  effect of successful, 81, 92, 133,
    141, 251
  failure to complete, 260, 279
  rehabilitation and, 81, 90-91, 141,
    279

therapeutic remands, 90-91
trivial offences and, 116-119
violence, escalation of, and, 119-120

CHARACTER OF OFFENDER
false testimony and, 184
generally, 69, 186
good character
  community contributions, and, 70
  conduit to fraud offences, as, 347
  entrapment, and, 74-75
  isolated offences, and, 75-80
  seriousness of offence, and, 71
isolated incident, 73, 75-80, 116
non-isolated offending, and, 78-80
overcoming challenges, 74
specific deterrence and, 69

COMMUNITY SERVICE ORDER,
  148-149

CONCURRENT SENTENCES, 16,
  90, 110, 255, 311-312, 318

CONDITIONAL SENTENCE
breach of court orders and, 273-274
criminal breach of trust and, 140
"dead time" and, 213, 219
denunciation and, 249, 250, 252,
  256, 260, 262
driving offences, for, 251-252
elderly offenders and, 25, 27, 28,
  29, 32
first offenders and, 76
general deterrence and, 15, 207,
  324-326, 250, 260, 262, 324
granted, 25, 29, 30, 32, 36-37, 38,
  83, 88, 132, 176, 235, 250,
  251, 253, 256, 261, 283, 290, 322,
  324, 344
poor health and, 235, 236
R. v. Proulx, 2, 96, 250, 260
refused, 27, 28, 75, 135, 137, 249,
  253, 259, 260, 261, 273, 274,
  286, 333
rehabilitation and, 253
remorse and, 135
re-incarceration following, 85, 253

CONDITIONAL SENTENCE —
continued
restraint principle and, 2, 76-77,
  96-98
secondary penalties and, 207, 213,
  219, 235
time served and, 219
tragic consequences of offence and,
  262
violent offence, for, 20, 88, 176, 235,
  249-250

COUNSELLING
successful, effect of, 81

CRIMINAL RECORD *see* **REPEAT
OFFENDERS**

CURFEW, 119, 142, 353

DANGEROUS OFFENDERS, 134

"DEAD TIME"
advocacy respecting, 231-232
conditional sentences and, 213, 219
crediting
  case by case basis, on, 226-228
  exceptions to "two for one" rule
    breach of bail order, 216-218,
      219
    custody not "as result of
      offence", 222
    discretionary, 214-216, 226
    nil credit, 219-222
    offender misconduct, 216-222
    segregation and, 224-225
  mathematical formula and,
    226-227, 231
  minimum sentences and, 210,
    215, 228-231
  parole eligibility and, 226
  post-conviction custody, 212, 226
  rationales for
    absence of rehab. programs,
      222-223
    absence of statutory scheme,
      222

avoidance of disparity,
  225-226
avoidance of unfairness, 226,
  231
  "dead time" is punishment, 225
  trying jail conditions, 223-225
re-trial, after, 212
"two for one" rule, 209-214, 227
Criminal Code, s. 719(3), 210, 215,
  222, 226, 228-230
generally, 208-209, 231-232
maximum sentences and, 220-222
minimum sentences and, 210, 215,
  228-231
parole eligibility and, 226
post-conviction custody, 212, 226
proportionality and, 213, 231
punishment, as 225
segregation and, 224-225
rehabilitation and, 210, 212,
  222-223, 231

DENUNCIATION
attitude and, 127
conditional sentence and *see*
  CONDITIONAL SENTENCE
driving offences and, 260
elderly offenders, and *see*
  ELDERLY OFFENDERS
first offenders and, 278
generally, 1, 3, 97, 120, 126, 133,
  199, 200
guilty plea and, 154, 177
planning and, 126
"sad life" principle and, 60, 66
secondary penalties and, 198, 199,
  200, 201
unforeseen consequences and,
  349-350
violence and, 120, 248, 268
youthful offenders, and *see*
  YOUTHFUL OFFENDERS

DETERRENCE
character and, 69
community service and, 149
conditional sentence and *see*
  CONDITIONAL SENTENCE

DETERRENCE — *continued*
continuing offences and, 254
driving offences and, 260
elderly offenders, and *see*
ELDERLY OFFENDERS
first offenders and, 11, 76, 278
"gap" principle and, 94, 113, 116
generally, 1, 3, 56, 63, 77, 97, 120, 126, 149, 199, 200
guilty plea and, 154, 177
planning and, 126
profit and, 295, 313
"sad life" principle and, 56, 59, 64, 66, 68
secondary penalties and, 198, 200-205, 243-244
"silly" offences and, 117
unforeseen consequences and, 349-350
violence and, 120, 248, 268
youthful offenders, and *see*
YOUTHFUL OFFENDERS

DISCHARGE
conduct of defence and, 190-193
employment and, 82
misconduct of accused and, 190-193
narcotics consumption in motor vehicle and, 349
perjury and, 190-193
secondary penalties and, 202, 204-205, 208

DISPARITY, 225-226, 340-342 *see also* **PARITY**

DRIVING OFFENCES *see also*
OFFENCES, PARTICULAR
behaviour of offender, 124, 251-252
breach of recognizance, 263-264
conditional sentences and, 259-261, 262
criminal record, absence of, 257-261
denunciation and, 260
deterrence and, 260
individualized sentences, 251-252
provincial driving records, 352
repeat offenders, 295-296, 352

road rage, 261
sprees, 281
tragic consequences, 261-263

DRUG OFFENCES *see also*
OFFENCES, PARTICULAR
addiction and, 264-266, 338
moral blameworthiness and
belief as to substance, 337-338
dangerousness of drug, 264-265
experimentation, 338
harm
individual, 265-266
social, 265-266
profit
actual, 265, 295-296
potential, 265
scale of offending, 264-265
suspended sentence for, 79, 338

EDUCATION
academic pursuits and sentencing, 320
imprisonment to enhance skills, 334
lack of, 104
upgrading of skills and, 82

ELDERLY OFFENDERS
age, as mitigating factor, 23, 26, 32-34
blameless life, 29-30, 33
conditional sentence
granted, 25, 29, 30, 32
refused, 27, 28
"death sentence"
avoidance of, 23, 24-27, 33
defined, 24
denunciation and, 24, 26
dependants, effect of sentence on, 31-32
deterrence and, 24, 26, 30, 34
generally, 22-23, 32-34
harshness of sentence, excessive, 34
health of, 22-24, 26, 28, 31, 32-34, 88-89
historical sexual violence, sentencing for, 22, 25, 26, 27-28

ELDERLY OFFENDERS —
continued
imprisonment
  availability, generally, 22, 27
  death during, avoidance of, 23,
    24-27
  place of confinement, selection
    of, 32
  sexual abuse, for, 27, 28
mitigating factors, combining, 32-34
parole and, 30-31
period of offending
  character and, 27-28
proportionality and, 26-27, 30
rehabilitation, and, 26, 30, 31
seriousness of offence, as factor in
  sentencing, 26, 27-28, 347
spared rigors of punishment, 23
time since offence, as mitigating
  factor, 29-30

ELECTION OF CROWN, 339

EMPLOYMENT
generally, 81-82, 315-317, 328-329
history, favourable
  exceptional situations, 317
  generally, 81-82, 315-317, 329
imprisonment to enhance skills, 334
lack of, 329-330
overcoming challenges in, 330-331
sliding scale, 331-332
temporary absence and, 333
welfare benefits and, 332-333

ENTRAPMENT, 74-75

EXPERT EVIDENCE
"gap" principle, and 115
rehabilitation, re, 246

FINE
automatic, 240-241
drug offences, for, 265
imprisonment in default of, 335
surcharges, 240-241

FIRST OFFENDERS
criminal record, absence of, 277-279
denunciation and, 278
deterrence and, 11, 76, 78, 278
drunk driving cases, in, 257-261
pre-sentence reports
  generally, 283-284
  unprosecuted prior offences and
    emerging view, 285-288
    generally, 283-284
    traditional view, 284-285
prior misconduct, unprosecuted
  domestic violence, 280
  generally, 279-280
  pre-sentence reports and,
    283-288
  sexual violence, 280-281
  similar act violence, 280-281
  sprees, 281-283, 351-352
  violence generally, 280-281
pro-social conduct, capacity for,
  277-280
re-attainment of first offender status,
  104
rehabilitation and, 11, 76, 78, 289
remorse, lack of, 165
serious offences by
  generally, 76
  moral blameworthiness, 288-290

FORFEITURE, 241-242

FULL ANSWER AND DEFENCE
conduct of trial and, 186, 187, 192,
  196, 198
not guilty plea and, 186, 187, 198

"GAP" PRINCIPLE
"assimilation element", 101-103, 116
combination with other mitigating
  factors, 108
context, importance of, 98-99, 109
custodial sentences, gap between,
  101
deterrence and, 94, 113, 116
expert evidence and, 115
"extreme" position, 103-104

"GAP" PRINCIPLE — *continued*
first offender status, re-attainment of,
   104
generally, 94-95, 108-110, 115-116
historical antecedents, 98
imprisonment, gaps created by,
   113-114
length of gap, critical
   precedents for quite lengthy
     period, 106-107
   review, general, 108-110
   youthful offenders, for, 107-108
limits as mitigating factor, 95-96,
   98-101, 102, 106-110, 114
multiple gaps, crediting
   generally, 110-111
   particular offences, with reference
     to, 111-112
post-gap offending, serious, effect of,
   114
pre-arrest gaps and sprees, 115,
   281-283, 351-352
pre-sentence report, influence of,
   114-115
presumption of good behaviour,
   327-328
prosecutorial delay and, 110
prosecutorial policy, gaps created
   by, 112
pro-social values, as demonstrative
   of, 101-103, 116
rehabilitation, and, 95, 103-104, 113
restraint principle and, 96-98, 113,
   116
seriousness of offence and, 100
severity justified notwithstanding,
   98-101
"spree" principle and, 115, 281-283,
   351-352
"stretching", 103-104, 108, 115
unprosecuted offences and, 115
violent offences and, 100, 105-106
youthful offenders and, 107-108

GUILTY PLEA
change in charges and, 154
Charter and, 180-181
credit for
   early *see* early, credit for
   fixed discount and, 166-168
   late or "later" *see* late or "later",
     credit for
   not guilty plea tantamount to
     guilty plea, 169-170
   where chance of acquittal waived,
     168-169
   where complaint validated, 170
   where evidence of guilt
     overwhelming, 174-183
denunciation and, 154, 177
deterrence and, 154, 177
early
   credit for
     after early confession, 156-157
     generally, 155-156
     with apology, 157
   fixed formula discount and, 168
   fixed percentage discount and,
     166-168
   generally, 151-152
   historic sexual assault case, in,
     168-169
   lack of remorse and, 165-166
late or "later"
   credit for
     after adverse ruling, 162
     after multiple appearances,
       159-160
     after preliminary hearing, 160
     after start of trial, 161
     change in charges, effect on,
       164
     fixed percentage discount and,
       166-168
     generally, 157-159
     lesser offence, plea to,
       162-163
     mixture of pleas, effect of, 164
     on day of trial, 160-161
     where chance of acquittal
       waived, 168-169
     where remorse lacking, 165
     where victims still testify,
       164-165

GUILTY PLEA — *continued*
lesser offence, to, 162-163
mixture of pleas and, 164
"*nolo contendere*", 169
promoting search for truth, 180-181
rehabilitation and, 160
remorse and, 152-154, 161, 163,
  165-166, 171, 177, 178-180
R. v. Spiller, rule in,
  application of, 175-181
  challenge to, emerging, 181-182
  Criminal Code, s. 718 and,
    178-179
  generally, 174-175, 177
saving court time and costs,
  173-174, 177-178
search for truth and, 180-181
societal interests and
  saving court time and costs,
    173-174
  sparing victims from testifying,
    171-173
  sparing witnesses from testifying,
    171-173
sparing victims from testifying,
  171-173, 180
timing
  early, 155-157
  general significance of, 154-155
  late or "later", 157-164
validating complaint, 170
waiving chance of acquittal, 168-169

INDIVIDUALIZED SENTENCE
drinking and driving offences, for,
  251-252
need for, 2, 42, 63-64, 249-250,
  340-341
violent offences and, 249-250, 278,
  294

INTERMITTENT SENTENCE, 18,
  137

"JUMP" PRINCIPLE, 321-323

MATURITY *see also* **ELDERLY
  OFFENDERS; YOUTHFUL
  OFFENDERS**
fortunate background, significance
  of, 62-63
generally, 47-49, 64-68, 107
individualized sentence and, 63-64,
  68
"moral compass", 60-62, 64-67
"sad life" principle
  denunciation, and, 60, 66
  general deterrence and, 56, 59,
    66
  generally, 47-50
  history of abuse and, 50-60
  limits as mitigating factor, 59-60,
    61
  "moral compass" and, 60-62
  relevance to sentencing, 50-54
  seriousness of offence and, 55,
    56
  variable factor, as, 63

MITIGATING FACTORS
absence of criminal record, 257
absence of generally, 189
absence of serious injury, relative,
  321
age, advanced, 23, 26, 27, 32-34
attitude, positive, 128-134
background, unblemished, 314
bail conditions, restrictive, 233
co-operation with police, 129-132
"dead time", 208-232
dysfunctional background, 340
economic hardship, 314-315
election of Crown, 339
employment, 81-82, 315-317,
  328-333
experimentation, 338
family background, favourable,
  318-319
gap in record, 94-116 *see also*
  "GAP PRINCIPLE"
good character, 69-80
good citizenship, 319-320
guilty plea, 157-183 *see also*
  GUILTY PLEA

MITIGATING FACTORS —
continued
history of abuse, 50-60
impulsive actions, 342-343
isolated offences, 75-80
not guilty plea, 183-198
personality defects, 343-346
planning to minimize injury, 348
poor health, 22-24, 26, 28, 31,
32-34, 88-89, 235-236
pre-sentence report, favourable,
133-134
profit, lack of, 313
provocation, 121-124
reputation, favourable, 320-321
residence, change in, 346
restraint principle and, 96-98
return to jurisdiction, voluntary, 339
role in offence, minimal, 313-314
"sad life", 47-62, 340
secondary penalties
adverse consequences of
conviction, 243-244
bail conditions, restrictive, 232
balancing of factors, 199-200
civil penalties, 242-243
confiscations, 241-242
costs, 200
damages (civil), 242
"dead time", 208-232
denunciation and, 198, 199, 200,
201
deportation, 239-240
deterrence and, 198, 200-205,
240, 243-244
driving penalties, civil, 242
family of offender, harm to,
236-239
fine surcharges, 240-241
fines, automatic, 240-241
flawed proceedings, 244, 324
forfeitures, 241-242
generally, 198-199
immigration consequences,
239-240
injuries suffered in course of
offence, 244-245
ostracism, 233-235

poor health and, 235-236
rehabilitation and, 200, 201,
203-204, 206, 210, 243
212, 222-223, 231
travel restrictions, 237
trial process, inherent in, 200-208,
245-246
support network, 141-146
technical breach of law, 327
time since offence, 29-30
unfairness in prosecution, 324
unlikely success in offence, 338-339

MORAL BLAMEWORTHINESS
attitude and, 127-149
behaviour and
awaiting sentence, during, 90,
118-119
breach of court orders, 263-264,
273-274
callous behaviour, 124
counselling, successful, 81
delay in sentencing, 118-119
driving behaviour, 124, 251-252,
263-264
education, 82
exploitative conduct, 249
"gap" principle, 94-116
generally, 80
parole, behaviour during,
113,120-121
passage of time since offence,
82-94
planning, 124-127, 348
probation, behaviour during, 121
provocation and, 121-124
therapy or treatment, failure to
complete, 260, 279
therapy or treatment, successful,
81, 133, 251
"trivial offences", 116-118
violence, escalation of, 119-120,
277
violence generally, 246-250,
266-270, 272
career criminals and, 299-301, 334
character and, 69-80
delay in sentencing and, 118-119

MORAL BLAMEWORTHINESS —
continued
duration of wrongdoing and, 254-256
exploitative conduct and, 249
first offenders and, 276-290
fortunate background and, 62-63
"gap" principle and, 94-116
history of abuse, and 50-60
intoxication and, 118, 251
maturity and, 47-68
neutralizing, 279
offender groups, distinct, and, 9-10,
  14, 17-20, 39-46, 276-301
personality defects and, 343-346
provocation and, 121-124
repeat offenders and, 291-301
"sad life" principle and, 47-62
"stark horror", 269-270
technical breach of law, 327
tragic consequences of offender's
  actions, and, 261-263
violence and, 119-120, 246-250,
  266-270

NEUTRAL FACTORS
conduct of defence, 186, 187, 194,
  195-197
criminal record, lack of
    drunk driving cases, 257-261
    unblemished background, 314
lack of willingness to make amends,
  146-147
not guilty plea, 186, 187, 197
passage of time, 91
spontaneous wrongdoing, 323
unemployment, 330, 334

NOT GUILTY PLEA
full answer and defence and, 186,
  187, 198
mitigation and
    generally, 183, 198
    R. v. Kozy, rule in
        Alberta, application in, 184
        British Columbia, application
          in, 196, 197
        generally, 183-187
        minority view, 196-198

Ontario, application in,
  187-193
Quebec, application in, 185,
  190-193
neutral factor, as, 186, 187
"*nolo contendere*", 169
rehabilitation and, 184, 192
remorse and, 183, 184, 185,
  189-190, 193-195

OFFENCES, PARTICULAR
abandoning child, 88
aggravated assault, 13, 18, 85, 123,
  214, 216, 271, 322
aiding escapee, 323
arson, 289
assault, 73, 85, 88, 99, 120,
  121-123, 139, 165, 272, 280, 294,
  297, 300, 302, 312, 321, 342, 347
assault causing bodily harm, 206,
  306, 309
assault peace officer, 347
assault with a weapon, 307
breaking and entering etc., 87, 94,
  99, 104, 113, 118, 159, 214, 282,
  302, 312, 326, 327, 330, 342, 353
car jacking, 266
care/control over .08, 109, 285
causing disturbance, 101, 107, 301,
  347
causing explosion of explosive
  substance, 245
child pornography, 4, 233
cocaine, importing, 129, 289
cocaine, possession for purpose of
  trafficking, 98, 104
conspiracy to commit robbery, 17
contempt, 186
controlled substance, possession of,
  214, 295
criminal breach of trust, 140
criminal harassment, 136, 292, 297,
  298, 322, 343, 344
criminal negligence causing bodily
  harm, 262
criminal negligence causing death,
  198, 238, 257-259, 262-263
dangerous driving, 243, 261, 262

OFFENCES — *continued*
dangerous driving causing bodily harm, 263
dangerous driving causing death, 72
driving over .08, 111, 262, 285
driving while disqualified, 101, 273
environmental offences, 176
extortion, 96, 100, 267, 316, 352
forcible confinement, 305
fraud, 23, 27, 32, 52, 74, 78, 88, 115, 137, 191, 240, 314, 328, 335, 347
gross indecency, 30, 59
"highgrading", 107
impaired driving, 99, 102, 109, 112, 124, 172, 281, 296, 300
impaired driving causing bodily harm, 71, 136, 251, 259-261, 262, 285
impaired driving causing death, 136, 251-252, 260-261, 262
incest, 22, 26-27, 36, 88-89, 327
indecent assault, 30, 283
keeping common gaming house, 241
kidnapping, 192, 266
libel, 89, 116
manslaughter, 52, 56, 80, 131, 157, 162-163, 168, 250, 269, 315
marijuana cultivation, 4
misappropriation of funds, 135
mischief, 98
murder, 50, 53, 98, 126, 162-163, 186, 226, 342
murder, attempt, 105, 120, 271, 289
narcotics trafficking, 75, 79, 90, 98, 148, 271, 320
obstructing justice, attempt, 85
offensive weapons, possession of, 79-80, 100, 111, 132, 297, 315, 320
passing spurious currency, 323
perjury, 184, 185, 189-193, 194, 196-197, 276
pointing firearm, 119
probation, breach of, 96, 263, 274, 326, 327, 343, 344
property obtained by crime, possession of, 214

rape, 9, 266, 269
recognizance, breach of, 85, 89, 116, 140, 221, 263, 274, 297, 343
robbery, 12, 17, 56, 176, 196, 211, 228-231, 238, 247, 267, 272-273, 287, 289, 293, 311, 321, 338, 348
sexual assault, 18, 25, 53, 57, 59, 61, 65, 71, 84-85, 126, 140, 168-169, 184, 192, 255, 256, 266, 283, 297
sexual assault causing bodily harm, 286
sexual assault with weapon, 254
sexual interference, 255
shoplifting, 100, 117, 172, 202
speeding, 352
taking automobile without consent, 263-264
theft, 16, 87, 99, 100, 107, 117, 118, 266, 277, 316, 348, 353
theft, attempt, 16, 316, 318
threatening, 125, 307, 267, 274, 297, 312, 350
unlawful confinement, 140, 267, 297
willful damage to property, 349

OVERINCARCERATION, 2-4, 40, 44, 45, 96-98, 325

PARITY, 271-272 *see also* **DISPARITY**

PAROLE
behaviour during, 113, 120-121
"dead time" and, 226
delay orders, 147, 267
elderly offenders, 30-31
ineligibility orders, 342-343
minimum sentences and, 229-230

PAROLE DELAY ORDER, 147, 267

PASSAGE OF TIME
awaiting sentence, 90
delayed arrest situation, 90
elderly offenders and, 29-30

PASSAGE OF TIME — *continued*
further intervention, need for, and,
   82-87
generally, 93-94
good post-offence behaviour, 82-87
historical prosecutions and, 88-89
learning necessary lesson and, 89
limits as mitigating factor, 91, 99
neutral factor, as, 91
progress in institution and, 92
rehabilitation in custody post
   offence, 87, 91, 92
reluctance to incarcerate and, 87-88
therapeutic remand, 90-91

PERJURY *see also* **OFFENCES,**
   PARTICULAR
conspiracy to commit, 191
negating remorse, 189-190, 193, 194
rehabilitation and, 192, 193

PRESUMPTION OF INNOCENCE,
   162

PRE-TRIAL CUSTODY *see* **"DEAD**
TIME"

PROBATION
behaviour of offender during, 121
breach of, 96, 263, 274, 326, 327,
   343, 344
condition re addiction, 245
youthful offenders, for
   deterrence and, 11
   preference for, 8, 203
   rehabilitation and, 11, 203

PROPORTIONALITY
Criminal Code, s. 718.1, 200, 246
"dead time" and, 213, 231
elderly offenders, and *see*
   ELDERLY OFFENDERS
generally, 15, 335-337
secondary penalties and, 200, 246
"trivial offences" and, 117
youthful offenders, and *see*
   YOUTHFUL OFFENDERS

PROVOCATION, 121-124

RANGE PRINCIPLE
exceptional cases and, 252,
   262-263, 341
scale of harm and, 249
undue hardship avoidance and,
   253-254

RECORD OF OFFENCES *see*
   REPEAT OFFENDERS

REHABILITATION
aboriginal offenders and, 37
attitude and, 127, 131, 132, 136,
   140, 141
community protection and, 254
conditional sentence and see
   CONDITIONAL SENTENCE
counselling and, 81
"dead time" and, 210, 212, 222-223,
   231
elderly offenders, and *see*
   ELDERLY OFFENDERS
expert evidence re capacity for, 246
first offenders and, 289
"gap" principle and, 95, 103-104, 113
generally, 1, 3, 63, 68, 97, 126,
   131, 199, 200, 331
guilty plea and, 160
marriage, long term, and, 143
not guilty plea and, 184, 192
passage of time and, 87, 91, 92
programs, absence of, 222-223
secondary penalties and, 200, 201,
   203, 206, 210, 212, 243
strict application of law and, 346-347
support network and, 141-146
therapy or treatment and, 81, 90-91,
   141, 279
undue hardship, avoiding, 253-354
youthful offenders, and *see*
   YOUTHFUL OFFENDERS

REMORSE
generally, 134-137
guilty plea and, 152-154, 161, 163,
   165-166, 171, 177, 178-180

REMORSE — *continued*
impact on sentencing, 134-137
lack of
    potential for reform and, 137-138
    recidivism and, 137
not guilty plea and, 183, 184, 185, 189-190, 193-195

REPEAT OFFENDERS *see also* **"GAP" PRINCIPLE**
career criminals, 299-301
double punishment
    duty to avoid, 350-351
driving prohibitions and, 298
generally, 291, 298-299
motivation
    addiction, 296
    animus, 296-298
    profit, 295-296
record of offences, impact of
    extensive record
        emerging rule, 300-301
        exceptional disposition, 300
        general rule, 299-300
    minor record, 292
    quasi-criminal record, 352
    recent record
        minor, 292
        substantial, 292-293
    unrelated record
        generally, 293-294
        lengthy unrelated, 294
    youth record, 291-292
"step" principle and, 321-323

"RESPITING" OF SENTENCE, 90

RESTITUTION ORDER, 148-149, 326

RESTORATIVE JUSTICE, 38, 40, 41, 148

RESTRAINT
aboriginal offenders and, 42
conditional sentences and, 2, 76-77, 96-98

Criminal Code, s. 718.2, 2-4, 96-98, 264, 325-326
"gap" principle and, 95-98, 113
general principle, 2-4, 76-77, 113
"step" principle and, 321-323

RETRIBUTION, 1, 63, 199

ROAD RAGE, 261

RUSE, USE OF, 349

"SAD LIFE" PRINCIPLE, 14, 36, 38, 43, 47-62, 64

SECONDARY PENALTIES
bail conditions, restrictive, 232
balancing of factors, 199-200
civil penalties, 242-243
confiscations, 241-242
costs, 200
"dead time" *see* **"DEAD TIME"**
denunciation and, 198, 199, 200, 201
deportation, 239-240
deterrence and, 198, 200-205, 243-244
driving penalties, civil, 242-243
family of offender, harm to, 236-239
fine surcharges, 240-241
fines, automatic, and, 240-241
flawed proceedings, 244
forfeitures, 241-242
generally, 198-199, 245-246
immigration consequences, 239-240
injuries suffered in course of offence, 244-245
ostracism, 233-235
poor health and, 235-236
pregnant offenders and, 237
pre-trial custody *see* **"DEAD TIME"**
professional disqualification, 234, 237
rehabilitation and, 200, 201, 203-204, 206, 210, 212, 222-223, 231, 243
travel restrictions, 237

SECONDARY PENALTIES —
continued
trial process, inherent in, 200-208,
245-246

SEPARATION PRINCIPLE, 40, 41,
97

SHAKEN BABY SYNDROME, 253

"STARK HORROR" CASES, 269

"STEP" PRINCIPLE, 321-323

SUSPENDED SENTENCE
criminal negligence causing death,
for, 198, 238
Crown's position on sentencing and,
339
drug offences, and, 79
generally, 16, 75, 76, 198, 238, 316,
318, 320, 338, 339, 342
youthful offenders, for *see*
YOUTHFUL OFFENDERS

SYSTEMIC RACISM, 39, 41, 43-46

TEST CASES, 139

THERAPEUTIC REMAND
Criminal Code, s. 721 and, 90
unavailability, 90-91

THERAPY
successful, effect of, 81, 92
therapeutic remand
unavailability, 90-91

TOTALITY PRINCIPLE, 19, 311-312

"TRIVIAL OFFENCES"
legislative background, 116-117
proportionality and, 117
"silly offences", 117-118

UNDUE HARDSHIP
avoiding, 253-254

UNEMPLOYMENT, 329-330,
332-334

VICTIM *see also* **AGGRAVATING
FACTORS**
apology to, 128-129, 136, 140, 157
guilty plea and, 160, 164-165,
170-171, 178, 180, 181
harm to
psychological, 267, 269
scale of, 248-250
secondary, 256-257
impact statement, 126, 145, 172,
280
protected status
convenience store employees,
272-273
generally, 270-271
internationally protected persons,
272
peace officers, 272-272
persons protected by court
orders, 273-274
taxi drivers, 272
vulnerable employees, 272-273
unprosecuted misconduct involving,
274-276
secondary harm to, 256-257
support from, 144-145
vigilantism and, 310
vulnerability, 257, 270-272

VICTIM IMPACT STATEMENT, 126,
145, 172, 280

VIGILANTISM
aggravating factor, as, 311
characterization, erroneous, 301
cycle of violence, 307-308
deliberation and, 309-310
extortion, as, 309
gang warfare, 308, 310
generally, 311
historical background, 303-305
innocent victim and, 310-311
lawlessness, fear of, and, 301-307
mob violence, concerns over, 308
multi-national perspective, 310

VIGILANTISM — *continued*
"Rambo style", 307-308
terrorism and, 310

"WORST-CASE" ANALYSIS, 266

WRONGDOING, DEGREE OF
aggravating factors, absence of, 4
moral blameworthiness, and, 4, 246-248
victim status, 270-274
violence and, 246-250, 266-270

YOUTHFUL OFFENDERS
character, and, 78-80
closed custody, 86, 123, 266
community supervision, 14
conditional sentence
    general deterrence and, 15
    violent offence, for, 20
defining, 11, 77-78
denunciation, and, 13, 14, 18, 20, 21
deterrence, and, 9, 11, 13, 14, 15, 17, 18, 20, 21, 76-78, 80
"gap" principle and, 107
generally, 7, 20-22
imprisonment
    minimization of, 7-9, 10-11, 15, 21, 76-77
    penitentiary terms, 8-9, 13, 19, 21
intermittent sentence, and, 18
isolated offences and, 76-78
mitigating factors, combining, 21-22
moral blameworthiness
    after-the-fact conduct, and 18

conspiracy and, 17
diminished, 9-10, 14
generally, 7, 17-20
planning, and 17
seriousness of offence, and, 12, 17, 18, 20, 78
sexual assault, and, 18
totality principle, and 19
nature of offence as sentencing
    factor, 11-12, 14, 17, 18, 20, 78
open custody, 67, 80, 92, 94, 266, 346
pre-sentence report, 133, 284
probation
    deterrence and, 11
    preference for, 8, 203
    rehabilitation and, 11, 203
"prodigal child" principle, 16
proportionality and, 15-16
pro-social values
    teaching
        amenability to, 12-13
        coercion and, 13-16
rehabilitation, and, 11, 12-16, 17, 19, 78, 79, 203-206, 256
secondary penalties and, 203-206
serious offences
    sentencing for, 11-12, 14, 17, 18, 20, 203, 288-290
suspended sentence, 12, 204-205
"taste of jail", and, 15
totality principle, and, 19
violent offences
    sentencing for, 11-12, 14, 17, 18, 20, 86, 138